2005

AMERICAN INDIAN EDUCATION

AMERICAN INDIAN EDUCATION

A History

Jon Reyhner
Jeanne Eder

University of Oklahoma Press : Norman

Also by Jon Reyhner

(ed. with Barbara Jane Burnaby) *Indigenous Languages Across the Community* (Flagstaff, Ariz., 2002)
(with Norbert Francis) *Language and Literacy Teaching for Indigenous Education: A Bilingual Approach* (Clevedon, UK, 2002)
(ed. with Joseph Martin, et al.) *Learn in Beauty: Indigenous Education for a New Century* (Flagstaff, Ariz., 2000)
(ed. with Gina Cantoni, et al.) *Revitalizing Indigenous Languages* (Flagstaff, Ariz., 1999)
(ed.) *Teaching Indigenous Languages* (Flagstaff, Ariz., 1997)
(ed.) Teaching American Indian Students (Norman, Okla., 1992)

Also by Jeanne Eder
The Dakota Sioux (Austin, Tex., 2000)
The Makah (Austin, Tex., 2000)

Library of Congress Cataloging-in-Publication Data

Reyhner, Jon Allan.
   American Indian education : a history / Jon Reyhner, Jeanne Eder.
     p. cm.
   Includes bibliographical references and index.
   ISBN 0–8061–3593–X (alk. paper)
   1. Indians of North America—Education—History.   2. Indians of North America—Government relations—History.   3. Indians of North America—Cultural assimilation.   4. Missions—North America—History.   5. Off-reservation boarding schools—United States—History.   I. Eder, Jeanne M. Oyawin.   II. Title.

E97.R49 2004
371.829'97—dc22
                                                                    2003063420

1 2 3 4 5 6 7 8 9 10

CONTENTS

Illustrations

FIGURES

TABLES

ACKNOWLEDGMENTS

No book that attempts a broad historical overview can be written without drawing on the work of other historians. We found Margaret Layman's 1942 dissertation, "A History of Indian Education in the United States," and Margaret Connell Szasz's two books, *Education and the American Indian* and *Indian Education in the American Colonies, 1607–1783*, particularly useful. Individual chapters drew heavily on various sources that are cited in the references, but we want to acknowledge some of them here. In chapter 1 the information on Mexico comes largely from Shirley Brice Heath's *Telling Tongues*. In chapter 5 we are indebted to Harry J. Sievers's 1952 article, "The Catholic Indian School Issue and the Presidential Election of 1892," for information on the battle between Catholics and Protestants, as well as Sister Carla Kraman's 1984 book, *A Portrait of Saint Labre Indian Mission through One Hundred Years*.

Several boarding school histories were very helpful, among them Robert Trennert's history of Phoenix Indian School, Scott Riney's study of the Rapid City Indian School, and K. Tsianina Lomawaima's study of Chilocco.

In chapter 9, Hildegard Thompson's *The Navajos' Long Walk for Education* was especially informative. In chapter 11, we are indebted to David K. Eliades and Linda Ellen Oxendine's *Pembroke State University*, John Williams and Howard L. Meredith's *Bacone Indian University*, Wayne Stein's dissertation, "A History of the Tribally Controlled Community Colleges," and his 1992 book based on that dissertation, *Tribally Controlled Colleges*.

Jon Reyhner received a Newberry Library Fellowship in 1990 for one month in residence at the D'Arcy McNickle Center for the Study of the American Indians that allowed him to examine original documents, such as the copies of the Carlisle Indian School student newspaper and returned student surveys done for the Bureau of Indian Affairs (BIA). He would also like to acknowledge his wife, Marie, who has stood by him for more than three decades while he learned about Navajo life. Her experiences as a student at a BIA school in Leupp, Arizona, and a boarding school in Shiprock, New Mexico, as a resident of the bordertown dormitory in Winslow, Arizona (which she eventually ran away from), as a student at Tuba City public schools, and as a graduate of a mission high school in Phoenix, Arizona, have brought him to a better if still incomplete understanding of what Indian education meant for Indian people.

Jeanne Eder wishes to express her gratitude to her husband, Stan Vlahovich, Jr., daughter, Kim Albea, and son-in-law, Joel Albea, and her grandsons, Brandon and Evan. She also thanks her administrative assistant, Penny Golden, for help with sources.

This book is a major expansion and revision of *A History of Indian Education* published by the Native American Studies Program of Eastern Montana College (now Montana State University–Billings) in 1989. Parts of chapter 8 appeared in Reyhner's essay "Teaching English to the Indians," which appeared in *Learn in Beauty: Indigenous Education for a New Century*, published by Northern Arizona University in 2000. Parts of chapter 10 are from Reyhner's article on Rock Point Community School in his 1990 monograph, *Effective Language Education Practices and Native Language Survival*; and parts of chapter 12 are from his 1993 article, "New Directions in United States Native Education," published in the *Canadian Journal of Native Education*.

We want to express our appreciation for all that we have learned from all our fellow students, teachers, administrators, and faculty over the years.

AMERICAN INDIAN EDUCATION

INTRODUCTION

This book describes the efforts of European immigrants to North America and their descendants to force the cultural assimilation of the continent's indigenous peoples through schooling, and it chronicles their resistance to as well as cooperation with these efforts under extreme conditions. In what the demographer Russell Thornton (1987) termed the "American Indian holocaust," the indigenous population of what is now the United States plummeted from several million before Columbus's arrival to a little over two hundred thousand at the beginning of the twentieth century. The European invasion that followed in Columbus's wake brought new diseases to which Indians lacked natural immunity and increased and more deadly (owing to guns) warfare that was often caused by the seemingly insatiable hunger for land and gold of the ever-growing white population. Even starvation took a toll as buffalo and other game disappeared and Indians were forced onto less desirable reservation lands not immediately wanted by frontier settlers.

Predictions of the Indians' ultimate demise led to the popularity of the term "Vanishing American" in the nineteenth century. Many humanitarians saw education and assimilation into non-Indian society as farmers as the only hope for Indians, although much of the reservation land left them was suitable for ranching at best. Both humanitarians and land speculators influenced U.S. Indian policy that was set by politicans and government bureaucrats in Washington, D.C., most of whom never ventured west of the Mississippi River to see how Indians lived and the results of their policies.

The U.S. government's goal of totally assimilating the first Americans into an alien, technologically advanced culture was repeatedly questioned by Native Americans—and sometimes even by their white teachers. Still, its accomplishment seemed inevitable as over the course of four centuries foreign diseases and superior organization and weaponry took their toll on Native peoples. However, missionaries, reformers, and teachers underestimated the strength of Native peoples and their resistance to assimilation. Mick Fedullo, a perceptive observer of Indian culture, quotes the Apache elder, Elenore Cassadore:

> [Many Indian parents had] been to school in their day, and what that usually meant was a bad BIA boarding school. And all they remember about school is that there were all these Anglos trying to make them forget they were Apaches; trying to make them turn against their parents, telling them that Indian ways were evil.
>
> Well, a lot of those kids came to believe that their teachers were the evil ones, and so anything that had to do with "education" was also evil—like books. Those kids came back to the reservation, got married, and had their own kids. And now they don't want anything to do with the white man's education. The only reason they send their kids to school is because it's the law. But they tell their kids not to take school seriously. (1992, 117)

Missionaries, in their ethnocentric zeal, assumed that once exposed to Christianity, "civilization," and the English language, Native peoples would be eager to change their lives "for the better." For example, the historian Althea Bass ([1936] 1996, 32) found that missionaries to the Cherokee had "supposed that non-Christian nations, given the opportunity to learn English, would embrace it promptly." Late-nineteenth-century reformers felt that assimilation could be accomplished quickly if the Indians were detribalized. They believed that if reservations were broken up and young people were educated in government boarding schools, Indians could, in the words of the historian Robert Utley (1984, 211), "leap into the mainstream of American life." Schooling in European ways was meant to destroy Indian tribal life, rid the U.S. government of its trust and treaty responsibilities, and repay Indians for land taken from them.

However, attempts at quick assimilation often led to failure. The rapid erosion of traditional culture by immersing students in an all-English environment in boarding schools often led to cultural disintegration, not cultural replacement. Students returned to their families unprepared to resume their tribal life but unable as well to carry on as "whites." Dillon Platero, director of the Navajo Division of Education, described "Kee," a student whose experience, according to Platero, was the rule rather than the exception:

> Kee was sent to boarding school as a child where—as was the practice—he was punished for speaking Navajo. Since he was only allowed to return home during Christmas and summer, he lost contact with his family. Kee withdrew from both the White and Navajo worlds as he grew older because he could not comfortably communicate in either language. He became one of the many thousand Navajos who were non-lingual—a man without a language. By the time he was 16, Kee was an alcoholic, uneducated, and despondent—without identity. (1975, 58)

As early as 1928, a government-sponsored investigation of the Interior Department's Indian Office (renamed the Bureau of Indian Affairs in 1947) called for a school curriculum based on "local Indian life, or at least written within the scope of the child's early experiences" (Meriam 1928, 33). And more recently, the anthropologist Clyde Kluckhohn (1962, 340) wrote of the impact of white culture and education on the nation's largest tribe: "Navajo culture is becoming an ugly patchwork of meaningless and unrelated pieces, whereas it was once a finely patterned mosaic." The Northern Cheyenne educator Richard Littlebear wrote:

> Our youth are apparently looking to urban gangs for those things that will give them a sense of identity, importance, and belongingness. It would be so nice if they would but look to our own tribal characteristics because we already have all the things that our youth are apparently looking for and finding in socially destructive gangs. We have all the characteristics in our tribal structures that will reaffirm the identities of our youth. Gangs have distinctive colors, clothes, music, heroes, symbols, rituals, and "turf." . . . We American Indian tribes have these too. We have distinctive colors,

clothes, music, heroes, symbols, and rituals, and we need to teach our children about the positive aspects of American Indian life at an early age so they know who they are. Perhaps in this way we can inoculate them against the disease of gangs. Another characteristic that really makes a gang distinctive is the language they speak. If we could transfer the young people's loyalty back to our own tribes and families, we could restore the frayed social fabric of our reservations. We need to make our children see our languages and cultures as viable and just as valuable as anything they see on television, movies, or videos. (1999, 4-5)

Only in the twentieth century, after four hundred years of Indian-white contact, was serious consideration given to allowing Indians to choose their own destiny and promote what has been called by the multicultural educator Sonia Nieto (1992) "mutual accommodation" through education.

MAINTAINING TRIBAL LANGUAGES AND CULTURES

There is a long history of opposition to forced assimilation, including efforts to maintain tribal languages and cultures. Sequoyah, a Cherokee, developed a syllabary in the early 1800s so that his people could write their own language. The tribe started its own bilingual Cherokee-English newspaper, but the state of Georgia confiscated the press. What happened next is referred to today as "ethnic cleansing." Over the objections of the U.S. Supreme Court, President Andrew Jackson used the U.S. Army to force the Cherokee to walk the "Trail of Tears" westward across the Mississippi River to what is now Oklahoma. Putting their lives back together in what was promised as their new permanent homeland, the Cherokee started their own schools, but the federal government again stepped in. It ended the self-government reestablished by the Cherokee and other tribes in Indian Territory and at the beginning of the twentieth century mandated that their schools were to be state-operated public schools. Fedullo writes:

For over a hundred years, the missionary and BIA schools had sought to reach the core of Indian inner life and destroy that which made it ethnically and culturally unique. Somehow many Indians had managed to steal away into the center of a complex maze of minimal outward adaptation and maximal inward adherence to their particular vision of the world. (1992, 54)

Wilcomb Washburn (1971, 218), director of the American Studies Program at the Smithsonian Institution, recalled that in 1952 he passed an Indian school whose motto was, "Tradition Is the Enemy of Progress." Under that motto students were forced to speak only English and sometimes had their mouths washed out with soap for speaking their Native languages. Many Indians felt that the loss of their language was one of the most critical problems they faced, for it leads to a breakdown in communication between children and their grandparents and cuts Indian people off from their heritage (Ahenakew 1986, 1). Tribal heritage provides a sense of group membership and belonging that is especially important to Indian people in today's increasingly individualistic and materialistic society, which the sociologist David Riesman (1950) termed the "lonely crowd."

What is being lost with assimilationist, English-only educational policies was brought home to Reyhner in 1996 at the annual meeting of the Alaska Association for Bilingual Education. At the meeting he picked up a card describing Iñupiaq Eskimo values. On one side the card read, "Every Iñupiaq is responsible to all other Iñupiat for the survival of our cultural spirit, and the values and traditions through which it survives. Through our extended family, we retain, teach, and live our Iñupiaq way." The other side read, "With guidance and support from Elders, we must teach our children Iñupiaq values." Then the card listed the following values: "knowledge of language, sharing, respect for others, cooperation, respect for elders, love for children, hard work, knowledge of family tree, avoidance of conflict, respect for nature, spirituality, humor, family roles, hunter success, domestic skills, humility, [and] responsibility to tribe." It concluded with the words, "OUR UNDERSTANDING OF OUR UNIVERSE AND OUR PLACE IN IT IS A BELIEF IN GOD AND A RESPECT FOR ALL HIS CREATIONS." It can be argued that, in the words of John Collier (1947, 17), President Franklin D. Roosevelt's Commissioner of Indian Affairs, modern society has lost the "passion and reverence for human personality and for the web of life and the earth which the American Indians have tended as a central sacred fire."

Decades ago, perceptive teachers saw the advantages of using Indian languages and recognized the gap between what Indians wanted and needed and what was forced on them in schools. The civil rights movement that began after World War II has focused the attention of political activists and researchers on the desires and needs of all American minorities and has led to a number of studies that point out that Indian schools were destroying the identity of the children they were supposed to serve. Among these were *Indian Education: A National Tragedy, a National Challenge* (1969), also known as the Kennedy Report, and critical examinations from an anthropological perspective (e.g., King 1967; Wolcott 1967). George Spindler (1987) maintained that Indian schools were ineffective because educators did not recognize and build on the tribal heritage of students and called for culturally appropriate teaching methods and materials, including instruction and materials in the students' Native languages.

In the last decades of the twentieth century there was danger on several fronts to linguistically and culturally appropriate curricula in the United States. Groups such as U.S. English advocated adopting English as the official language of the United States and the exclusive use of English as the language of instruction in public schools. English-only propositions were passed in California in 1998, in Arizona in 2000, and in Massachusetts in 2002 that severely limited bilingual education programs, although Arizona's attorney general issued an opinion after adoption of the "English for the Children" proposition in her state specifically exempting Indians (Reyhner 2001). In addition, the "cultural literacy" movement received a great deal of media attention following the 1987 publication of E. D. Hirsch Jr.'s *Cultural Literacy: What Every American Needs to Know*. This movement, with its emphasis on teaching mainstream Euro-American culture, jeopardized the teaching of non-Western, non-European, non-Judeo-Christian heritages in U.S. schools.

These assimilationist forces have been countered by American Indians who lobbied and won passage of the Indian Religious Freedoms Act of 1978 and the Native American Languages Act of 1990. In addition, the U.S. Secretary of Education's Indian Nations at Risk Task Force (INAR 1991, 16) found that "schools that respect and support a student's language and culture are significantly more successful in educating those students."

CONFLICTING EXPLANATIONS OF INDIAN STUDENT FAILURE

The little national attention that Indian education receives tends to focus on the continued poor academic performance of American Indian and Alaska Native students. The performance of Native students mirrors that of African American and Hispanic students. Researchers have debated why some minority groups experience relative school success and others do not (Jacob and Jordan 1987; Ledlow 1992). Some have examined the differences between dominated minorities, who resist "colonial" education, and voluntary minorities, who view education as a path to economic success (e.g., Ogbu 1978, 1995). Others focus on cultural differences between home and school (e.g., Reyhner 1992a). Fedullo (1992) described assimilationist teachers who are still at work in Indian schools and the continuing passive and direct student resistance to their efforts. While sitting in a teachers' lounge, he overheard teachers complaining about their students. After using several "four-letter" words to describe his students, one teacher said,

> The thing that gets me most is they got no respect for anything. They don't want to listen to you. They don't want to do their work. They don't want to settle down an' be polite. Even if they're not gonna listen, they could at least be polite. They just don't want to learn, period. How can I teach them anything if they don't want to learn? (Fedullo 1992, 186)

In order for teachers to be successful, they must both overcome their students' resistance to education and master the art of intercultural communication. Jim Cummins (1992, 2000) studied four factors that need to be addressed if Indian and other minority students are to see the importance of education and feel a sense of empowerment: cultural and linguistic incorporation, community involvement, experiential and interactive teaching methods, and testing programs that emphasize student advocacy. Cummins calls for a move from a subtractive assimilationist approach to education to an additive bilingual "English Plus" approach. According to Fedullo,

> [Successful educators] demonstrate their belief in the move toward Indian self-determination, while the worst are full of the passionate intensity of

the old assimilationists. The best go about learning as much as they can about the tribe they work for and attempt to become culturally sensitive, respecting tribal customs and beliefs. The worst fiercely adhere to the paternal idea that Indians must be "civilized." They approach education as though it embodied their own personal mission to convert Indians to thinking that the only way to happiness is the "White Way." (1992, 184)

Recent research on American Indian dropouts demonstrates that students give up on school because they perceive their teachers as uncaring and do not see the relevance to their lives of what they are being taught. Donna Deyhle quotes a number of American Indian students:

The way I see it seems like the whites don't want to get involved with the Indians. They think we're bad. We drink. Our families drink. Dirty. Ugly. And the teachers don't want to help us. They say, "Oh, no, there is another Indian asking a question" because they don't understand. So we stop asking questions. (1992, 24)

It was just like they [teachers] want to put us aside, us Indians. They didn't tell us nothing about careers or things to do after high school. They didn't encourage us to go to college. They just took care of the white students. They just wanted to get rid of the Indians. (1992, 24-25)

W. G. Secada (1991) reports meeting high school mathematics teachers who did not want anything to do with limited English proficient students. One teacher said to him, "I was trained to teach mathematics, not to teach *those* students" (1991, 35; original emphasis). The Indian Nations at Risk Task Force reported in 1991 that Indian students are faced with "an unfriendly school climate that fails to promote appropriate academic, social, cultural, and spiritual development among many Native students," and one of its ten national goals was that "by the year 2000 all schools [would] offer Native students the opportunity to maintain and develop their tribal languages" (INAR 1991, 7). Deyhle's and Secada's findings also reinforce the Indian Nations at Risk Task Force's recommendation that teachers of Indian students should have special training (Reyhner, Gabbard, and Lee 1995; Reyhner, Lee, and Gabbard 1993; Reyhner and Jacobs 2002).

In 1990 about one-third of American Indian students dropped out of school, and the Hispanic dropout rate was not far behind (INAR 1991). The Navajo Area Dropout Study (Brandt 1992), an extensive study performed on the largest Indian reservation in the United States, found that 37 percent of students who planned to drop out were bored with school and that 24 percent of school administrators reported students dropped out of school because they were not interested in education. Only 8 percent of students gave academic failure as a reason for dropping out.

Although students themselves do not report language as a major reason for their lack of school success, studies have shown a different picture. Deyhle (1992) found that many Navajo and Ute high school students did not have the necessary academic skills, specifically reading, to do the required assignments, which usually involved reading grade-level textbooks and answering questions at the end of each chapter. This common type of classwork tends to bore students who have the language skills to perform it, but it is even more boring for students who are frustrated by their inability to read well enough to do the assignment. Typically, underperforming students are shunted into remedial programs in which lessons are broken down so that they have more time to complete their classwork. These programs have a number of disadvantages: they increase students' boredom, and they pull students out of mathematics and science classes.

DANGERS OF MODERN EDUCATIONAL "REFORMS"

Perhaps the greatest danger facing Indian education at the beginning of the twenty-first century is the push for outcomes assessment, state and national standards, and the associated increased use of high stakes testing in all facets of education but especially for promotion to the next grade. Young minority students who do poorly on tests are often placed in special education and basic skills programs instead of culturally appropriate programs. High school students get tracked into non-college-bound curricula based on achievement tests (Oakes 1985) and are denied diplomas when they cannot pass exit examinations. As the anthropologist Ruth Underhill and the Indian Office's director of education, Willard Beatty, noted in 1944, "[S]tandard tests of intelligences are not measures of native ability but of cultural experience" (2).

Another complicating factor in Indian education historically has been economics. Colonists used Indian education as a way to obtain donations from England that were then sometimes used to pay for the education of white children. In the nineteenth century corruption in the Office of Indian Affairs diverted money into the pockets of contractors and Indian agents. This corruption was a notorious problem that received national attention. After Civil Service reforms brought corruption under control in the 1890s, the increasingly large Indian education budget seemed to give the Indian Office bureaucracy a life independent of the students it served. In the beginning public school districts were often not interested in serving Indian students. If they were interested at all, it was because of the receipt of federal moneys.

LOOKING FORWARD

In order for educators and policy makers to understand why the various programs in Indian schools exist and why certain curricula are more likely to lead to success, they must know about the past failures and successes of Indian education. They must know the roots of Indian resistance to schooling and the educational empowerment that Indians are striving for.

Following the lead of Ivan Illich, some theorists have recommended that indigenous people reject schooling because it destroys their cultures and communities (see, e.g., Prakash and Esteva 1998). But others see community-controlled schools as the only way that indigenous people can protect their lands and communities from the onslaught of mainstream society (Enos 2002). Supporters of Indian self-determination call on educators to be advocates for Indian students, to protect them from culturally insensitive textbooks, curricula, and tests and promote place- and community-based teaching methods and curricula that recognize and value tribal knowledge (Deloria and Wildcat 2001).

The five centuries of white ethnocentrism, cultural chauvinism, and insensitivity to Indian needs described in this book still exist. Teachers who go beyond teaching, who learn about their students' cultures, can change their students' lives for the better. Rather than justify a one-way monocultural, "English only" education for assimilation that has dominated the historical record, this book documents the advantages of an "English Plus" education, one that involves mutual accommodation and a two-way exchange between Indian and white societies.

Looking backward, as this book does, offers insight into what works in Indian education. Although the 1969 Kennedy Report called Indian education "a national tragedy," there have always been Indian students who are eager to learn and responsive teachers, Indian and white, who have worked to overcome Indian resistance to schooling and to meet the special needs of Indian students. American Indians were becoming teachers and ministers two centuries ago and doctors and anthropologists a century ago. Today an increasing number of Indians are successfully attending universities and colleges and returning to their communities to teach in and administer their own schools and colleges. They are discovering for themselves what works in Indian education and expressing their ideas in both words and acts.

CHAPTER ONE

COLONIAL MISSIONARIES AND THEIR SCHOOLS

Before the arrival of European colonists North American tribes spoke more than three hundred languages, had different beliefs, and lived in different ways. But there were certain similarities among all the tribes. The anthropologist George A. Pettitt (1946), for example, documented similarities in child-rearing practices. He found that training for survival was central to Native education. Babies were taught not to cry by cutting off their air supply; this would prevent them from revealing the band's whereabouts to an enemy. The struggle for survival taught the Indians humility. They understood that, contrary to the teachings of Christianity, humans did not hold dominion over the earth but must live in harmony with it. A Cree hunter stated this philosophy thus:

> The man who earns his subsistence from hunting, who survives, as the Indians say, from the land, depends on knowing where he must stand in the strangely efficient and mysterious balance that is arranged for the propagation of all life. . . . In this scheme of things the man is not dominant; he is a mere survivor, like every other form of life. (Quoted in Szasz 1988, 12)

Agricultural tribes of the East and Southeast had a similar attitude toward growing corn, melons, and beans.

Knowledge of tribal traditions was another component of children's education. Through ceremonies, storytelling, and apprenticeship, children learned the culture of their parents. Play was yet another means to educate Indian children. Some games, called "the little brother of war," taught boys the skills necessary to handle weapons and developed physical endurance. Pretty Shield described to Frank Linderman (1932) how as a child before the white people had changed Crow culture she and her friends put up a tent and played at carrying out all the household activities she would later take on when she married. Children learned by observing and then mimicking their parents.

The first European teachers of Indians were Christian missionaries who generally did not understand Indian child-rearing practices. The Jesuit father Paul le Jeune wrote in 1634, "These Barbarians cannot bear to have any of their children punished, nor even scolded, not being able to refuse anything to a crying child. They carry this to such an extent that upon the slightest pretext they would take them away from us, before they were educated" (quoted in Thwaites 1896–1901, vol. 6, 153–54). Le Jeune wrote again in 1639 that "the Savages love their Children above all things" (quoted in Thwaites 1896–1901, vol. 16, 67). The Jesuit priest Joseph Jovency recorded in a book published in 1710, "They treat their children with wonderful affection, but they preserve no discipline, for they neither themselves correct them nor allow others to do so. Hence the impudence and savageness of the boys, which, after they have reached a vigorous age, breaks forth in all sorts of wickedness" (quoted in Thwaites 1896-1901, vol. 1, 277).

Missionaries sought to Christianize, civilize, and assimilate Indians into European culture. They criticized Indian cleanliness and ceremonies, but they were even more critical of the apparent lack of discipline among Indian children. Contrary to European practice, in many tribal cultures the use of corporal punishment to discipline children was unacceptable. Indian children were taught that to endure pain without showing emotion was a sign of maturity. Therefore, using pain as a form of punishment did not make sense. Flora Greg Iliff (1954, 144), who taught on the Havasupai and Hualapai Reservations starting in 1900, observed, "Physical punishment was seldom inflicted on a child. In all my experience I never saw an Indian parent strike a child. A whipped child loses courage, they said, and his soul withers and dwindles away until he dies, for the soul of a child is a tender thing and easily hurt."

Instead discipline was enforced through teasing, ostracism, and peer pressure. In addition, tribal stories that described how children who went outside the bounds of tribal custom were severely punished by supernatural powers served as object lessons.

Missionaries attempting to transform tribal societies rarely studied Native child-rearing practices and other customs before seeking to change them. Some learned one or more tribal languages, but few understood, must less appreciated, tribal cultures. Indian religions were viewed as false and the work of the devil. For most Indian students being taught by missionaries, parental influence far outweighed the influence of missionaries. Since this frustrated their efforts at conversion to Christianity and the European way of life, missionaries soon sought to separate Indian children from their parents by placing them in white homes or boarding schools. Missionaries had the most success when Indian societies began to disintegrate from the onslaught of war, alcohol, European diseases, and famine. Conditions were made worse for the Indians when increasing numbers of immigrants caused their dislocation from ancestral homelands and lifestyles.

In addition, missionaries represented one segment of the white frontier population. Indians were confused when other "Christians," and even some missionaries, cheated and sexually abused them and did not practice what the missionaries preached. The Sioux author and physician Charles Eastman (1915) felt that the real civilizing influences on the Indians were whiskey and gunpowder, with the result that Indians often learned the whites' worst habits. Lewis Meriam (1932, 30), who headed an extensive study of the Indian Bureau (see chap. 8) was told repeatedly by missionaries that their "real difficulties" lay with "sinister white influences" rather than with the Indians.

CATHOLIC MISSIONS

After 1492, the Spanish sought both to exploit Indians through forced labor and to convert them to Catholicism. Whereas the English colonists who came later saw Indians as an impediment to settlement, the French and Spanish saw them as a cheap source of labor. The Spanish *encomienda* system gave the conquistadors grants of land, and local Indians went with the land in semislavery as the "spoils of conquest." According to the Law of Burgos of 1512, all Spaniards owning more than fifty Indians were required to provide for "the salvation of their souls . . . and the conservation of their lives" (quoted in Heath 1972, 8). The Spanish government idealistically intended holders of land grants to civilize and Christianize "their" Indians, but the Spanish conquerors often worked the Indians to death in mines and fields in their rush to return to Spain rich.

Bartolomé de Las Casas, perhaps the first Catholic priest ordained in America, claimed that in the first fifty years of the Spanish conquest more than 12 million Indians died (Las Casas [1542] 1992). Las Casas protested the mistreatment of Indians and their portrayal as irredeemable savages, and he fought against the encomienda system that he originally practiced himself, pleaded for religious toleration, and led the academic debate to recognize Indians as rational human beings with souls. In 1537 the pope gave them this recognition:

> God created these simple people without evil and without guile. They are most obedient and faithful to their natural lords and the Christians whom they serve. . . . Surely [they] would be most blessed in the world if only they worshipped the True God. . . . [T]he Indians are truly men and . . . they are not only capable of understanding the Catholic Faith, but according to our information, they desire exceedingly to receive it. (Quoted in McAlister 1984, 154)

Unfortunately for the Indians, this liberal view of their humanity and optimistic view of their willingness to convert to Catholicism was more prominent among intellectuals in Europe than among colonists in the Americas. Yet the colonial attitude that Indians were savages, little or no better than animals, did not stop large-scale intermixing of races. Unlike the later English colonists, most of whom immigrated as family units and planned to settle permanently in the New World, many French and Spanish men came to make their fortunes and then return to Europe. Harold Driver (1969, 476-77) writes, "Since about 90 per cent of Spanish colonists were unmarried men, they cohabited with and married Indian women in large numbers. . . . Although almost everyone in Mexico today is of mixed ancestry, the Indian genes that went into the mixture are about 80 per cent of the total." This intermixing created new groups of people, including the métis of Canada and the mestizos of the American Southwest and Central and South America.

Because of the failure of landowners to look after the education of Indians on their lands, in 1542 Charles V of Spain transferred the responsibility to Catholic friars. The Spanish colonial government's purpose was to Hispanicize the Indians, but friars sought to Christianize them. To separate Indians from both their nomadic way of life and the corrupting influence of frontier whites, the friars settled Indians around churches in a feudal pattern. When Pánfilo de Narváez took possession of the coast around Pensacola Bay, Florida, he had with him four Franciscan fathers who came to start missions. In 1568 the Jesuits established a school in Havana for Florida Indian youths (*Indian Education* 1969). Jesuits and Franciscan Gray Friars established several missions in what is now Florida after 1573 that lasted until the English attacked in 1703 and 1704.

Colonial Mexico

In 1529 a secondary school for Indians was established in Mexico City. The Franciscan Bernardino de Sahagún early on learned to speak Náhuatl, the language of the Aztecs, and to appreciate their culture. In 1536, seventeen years before the University of Mexico was founded, he helped to establish the Colegio de Santa Cruz de Tlatelolco for eighty Indian boys. The colegio was supported by the Law of the Indies and was largely turned over to the Indians in 1545. Latin, the language of the Catholic Church, was taught through the medium of Náhuatl.

However, by 1595 the school was in ruins and taught only elementary subjects. Colonial administrators had found that whereas non-Spanish-speaking Indians were "humble," those who spoke Spanish and especially those who knew Latin were "impudent." The average Spanish layman "strenuously objected to the Indian's use of Spanish [for] Indians who learned Spanish threatened the social stratification system which assumed Spanish superiority and Indian inferiority" (Heath 1972, 43). On the other hand, a little education was seen as good: it motivated Indians to move to cities, where they could be further exploited.

In 1550 Charles V ordered all Indians to learn Castilian Spanish. However, missionaries thought their work would be impeded if Indians were to be first taught Spanish, and a friar presented the case for indigenous-language teaching to Charles V:

Your Majesty has ordered that these Indians learn the language of Castile. Can you understand that some Indians will never learn it, while others will learn it badly? After all, we know that although the languages of Castile and Portugal are almost the same, a Portuguese gentleman may spend thirty years in Castile and never learn the language. Then how are these people whose language is so different from ours and who have such elaborate ways of speaking ever to learn Castilian? It seems to me that Your Majesty should command that all the Indians learn the Mexican language [Náhuatl], for in every village there are many Indians who know this language and learn it easily, and many confess in it. (Quoted in Heath 1972, 19)

Friars took over from the Aztec government the promotion of Náhuatl as a common Indian language; it was easier to teach and learn than Spanish, and there were not enough translators available for all the local indigenous languages. The friars spoke of Náhuatl's "authority, stylistic variety, and expressiveness" (quoted in Heath 1972, 24) and of how Indians learned quickly how to write it in roman letters. Faced with these facts from the hinterland, in 1570 King Philip III of Spain declared Náhuatl the official language of New Spain's Indians and ordered that the University of Mexico establish a chair of Náhuatl and that all clerics should learn it. By then Franciscan friars had produced more than eighty grammars, vocabularies, catechisms, and scriptural translations in Mexico's indigenous languages. Chroniclers from the sixteenth century wrote of friars who preached in as many as ten languages (Heath 1972).

In 1603 Philip revived his father's 1565 order that all missionaries learn the language of their charges. King Charles II again promoted Spanish for Indians in the 1690s but was not supported by either religious or lay colonial leaders. In 1728 descendants of Indian nobles asked the archbishop of Mexico City to reopen the Colegio de Santa Cruz de Tlatelolco. Primary education of Indians was considered poor, and "precision in penmanship and Latin oratory" were considered the "supreme goals" (Heath 1972, 59).

The Northeast

After 1611 Jesuits established missions in present-day Maine, New York, Wisconsin, Michigan, Ohio, Illinois, and Canada, plus one in

Louisiana that was reached by traveling down the Mississippi River. A description of a Jesuit Indian seminary is found in the Jesuit Relations of 1637. Students rose in the morning to say their prayers and then went to mass. After breakfast they were taught reading and writing. After a brief recess, they were taught the catechism. Midday dinner was followed by more prayers and afternoon reading. Then there was a recreation period, supper, more prayers, and bed. Of the six young men who constituted the first class, two died of sickness after being "purged and bled" and one left the seminary. Both of the students who died had been involved in fights with Frenchmen. The priest claimed the students died from overeating (Thwaites 1896–1901, vol. 12, 49).

Early New Mexico and California

The first permanent mission in New Mexico was founded in 1598. Over the next three centuries nearly three hundred Franciscans, thirty-eight of whom were killed by Indians, served in the Southwest. The Indians of the Southwest tended to be more agrarian and peaceful than those of the Northeast, but they did not take kindly to domination by the Spanish. When in 1599 Acoma Pueblo resisted a Spanish military expedition's demands for food, finally by armed resistance, Spanish retribution was drastic. An estimated 800 villagers were killed and 580 survivors placed on trial. The survivors were convicted of killing eleven Spaniards and two servants. Men over the age of twenty-five had one foot cut off and were sentenced to twenty years of servitude. Men between the ages of twelve and twenty-five and women over twelve were punished with twenty years of servitude. Two visiting Hopis had their right hands cut off (Knaut 1995).

Hopis opposed Franciscan missionaries who established a mission in Awatovi in 1629 and later at Shongopavi and Oraibi. An apostate from one of the Christian pueblos had told the Hopis that "some Spaniards, whom they would meet shortly, were coming to burn their pueblos, steal their property and behead their children, and that other Spaniards with the tonsures and vestments were nothing but imposters and that they should not allow them to sprinkle water on their heads because they were certain to die from it" (quoted in Whiteley 1988, 17).

Records show there was good reason for the Hopi's hatred of missionaries, as savagery was widespread in New Mexican missions. The historian France V. Scholes describes one occurrence in 1655. "Indian captains" appeared before Custodian Ibargaray and testified:

[A]n Oraibi Indian named Juan Cuna had been discovered in some act of idolatry. In the presence of the entire pueblo, Father Guerra gave him such a severe beating that "he was bathed in blood." Then, inside the church the friar administered a second beating, following which he took burning turpentine and larded the Indian's body from head to feet. Soon after receiving this brutal punishment the Indian died. (Scholes 1937, 145)

The deep hostility the Pueblos felt toward the newcomers led to the Pueblo Revolt of 1680, which resulted in the ousting of the Spanish from New Mexico. The Spanish were not able to muster the strength to return until 1692 (Knaut 1995). When the Hopi pueblo of Awatovi took back Franciscan missionaries after the Pueblo Revolt, the other villages came together and destroyed it, massacring its male villagers. The Spanish sent a punitive expedition in 1701, but the Hopis easily repulsed it (Whiteley 1998).

Father Junípero Serra founded the first Upper California mission in 1769 at San Diego. In 1808 there were nineteen California missions, and in 1823 there were twenty-one, stretching up the coast along El Camino Real (the Royal Road) from San Diego to San Francisco. The Spanish government financed the Catholic missions to pacify the frontier and protect California from Russian encroachment. The missions reduced the cost of stationing soldiers in California by supplying them with food, which otherwise had to be shipped from Mexico at great expense (Jackson and Castillo 1995). Mission lands were held in common, and Spanish was the lingua franca. Agricultural training as well as religious instruction was important, as the missions were largely self-sufficient using Indian labor. Early Spanish mission efforts focused on *reducción*, the gathering of nomadic Indians onto a mission compound ruled by missionaries, as was practiced in Paraguay from 1610 to 1757. An unintended consequence of concentrating Indians into mission villages was the promotion of virgin ground for epidemics of new diseases brought from Europe.

On his first Indian mission in Mexico, Father Serra learned the language, translated catechisms and prayers, and fought colonial encroachment on Indian lands. He was also an inquisitor for the Spanish Inquisition, though he sent no one to burn at the stake. Serra told the Indians that if they were baptized they would become "equal to the Spaniards" (Forbes [1839] 1972, 98).

Under Spanish law the missions were required to be secularized after ten years. The military governor of California, Filipe de Neve, tried to force this secularization but was opposed by Serra. According to Daniel Fogel (1988), the missionaries' efforts to educate the Indians were doomed because they continued to treat Indian men and women like children. The Franciscan order rigidly excluded Indians from the priesthood. Alexander Forbes ([1839] 1972), a British merchant and author of the first comprehensive history of California, described the California missions as a system of "ecclesiastical slavery" wherein the missionary was a slave master supported by a few soldiers, the students were hostages, and the Indians were more interested in food they received for going to Catholic services than the prayers. Each mission comprised about fifteen square miles and functioned as a self-supporting agricultural and industrial school.

"Wild" Indians were brought in for conversion by force, the women and children generally captured first. Once at the missions, they were expected to work seven hours a day and pray two hours, though there were many saints' holidays. Priests received twice the rations of Indians, and soldiers received one and a half times that of priests (Tinker 1993). A convert described the Indians' diet:

> The Indians at the mission of Santa Cruz, after prayers in the morning at church, received their orders as to their labors at the church door; then they went to breakfast, and had their meal altogether of boiled barley, which was served out to them from two large cauldrons, by means of a copper ladle. This full was the ration to each in a cora (a small kind of basket), from which they ate with a shell or the fingers. Some had small gourds into which they received their rations. Boiled barley was all that they had in the mornings. . . . At eleven A.M., the bell was rung to call them together. . . . The dinner consisted of cooked horse beans and peas. At the end of an hour the bell was rung again, and all went to work until about sunset, when each

received his rations of boiled corn. Such of the Indians as had families were given meat also. (Quoted in Jackson and Castillo 1995, 32)

Unmarried girls over eight years old were locked in a dormitory at night (Fogel 1988). A German naturalist described the treatment of widows and girls at the San Francisco mission in 1806:

All the girls and widows are in separate houses, and are kept at work under lock and key; they are only sometimes permitted, by their superiors, to go out in the day, but never at night. As soon, however, as a girl is married she is free, and lives with her husband in one of the villages of Indians belonging to the mission. . . . About a hundred paces from the buildings called the mission, lies one of the villages or barracks for Indians, which consist of eight long rows of houses, where each family lives entirely apart from the rest. (Quoted in Jackson and Castillo 1995, 81)

The friars punished lesser infractions of their rules, such as missing Mass, with whipping and more serious infractions with imprisonment or the stocks. They used soldiers to quell any Indian opposition. Forbes ([1839] 1972) described these soldiers as "deported felons and persons of low quality who raped Indian women, spreading syphilis." In contrast to the brutality of mission life, Forbes ([1839] 1972, 195) noted "the extreme tenderness and love shewn by the [Indian] parents to their children."

According to the friars, hell was the destination of all Indians who did not give up their former way of life, even their harmless or good customs—taking all the fun out of life. Religious instruction given neophytes was rudimentary, limited to repeating "in Spanish and Latin the offices of the church" from memory without understanding their meaning (Forbes [1839] 1972, 235). Under such harsh conditions, deaths among Indians outnumbered births, and the missions were only kept going by rounding up replacements from Indians who had not yet been colonized. According to Robert H. Jackson and Edward Castillo, the friars were not alarmed by the mortality rate. On the contrary: "The general belief held by missionaries that epidemics were a punishment sent by God, frequently limited their response to outbreaks. . . . [S]uffering on earth merely prepared Indian converts for a better life in heaven, in God's grace. These attitudes contributed to a rejection of innovations in medicine that could save lives" (1995, 42). The Franciscans tended to become "tied into a routine of acting as labor and estate managers responsible for the administration of the mission" (Jackson and Castillo 1995, 35).

In 1795 the Spanish monarchy decreed that Native languages be suppressed, overturning the Law of the Indies. However, even before that time most Catholic missionaries did not learn the Native languages of California. They held Indian cultures in contempt and provided little academic instruction of any kind. Mission Indians were described by visitors as "sullen, listless, and dull." Forbes ([1839] 1972) estimated that in 1802 there were 15,562 Indians on eighteen missions, compared to only 4,342 soldiers and settlers (who were discouraged from entering the missions). In 1833 the California missions were secularized, and many Indians promptly fled. The end of Mexican rule in 1846 did not improve the situation for California's Indians. In 1850 Indians and blacks in California were barred from testifying in court against whites, and in 1854 the Chinese were included in this restriction (Fogel 1988).

Independent Mexico

The only schooling the Indians of Mexico received in the early nineteenth century was religious. The 1857 Constitution called for free and secular education, and the governor of the state of Mexico called for publication of indigenous-language teaching materials. During the last half of the nineteenth century, more than one hundred scholars were writing in Mexico's indigenous languages. However, Spanish was considered the language of national unity. In the 1920s, at a time when the nation's four million Indians constituted almost one-third of the population, the minister of education under the conservative Diaz government called for the extermination of Indian languages. The use of indigenous languages was banned in favor of the "direct method" of teaching Spanish with no translation. However, the failure of this direct method was documented in 1927. A successful bilingual school existed in the 1920s, but the graduates wanted to stay in the city rather than return to rural Mexico where Spanish was useless outside the classroom (Heath 1972).

In 1931 Mexico's undersecretary of education met William Cameron Townsend, a missionary from the United States who advocated bilingual education. In 1934 Townsend started Camp Wycliffe (named after the English theologian who promoted the first translation of the Bible into English in the 1380s), which became the Summer Institute of Linguistics (SIL) at Sulfur Springs, Arkansas, to train linguists to work among Indian tribes in Mexico. SIL helped to prepare indigenous-language texts for Mexico's Department of Indian Affairs, which was founded in 1936. At that time the national illiteracy rate was nearly 60 percent. The Third Inter-American Conference on Education held in 1937 passed a resolution supporting bilingual education. A 1939 experiment showed that students could learn to read their own language after thirty to forty days of instruction, faster than they could learn to read Spanish. It was suggested that instruction in Spanish not begin before second or third grade (Heath 1972).

In 1940 the First Inter-American Indigenist Congress was held and the journal *America Indígena* started. However, right-wing politicians bitterly opposed bilingual education. UNESCO, an arm of the new United Nations after World War II, advocated a local approach to local problems and promoted bilingual education over the direct method of teaching national languages. Mexico's minister of public education again endorsed bilingual education in 1993 (Heath 1972).

PROTESTANT MISSIONARIES

Protestant missionary efforts among the Native population began soon after the arrival in the Americas of the first Protestant colonists (Bowden 1981). The first royal Charter for the Colony of Virginia in 1606 commended the founders for their "desires for the Furtherance of so noble a work . . . in propagating the Christian Religion to such People, as yet live in Darkness and miserable Ignorance of the true Knowledge and Worship of God [with the hope that they] may in time bring the infidels and Savages, living in those Parts, to human Civility" (quoted in Vogel 1972, 45–46).

In 1617 King James of England asked Anglican clergy to collect money "for the erecting of churches and schools for ye education of ye children of these barbarians in Virginia" (*Report* 1976, 26). However, the English colonists produced fewer missionaries and spent less money on missionary work than other Europeans (Bowden 1981).

Some Protestant missionaries, like some of their Catholic counterparts, found that the best way to explain Christianity was in their subjects' own languages. With Indian help, these missionaries translated the Bible and other religious works into Indian languages, as they had been translated in the preceding centuries into the many languages of Europe.

John Eliot and the Indian Bible

The first Charter for Massachusetts Bay Colony declared in 1629 the "principall ende of this plantation" to be to "win and incite the natives of that country to the knowledge and obedience of the onlie true God and Savior of mankinde, and the Christian Fayth" (quoted in Vogel 1972, 46). While converting the Indians was never the principal goal of the colonists, some missionary efforts were undertaken by the Puritans (later Congregationalists) in Massachusetts. In 1631 the Reverend John Eliot arrived in America and established a school in Roxbury near Boston. Five years later he instructed Pequot war captives "in the habits of industry." Although he used the Native language, he did not try to draw any connection between Christianity and traditional culture. Instead, he encouraged converts to come together in small, self-governing towns where they could be instructed in Christian ethics and arts. In these "praying towns," Indians were to dress and live like the colonists.

From 1651 to 1674 he helped to found fourteen praying towns with an estimated 1,111 inhabitants, 142 of whom could read in their own language and 72 of whom could write in English. Natick was the first praying town, and there Eliot conducted a sort of summer teacher training program for young Indians, who were taught English, Latin, and Greek. Eliot's teaching method was to deliver lectures, after which student questions were discussed. Eliot's work was most successful with those Indians who had been debilitated by war and disease. The Puritans insisted that the Indians give up their traditional lifeways, including long hair for men and short hair for women (Layman 1942; Szasz 1988). Missionaries usually insisted that schoolchildren "cut their hair, wear trousers and dresses, use soap, water, and combs, adopt English names, sit in chairs, eat with forks, and perform chores around the house and farm" (Bowden 1981, 169).

Eliot's interest in converting Indians was instrumental in the chartering by the English Parliament in 1649 of the Society for the Propagation of the Gospel in New England (called the New England Company after 1770) to support missionary efforts. Harvard University was founded in 1636 in part to provide education for Indian youths. In 1653 the Society funded the construction at Harvard of "a small brick building, known as the Indian College," but this effort was a failure (McCallum 1932, 300), and the building was demolished in 1698. With the restoration of the English monarchy, the Society was given a new charter in 1661 under the name Company for the Propagation of the Gospel in New England and the parts adjacent in America. In 1663 the Company provided funds raised in Great Britain to print fifteen hundred copies of the Indian Bible in the Massachusetts dialect of the Algonquian language at Harvard.

A number of Indians helped Eliot with his work. They taught him the Massachusetts language and served as translators. The first was a Montauk captive named Cockenoe who learned to read and write. He went on to make his living as an interpreter and defended Montauk ownership of Manhansick (Shelter) Island from claims by the colonists. Although Eliot was willing to work with Indians and eager to convert them, he did not treat them as equals. For example, they received far less pay than whites for similar work (Szasz 1988). In 1646 Eliot arranged for two young Massachusetts Indians to be educated. One of these, Job Nesuton, became an interpreter, teacher, and translator. A five-year-old Nipmuc Indian, Wowaus, was sent by his family to get an English education. He probably spent a few years at Corlet's Cambridge Grammar School and at Harvard. Under the English name James Printer, he was apprenticed as a printer and probably helped Eliot print the first Indian Bible and many other books. Only five Indian students attended Harvard's Indian College. Caleb Cheeshahteaumauk from Martha's Vineyard was the only Indian to graduate from Harvard in the colonial period; he died soon after from tuberculosis (Wright 1985; Szasz 1988).

The attack on the New England colonists led by the Indian leader King Philip in 1675–76, known as King Philip's War, caused the destruction of most of Eliot's praying towns, even when the inhabitants tried to remain neutral. Most of the Algonquian-language books were destroyed in the war. Fearful colonists interned most of the converts in Boston Harbor, where, under crowded, unhealthy conditions, many died. James Printer had sided with King Philip, but he took advantage of an amnesty and after the war helped Eliot reprint the Indian Bible, primers, and other missionary materials (Szasz 1988).

Thomas Mayhew Jr. and the Wampanoags

The experiences of the Indians who lived in relative isolation on Martha's Vineyard reveal an alternate model of Indian-white contact. Puritan missionaries there did not demand cultural suicide, and its isolation protected its inhabitants from the destruction of King Philip's War.

Thomas Mayhew and his son Thomas Mayhew Jr. worked with the fifteen hundred to three thousand Wampanoags on Martha's Vineyard in the 1640s. Whites did not become a majority on the island for another eighty years (Ronda 1981). Unlike Eliot's praying towns, where the focus was only on Christianizing the Indians, in Martha's Vineyard Christianity was also Indianized. Eliot identified Christianity with civilization, whereas Mayhew's priority was belief in God. Mayhew wanted Indians to think about theological questions such as what kind of being God was (Szasz 1988).

Once a few Wampanoags converted, they became the nucleus for further conversions that continued from generation to generation. Christianized Indians served as deacons, magistrates, and preachers. A few became voracious readers of religious books in both English and Algonquian. The new religion did not stop all Indians from abusing alcohol, but it helped to control the scourge. Thomas Mayhew Jr.'s brand of Christianity and that of his Indian successors, according to the historian James Ronda (1981, 385–86), "tended to elevate and honor the roles and tasks of Indian women" and "attracted Indian women by valuing their traditional roles." Ronda continues: "Christianity on the island was closely linked to formal schooling for converts. Educational opportunities extended to Indian women proved a powerful incentive for both conversion and continued Christian affiliation. The Indian churches promoted literacy among women and gave educated women a place to use their learning" (1981, 387). Ronda's research indicates that the literate Christian Indians of Martha's Vineyard, unlike many Christian converts elsewhere, had a good understanding of Christian theology.

In 1734 John Sergeant, a Congregationalist minister and former Yale University tutor who became fluent in the Muhhakaneok language, opened a school in Stockbridge, Massachusetts, with twenty Indian students. He described his philosophy of education thus:

> [It] is to take such a *Method* in the Education of our *Indian Children*, as shall in the most effectual Manner change their whole Habit of thinking and acting; and raise them, as far as possible, into the Condition of civil industrious and polish'd People; while at the same Time the Principles of Vertue and Piety shall be carefully instilled into their Minds in a Way, that will make the most lasting Impression; and withal to introduce the *English Language* among them instead of their own imperfect and barbarous *Dialect.* (Sergeant [1743] 1929, 3; original emphasis)

When Sargeant died in 1749, the school had fifty-five students, and it was supported in part by gifts from rich Londoners and a grant from the Massachusetts General Assembly. The school continued to operate for only a few years after his death. Some of its students went on to Dartmouth College, which was founded by Eleazar Wheelock (Layman 1942).

Eleazar Wheelock and Samson Occom

Eleazar Wheelock and Samson Occom (fig. 1) were among the most prominent colonial missionaries of the eighteenth century. Wheelock was born in Windham, Connecticut, in 1711, graduated from Yale in 1733, and became a leader of the religious revival called the Great Awakening that swept through the colonies in the 1740s. Although there was no popular support for Christianizing Indians and some support for exterminating them, Wheelock became interested, as had John Eliot, the Mayhews, and John Sergeant before him, in converting them. His greatest success was with one of his first Indian students, a young Mohegan named Samson Occom. The evangelical enthusiasm of the Great Awakening caught up Occom when he was about sixteen.

Portrait of the Reverend Samson Occom, circa 1751–1756, by Nathaniel Smibert. Bowdoin College Museum of Art, Brunswick, Maine. Bequest of the Honorable James Bowdoin III (1813.4).

In 1743, when he was twenty, he asked his mother to go to the Reverend Mr. Wheelock and ask him to teach her son reading (Occom 1994).

Wheelock's idea of Indian education was to remove children from their homes to Moor's Indian Charity School. There, the basics of a secular and religious education and husbandry were taught to boys. Girls were taught subjects suitable for their future roles as wives and mothers (Layman 1942). Among other things, Wheelock taught Occom and his other male students Greek and Latin, which he felt were essential for future missionaries. The Protestant emphasis on each person interpreting the Bible for himself led to an emphasis on each person being able to read the original Greek, Latin, and Hebrew biblical texts. Margaret Szasz gives the following description:

> At Moor's School, the day began before sunrise. Following early morning prayer and catechism, the boys remained in the classroom until noon, where they received a classical training in Latin and Greek, and sometimes Hebrew. After a two-hour break, they returned to work until 5:00 P.M. Just before dark, they attended evening prayers and public worship, and then studied until bedtime. This schedule was altered only on Sunday, when they spent the day in meetings and catechism classes. (1988, 223)

The father of one of Wheelock's Indian students wrote to complain that if his son was to spend his time doing farm chores he might as well be back home. Indian girls spent only one day a week at the school. During the rest of the week, they worked in area homes, where they were probably treated little better than servants. While primarily motivated by religion, Wheelock also argued in 1762 that missionaries and schoolmasters were cheaper than fortresses and wars, and he insisted that whites and Indians be taught the same subjects (Layman 1942). A visiting Boston merchant in 1764 reported finding at the school twenty or more Indian boys and girls who rose at 5:00 A.M. to read verses and pray. He also observed four or five men in their early twenties who were training to start their own schools and preach (Smith [1764] 1932).

Occom was ordained a Congregational minister in 1759. He went to Long Island as a missionary and teacher for twelve years. He wrote:

> I kept School as I did before and Carried on the Religious Meetings as often as ever, and attended the Sick and their Funerals, and did What Writings they wanted, and often Sat as a Judge to reconcile and Decide their Matters between them, and had Visiters of Indians from all Quarters; and, as our Custom is, we freely Entertained all Visters, And was fetched often from my Tribe and from others to See into their Affairs Both Religious & Temporal. (Quoted in Blodgett 1935, 45)

Although he was not paid as well as white missionaries who did less work among the Indians, Occom managed to raise a family of six children and minister to and teach his congregation. He left the following description of his teaching method:

> My Method in the School was, as Soon as the Children got together, and took their proper Seats, I Prayed with them, then began to hear them. I generally began (after Some of them Could Spell and Read) with those that were yet in their Alphabets; So around, as they were properly Seated, till I go through; and I obliged them to Study their Books, and to help one another; When they Could not make out a hard word, they Brought it to me—and I Usually heard them, in the Summer Season 8 Times a Day 4 in the morning and in ye after Noon. In the Winter Season 6 Times a Day, as Soon as they could Spell, they were obliged to Spell whenever they wanted to go out. I Concluded with Prayer. . . . I found Difficulty with Some Children, who were Somewhat Dull. Most of these can soon learn to Say over their Letters, they Distinguish the Sounds by the Ear, but their Eyes can't Distinguish the Letters, and the way I took to Cure them, was by making an Alphabet on Small bits of paper, and glued them on Small Chips of Cedar—after this Manner—A B etc. I put these Letters in order on a Bench, then point to one Letter and bid a Child to take notice of it, and then I order the Child to fetch me the Letter from ye Bench. . . . When they can bring any Letters, this way, then I Just Jumble them together, and bid them to Set them in Alphabetical order, and it is a Pleasure to 'em; and they soon Learn their Letters this Way. (Quoted in Blodgett 1935, 45–46)

Occom's methodology is similar to other descriptions from the eighteenth century. A hornbook, a three-by-five-inch paddle printed with the alphabet and the Lord's Prayer, was often a child's first "book." The emphasis on learning the names of letters continued into the nineteenth century, and the purpose of learning to read was to memorize Bible verses (Goodman et al. 1988). Later, Occom's involvement in helping his tribe keep their lands caused a rift with the church. He also tried to resettle southern New England Indians in upstate New York in a religiously oriented community, Brothertown, which he may have patterned after one of Eliot's praying towns that he had visited years before.

Two of Occom's brothers-in-law, the Montauks David and Jacob Fowler, who were Occom's students and attended Moor's Charity

School, also became teachers and went on to become leaders in Brother-town. Occom's daughter married a Mohegan teacher, Joseph Johnson (McCallum 1932). Another famous student at Wheelock's school was Joseph Brant, a Mohawk. He learned to write his own language from Anglican missionaries and teachers. Occom recruited the sixteen-year-old Brant and two other students to attend Moor's Charity School, where Brant stayed for two years. His sister lived with Sir William Johnson, the British Indian superintendent, in upstate New York. In 1763 Brant returned home and became a leader of the pro-British tribes during the American Revolution. Later, living in Canada, he collaborated on the 1786 edition of the *Mohawk Prayer Book*, which contained his translation of the *Anglican Book of Common Prayer* and the Gospel of Mark (O'Donnell 1980). Brant's sons attended Dartmouth College (Layman 1942).

Colonial Colleges

In 1766, at the behest of Wheelock, Samson Occom went to England to preach and raise money for Indian education. The English gave Occom much more respect than the colonists had. He raised more than eleven thousand pounds, which was used by Wheelock to found Dartmouth College. The college's charter established it "for the education and instruction of youth of the Indian Tribes in this Land in reading, writing, and all parts of Learning which shall appear necessary and expedient for civilizing and christianizing Children of Pagans as well as in all Liberal Arts and Science; and also of English youth and any others" (quoted in Layman 1942, 87–88)

Occom became upset when the college accepted more white than Indian students. However, Dartmouth has continued to educate a few Indians to this day. It was the only college in the colonies that remained open throughout the American Revolution. In 1775, in an attempt to garner Indian support for the Revolution, the Continental Congress appropriated $500 to support Indian youths at Dartmouth.

According to Margaret Layman (1942), Wheelock's failure to provide his students with living conditions that would make them feel more at home and to adapt the curriculum to meet their special needs prevented his efforts from being successful. Algonquian Indian missionaries trained by him shared his prejudices. When they were sent among the Iroquois, for example, they regarded them as foreign savages (Szasz 1988). Wheelock died in 1779. Toward the end of his life he wrote:

> I have turned out forty Indians who were good readers, writers, and instructed in the principles of the Christian religion. . . . Well behaved while with me[,] . . . by contact with the vices of their tribes, not more than half preserved their characters unstained. The rest were sunk into as low, savage, and brutish a way of living as they were before and many of the most promise have fallen lowest. (Quoted in Layman 1942, 92)

Wheelock's failure to note that his students' fall from grace was probably a result of their contact with frontier whites rather than with their own people is symptomatic of missionaries' general inability to see traditional tribal practices as anything but evil.

Harvard and Dartmouth were not the only colonial colleges set up in part to Christianize Indians. The College of William and Mary was founded in 1693, and the first Indian students attended in 1700. In 1723 a three-story house for Indian students known as Brafferton was built there and remained open until the American Revolution.

OTHER MISSIONARY EFFORTS

Missionaries representing other religious groups worked with various tribes during the colonial period. The pacifist Quakers gained a reputation for dealing fairly with Indians and insisting on purchasing Indian lands from the Indians themselves rather than land speculators. Another pacifist group, the German-speaking Moravians, established Indian missions in New York and Connecticut. Moravian schoolmasters, working primarily in Pennsylvania, learned the Indian languages and tried to maintain their use. They also taught their students German. For protection in the French and Indian War of 1764, Indian converts were put in barracks in Philadelphia, where sickness killed many of them (Layman 1942).

Russian missionaries arrived in Alaska in 1794, and by 1867, when the United States bought it from Russia, the Russian Orthodox Church operated some fifty schools there. These schools were gradually phased out, and the last one closed in 1916. Moravian, Presbyterian, Episcopalian, and Catholic missionaries took the place of the Russian Orthodox Church.

In 1884 the Alaska Organic Act charged the U.S. secretary of the interior with establishing schools. The Presbyterian missionary Dr. Sheldon Jackson (1834-1909), who had lobbied Congress for passage of the act, was appointed general agent for education in 1885. Missionaries were paid to educate Alaska Native students into the mid-1890s. Jackson helped to raise funds to found and maintain a Presbyterian mission school in Sitka, Alaska, which in 1966 became Sheldon Jackson College (*History* 2003).

Jackson worked to prevent Alaska Natives from being placed on reservations, as had been the fate of Indians in the lower forty-eight states. But he supported English-only education and putting Native students in boarding schools. When gold was discovered in Alaska in the 1880s, the non-Native population of Alaska increased considerably, and in 1900 Congress permitted towns with a population of three hundred or more to incorporate and elect school boards (Dauenhauer 2000; Getches 1977).

CANADIAN RESIDENTIAL SCHOOLS

Canada has been described as having a better Indian policy than the United States, one that led to fewer Indian wars. In many ways, however, its efforts paralleled those of the United States—with even worse consequences that have lasted longer. Instead of giving Indians large reservations and slowly whittling them away as in the United States, the Canadian government started with small reserves. The schools the government funded were unrelentingly assimilationist and designed to separate parents from their children so that the children could join modern society. However, the schools were inadequate in preparing students to live in white society or to return to their reserves. In *A National Crime* (1999), the historian John S. Milloy uses government records to document the unhealthy, brutal conditions in Canada's church-run residential schools. His research found that these schools were "marked by the persistent neglect and abuse of children and through them of Aboriginal communities in general" (xiii) and were characterized by widespread physical and sexual abuse (both by staff and by other students) until the last one closed in 1986. In the "mini-monarchies" that were residential schools, "discipline was curriculum and punishment was pedagogy" (44, 134). The Canadian government chronically underfunded their system of church-run residential industrial schools (started in 1879), which were patterned in part after similar schools in the United States, and it left them under church control, mainly Catholic and Anglican, without adequate government oversight throughout most of the twentieth century.

Under British rule the Proclamation of 1763 recognized Indian self-government, which continued into the nineteenth century. The 1857 Act to Encourage the Gradual Civilization of the Indian Tribes in the Province promoted allotment of Indian lands. This act, according to Milloy (1999), redefined civilizing Indians from developing community self-sufficiency to assimilating them individually. The passage of the British North American Act of 1867 defined the government's "respon-sibility" for Indians and Inuits and abolished their self-government. Canada did have fewer Indian wars than the United States, and after the second Riel rebellion of métis in 1885 schooling was viewed as pacification.

The 1924 Memorandum of the Convention of Catholic Principals declared:

> All true civilization must be based on moral law, which christian religion alone can give. Pagan superstition could not . . . suffice to make the Indians practice the virtues of our civilization and avoid its attendant vices. Several people have desired us to countenance the dances of the Indians and to observe their festivals; but their habits, being the result of free and easy mode of life, cannot conform to the intense struggle for life which our social conditions require. (Quoted in Milloy 1999, 36–37)

Indians in Canada did not benefit from the loosening up of assim-ilationist efforts that occurred in the United States in the 1930s (see chap. 8), and they were not granted the right to vote in federal elections until 1960. Unlike U.S. Indians, the Indians of Canada had little choice about where to send their children to school, which put less pressure on the schools to accommodate the desires of parents. In 1938 a joint delegation of churches called on the government to provide school uniforms: "There would be no true cohesion without a uniform. Further if modern Dictators [Hitler and Mussolini] find that a coloured shirt assists in implanting political doctrines and even racial and theological ideas, it would be obvious that the adoption of a bright and attractive uniform would assist in implanting all that we desire in the children under our care" (quoted in Milloy 1999, 125).

In 1939 there were 9,027 students in seventy-nine residential schools. As in the United States, after World War II Canada worked to close Indian schools and integrate Indians into the provincial school systems. Some residential schools were closed and day schools received more government support. The Catholic Church staunchly opposed closing its residential schools. Over the course of the 1950s an effort was made to start parent committees and the Canadian Parliament dropped sanctions against some Indian traditional practices that had been banned in its 1951 Indian Act. In 1969 Canada's Department of Indian Affairs took complete control of its schools for Indians and Inuits. As in the United States, orphans and children from dysfunctional families who were seen as having nowhere else to go increasingly filled the remaining residential schools. Many students lacked adequate preparation for provincial schools, which often did little to accommodate their special needs, leading to an increased dropout rate. By 1969 there were only 1,899 students in twelve residential schools. In 1970 the Blue Quills School in Alberta was taken over by local Indians nonviolently when the government tried to close it.

As in southern Canada and in the United States, local school advisory committees were established after World War II in Canada's far north, but they had little real power at first. In 1975 the James Bay and Northern Quebec Agreement provided for Inuit and Cree self-governance, including running the schools serving their children. In 1978 the Kativik School Board serving schools in fourteen villages became the first Inuit-controlled school board in Canada. In 1989 the Nunavik Educational Task Force was formed to review language, curriculum, teacher training, postsecondary education, adult education, and the role of family and community in education in northern Quebec. It found that self-governance did not automatically lead to more culturally relevant education or higher student academic achievement.

Ann Vick-Westgate (2002, 13), in her study of Inuit-controlled education in northern Canada, notes that the "village school was, and still too often is, a Westernized formal institution that has excluded the knowledge and values of the community it serves and done a poor job of preparing young people for future roles."

The Royal Commission on Aboriginal Peoples reported in 1997 on the "grievous harms suffered by countless Aboriginal children, families, and communities as a result of the residential school system." And in 1998 the Canadian minister of Indian affairs declared:

> One aspect of our relationship with Aboriginal people over this period that requires particular attention is the Residential School system. The system separated many children from their families and communities and prevented them from speaking their own languages and from learning about their heritage and cultures. In the worst cases, it left legacies of personal pain and distress that continue to reverberate in Aboriginal communities to this day. Tragically, some children were the victims of physical and sexual abuse. (Quoted in Milloy 1999, 303–4)

While the indigenous peoples of America were still fighting colonialism in the second half of the twentieth century with the support of the civil rights movement, the English colonies south of Canada had thrown off British rule two hundred years earlier.

THE END OF BRITISH RULE
IN THE THIRTEEN COLONIES

The threat of Indian attack helped to unify the thirteen British colonies south of Canada for their common defense. Both the 1643 New England Confederation and the 1754 Albany Plan of Union were spurred by fears of Indian attacks. Ironically, the colonists patterned the Albany Plan, Articles of Confederation, and Constitution in part on the Iroquois Confederacy, which provided a model of unity, equality, and legislative decorum (Grinde and Johansen 1991).

Because of the expense of the Indian wars and the desire to preserve a profitable trade in furs, colonists were not allowed to buy Indian land in 1761. In 1763 King George issued a royal proclamation closing the west to white settlement in a further attempt to reduce friction between colonists and Indian tribes. The extra taxes colonists were forced to pay to support the cost of Indian wars and the standing army needed to enforce the provisions of the 1763 proclamation were one of the major causes of the American Revolution.

CHAPTER TWO

TREATIES AND WESTERN REMOVAL
1776–1867

During the American Revolution (1776–81), the united thirteen colonies sought to have Indian tribes fight on their side or at least remain neutral. The Continental Congress approved its first treaty, with the Delaware, in 1778. In 1775 the Continental Congress had recommended the employment of Samuel Kirkland to work with the Iroquois Confederacy. In 1784 Kirkland worked as a missionary for the Society in Scotland for Propagating the Gospel, setting up small schools in the Oneida villages where reading, writing, and arithmetic were taught in Oneida and English (Layman 1942).

In an attempt to avoid costly new wars, one of the first concerns of the postrevolutionary leadership was dealing with Indian tribes, especially those that had fought alongside the British. The Constitution that went into effect in 1788 gave the federal government the power to regulate commerce with Indian tribes and make treaties with them. With fine rhetoric, the Congress established by the Articles of Confederation had in the previous year adopted the Northwest Ordinance, which outlined how lands west of the Appalachians could become states. Article III stated, "The utmost good faith shall always be observed towards the Indians, their lands and property shall never be taken from them without their consent; and in their property, rights and liberty, they never shall be invaded or disturbed, unless in just and lawful wars authorized by Congress" (Thorpe 1909, 961).

There was a consensus, at least among humanitarians, that it was necessary to civilize Indians so that they would live in harmony with the settlers who were taking their lands. In exchange, the Indians would receive civilization and education. Education would make them independent yeoman farmers, thus freeing up their vast hunting grounds for white settlement. There were only a dozen missionaries left at the end of the American Revolution, but another religious revival, the Second Great Awakening, led to the creation of the American Board of Commissioners for Foreign Missions in 1810 whose purpose was to evangelize Indians and others (Prucha 1984).

In his fourth annual address to Congress in 1792, President George Washington declared, "I can not dismiss the subject of Indian affairs without again recommending to your consideration the expediency of more adequate provision for giving energy to the laws throughout our interior frontier and for restraining the commission of outrages upon the Indians, without which all pacific plans must prove nugatory" (Richardson 1910, 119). A year later, he issued a proclamation offering a reward for the apprehension of Georgians who had destroyed a Cherokee town. But the newly independent United States had no more success controlling frontier whites than had the British. Speculators, settlers, traders, and trappers often took advantage of Indians, who would then retaliate. Then there would be a cry for the army and a new Indian war would start, usually with the Indians losing. The Indians would give up more land and be forced farther west.

TREATY MAKING

The 1794 treaty with the Oneida, Tuscarora, and Stockbridge Indians provided for "employing one or two suitable persons . . . to instruct some young men of the three nations in the arts of the miller and sawyer" (Washburn 1973, 2293). The 1803 treaty with the Kaskaskias of Indiana Territory stated:

> Whereas, The greater part of the said tribe have been baptized and received into the Catholic church to which they are much attached, the United States will give annually for seven years one hundred dollars towards the support of a priest of that religion, who will engage to perform for the said tribe the duties of his office and also to instruct as many of their children as possible in the rudiments of literature. (Washburn 1973, 2310)

As the U.S. government and Indian nations negotiated more treaties, provisions for education and civilization increased, sometimes at the request of the tribes, which saw they would have to change to survive. Over the next eighty-two years, the Senate approved almost four hundred treaties, one hundred twenty of which contained educational provisions. In these treaties, tribes ceded almost a billion acres to the United States (*Indian Education* 1969; Task Force 1976). The U.S. government saw the provision of education as a proper trade-off for land given up by the tribes. Throughout the nineteenth century the government did not always consult with tribes when their treaty money was used for the support of mission schools (Adams 1988).

THE FACTORY SYSTEM

In 1795 Congress set up a system of government-operated trading posts called factories to provide Indians with trade goods at a fair price so as to tie them to the United States economically and avoid further warfare. The Trade and Intercourse Act of 1802, which remained in effect until 1834, defined the boundaries of Indian lands and penalties for trespassers, authorized the death penalty for anyone killing friendly Indians, allowed the president to prevent the selling of "spiritous liquors" to Indians, and authorized up to $15,000 per year "to promote civilization among the friendly Indian tribes, and to secure the continuance of their friendship" (Peters 1845, vol. 2, 143).

The factory system worked relatively well until the War of 1812 made it impossible to continue to supply superior British-made goods. Thomas J. McKenney was appointed superintendent of Indian trade in 1816 and served in that office until 1822. McKenney broadened the duties of the position to advise the secretary of war and work with humanitarian and church groups concerned with the welfare of Indians (Viola 1979).

THE CIVILIZATION FUND

McKenney "fought hard" to establish "a national school system for the Indians, to be supported by profits from an expanded factory system"

(Prucha 1984, 150). Along with missionaries, he lobbied Congress for funding. In 1818 a House committee declared:

> In the present state of our country, one of two things seems to be necessary: either that these sons of the forest should be moralized or exterminated. Humanity would rejoice at the former, but shrink with horror from the latter. Put into the hands of their children the primer and the hoe, and they will naturally, in time, take hold of the plough; and, as their minds become enlightened and expand, the Bible will be their book, and they will grow up in habits of morality and industry, leave the chase to those whose minds are less cultivated, and become useful members of society. (Quoted in Prucha 1984, 150)

Examples of missionary successes in Asia and Africa were used in support of the argument that Indians could also be converted and civilized.

In 1819 McKenney succeeded in getting Congress to pass the Indian Civilization Act to provide financial support to religious groups and other interested individuals willing to live among and teach Indians. Ten thousand dollars a year was authorized under the act, in addition to money for education provided to tribes by treaties "for the purpose of providing against the further decline and final extinction of the Indian tribes, adjoining the frontier settlements of the United States, and for introducing among them the habits and arts of civilization." The money was to be used with the consent of the Indians "to employ capable persons of good moral character, to instruct them in the mode of agriculture suited to their situation; and for teaching their children in reading, writing, and arithmetic, and performing such other duties as may be enjoined" by the president (Peters III 1848, 516). To implement the act, President James Monroe's secretary of war, John C. Calhoun, issued a circular to all missionary agencies offering to pay two-thirds of construction costs and providing operating expenses for any of them willing to educate Indians. Congress discontinued the factory system in 1822 because of opposition by private companies, especially the American Fur Company.

At that time there were fourteen schools with 508 students, and only the Creeks were reported to not want schools. Within five years of the establishment of the so-called Civilization Fund, eighteen new Indian schools were opened, bringing the total to twenty-one schools with 800 students (Fishbacher 1967; Layman 1942). Funding continued to be provided under this act until it was repealed in 1873.

The Reverend Jedidiah Morse, a well-known Congregationalist minister and author, visited Indian tribes in 1820 at the request of two missionary societies. Secretary of War Calhoun gave Morse an official commission after President Monroe approved the plan. As could be expected, Morse's 1822 *Report to the Secretary of War of the United States on Indian Affairs* called for greater efforts to civilize and convert Indians using "'education families' composed of missionaries, teachers, and mechanics" and included a proposal for an Indian college to be funded by the government and run by missionaries. Morse felt Indians were "an intelligent and noble part of our race, and capable of high moral and intellectual improvement" (Prucha 1984, 156).

The government expected teachers in mission schools to promote government policy, including the policy of removing eastern tribes west of the Mississippi River. In 1820 Calhoun declared it the duty of Indian school employees "to impress on the minds of the Indians the friendly and benevolent views of the government towards them, and the advantages to them in yielding to the policy of the government, and co-operating with it in such measures as it may deem necessary for their civilization and happiness" (New American State Papers 1972, 581). (Calhoun's grandmother had been killed by Cherokees in 1760.)

THE OFFICE OF INDIAN AFFAIRS

At the same time that missionary groups were expanding their efforts among Indian tribes, the U.S. government formalized its handling of the tribes. In 1824 Secretary of War Calhoun created within his department the United States Office of Indian Affairs under the direction of McKenney. The new office began issuing annual reports that year and continued to do so until 1949. McKenney wrote in his first annual report that there were thirty-two Indian schools in operation with 916 students, including two schools for the Cherokee operated by the United Brethren, fifteen schools for the Cherokee and Choctaw operated by the American Board of Commissioners for Foreign

Missions, four schools for the Cherokee and Creek run by the Baptists, and one school run by the Catholic Church (*ARCIA* 1824).

McKenney declared optimistically that school superintendents' reports "demonstrate that no insurmountable difficulty is in the way of a complete reformation of the principles and pursuits of the American Indian" and that the "entire reformation" was possible in the present generation (*ARCIA* 1824, 1-2). In 1825 he was able to report that six more schools were in operation (*ARCIA* 1825). In 1826 he reported that $10,000 a year from the Civilization Fund was not enough and asked for more money. That year he reported to Congress that there were about twelve hundred students being educated in farming, mechanical arts, and domestic economy (*ARCIA* 1826). In addition, he reported that he had visited schools and seen that Indian students were receiving great benefits from their education and that graduates needed sections of land on which to live.

In 1830 McKenney was forced out of the Indian Office by the new president, Andrew Jackson, whom he had previously opposed politically. His replacement wrote in the 1831 annual report:

[Indians are] gradually diminishing in numbers and deteriorating in condition; incapable of coping with the superior intelligence of the white man; ready to fall into the vices, but unapt to appropriate the benefits of the social state; the increasing tide of the white population threatened soon to engulf them, and finally cause their extinction. (*ARCIA* 1831, 172)

His antidote for this depressing situation was schooling and the removal of the Indians west of the Mississippi River.

The status of the Office of Indian Affairs inside the War Department was formalized by Congress in 1832, which at the same time created the post of Commissioner of Indian Affairs. In 1834 the Indian Office was reorganized by Congress into the Department of Indian Affairs, still inside the War Department. The first Commissioner, Elbert Herring, wrote in his 1832 annual report that "Indian children evince a facility of acquirement no wise inferior to those of European origin" (*ARCIA* 1832, 160). By 1832 Catholics were running three of the fifty-one schools, which now served 1,865 students. The church was teaching children in their own language at Green Bay so that they could learn more readily and pass on their education to other members of the tribe.

The 1832 report also indicated that Indians were being vaccinated against diseases. In 1833 Herring emphasized the need to keep alcohol away from Indians and to provide employment to Indian students after they left school to keep them from returning to their traditional ways. According to Herring's 1835 report, $42,000 in treaty money was going to help support the operation of twenty-nine schools and that one school, the Choctaw Academy, was receiving $31,000.

In 1836 the new Commissioner of Indian Affairs, Carey Allen Harris, reported that there were fifty-two schools with 1,381 students, 156 of whom attended the Choctaw Academy. The American Board was running nineteen schools, the Choctaw Nation five schools, and the Catholic Church four schools (*ARCIA* 1836). Harris was forced out of office in 1838 under charges of corruption involving speculation on Indian lands (Satz 1979). His successor, T. Hartley Crawford, formalized development of manual labor schools to educate Indian children in farming and homemaking (*ARCIA* 1838). Crawford even took four Indian boys into his home.

In 1842 Crawford stated that "the greatest good we can bestow upon" Indians "is education, in its broadest sense—education in letters; education in labor and the mechanic arts; education in morals; education in Christianity" (*ARCIA* 1842, 379). His successor, Commissioner William Medill, reported in 1845 that the Choctaw were supporting twenty-eight neighborhood schools with treaty funds. He wrote:

Experience has clearly demonstrated the superiority of schools conducted on the manual labor system. The mere teaching of letters to the savage mind is not sufficient to give a new direction to his pursuits, or render him useful to his people. It is known that strong prejudices exist among many of the tribes against schools, and it is only by actual observation, by demonstrating the advantages of learning, that the Indian can be made to feel its importance. This can only be done by combining with letters such studies as call forth the energies of the body, and inspire a taste for the arts of civilized life; for to the same extent that the educated Indian appreciates his own knowledge, it frequently occurs that he is depreciated in the estimation of his tribe. He is viewed as unfitted for the chase, and is condemned and ridiculed by his fellows, who are unable to understand, and, of course, attach no importance to his acquirements. (*ARCIA* 1845, 453–54)

Because of this lack of appreciation, the former students then, according to Medill, start to associate with "depraved white men." The Creek Indian Agent described returned students as drunken idlers in the same report and detailed the fate of one student returning from the Choctaw Academy who wanted to help his people but was rejected as a "white man" and turned to drink. His tribe wanted him to become an Indian again before they would listen to him. He served as an interpreter for a time but was killed in "drunken frolic" (*ARCIA* 1845, 520). Medill deplored the "inadequacy of existing laws to suppress the whisky trade" carried on by "abandoned white men" (452). One of his Indian agents wrote:

> It is not a subject of astonishment that the education, the civilization, and especially the glorious religion of the white man, are held by them in so little estimation. Our education appears to consist in knowing how most effectually to cheat them; our civilization in knowing how to pander to the worst propensities of nature, and then beholding the criminal and inhuman results with a cold indifference—a worse than heathen apathy; while our religion is readily summed up in the consideration of dollars and cents. (485)

By 1842 there were fifty-two Indian schools; the forty-five schools reporting enrollment had 2,132 students. In 1848 there were sixteen manual labor schools with 2,873 students, and after 1848 treaties specified schools as manual labor or agricultural and industrial schools. In 1861 there were 147 Indian schools, and ten years later, near the end of the treaty period, 286 with 6,061 students. Almost half those schools were in the Cherokee, Choctaw, Chickasaw, and Creek Nations in Indian Territory, present-day Oklahoma. The difficulty of convincing parents to send their children to schools can be seen in the 1857 Pawnee treaty that stipulated that parents who refused to send their children to school regularly would have money deducted from their annuities (Layman 1942).

In 1849 Congress created the Department of the Interior and transferred into it the Office of Indian Affairs. This move had little effect on Indian education, as missionaries continued to be the major influence on Indian children. As time went on, the forced relocation and settlement of tribes on reservations caused them to become almost totally dependent on the federal government's Indian Office for food, shelter, and clothing. The developing system of Indian reservations brought on the growth of a government bureaucracy headed by the Commissioner of Indian Affairs in Washington, D.C., and managed at the reservation level by Indian agents.

Frequent changes in Indian Commissioners hampered U.S. efforts to develop a consistent and effective Indian policy. Most Commissions of Indian Affairs remained in office for only a few years and left just when they were becoming proficient in discharging their duties.

WESTERN REMOVAL

It is ironic, given the success of the missionary and government efforts to "civilize" the Cherokee, that in 1820 congressional leaders began to develop plans to move eastern tribes, including the Cherokee, west of the Mississippi River. In a special message to Congress in 1825 President Monroe gave his support to removal as a way to protect Indians from whites. Although the Cherokee fought the issue all the way to the Supreme Court, the discovery of gold in the Georgia portion of the Cherokee Nation doomed their chance to retain their ancestral lands. In 1830 Congress passed the Indian Removal Act, authorizing President Andrew Jackson to exchange lands in the west for those held in the eastern states. In the 1831 Supreme Court case *Cherokee Nation* v. *Georgia*, Chief Justice John Marshall opined,

> Though the Indians are acknowledged to have an unquestionable, and, heretofore, unquestioned right to the lands they occupy, until that right shall be extinguished by a voluntary cession to our government; yet it may well be doubted whether those tribes which reside within the acknowledged boundaries of the United States can, with strict accuracy, be denominated foreign nations. They may, more correctly, perhaps, be denominated domestic dependent nations. They occupy a territory to which we assert a title independent of their will, which must take effect in point of possession when their right of possession ceases. Meanwhile they are in a state of pupilage. Their relation to the United States resembles that of a ward to his guardian. (5 Pet. 1, 12 [1831])

By appointing its own leaders for the Cherokee, the U.S. government obtained a "voluntary cession" of Cherokee land in the east in the 1835 Treaty of New Echota, but the U.S. Army had to enforce removal at gunpoint after the Georgia Guard terrorized the Cherokee. The Guard was a state militia formed in January 1831 to "protect" gold mines in the Cherokee Nation. In 1830, with President Jackson's support, Georgia passed a law stipulating that missionaries had to have licenses and take an oath of allegiance to the state of Georgia. However, in 1832, in *Worcester* v. *Georgia*, the Supreme Court struck down this attempt by Georgia to keep missionaries and white friends out of the Cherokee Nation. Again, Chief Justice Marshall held:

> The treaties and laws of the United States contemplate the Indian territory as completely separated from that of the states; and provide that all intercourse with them shall be carried on exclusively by the government of the Union.
>
> The Indian nations had always been considered as distinct, independent, political communities, retaining their original natural rights, as the undisputed possessors of the soil, from time immemorial. . . . The words "treaty" and "nation" are words of our own language, selected in our diplomatic and legislative proceedings, by ourselves, having each a definite and well understood meaning. We have applied them to Indians as we have applied them to the other nations of the earth. They are applied to all in the same sense. (6 Pet. 500 [1832])

Jackson is reported to have remarked, "John Marshall has made his decision, now let him enforce it" (Vogel 1972, 124). The Georgia Guard forced missionaries to leave or arrested them. According to the historian William McLoughlin (1984, 25), "[T]he imprisonment of white missionaries pursuing their religious duty aroused far more vehement reaction from the general public, North and South, East and West, than any oppression of the red man." Despite winning his Supreme Court case, the Reverend Mr. Worcester received four years at hard labor for his support of the Cherokee. Eventually he agreed to leave Georgia and was pardoned.

Despite the fact that he supported the Cherokee in their resistance to removal from their ancestral lands, Dr. Worcester felt Cherokee youth who did not speak English should be removed to boarding schools because they learned nothing in day schools. In the words of a missionary's wife, "In a neighborhood school the children were constantly under the influence of their Heathen parents" (McLoughlin 1984, 306). After his release from prison, Worcester established a printing press in western Cherokee country. Between 1835 and 1861 almost fourteen million pages were printed by this press, many of them using Sequoyah's Cherokee syllabary (Foreman 1938). However, despite having spent thirty-four years among the Cherokee, Worcester never learned to speak their language well enough to preach without an interpreter (Bass [1936] 1996).

Methodist ministers went so far as to preach that President Jackson would go to hell for his actions against the Cherokee. However, many Cherokees were now disillusioned with Christianity; a Christian nation had taken their lands, including mission lands, by force and given it to the "offscouring of American society" (McLoughlin 1984, 302). As a side effect of removal, federal support for mission schools east of the Mississippi River ended in 1832, and the government offered generous subsidies to move missions west. Jackson's support of Georgia's "nullification" of Supreme Court decisions helped to create the climate that led Southern states to secede from the Union.

Congress approved the forced removal of the remainder of the Cherokee in 1838. Assembled at bayonet point and marched west, an estimated 4,000 of the 11,500 Indians who started on what became known as the Trail of Tears died from dysentery, malnutrition, exposure, or exhaustion before they reached Oklahoma (Woodward 1963). Alexis de Tocqueville, who witnessed the removal, wrote in *Democracy in America* of the great evils of the young Republic's treatment of Indians. According to Tocqueville, the tribes stood in the path of the greediest nation on earth, a nation destitute of good faith:

> At the end of the year 1831 I was on the left bank of the Mississippi, at the place the Europeans call Memphis. While I was there a numerous band of Choctaws . . . arrived; these savages were leaving their country and seeking to pass over to the right bank of the Mississippi, where they hoped to find an asylum promised them by the American government. It was then the depths of winter, and that year the cold was exceptionally severe; the snow was hard on the ground, and huge masses of ice drifted on the river. The Indians brought their families with them; their were among them the

wounded, the sick, newborn babies, and old men on the point of death. They had neither tents nor wagons, but only some provisions and weapons. I saw them embark to cross the great river, and the sight will never fade from my memory. Neither sob nor complaint rose from that silent assembly. Their afflictions were long standing, and they felt them irremediable. ([1835] 1966, 298–99)

Despite the hardship and internal conflict produced by removal, the Choctaw, Cherokee, and other tribes soon established schools in Indian Territory.

TEACHERS AND SCHOOLS

A teacher's description of the Baptist school at Sault Ste. Marie, Michigan, illustrates a teaching method used in the 1830s:

I attached a large sheet containing the alphabet to the side of my room, formed the small scholars into classes and placed a monitor over them, whose business it was, through the day, to march those classes one after another to the card and teach them, the whole class speaking at once. In a few weeks we had them all nicely through their alphabet. (Quoted in Layman 1942, 128–29)

This missionary reported opposition from the local liquor dealers and the longer-established Catholic missionaries. Another Northwest mission was that of Frederick Ayer, who reestablished a mission for the Western Evangelical Missionary Society of Oberlin College at Red Lake, Minnesota, in 1843. In the early years, only books written in the Ojibwa language were used. When the missionaries later switched to instruction in English, the quality of education reportedly declined (Layman 1942).

Stephen R. Riggs and his wife, Mary, started missionary work with the Sioux in 1837. In 1852 Riggs published the *Grammar and Dictionary of the Dakota Language.* The couple found teaching English "to be very difficult and not producing much apparent fruit." It was not the students' lack of ability but their unwillingness that prevented them from learning English. According to Riggs (1880, 61), "Teaching Dakota was a different thing. It was their own language. The lessons, printed with open type and a brush on old newspapers, and hung round the walls of the school-room, were words that had a meaning even to a Dakota child." The success of these missionaries is indicated by the report of a Hicksite Friend (Quaker) that "[a] very small portion of the [Santee Sioux] . . . speak or write the English language, but a large number speak and write their own, and are able to hold correspondence with those who are in Minnesota and Wisconsin" (*ARBIC* 1871, 161). The success of this method can be attributed not just to the fact that students were learning in their own language; it was also because the writing system developed corresponded closely with the sounds of their language, unlike English, in which many words are not spelled the way they sound: "Theirs is a phonetic language, and a smart boy will learn it in three or four weeks; and we have found it far better to instruct them in their own language, and also to teach them English as fast as we can" (*ARBIC* 1871, 168).

The Riggses' children carried on their work at Santee Training School in the second half of the nineteenth century, and a Bible in Dakota was printed in 1880. Their work had many hazards, including being caught up in the Minnesota Sioux Uprising of 1862 in which one government teacher was shot and killed. Stephen Riggs was spit on by some whites for working with the imprisoned Sioux, and he acted as interpreter and clerk of the military court that tried and condemned three hundred of them for their part in the uprising (Howard 1958). Charles Eastman (1915) dates the beginning of a positive change in the popular attitude toward Indians to President Abraham Lincoln's sparing all but twenty-nine of the condemned from hanging, including Eastman's father.

Cherokee Schools

The Cherokee tribe of the southeastern United States was one of the most successful in accepting civilization. However, "few Cherokee found the Christian religion particularly relevant or helpful when they first heard it," according to McLoughlin (1984, 22), because it "lacked the sense of balance and harmony between man and nature which was so central" to the Cherokee. Many Cherokee wanted education without Christianity. One person told the Baptists in 1824, "We want our children to learn English so that the white man cannot cheat us" (McLoughlin 1984, 155). Mixed-blood Cherokee were more in favor of education and more accepted by missionaries.

The Cherokee mission schools were run on the new Lancastrian plan, developed in about 1800 in England by Joseph Lancaster. The American Board of Commissioners for Foreign Missions (established in 1810 with support from the Congregational, Dutch Reformed, and Presbyterian Churches in 1816) sent a teacher to a Lancastrian school to learn the system. It provided very structured instruction and used advanced students as "monitors" to teach younger students. The curriculum consisted of reading, writing, arithmetic, and morals (religion). The goal of the education was to give the students information and develop their memory (Layman 1942). Students were given tickets for good behavior and learning that could be exchanged for additional clothing or books (McLoughlin 1984).

According to missionaries, it took three to four years of regular school attendance for Cherokee children to master the rudiments of English reading and writing. Students learned by rote, first memorizing the sounds of English. The mission schools had rigid discipline, including whipping. A Moravian missionary wrote, "During school no one dare look off from his book or talk to his neighbor" (quoted in McLoughlin 1984, 60). The Moravian school in 1804 had a model farm, and students were kept busy from dawn to dusk. The Moravians did not learn Cherokee, even though some lived among the tribe for twenty-five years. Missionaries preferred preaching to dreary teaching, and the Cherokee felt that elders should be teachers (McLoughlin 1984).

There were class distinctions in the missionary work of the various denominations. The Moravians (United Brethren) and the Presbyterian Board of Missions taught the slave-owning, mixed-blood Cherokee elite, whereas the Methodists and the Baptists learned Cherokee and lived with the common people, usually full-bloods, as itinerant ministers. In contrast to the Calvinist Moravians and Presbyterians, the Baptists and Methodists used Cherokee exhorters (lay preachers) and were able to convert the poor. According to McLoughlin (1984, 60), "[A] native ministry was the key to giving vital new power to God's word among the Cherokees." Speaking English was not a requirement for becoming a Methodist or a Baptist. In contrast to the Calvinist belief that people were predestined before birth to go to heaven or hell,

Wesleyan Methodism allowed for free will and the potential for all persons to be saved. It was the latter that the Indians found more attractive.

Some Cherokee traveled to Cornwall Academy in Connecticut for their education. But when two mixed-blood Cherokee students, Elias Boudinot and John Ridge, married local white girls in 1826, public outrage forced the closure of the school. Boudinot became editor of the *Cherokee Phoenix*. Started in 1828, this newspaper is reportedly the first published in English and an Indian language. Conservative Cherokees assassinated Boudinot and Ridge in 1839 for agreeing to removal by signing the Treaty of New Echota negotiated by a minister in 1835. This was the traditional Cherokee punishment for treason.

The Cherokee adopted a constitution in 1827 that provided for the free exercise of religion and contained the following education clause modeled after the Massachusetts constitution: "Religion, morality and knowledge being necessary to good government, the preservation of liberty and the happiness of mankind, schools and the means of education shall forever be encouraged in this Nation" (quoted in McLoughlin 1984, 232). The next year the Cherokee government attempted to inspect mission schools. In 1824 Georgians forced a congressional inquiry into whether the U.S. government should support Indian missions because the latter worked against removal. John Quincy Adams's secretary of war denounced Indian missionaries in 1828 for opposing removal.

Unique among the Indians of the United States, the Cherokee developed their own written language. Working independently, a non-English-speaking Cherokee, Sequoyah, developed a syllabary with eighty-five symbols representing sounds in his language. Samuel Worcester printed Sequoyah's syllabary in 1821, and the Cherokee used it in both private correspondence and the tribal newspaper, the *Cherokee Phoenix*. Sequoyah, who later moved west to avoid whites, hoped his writing system would help to preserve Cherokee heritage and religion (McLoughlin 1984). In 1836 the first *Cherokee Almanac* was printed. In 1872 John B. Jones, the Indian agent at Tahlequah in Indian Territory who favored bilingual education, noted, "Almost the whole of those Cherokees who do not speak English can read and write the Cherokee by using the characters invented by Sequoyah" (*ARBIC* 1872, 159). Jones was a Baptist missionary who helped to translate the Bible into Cherokee and was granted tribal citizenship along with his missionary father by the Cherokee National Council in 1865 (McLoughlin 1990).

Cherokee Schools after Removal

In 1841 the Cherokee National Council set up a national school system under a superintendent of education with eleven schools in eight districts. The schools taught reading, writing, arithmetic, bookkeeping, English grammar, geography, and history. Within ten years, locally trained teachers in most cases had replaced eastern-educated missionaries. The tribes financed these schools, often with money granted them by the U.S. government for land they had ceded. The Cherokee passed a law in 1845 encouraging mechanics to come into the nation and take on apprentices. By 1852 the Cherokee Nation had a better common school system than the neighboring states of Arkansas and Missouri (Bass 1937; Layman 1942).

The Cherokee National Council opened male and female seminaries near Tahlequah, Oklahoma, in 1851 to provide instruction at the high school level. The seminaries served only tribal members, though some had as little as 1/128 Cherokee blood. Less than 10 percent of the students were full-bloods, and one-third of the students were 1/16 Cherokee or less. The Cherokee Female Seminary was open from 1851 to 1856 and then reopened from 1872 to 1909, when it was sold to the state of Oklahoma and became the nucleus of what is now Northeastern State University (Mihesuah 1993).

The Female Seminary was patterned after Mount Holyoke Seminary in South Hadley, Massachusetts, where some of the missionaries to the Cherokees went to school. In its forty years of operation it served 3,000 students, but only 212 graduated. Graduates tended to marry white men or Cherokees with less Indian blood than they had. In the early years, fifteen of the twenty-six seminary graduates became teachers in the Cherokee public school system. Twenty-eight of the seminary's graduates and seventeen of the nongraduates went on to teach at the seminary (Mihesuah 1993). In 1852 fifty students were studying Latin, algebra, arithmetic, grammar, geography, botany, and vocal music (Bass 1937).

The history of the Cherokee Female Seminary indicates that left to their own designs and volunteer missionary efforts, tribes could effectively assimilate themselves. The Cherokee Female Seminary had no Cherokee curriculum. The Cherokee historian Devon Mihesuah (1993, 80) documented that a mixed-blood seminary superintendent in 1908 castigated full-blood students for their "pathetic attachment to home." Another superintendent in 1889 declared, "[I]t is the white blood that has made us what we are," and encouraged intermarriage with whites (81). According to Mihesuah, "[T]he teachers . . . relentlessly reinforced the importance of learning and retaining the values of white society. At the same time they repressed Cherokee values" (81).

The enforcement of white values did not go unnoticed by the more traditionally oriented Cherokee, and, in fact, some full-blood students were expelled for trying to burn the seminary to the ground in protest of its "white atmosphere." Despite the Cherokee Nation's support of "civilization," the U.S. government increasingly interfered with internal tribal affairs. For example, in 1900 President McKinley refused to accept the seminary principal appointed by the Cherokee National Council. Such an action makes it clear that control, at least as much as "civilization," was the real policy of the U.S. government. The government was also interested in giving the Indians a second-class "manual labor" or "industrial" education. The Department of the Interior's 1899 annual report complained that the seminary's curriculum was too academic and that girls were learning Latin and math instead of the "domestic arts" they needed (Mihesuah 1993).

Creek and Choctaw Schools

The Creeks, another of the Five Civilized Tribes, responded to removal by expelling missionaries in 1836 and persecuting converts to Christianity. A Creek spokesman informed the Presbyterian Board of Foreign Missions, "We want a school, but we don't want any preaching, for we find that preaching breaks up all our old customs—our feasts, ball plays, and dances—which we want to keep" (quoted in Layman 1942, 152).

Afraid by 1817 that American Indians might become extinct if they were not civilized, the American Board of Commissioners for Foreign Missions had become increasingly involved in missionary work in the West. Its stated goal in 1816 was to make Indians "English in their language, and Christian in their religion," though they later saw that Native languages needed more attention (Bass 1936, 31). In 1818 missionaries set off on a four-hundred-mile overland journey to Choctaw country in present-day Mississippi. To their dismay, the missionaries found the Choctaw more interested in education than Christianity. A letter sent to the board by a missionary stated, "The expectation of this people has been that all our efforts would be directed toward the commencement of a school" (quoted in Kidwell 1987, 55).

Choctaw discontent with American Board missionaries was given vent in 1825 when the tribe gave its treaty education funds to the Choctaw Academy in Kentucky. The Choctaw Academy was originally founded in 1818 by Baptists. Using $6,000 per year authorized for twenty years by Article II of the treaty with the Choctaw, the school was revived in 1825 by the flamboyant politician Col. Richard M. Johnson, who became vice president of the United States in 1837. His purpose in establishing the school seems to have been financial gain from treaty education funds. However, the school is reported to have given students a good education. Johnson sent representatives to treaty councils to secure students and educational annuities for his school (Layman 1942). The Baptist General Convention undertook to run the school on Johnson's property and appointed the Reverend Thomas Henderson as superintendent. The revived school "flourished" for fifteen years and reached a top enrollment of 188 students (Prucha 1984).

The Choctaw Academy offered reading, writing, arithmetic, English grammar, geography, practical surveying, astronomy, natural philosophy, history, moral philosophy, and vocal music. In 1828 the Lancastrian system was introduced to reduce costs. Under this system, students competed for position in the school's hierarchy. At first, sons of chiefs were not to have "menial" work; however, by 1833 manual training was provided, and in 1838 boys were required to work in the shops (Foreman 1931; Layman 1942)

In 1834 the Academy had 156 students: 62 Choctaws, 24 Pottawatamies, 15 Cherokees, 15 Creeks, 8 Miamies, 8 Seminoles, 4 Quapaws, and 20 Prairie du Chiens. The oldest student was twenty-six, the youngest 7; most students were in their teens. They were divided into four classes of approximately equal size. The first class learned "the alphabet and the first elements of learning"; the second, "spelling, reading, and writing"; the third, "arithmetic, grammar and geography"; and the fourth, "all the higher branches of English education" (Foreman 1931, 406–9).

A Lycurgus court, named after the legendary Greek king of Sparta, was organized to promote student self-government. Students were instructed in etiquette, and there was a singing society and Native band. Students were encouraged to write home weekly and to support government policies such as removal in their letters. There were problems with Indian boys consorting with mulatto girls on Johnson's plantation. Johnson, who had a mulatto mistress and two mulatto daughters, was not anxious for publicity over these matters and wanted the students dealt with severely and quietly (Layman 1942).

In 1839 thirty-three students sent a letter to the Indian Office complaining that the school's subsuperintendent was a "profane man," that there was a great deal of drunkenness, that the Sabbath was not observed, and that there was no supervision at night. The Board of Inspectors deemed the complaint unfounded, but when Johnson left the vice presidency in 1841 the school lost its political support and remained open for only a few more years (Foreman 1932; Layman 1942).

The American Board schools in Mississippi became feeder schools for the Choctaw Academy, and like the Academy, these schools had their problems. In 1828 a teacher in an American Board mission school admitted seducing and impregnating one of his students. However, the schools had successes as well. According to the Choctaw historian Clara Sue Kidwell (1987, 69), "[T]he most lasting result of missionary activity among the Choctaw in Mississippi was the preservation of the Choctaw language." Translations of the Bible introduced the Choctaw to literacy in their own language.

In 1842, after removal, the Choctaw set up a system of tribal schools. By 1848 there were nine boarding schools operated by mission boards and a system of neighborhood schools. Despite the destruction caused by the Civil War, the Choctaw school superintendent reported in 1870 that 1,764 students were attending eighty-four neighborhood schools most of whose teachers were Choctaws (Layman 1942).

CHAPTER THREE

RESERVATIONS, 1867–1887

When U.S. troops were withdrawn from the West during the Civil War, the Indians tried to take advantage of the situation, which led to renewed fighting. At the end of the war eastern reformers turned their attention to ending the mistreatment of Indians and halting the Indian wars (Mardock 1971). In 1865 the Republican-controlled Congress approved the Joint Special Committee on the Conduct of the Indian Tribes, also called the Doolittle Committee, after its chairman, James R. Doolittle. The committee toured the West in three groups and recommended leaving Indian affairs under the jurisdiction of the Department of the Interior and setting up five inspection districts to prevent corruption (Prucha 1984). They reported that there was a rapid decline in Indian population everywhere but in Indian Territory and that the Indian wars were a result of "the aggressions of lawless whites" ("Report" [1867] 1990, 103). By then the federal government had removed most of the eastern tribes to Indian Territory, and the western tribes were being confined to reservations. Because professional hunters had decimated the vast buffalo herds on which the Plains Indians depended for food, as well as for shelter and clothing, the latter were being starved into submission. In addition, the survival of seminomadic tribes was threatened by the fencing off of land by farmers.

In 1867 Congress established the Peace Commission to deal with hostile tribes. Among its members were Commissioner of Indian Affairs Nathaniel G. Taylor and Generals William T. Sherman, William S. Harney, John B. Sanborn, and Alfred H. Terry. In its 1868 report to President Andrew Johnson, the Commission declared:

While it cannot be denied that the government of the United States, in the general terms and temper of its legislation, has evinced a desire to deal generously with the Indians, it must be admitted that the actual treatment they have received has been unjust and iniquitous beyond the power of words to express.

Taught by the government that they had rights entitled to respect; when those rights have been assailed by the rapacity of the white man, the arm which should have been raised to protect them has been ever ready to sustain the aggressor.

The history of the Government connections with the Indians is a shameful record of broken treaties and unfulfilled promises.

The history of the border white man's connection with the Indians is a sickening record of murder, outrage, robbery, and wrongs committed by the former as the rule, and occasional savage outbreaks and unspeakable barbarous deeds of retaliation by the latter as the exception. . . .

The testimony of some of the highest military officers of the United States is on record to the effect that, in our Indian wars, almost without exception, the first aggressions have been made by the white man, and the assertion is supported by every civilian of reputation who has studied the subject. (Quoted in *ARBIC* 1869, 7)

According to the Jesuit historian Francis Paul Prucha (1985, 16), Taylor, chair of the Peace Commission in 1867 and 1868 and a Methodist minister, "epitomized the paternalistic outlook of Washington official-dom [and] sought the 'civilization' of the Indians with a vengeance." Taylor told the Crow Indians at Fort Laramie in 1867,

Upon the reservations you select, we propose to build a house for your agent to live in, to build a mill to saw your timber, and a mill to grind your wheat and corn, when you raise any; a blacksmith shop and a house for your farmer, and such other buildings as may be necessary. We also propose to furnish to you homes and cattle, to enable you to begin to raise a supply of stock with which to support your families when the game has disap-peared. We desire also to supply you with clothing to make you comfort-able and all necessary farming implements so that you can make your living by farming. We will send you teachers for your children. (*Proceedings* 1975, 86–87)

Article 7 of the 1868 treaty made with the Sioux and their allies at Fort Laramie embodied Taylor's ideas:

> In order to insure the civilization of the Indians entering into this treaty, the necessity of education is admitted, especially of such of them as are or may be settled on said agricultural reservations, and they therefore pledge themselves to compel their children, male and female, between the ages of six and sixteen years, to attend school; and it is hereby made the duty of the agent for said Indians to see that this stipulation is strictly complied with; and the United States agrees that for every thirty children between said ages who can be induced or compelled to attend school, a house shall be provided and a teacher competent to teach the elementary branches of an English education shall be furnished, who will reside among said Indians, and faithfully discharge his or her duties as a teacher. The provisions of this article to continue for not less than twenty years. (Washburn 1973–79, vol. 4, 2571)

Article 7 of the treaty with the Navajo made the same year contained almost verbatim provisions, but the promised teachers were very slow in coming.

When Gen. Ulysses S. Grant, who had served in the West, became president in 1869, he began a "peace policy." In his first inaugural address he declared, "The proper treatment of the original occupants of this land—the Indians—is one deserving of careful study. I will favor any course toward them which tends to their civilization and ultimate citizenship" (Richardson 1910, 3962).

Grant appointed his Civil War aide, Brig. Gen. Ely S. Parker Commissioner of Indian Affairs. Parker, a Seneca, was the first Indian to head the Indian Bureau and served from 1869 to 1871. Denied entrance to law school because he was not a citizen, a privilege then denied Indians, he chose civil engineering as an alternative (Vogel 1972). In 1869 Grant also established the Board of Indian Commissioners to supervise the appointment of Indian agents, teachers, and farmers as well as the buying of supplies. Although the Board remained in existence until 1933, it lost most of its power soon after it was created. It divided up Indian agencies among thirteen religious groups that were given the authority to nominate the agents. Because of their long and active history of missionary work among the Indians, the Catholics had expected thirty-eight reservations, but they were given only eight (all board members were Protestants).

Grant believed the Quakers had had the best success among the Indians and assigned them the largest number of agencies (sixteen) (Prucha 1984, 517–19): "The Society of Friends is well known as having succeeded in living in peace with the Indians in the early settlement of Pennsylvania, while their white neighbors of other sects in other sections were constantly embroiled" (quoted in Layman 1942, 356). During the colonial period, the Quakers bought rather than just took Indian lands. In 1850 Quakers had told a group of Indians:

> With your religious concerns we have studiously avoided to interfere, not because we have deemed Religion an unimportant subject, but because we have not been called upon by our position or sent among you to teach it. . . . It is not the extent of our theological instruction but our fidelity in the performance of manifest duty that is the measure of our acceptance in the Divine Sight. (Quoted in Layman 1942, 182)

JOHN HOMER SEGER

John Homer Seger was born in 1846 in Ohio and enlisted to fight in the Civil War at the age of seventeen. He was with General Sherman as he marched through Georgia to the sea. In 1872 Seger worked on the Cheyenne-Arapaho Agency at the site of present-day Darlington, Oklahoma, as a stone mason and carpenter and continued to work with the Arapaho until his death in 1928. At the agency he observed that the Quakers hired to teach under Grant's Peace Policy had their hearts in the right place but had to cope with conditions beyond their control. He described the attempt to have an agency school in 1871:

> The schoolhouse was an unpainted cottonwood shack, and the furniture consisted of a couple of tables and a few benches with no blackboard. . . . One of the first difficulties which had to be met was getting the children to come at the right hour. They were not used either to going to bed or getting up any specified time, and as they had no timepieces, punctuality was out of the question, so Mr. Standing [the teacher] summoned them by going through the camp blowing a cow's horn. (Seger [1924] 1979, 6-7)

School lasted three months, and then the Indians went on their summer buffalo hunt with all their children. Seger ([1924] 1979, 7) wrote, "At times Mr. Standing went out to the camps with pictures and books and taught wherever he could collect a class. In this way he got acquainted with the children and cultivated friendship of parents." He was invited to go on the hunt and continue his teaching, but the agent vetoed the idea. Standing went on to be assistant superintendent at Carlisle Indian Industrial School under Pratt.

Finding a Quaker teacher in the midst of noisy students doing everything but paying attention, Seger made humorous faces to get their attention and then taught them a "round" called "Johnny Smoker" based on a German song. This was a song whose "words were accompanied with gestures of how Johnny Smoker blew his horn, beat his drum and triangle, and played his violin and cymbal. It ended up by showing how he smoked his pipe" (Seger [1924] 1979, 23). He was asked for an encore, and after several repetitions the students tried to sing the song. He also found that students who would not do schoolwork were willing to help him lay a stone foundation. Having shown some success with children, in 1874, at the suggestion of the agent's wife, Seger became the teacher at the agency. He introduced industrial education and in his second year contracted with the government to run the school and shared the profits of the agency's school farm with the students (Peery 1932–33). When the agency doctor's son was killed and it was reported that the killers were looking for the school superintendent, the latter decided to return to Indiana. Thus Seger became superintendent. He found the students unresponsive and told the agent he would rather be a mason. But based on reports of the Arapaho, over time Seger was able to win the students' attention. The Arapaho artist Carl Sweezy recalled, "[Seger's] children played with us and went to our Arapaho school and learned our language and songs and games and stories. Some people said they even came to look like us" (quoted in Bass 1966, 9-10). Sweezy also recalled that Seger was a popular Santa Claus at Christmas time and could speak Arapaho. As a teacher, Seger introduced a variety of games at Darlington, and he "got friends from outside to send magazines and newspapers and books, which he used in the schoolroom to make the Indian children realize that reading was something more than a hard chore and was a means of finding out what was going on in the world" (Bass 1966, 57).

According to Sweezy, Seger "thought that games and songs would help [the children] to learn to use English and like it, as studying it only in books would not do, and in this he was right" (Bass 1966, 57). Seger also used magic tricks he had learned as a boy to impress both his students and their parents (Peery 1932–33).

Hamlin Garland (1923, 11–12) describes how Seger risked his life whipping a Cheyenne chief's son in order to get his classroom under control. The editor of Seger's autobiography recounts when a chief asked Seger for a pass to leave the agency to hunt buffalo:

> Seger answered, "Give me your son."
> The Chief protested, "Why should I give you my son?"
> Seger replied, "So that I can make a white man of him."
> The chief laughed at this absurdity. He had heard that song before. Said he, "Then give me a white boy to make an Indian of."
> As the chief had expected, Seger replied, "I have no white boy to give you." Then, to the chief's surprise, Seger added, "But if you will give me your son to put to school this winter, I will come to your camp next summer and you can make an Indian of me." (Seger [1924] 1979, v–xi)

Seger learned a lot by asking "Why?" that next summer in the Indian camp when he did not understand what he observed (Seger 1979).

Although the Arapaho and Cheyenne chiefs brought to Washington, D.C., in 1880 to be impressed by the white man's civilization had promised their "Great Father" that they would put their children in school, at first they volunteered only orphans. Schoolboys were taunted as white men: "To call a Cheyenne a white man was considered one of the worst insults that could be offered him" (Seger [1924] 1979, 36). Not only the schoolboys were intimidated. Older boys attempted to gang up on Seger, and he was forced to knock down the ringleader. The next day a student threatened his life. Students even drew their revolvers. When he went to the Indian agent for advice, the agent had none to give. Wisely, Seger decided not to press the issue with the students and slept with his rifle. Seger talked to the students the next day, comparing his discipline, which was whipping, with the rules of the chief or the Dog Soldiers. After his lecture he shook hands with the students. Over time some Indians began to appreciate education. Henrietta Mann, a

Cheyenne university professor, quotes the recollections of White Buffalo Woman on what the elders said about education:

> Perhaps this education the White Man talks to us about is not all bad. We need to understand the Veho. We have to live with him. We have to deal with him. If our children go to his school they [will] learn his language; they will know how he thinks. They will become our eyes, our ears, our mouths. Through our children we will listen, and we will speak. Thus we can better protect our ways, our culture as it has come down to us through many generations. (1997, 44)

In 1879 Seger left his post to run a freight and mail business on the reservation. The agents appointed in Washington varied in character; some had little understanding of Indians. Seger was present at one incident when a group of Indians rode into Darlington firing their guns. The agent was frightened and called for troops, but Seger explained that firing guns was a sign of a friendly visit because it proved that their guns were now empty (Peery 1932–33). In 1886 a new Indian agent asked Seger to start a farming "colony" sixty miles from the agency, which he did with a nucleus of sixteen of his former students. In 1893 he opened a school at Seger Colony. Eighty percent of his students had never been to school before (*ARCIA* 1893). "Because the school was new and policy had to be set, parents were invited to determine how to enforce discipline, and they voted to leave it to the discretion of the superintendent" (Mann 1997, 97). The discussion included the idea of expelling unruly students, but Seger thought they were the ones most in need of discipline. He did not believe in rushing things. He stated that students needed time to learn school rules, that parental visits to the school were helpful, and that his experience told him that civilizing the Indian could not be accomplished in just a few years (*ARCIA* 1893). Like other government Indian schools of the period, students received an elementary education along with vocational instruction, including animal husbandry (see fig. 2). A visitor recalled that when the school was in session there was a morning chapel service at which the "work of the school and business of all kinds was discussed by the superintendent, the teachers and the students" (Peery 1932–33, 351). Seger remained superintendent of the school until 1905. It closed in 1932.

Branding cattle, Seger Colony School in Oklahoma, 1900. Photograph courtesy of the National Archives NWDNS-75SE-32B.

Seger reported to the Commissioner of Indian Affairs in 1894 that some of the older girls who were "saucy, insolent, and disobedient" were responding to an employee in charge of them who was "injudicious" and lacked "tact and discretion" (*ARCIA* 1894, 403–4). The next year he reported that "the matter of discipline has ceased to be a problem. Perhaps it is because rules are not made unless there is a reasonable probability of enforcing them" (*ARCIA* 1895, 393). Seger's mixture of strict discipline and real concern for his students led Mann (1997, 178) to describe him as "the beloved school superintendent 'Johnny Smoker.'" Sweezy reported, "Some people said that Mr. Seger couldn't spell any better than the Arapaho could, but we were more in need of other things than we were of a good speller" (quoted in Bass 1966, 58).

THE "OPENING" OF THE WEST

Despite President Grant's and the Quakers' good intentions, the flood of immigrants wanting land after the first transcontinental railroad was completed in 1869 spelled the end of protective isolation for western tribes. The driving of the "Golden Spike" at Promontory, Utah, the last spike in the railroad linking California to the East Coast, was the start of the opening of the entire West to white settlement. White Americans came to feel that their continued success was God's will and that it was their "manifest destiny to overspread and to possess the whole continent which Providence" had given them (O'Sullivan 1845). In addition, the railroad allowed the military to quickly move to meet any Indian resistance to white encroachments. Although a few battles were yet to be fought, tribes were no longer military powers to be negotiated with.

In 1871, in a dispute over power between the House and the Senate, Congress ended all treaty making with Indian tribes. The House did not like having to appropriate money for treaties made by the Peace Commission that only the Senate approved. After 1871 all "agreements" made with tribes required approval by both houses of Congress. This change reflected a shift in government policy from relocating Indians to the previously unsettled West to segregating them on reservations and treating them as government wards. This status did not end until passage of a congressional resolution in 1953 (Fischbacher 1967).

In his 1871 *School History of the United States,* William Swinton (1875, 21) wrote, "[Indians] were destitute of all that constitutes civilization. Their main delight was war." Although he admitted that "whites were not always just and true and prudent in their dealings with Indians," he felt there was "hostility between the Indian character and civilization." Further, in his view,"it is not to be doubted that in a few more years the Red Men will have disappeared from the American continent." In 1870, while the country was waiting for the "vanishing American" to vanish, Congress appropriated $100,000 for the support of industrial and other schools among the Indian tribes. This started the shift of Indian education from a largely missionary activity partially funded by the government to an activity directly managed by the Office of Indian Affairs. Emphasis was on day, boarding, and industrial schools whose curricula focused on basic skills in arithmetic and in speaking, reading, and writing English. In 1872 Commissioner of Indian Affairs Edward P. Smith estimated that almost one hundred thousand Indians were "wild," that just over fifty thousand labored and were "tractable," and just over one hundred thousand had land, property, stock, and implements (Fischbacher 1967, 172).

Just as the discovery of gold in 1828 in Georgia had led to the removal of the Cherokees and in 1848 in California had spelled disaster for its Indians, the discovery of gold in the Black Hills in 1873 set the stage for the conflict between the United States and the Sioux and Cheyenne Nations. This conflict, which included the famous Battle of the Little Big Horn in 1876, went on at the various Indian agencies serving the Plains Indians. On the one side were miners and settlers who, in their pursuit of wealth, saw Indians only as obstacles to be exterminated or moved out of the way. On the other side were the Indians and some missionaries and easterners who were interested in Indian rights and avoiding genocide. The federal government continued to see education as the solution to the "Indian problem." In 1876 a training institute was held on the Cattaraugus Reservation in New York for thirty-five teachers. The Indian Office estimated that of the 266,151 Indians living in the United States, excluding Alaska, 104,818 Indians wore "citizens dress" and 25,622 could read. Four hundred thirty-seven teachers were educating 6,028 boys and 5,300 girls in 63 boarding schools and 281 day schools. However, average attendance was only 7,094 students (*ARCIA* 1876).

While many Indians accepted citizens dress and schooling, bowing to the seemingly inevitable, many others continued to resist the growing demands placed on them by the settlers and the government. In 1877 the Nez Perce fought a long retreat through Idaho, Wyoming, and Montana that received extensive newspaper coverage and won them some public sympathy. In the winter of 1878–79, the Northern Cheyenne fled Indian Territory (Oklahoma). At Fort Robinson, Nebraska, they gave the government the choice of killing them off or letting them return to their homeland in Montana. In 1884 the government temporized and gave them the present Northern Cheyenne Reservation in south-central Montana.

Pressure to remove Indians to Oklahoma arose from the growing demand for land for immigrants brought in by the new railroads. Indian land speculation, in which even George Washington had been involved, was rampant on the frontier. The 1878 *Annual Report of the Commissioner of Indian Affairs* noted that Indians did not trust whites because of broken promises and that "every means that human ingenuity can devise, legal or illegal, has been resorted to for the purpose of obtaining possession of Indian lands" (vii). What a correspondent for the Indian Bureau wrote the following year about Nebraskans was true elsewhere in the West:

The people of that portion of Nebraska which is contiguous to the Santee reservation are clamoring for the removal of that tribe of Indians. There is no reason for this whatever except the desire to crowd the Indians out that their lands may be seized by speculators. There are thousands of acres of unbroken prairie in every section of the State, and this demand for the removal of the Santees proceeds from the most criminal selfishness. The Indians are not troublesome, and are just now making rapid strides toward a better civilization than that professed by those who are striving to despoil and drive them into the wilderness. It will be a national disgrace if Congress should listen to the voice of these Western land speculators and force the Santees to abandon their present home and their bright prospects in the near future. (*ARBIC* 1879, 78)

Most contemporary westerners had a dim view of Indians and the Indian Bureau officials and eastern humanitarians who sought to protect Indian lands. In 1866 the editor of the *Kearny (Nebraska) Herald* wrote,

Nothing is more absurd to the man who has studied the habits of the Indian savage than to talk of making permanent treaty negotiations with these heartless creatures. They are destitute of all the promptings of human nature, having no respect for word or honor. Their only creed is that which gives them an unrestricted license to use and abuse beings, brutes and things, as through earth and its contents were inanimate wooden heaps, made purposely to gratify a heathenish pleasure. To the Indian destruction is gain; it is a generative instinct and one which goes from infancy to the grave. Educated to look upon the white man with inveterate enmity, he ignores peace and civil associations. Now and then you will hear a chicken-hearted historian, who knows nothing of the red savage, extolling his noble characteristics and praising his natural knightly endowments. The earnest defenders of this barbarian monster would turn away in disgust could they see him in all of his original desperation. (Quoted in Mardock 1971, 86)

Col. Frank Triplett wrote in 1883:

[The Indian Bureau] is responsible for arson, murder and rape; it is a refuge of incompetents and thieves. . . . From the Indian agent the savage obtains his supplies of food to enable him to make his raids; from some creature of the agent, he obtains his supplies of ammunition and improved arms, that make him more than a match for the raw recruit, that the American government enlists from the city slums, dignifies by the name of soldier, and sends out to meet these agile warriors.

The whole system of Indian management is a fraud: the Indian Department rotten from the outmost edge to the innermost core.

[Putting the Indian Bureau back under the army] would do away with our junketing peace commissions, composed of low-brow, thick-lipped, bottle-nosed humanitarians, the inferiors of the savages in every manly trait and objects of unlimited contempt by these shrewd marauders. (Triplett 1883, 347)

In his 1857 novel, *The Confidence Man*, Herman Melville described a westerner who was brought up from an early age to hate Indians:

He hears little from his schoolmasters, the old chroniclers of the forest, but histories of Indian lying, Indian theft, Indian double-dealing, Indian fraud and perfidy, Indian want of conscience, Indian blood-thirstiness, Indian diabolism—histories which though of wild woods, are almost as full of things unangelic as the Newgate Calendar or the Annals of Europe. . . . The instinct of antipathy against an Indian grows in the backwoodsman with the sense of good and bad, right and wrong. In one breath he learns that a brother is to be loved, and an Indian to be hated. ([1857] 1971, 126–27)

With the repeal of the Civilization Fund in 1873, the federal government became more directly involved in the operation of Indian schools. The Fund's $10,000 a year had from the beginning covered only a fraction of the costs, which treaty funds and missionary contributions supplemented. With its repeal, Congress appropriated ten times the Fund's amount to more directly provide Indian education (Fischbacher 1967).

In the 1878 *Annual Report of the Commissioner of Indian Affairs*, "education of their children" was seen as the quickest way to civilize Indians, and education could only be given "to children removed from the examples of their parents and the influence of the camps and kept in boarding schools" (xxv–xxvi). In the same report, Lt. Richard Henry Pratt described Indian schoolchildren as "hostages for good behavior of [their] parents" (174). The parents themselves were, in the words of Col. Richard Irving Dodge (1882, 644), an aide-de-camp to General Sherman, "held on reservations, actually prisoners of war." Indians needed passes signed by the Indian agent to leave reservations, and non-Indians needed permission to visit reservations. The absence without permission of thousands of Sioux and Cheyenne from their new reservations was the reason General Custer was looking for them on the banks of the Little Big Horn in 1876. This requirement for permits, which made Indian agents essentially prison camp directors, continued into the early twentieth century.

In his second inaugural address on March 4, 1873, President Grant declared:

Our superiority of strength and advantages of civilization should make us lenient toward the Indian. The wrong inflicted upon him should be taken into account, and the balance placed to his credit. The moral view of the question should be considered and the question asked, Can not the Indian be made a useful and productive member of society by proper teaching and treatment? If the effort is made in good faith, we will stand better before the civilized nations of the earth and in our own consciences for having made it. (Richardson 1910, 4176)

Grant's successor, Rutherford B. Hayes, continued his Peace Policy.

REFORM AND GROWTH

In 1866 Commissioner of Indian Affairs Dennis Cooley conducted an extensive survey of school conditions. He had become aware of German kindergartens and sent books on it to agency teachers, hoping that younger Indian children could be attracted to schools (Prucha 1984). He also noted the need to introduce efficiency and to stamp out corruption in the Indian Office. In 1871 during Grant's presidency, Missouri Senator Carl Schurz introduced a civil service bill to reduce government corruption and end the "spoils system" of awarding government jobs and contracts to political supporters. In 1877 President Rutherford B. Hayes appointed Schurz his secretary of the interior. Schurz sought to clean up the corruption in the Indian Bureau. Appointments in the pre–Civil Service Indian Bureau were often made for political rather than educational reasons. Mrs. Horace Mann wrote in Sarah Winnemucca's (Piute) 1883 autobiography, "Salaries are paid teachers year after year, who sit in the school-rooms . . . and read dime novels, and the children play around, and learn nothing from them, except some few hymns *by rote*, which when visitors come they sing, without understanding one word of it" (Hopkins 1883, 52; original emphasis). Schurz started an investigation that uncovered many problems and led to the dismissal of some Bureau employees. He won the fight to keep the Bureau out of the War Department and helped to start several successful programs, including the Indian police and Carlisle Indian School (see chap. 6). When in 1879 the Omaha Indian Standing Bear, in *Standing Bear v. Crook*, renounced his tribal affiliation and won a writ of habeus corpus to keep from being forcefully returned to Indian Territory, Schurz did not appeal the local court's decision (Fuess 1932).

In 1879, near the end of Schurz's term of office, the *Annual Report of the Board of Indian Commissioners* estimated there were 500 teachers in 64 boarding schools and 292 day schools teaching 13,343 students (out of 46,000 school age Indian children) for a total cost of $379,354. An estimated 44,731 Indians could read. The commissioners wrote: "The progress of the pupils in industrial boarding schools is far greater than in day schools. The children being removed from the idle and corrupting habits of savage homes are more easily led to adopt the customs of civilized life and inspired with a desire to learn" (*ARBIC* 1879, 14).

Secretary of the Interior Henry Teller continued Schurz's interest in Indian education. In 1884 Teller wrote:

> The greatest agency for the civilization of the Indian is the manual-labor school. Indeed, I do not think I shall be far out of the way if I say the only agency for that purpose is the manual-labor school. . . . The history of the few manual-labor schools established for the education of Indian children has demonstrated their great value, and that it is only necessary to multiply their number, so as to include all the Indian children of school age, to forever set at rest the question as to "what shall be done with the Indians." (Quoted in Prucha 1984, 689)

J. D. C. Atkins, Commissioner of Indian Affairs from 1885 to 1888, listed in his 1887 *Annual Report of the Commissioner of Indian Affairs* 68 government boarding schools with 5,484 students enrolled, 90 government day schools with 3,115 students (but an average attendance of only 1,896), and 5 industrial boarding schools with 1,573 students. In addition, 41 boarding schools with 2,553 students and 20 day schools with 1,044 students were operated under contract, mostly by religious organizations, with the Indian Bureau. These schools cost $1,166,025 to operate (xv). Of this money, about 94 percent went to operate the boarding schools; the remainder was used for day schools. Government-operated schools received 70 percent of the funding and contract schools 30 percent. The industrial schools cost $170 per student to operate in contrast to $121 for the agency boarding schools and $119 for the contract boarding schools. Government day schools cost $30 and contract day schools $16 per student (Fischbacher 1967).

In his 1887 report, Atkins commended Congress's requirement that schoolbooks "teach the baneful influences of ardent spirits and narcotics" (xxv). He concluded:

It is apparent that we have advanced far enough in the education of Indian children to be able to say that what for a time was an experiment no longer admits of uncertainty. The Indian can be educated equally with the white or the colored man, and his education is gradually being accomplished, and at a less cost per capita from year to year as the work proceeds. . . . One thing is clear, the Government has made a wonderfully economic move in undertaking to educate these people in any kind of schools instead of fighting them. The cost of the schools is immeasurably less than that of the wars which they supplant. (*ARCIA* 1887, xvi–xvii)

The experiment in education was decidedly an ethnocentric one. Through education, Indians were to lose their heritage, in particular, their native religion and language.

ENGLISH ONLY

The Peace Commission reported in 1868:

[It is the] difference in language [between Indians and whites], which in a great measure barred intercourse and a proper understanding each of the other's motives and intentions.

Now, by educating the children of these tribes in the English language these differences would have disappeared, and civilization would have followed at once. . . .

Through sameness of language is produced sameness of sentiment, and thought; customs and habits are moulded and assimilated in the same way, and thus in process of time the differences producing trouble would have been gradually obliterated. . . . In the difference of language to-day lies two-thirds of our trouble. . . . Schools should be established, which children should be required to attend; their barbarous dialect should be blotted out and the English language substituted. (*Report of Indian Peace Commissioners* 1868, 16–17)

Francis La Flesche, who in the mid-1860s attended a mission school run for the Omaha by the Board of Foreign Missions of the Presbyterian Church, was faced with a rigid English-only rule. He wrote in the foreword to his fictionalized account of his boarding school experiences, *The Middle Five:*

> When we entered the Mission School, we experienced a greater hardship, for there we encountered a rule that prohibited the use of our own language, which rule was rigidly enforced with a hickory rod, so that the new-comer, however socially inclined, was obliged to go about like a little dummy until he had learned to express himself in English. ([1900] 1963, xvii)

As the government geared up its educational efforts, there was early optimism regarding how easy it would be to assimilate Indians into the general population by giving them a white man's education for a few years in a boarding school (Hoxie 1984). This optimism was based largely on the apparent success of students of the first government-operated boarding school at Carlisle, Pennsylvania, after its founding in 1879. In 1885 the Indian Office's superintendent of Indian schools, John H. Oberly, predicted optimistically: "If there were a sufficient number of reservation boarding-school-buildings to accommodate all the Indian children of school age, and these building could be filled and kept filled with Indian pupils, the Indian problem would be solved within the school age of the Indian child now six years old" (*ARCIA* 1885, cxiii). Oberly complained that Indian agents were selecting inappropriate textbooks and called for the publication of a "series of uniform Indian school text-books" to be printed by the Government Printing Office. These textbooks would not "on one page represent the Indian as a monster, and on the next page represent him as a hero of romance" (*ARCIA* 1885, 101).

Secretary of the Interior Schurz felt that the alternatives for Indians were extermination or civilization. The object of Indian policy was "unquestionably the gradual absorption of the Indians in the great body [of] American citizenship." Reservations were seen as "socialism" (Prucha 1973, 14-15, 73); a charge repeated more than a century later by Secretary of the Interior James Watt during Ronald Reagan's presidency. Some observers believed that by concentrating individual tribes on small reservations, the government was actually supporting Native language use (Dodge 1882).

Under Schurz, the Indian Bureau issued regulations in 1880 that "all instruction must be in English" in both mission and government schools under threat of losing government funding (Prucha 1973, 199). In 1883 Indian Commissioner Hiram Price wrote that it was beyond controversy that "the Indian must be taught to work for his own support, and to speak the English language, or he must give place to people who do" (*ARCIA* 1883, iii). The following year he declared, "Taken altogether, an impartial view of the situation warrants the belief that some time in the near future it is fair to presume that, with the aid of such industrial, agricultural, and mechanical schools as are now being carried on, the Indian will be able to care for himself, and be no longer a burden but a help to the Government" (*ARCIA* 1884, iii). That year a specific order went out to a school teaching in both Dakota and English that the "English language only must be taught the Indian youth placed there for educational and industrial training at the expense of the Government. If Dakota or any other language is taught such children, they will be taken away and their support by the Government will be withdrawn from the school" (quoted in *ARCIA* 1887, xxi).

Atkins (1887, xxiii) felt that "to teach Indian school children their native tongue [their "barbarous dialect"] is practically to exclude English, and to prevent them from acquiring it." The ethnocentric attitude that prevailed in the late nineteenth century is evident in Atkins's 1887 report and merits quoting at length:

Every nation is jealous of its own language, and no nation ought to be more so than ours, which approaches nearer than any other nationality to the perfect protection of its people. True Americans all feel that the Constitution, laws, and institutions of the United States, in their adaptation to the wants and requirements of man, are superior to those of any other country; and they should understand that by the spread of the English language will these laws and institutions be more firmly established and widely disseminated. Nothing so surely and perfectly stamps upon an individual a national characteristic as language. . . . Only English has been allowed to be taught in the public schools in the territory acquired by this country from Spain, Mexico, and Russia, although the native populations spoke another tongue. All are familiar with the recent prohibitory order of the German Empire forbidding the teaching of the French language in either public or private schools in Alsace and Lorraine. . . . If the Indians were in Germany or France or any other civilized country, they should be instructed in the language there used. As they are in an English-speaking country, they must be taught the language which they must use in transacting business with the people of this country. No unity or community of feeling can be established among different peoples unless they are brought to speak the same language, and thus become imbued with like ideas of duty. . . .

The instruction of the Indians in the vernacular is not only of no use to them, but is detrimental to the cause of their education and civilization, and no school will be permitted on the reservation in which the English language is not exclusively taught. . . .

It is believed that if any Indian vernacular is allowed to be taught by the missionaries in schools on Indian reservations, it will prejudice the youthful pupil as well as his untutored and uncivilized or semi-civilized parent against the English language, and, to some extent at least, against Government schools in which the English language exclusively has always been taught. (*ARCIA* 1887, xxi–xxiii)

A number of missionaries, supported by their national organizations, objected strenuously to Atkins's pronouncements, claiming that he lacked knowledge of their successes in the field. Missionary societies engaged in foreign missions were aware of the importance of vernacular languages in their work. The president of Dartmouth College declared that "the idea of reaching and permanently elevating the great mass of any people whatever, by first teaching them all a foreign tongue, is too absurd ever to have been entertained by sane men" (Bartlett 1887, 1254). Observers in the field such as Gen. Oliver O. Howard (1907) reported that successful missionary teachers learned the tribal language that so they could communicate with their students. Luther Standing Bear (1928), a former Carlisle student who started teaching in 1884, reported:

At that time, teaching amounted to very little. It really did not require a well-educated person to teach on the reservation. The main thing was to teach the children to write their names in English, then came learning the alphabet and how to count. I liked this work very well, and the children were doing splendidly. The first reading books we used had a great many little pictures in them. I would have the children read a line of English, and if they did not understand all they had read, I would explain it to them in Sioux. This made the studies very interesting. (1928, 192–93)

A teacher at a Rosebud Agency day school reported that one student who had been at a boarding school spoke some English. When he asked that student how he learned English, saying "no doubt you had a good teacher," the student replied, "Yes, but she did not learn me to talk. When I heard something in English I asked the other boys 'on the sly' what it meant and they told me. We did not tell on each other for we were not allowed to talk Indian" (*ARCIA* 1892, 465).

Enforcement of English-only regulations was often strict. Lawrence Horn, a Blackfeet who attended the government school at Heart Butte, recalled students getting a stroke of a leather strap with holes in it every time they spoke "Indian" (Parsons 1980).

MISSIONARIES AND NATIVE LANGUAGES

Missionaries favored ending tribal traditions, but some were more willing than the government to use tribal languages in their educational efforts. They saw through some of the apparent rapid success at teaching English. The Reverend S. D. Hinman (1869, 15, 29) reported, "It is a wonder to me how readily they learn to read our language; little fellows will read correctly page after page of their school books, and be able to spell every word, and yet not comprehend the meaning of a single sentence," and he complained about the "monotony and necessary sameness of the school-room duty." In contrast to the problems associated with getting Indians to learn English, Hinman reported that three adult Yankton (Sioux) warriors rode back and forth from their agency forty miles every week to learn to read and write their own language (33).

In 1871 the American Board of Commissioners for Foreign Missions and the Presbyterian Board of Foreign Missions started publishing with the Dakota mission a monthly newspaper, *IAPI OAYE* (The Word Carrier), mostly in the Dakota language. An editorial in an early edition of that paper declared:

It is sheer laziness in the teacher to berate his Indian scholars for not understanding English, when he does not understand enough Indian to tell them the meaning of a single one of the sentences he is trying to make them understand properly, though they have no idea of the sense. The teacher with his superior mind, should be able to learn half a dozen languages while these children of darkness are learning one. Even though the teacher's object were only to have them master English, he had better teach it to them in Indian, so they may understand what they are learning. (Editorial 1874, 4)

In 1884 the paper was split into an all-Dakota edition and an all-English edition. The mission schools for the Santee Sioux, including the Santee Sioux Normal School, started in 1870 by Stephen R. Riggs's son Alfred, to train Sioux teachers, made extensive use of the Dakota language. A correspondent who visited schools with Secretary of the Interior Schurz reported that the educational facilities of the Santee Sioux in Nebraska "are perhaps better than those of any other of the northern tribes" (*ARBIC* 1879, 77). There was a government school, an Episcopal girls' boarding school, and the American Mission male and female boarding schools. At the mission school Dakota was taught, and all the elementary books and the Bible were in Dakota. After the children learned to read in Dakota, they received a book with illustrations explained in Dakota and English. The correspondent reported:

> Mr. Riggs is of the opinion that first teaching the children to read and write in their own language enables them to master English with more ease when they take up that study; and he thinks, also, that a child beginning a four years' course with the study of Dakota would be further advanced in English at the end of the term than one who had not been instructed in Dakota. (*ARBIC* 1879, 77)

A Dr. Alden testified before the Board of Indian Commissioners:

> Our missionaries feel very decidedly on this point, and that is as to their work in the teaching of English. They believe that it can be better done by using Dakota also, and that it will be done by them in their regular educational methods. While it is not true that we teach *only* English, it is true that by beginning in the Indian tongue and then putting the students into English studies our missionaries say that after three or four years their English is better than it would have been if they had begun entirely with English. So our missionaries say that if this experiment is to be carried out at Hampton and Carlisle, let us have the same opportunity to show at our

school at Santee what can be done there. And we think, after so large experience, that the same work can be accomplished at that Santee Agency, and reaching far more in number than can be done by simply transporting them to a distance [to an off-reservation boarding school]. But with the two together we believe that a splendid work will be done both in the way of English education and civilization of the Indian. (*ARBIC* 1879, 98)

Although these missionaries used the Dakota language, they had no sympathy for Native culture. It was simply a means to Christianize and civilize their charges rapidly.

Despite the experiences of some missionaries that showed Native languages could be used effectively in schools, the Indian Office continued its efforts to eradicate them along with all Indian customs and religions. In 1881 the U.S. government banned the Plains Indian Sun Dance, and in 1885 this ban was extended into a general policy forbidding traditional Indian religious ceremonies and related customs. However, this federal policy of forced assimilation, which suppressed Native languages and cultures, did not extend to giving Indians the rights of U.S. citizenship. When John Elk renounced his tribal membership and tried to vote, the Supreme Court held in 1884 in *Elk* v. *Wilkins* that he could not (Prucha 1975). Self-styled "Friends of the Indians" threw their support behind Elk and lobbied Congress to break up Indian reservations and allow Indians to take an equal place beside other Americans, with all the rights of citizenship.

CHAPTER FOUR

ALLOTMENT AND DEPENDENCY
1887–1924

Deprived of their traditional lands, foods, and lifestyles, Indians began to feel that the government, which was responsible for this situation, owed them compensation in the form of annuities and rations. Many treaties specifically provided for annuities for a transitional period as Indians were expected to learn quickly to be farmers. However, the marginal quality of most reservation land, even for grazing, and the Indians' lack of interest in becoming farmers frustrated the government's attempts to make Indians self-sufficient on their reservations.

The 1887 General Allotment Act, also called the Dawes Act, was an attempt to force European values of individualism and private initiative on Indian people, who traditionally lived under a communal system. It granted 160 acres to each family head and 80 acres to single persons over the age of eighteen and orphans under the age of eighteen. Fee patent title was issued to each allottee to be held in trust by the government for twenty-five years. The government allowed Indians four years to decide what land they wanted; if they did not decide by then, the secretary of the interior was directed to decide for them.

Henry L. Dawes (1816-1903), Massachusetts senator and chair of the Senate's Committee on Indian Affairs, sponsored the General Allotment Act. He considered himself a friend of the Indians and advertised the act as the American Indians' Emancipation Proclamation. In a speech reported in 1883 Dawes declared that he wanted to civilize the Indian and estimated that it cost "well-nigh a million dollars for every Indian we have exterminated, and many white lives in the process, and yet he has increased in number." Dawes saw the communal way of life and the Indian value of generosity as antithetical to civilization. According to Dawes, "The last and the best agency of civilization is to teach a grown up Indian to keep" (quoted in Prucha 1973, 29).

All allottees were to be given citizenship within twenty-five years. After tribal members received their allotments, the federal government bought the "surplus" land and resold it to whites, with the tribal profits used for "education and civilization." Over the next four decades the Dawes Act reduced tribal holdings from about 140 million to 50 million acres. Three goals of the supporters of the Dawes Act were to break up tribal life, to enable Indians to receive the benefits of civilization, and to protect their remaining landholdings ("Report" 1976, 43). Dawes admitted in 1895 that "thieves got hold" of his act (*ARBIC* 1895, 41).

The Dawes Act did not result in the assimilation of Indians. Instead, it perpetuated the status of many of them as a permanent underclass even more dependent on the federal government. According to Susan La Flesche, "voting and citizenship marked the beginning of alcohol abuse on the reservation. Local politicians with whiskey to dispense came to solicit the Omaha's vote, explaining to them that since they had the same rights as white men they could drink all they wanted" (quoted in Mathes 1985, 75).

Another example of the negative impact of the Dawes Act is the experience of one family with four middle-aged sons who received allotments fifty miles apart and one hundred miles from their seventy-year-old grandfather. Geographic isolation prevented the family from providing mutual aid in the traditional way. The marginal quality of much of the allotted Indian land on the Great Plains became apparent during droughts in the early nineteenth century, the Depression years, and the 1980s when many white farmers were forced off holdings much larger than 160 acres.

Over the years allotments were split up through inheritance to the extent that it was economical only to have them leased out by the owners' trustee, the Indian Office, later known as the Bureau of Indian Affairs (BIA). In 2002 the BIA was sued by allottees because it was not keeping adequate track of lease payments.

The speed with which a reservation was allotted was directly proportional to how much the land was desired by whites. The desert reservations of Arizona, without any then-known mineral resources, escaped allotment. The Navajo Reservation was the largest exception to allotment, and it actually expanded greatly under executive orders even after 1900. The communal orientation of most Indians was strong. A delegate from Indian Territory to Washington, D.C., in an 1886 article in *The Indian* reprinted from the *Cherokee Advocate*, protested the efforts of Dawes and his allies:

> We were sent to the wilderness because the whites wanted our country in the States. Now we have developed the new country and built for ourselves homes in it, and the whites want that. We are doing well. We are happy and prosperous. We are working out the problem of civilization. We have schools and churches and governments patterned after your own. Our lands are patented to tribes, and our people hold it in common. We all have names. There are no paupers among us. We never see anybody begging for pennies in our country as we do here [in Washington, D.C.]. Let us alone. Don't break us up. (*Indian* 1886, 25)

Despite their opposition, the Five Civilized Tribes of Oklahoma were forced into allotment with the passage of the Curtis Act (30 U.S. Stat. 495–503) in 1898. Their self-government was replaced by principal chiefs appointed by the president of the United States, and their schools were taken over by the Department of the Interior and transformed into state-operated public schools (Debo 1970).

Under the allotment program, it was hoped that Indians would attend public schools. In 1904 Indian Commissioner W. A. Jones found that "too frequently where contracts are made with [public] school districts the money to be paid by the Government is the main thing sought, and not a sincere desire to benefit the Indian" (*ARCIA* 1904, 44). The contracts required Indian students to be educated alongside white students and to be treated the same way, but this was not always done, with the result that some contracts were ended (ARCIA 1905). Indian students were often too poor to buy clothes for school and did not speak English well enough to do the required classwork.

Anna Moore Shaw (1974) was an exceptionally successful Pima student. In her junior year she started attending Phoenix Union High School while staying at the Phoenix Indian Boarding School dorm. She recalled liking her teachers and the special efforts they made to help her pass subjects that had been "a bit neglected . . . at the Indian school" (141). One teacher especially, Miss Summers, stood out for helping her with American history. She recalled, "[T]hroughout my days in high school I never noticed any prejudice directed at me because of my Indian blood," which was particularly important to her because her boyfriend in the Phoenix Indian School's National Guard unit was called up to fight Pancho Villa and she missed him intensely (141-42). In 1920 she was the first full-blooded Pima girl to graduate from Phoenix Union High School. Although she had assimilated into white culture, she "felt deep sadness" that the old beliefs were dying out and she noted that the "missionaries' belief that the traditional customs were sinful was gradually dying out," especially since the Pimas were now "staunch Christians" (172-173).

In 1924 the Committee of One Hundred report on Indian Affairs noted that the attendance of Indian students in public schools was poor (Otis 1924). Despite problems, there was a rapid increase in Indians attending public schools alongside non-Indian students in the twentieth century. In 1909 the figure was only 900, but by 1926 it was 37,730 and in 1932 48,000 according to government figures. In 1916 enrollment in government (federal) schools reached a high of 27,764 and then began to slowly decline, and the Indian enrollment in public schools surpassed that in the federal government's schools. (Fischbacher 1967; Schmeckebier 1927). Public school attendance was part of the plan for total assimilation that also included the passage by Congress in 1924 of the Indian Citizenship Act, which made all U.S.-born Indians U.S. citizens. However, the Act had little impact on the status of Indians. Luther Standing Bear declared:

> The greatest hoax ever perpetrated upon him [the Indian] was the supposed citizenship of 1924 when President Coolidge signed a bill that freed the Indian. The signing of that bill changed not in the slightest measure the condition of the Indian. Not one agent was removed from office, Indian boys and girls are still segregated in school life, and the reservation and reservation rule still exist. (1933, 229)

In South Dakota, New Mexico, and Arizona, Indians were not allowed to vote until after World War II because voters had to own property, pay taxes, or meet other requirements.

THE CATHOLIC-PROTESTANT FIGHT

Although allotment had the ideological purpose of detribalizing Indians and making them citizens, its real purpose was to open more of the West to white settlement. The Indians were not only victims of immigrants' unrelenting demand for more land, they were also pawns in political battles that were unrelated to Indian people. One such battle in late-nineteenth-century America was the continuation of the long war between Catholics and Protestants that dated from the Protestant Reformation in the sixteenth century. The Catholic Church has had a continuing interest in Indian education from the time of Columbus. Protestantism, as a breakaway religion, has been antagonistic to Catholicism from the beginning. Colonial schoolchildren were taught in the 1727 *New England Primer*, "Abhor that arrant Whore of Rome, and all her Blasphemies" (Ford 1962, n.p.). In the 1850s the anti-immigrant American (Know-Nothing) Party went so far as to burn urban Catholic schools. In 1887 the American Protective Association (APA) was formed to combat Catholicism in the United States through a strategy of placing anti-Catholics in important government offices (Sievers 1952).

While the presidentially appointed Board of Indian Commissioners was all Protestant, the Bureau of Catholic Indian Missions (BCIM), formed in 1874 in Washington, D.C., through an organized drive to establish mission schools, garnered the lion's share of government funding. In 1884 Catholic Indian schools received $62,250 in government funding. In 1886, of the fifty religious schools receiving support from the government, thirty-eight were Catholic. With their head start and better organization, by 1889 Catholic Indian schools were receiving $347,672, almost 75 percent of all contract funds and $300,000 more than the next largest group, the Presbyterians.

The Catholics were greatly helped by Katherine Drexel (1858–1955). Soon after her banker father died in 1885, leaving her and her two sisters several million dollars, Father Joseph Stephan, director of the BCIM, and Bishop Martin Marty met with them about supporting Indian missions. Stephan and Marty got the sisters to visit the western missions in 1887 and 1888, and Katherine began to donate money for building Indian schools, which could then receive $100 per student per year from the government. In 1889 she became a postulant, and in 1891 she became the first sister of the Blessed Sacrament for Indians and

Colored People. This order would provide badly needed teachers for the schools she built. The first four nuns overcame the vicissitudes and violence of the Pullman strike and arrived by train in 1894 to reopen St. Catherine's Indian School in Santa Fe, New Mexico. In 1897 Katherine agreed to cover the costs of a mission to the Navajo, and in 1902 St. Michael's School was opened on the reservation. By 1907 Katherine and her sisters had donated $1.5 million to Indian missions (Duffy 1966).

The success of the BCIM, the doctrine of papal infallibility established by the Vatican Council of 1869–70, the success of parochial schools in the cities, and the electoral gains of Irish Catholics in some of the nation's largest cities infuriated many Protestants. As a result, government funding of Catholic Indian schools became an issue in the 1884 presidential election. The backlash to a Presbyterian minister's comment that the Democratic Party was the party of "rum, Romanism and rebellion" helped Grover Cleveland get elected president. Protestants grouped Catholic Indian schools with urban Catholic parochial schools and labeled both un-American, in contrast to the nondenominational locally run public schools. James M. King, representing the National League for the Protection of American Institutions, declared that "much Roman Catholic teaching among the Indians does not prepare them for intelligent and loyal citizenship" (*ARCIA* 1892, 65).

The conflict was aggravated by the appointment of the Baptist minister and educator Thomas Jefferson Morgan as Commissioner of Indian Affairs in 1889 by his old Civil War commander, President Benjamin Harrison, who replaced Cleveland that same year. Morgan left Franklin College in 1861 to enlist as a private in the Union Army, and he finished the Civil War as a brigadier general commanding black troops. After the war he served as principal of several normal schools, taught at the Baptist Union Theological Seminary in Chicago, and was vice president of the National Educational Association (NEA) from 1887 to 1889 (Prucha 1984, 1997b). In his 1889 book, *Studies in Pedagogy*, published just before his appointment, Morgan argued against legislation discriminating against Chinese immigrants and for educating Indians, and he saw the purpose of schools as assimilation and unification, with "the first bond of union . . . a common language" (152).

The journal *Education* greeted Morgan's appointment and that of his superintendent of Indian schools, Daniel Dorchester, a Methodist minister, by saying they were in "hearty sympathy with American ideas, and the American theory of education and system of public schools" (Editorial 1890, 449). Morgan favored "[a] comprehensive system of education, modeled after the American public school system[,] . . . embracing all persons of school age, compulsory in its demands and uniformly administered" (quoted in Sievers 1952, 142). In an interview in 1889, Morgan elaborated:

> I am not sure that it is wise to place any public school entirely in the hands of a religious order. . . . [I]t seems to me it would be far better to take American Catholics with experience in public schools and with normal school training for such places in preference to either jesuits or sisters educated in foreign lands, who speak the English language indifferently, who know nothing by experience or training of public school work, who are not imbued with American ideas. (Quoted in Sievers 1952, 142)

The Carlisle Indian School publication, the *Red Man*, supported Morgan's 1889 declaration that "the public school system has come to be recognized as an essential factor in training of American citizens" (Sievers 1952, 143). Morgan tried to control the curriculum to be used in mission schools and to send the brightest pupils to government boarding schools. The Catholics got around Morgan by obtaining a special congressional appropriation of $535,000 earmarked for contract schools.

Superintendent of Indian Schools Dorchester had published *Romanism versus the Public School System* in 1888. When Dorchester inspected the federal schools, he dismissed some Catholics, and Morgan did the same back in Washington. Morgan's 1892 *Annual Report* to the secretary of the interior revealed the bitterness of his fight with the Catholics. For example, the Catholic priest J. B. Boulet discouraged Indians from allowing their children to be transferred from a reservation Catholic school to Salem (Chemawa) Indian School. Boulet wrote the editor of the *Catholic News*, "Morals are said to be very low in that [Salem] school; too much freedom among the sexes and followed by many breaches against chastity. Graduates of this school are generally proud, haughty—polished heathens" (*ARCIA* 1892, 156). The U.S. Indian agent responded to these attacks, "As a result of the outrageous and treasonable interference of this foreign missionary the supervisor of education William T. Leeke, and I were unable to get a single pupil for the Salem school from the Lummi" (*ARCIA* 1892, 154). Leeke asked that the priest be banned from all Indian reservations. The archbishop of Santa Fe took issue with Morgan's claims of the lack of industrial training and English usage at St. Catherine's Indian School in Santa Fe and called him a liar (*ARCIA* 1892). Soon after, Morgan accused Catholics of "treason" and declared, "We ought to insist that the flag shall float over every schoolhouse, that American songs shall be sung" (*ARCIA* 1893, 130).

All relations broke down between the Indian Bureau and the BCIM in 1892 as the presidential electioneering heated up. Anti-Catholics quoted the BCIM director as referring to the "bigoted Indian Commissioner, Morgan, and the not-much-less bigoted [President] Harrison" (quoted in Sievers 1952, 132), and Morgan stopped direct government relations with the BCIM, forcing each Catholic school to negotiate a separate contract. The Catholics brought up Morgan's Civil War court martial for perjury, theft, and forgery (Sievers 1952). Thus Indian education, as a sidelight of the Protestant-Catholic debate, became an issue in the 1892 presidential election that Cleveland won, thereby becoming the only president to serve two nonconsecutive terms. Cleveland promptly replaced Morgan with Daniel M. Browning, who was inexperienced in Indian affairs and had no clear policy (Hagan 1979). The Jesuit father L. B. Palladino (1837-1927) wrote his 1894 book, *Indian and White in the Northwest*, in part to attack Morgan's policy. He wrote, for example, "[T]o make Indian schools non-sectarian, as the word goes, is simply to eliminate Christianity from the education of the Indian, and to eliminate Christianity from Indian education is to eliminate the one factor without which . . . the civilization of the red man is an utter impossibility" (1922, 90). Palladino was especially upset with the founding by Morgan's administration of Fort Shaw Indian School in Montana in 1892, because it would draw students from the existing Catholic boarding schools.

To help end government funding of Catholic mission schools, the parent mission societies of most Protestant mission schools ceased applying for government funds. Between 1895 and 1900 direct government funding of mission schools was phased out, with the result that many mission schools either closed or were reduced in size. In 1901 Indian Commissioner W. A. Jones stopped the distribution of rations to students in mission schools. Congress restored rations to mission school children in 1904, and missionaries won the right in court in 1908 in *Quick Bear* v. *Leupp* to continue to get tribal treaty and trust funds held by the U.S. government if they could obtain tribal approval. After a sharp decline, attendance in mission day and boarding schools slowly increased between 1900 and 1926, from 4,081 to 7,571 students. While only about 6 percent of these students were attending day schools in 1900, that figure had risen almost 22 percent in 1926. Government school enrollment during this period was near or over capacity, but the mission schools were only at about 70 percent capacity (Schmeckebier 1927).

REFORM EFFORTS

Congress had written into law in 1888 the position of superintendent of Indian schools with the intention that it would be filled by a professional educator. Later, it authorized field supervisors. In 1891 Congress authorized compulsory education for Indians, and in 1892 it started to pass laws to improve the quality of teachers in Indian schools (Fischbacher 1967). In the 1880s and 1890s there was a major shift in the focus of the Indian Office. In 1881 only 238, or 11.3 percent, of its employees were in education; in 1897 the number was 1,936, or 49.4 percent (Prucha 1984). This shift necessitated a close examination of what was actually being accomplished by the education program.

In addition to his involvement in the religious dispute, Commissioner Morgan sought to remake the Indian school system according to the model of the developing U.S. public school system. He asked Dorchester, his new superintendent of Indian schools, to begin with a two-month, six-thousand-mile inspection of Indian schools, which resulted in "the first official comprehensive field report on Indian education" (Adams 1946, 54–55). He found incompetent teachers, schools that had never been inspected, and poor sanitary conditions. Morgan made his own inspection the next year and divided Indian country into four districts, each with a supervisor responsible for inspecting schools (Adams 1946). In 1889 Morgan estimated there were 50,000 Indian children between the ages of six and sixteen, 21,000 of whom were still not in school (Fischbacher 1967). Morgan's reforms included codification of school rules, compulsory attendance, establishment of the merit system for personnel, and standardization of curriculum, textbooks, and instruction. He also created the position of "field matron" in 1892 to teach Indian women in the home "the preparation and serving of food, sewing, laundry, care of domestic animals, care of the sick, and proper observance of the Sabbath" (Mathes 1985, 65; see also Golden 1954). In 1893 the Rosebud field matron reported getting no supplies but spending 181 days visiting 325 families, instructing 420 women, and traveling 1,653 miles (*ARCIA* 1893). In 1895 the appropriation for field matrons was increased (*ARCIA* 1895).

Congress also passed laws permitting Morgan to enforce school attendance through the withholding of rations and annuities from Indian families who did not send their children to school. Dorchester wanted to have students attend day school for the first four years and then boarding school for four years. He supported reservation boarding schools while Carlisle's Richard H. Pratt saw them as only a way to appease westerners by putting government money into their pockets. Dorchester's reforms also included having the power to enforce student attendance moved from the agent to the secretary of the interior so as to provide greater uniformity and prevent abuses. In 1893 the post of Indian agent was abolished at the Cherokee Agency and the duties were given to the school superintendent. The next year, with the approval of the secretary of the interior, the Commissioner of Indian Affairs was allowed to replace Indian agents with bonded superintendents of agency training schools, who received the honorary title Major. The old school superintendents now became principals. In 1894 there were fifty-eight Indian agencies (*ARCIA* 1901).

The political spoils system that Carl Schurz and others had fought in the 1870s continued, and reforms were certainly needed. A longtime inspector of Indian schools reported to the Board of Indian Commissioners at their nineteenth annual conference with the representatives of Indian missions that "the Indian Bureau has been made the dumping-ground for the sweeping of the political party that is in power" (*ARBIC* 1889, 139). In an *Educational Review* article, Elaine Goodale (1891, 58), soon to be the wife of Charles Eastman (Sioux), criticized education in Indian schools: "Four fifths, if not nine tenths, of the work done is purely mechanical drill. . . . The child reads by rote, he memorizes the combinations in arithmetic, he copies letters and forms, he imitates the actions of his teacher." The same year the Dakota Mission's *Word Carrier* reprinted an article from the *School Journal* declaring the "chief difference between English-speaking and Indian children [is] the need of grinding, drilling, and driving English into them" and commenting on the "deadness" of Indian classrooms (North 1891, 35).

Albert H. Kneale remembered monotonous lessons at the turn-of-the-century Oklahoma boarding school where he worked:

> Few of the pupils had any desire to learn to read, for there was nothing to read in their homes nor in the camp; there seemed little incentive to learn English, for there was no opportunity to use it; there seemed to be nothing gained through knowing that "c-a-t" spells cat; arithmetic offered no attraction; not one was interested in knowing the name of the capital of New York. (1950, 52-53)

He remembered students being more interested in the afternoon vocational training. Estelle Brown (1952) replaced a kindergarten teacher in 1897 who took one look at the Crow Creek School in South Dakota and left. She found the Indian Bureau preoccupied with paperwork and staff morals rather than responsive to the firsthand advice of their field-workers or the Indians they were supposed to serve. "A knowledge of the pupils' home environment was not considered necessary since their education aimed to make that environment unsuitable to them" (204). She never heard any of her fellow employees express an interest in improving reservation conditions.

Soon after Brown started teaching kindergarten at Crow Creek Indian School in 1897, another employee told her that "there ain't nobody here who could earn a living anywhere else. They're the only kind of people who ever come into this dirty Indian Service" (43). By 1897 more than two-thirds of the teachers employed in 1892 and three-fourths of the school superintendents had left the Indian Service, probably owing to the isolation, monotony, and poor living conditions. The average teacher was a single woman in her late twenties, from the Midwest and the Great Plains. The historian David Wallace Adams (1995) describes an incident on Nevada's Duck Valley Reservation in 1899 in which the red-headed female Catholic school superintendent had a shootout with the Indian agent, who was anti–Civil Service. His daughter was a matron at the school and his wife an agency clerk (Adams 1995).

High rates of teacher turnover continued into the late twentieth century, and teaching on reservations was rarely the first choice of non-Indian teachers, who usually had no special training to work with Indian students (Deyhle 1992; *Report on BIA Education* 1988; *Indian Education* 1969). The continued seriousness of this problem can be seen in Gary Plank's 1993 study of Navajo schools. Plank reported that the annual teacher turnover rate ranged from a high of 57 percent to a low of 25 percent, with 77 percent of new teachers getting no orientation to Navajo education. One of the teachers Plank interviewed stated, "They hired me over the phone you know. I looked good on paper. I didn't know they didn't speak English too much and had to learn a different language. I didn't know it was a boarding school and that was a surprise" (Plank 1993, 30-31).

William N. Hailmann

On the recommendation of U.S. Commissioner of Education William T. Harris, President Cleveland appointed Dr. William N. Hailmann superintendent of Indian schools. Hailman, a professional educator with no denominational affiliation and a proponent of Froebel's educational philosophy, having translated his work from German in 1887, served from 1894 to 1898. According to his biographer, Dorothy Hewes (1981, 64), he "stressed student self-government, activity learning from kindergarten through high school, the importance of family life, and of community involvement in schools." A German-speaking immigrant from Switzerland, Hailmann was more familiar than most Americans with the problems of learning English.

In a major address at the 1895 National Education Association (NEA) annual meeting in Denver, Hailmann expressed his support for an assimilationist policy, including abolishing reservations and putting Indians in public schools. As superintendent he favored ending corporal punishment and improving teaching, for example, by using more cooperative teaching methods and an integrated curriculum. Teacher institutes, reading circles, educational leave with pay, and the extension of Civil Service improved the quality of school staff during Hailmann's tenure (Adams 1946; Hewes 1981). During Hailmann's term of office, twenty-four new day schools were opened and four boarding schools were closed. He supported the establishment of kindergartens and "encouraged the telling of tribal legends by older students and Indian staff members" (Hewes 1981, 70). However, the economic depression started by the Panic of 1893 meant that little money was available to improve Indian education. In a book edited by Nicholas Murray Butler, president of the NEA in 1895 and first president of Teachers College, Columbia University, Hailmann criticized the military and anti-Indian culture aspects of Indian schools as well as the "unintelligent warfare against the Indian idiom" (Hailmann 1990, 942).

In 1895 he reported to the Board of Indian Commissioners that he was supplying schools with sets of forty books chosen for pleasure reading, that many schools were closing their "jails," that bathtubs were being replaced with showers, and that more students were getting milk and individual towels (*ARBIC* 1895). In his 1896 report to the Commissioner of Indian Affairs, Hailmann criticized workers in Indian schools for knowing "little about the Indian as an Indian," and he went on to say that the change in view from the Indian as a savage to the Indian as a human being had led to greater use of native languages in schools (*ARCIA* 1896, 119-20). The following year he declared:

> In accordance with suggestions made at summer institutes, a number of teachers have commenced to take an interest in the study of the Indians upon their reservation, acquainting themselves with the home environment of the children, as well as the habits, wisdoms, ideals and in a measure even with the language of the Indians. (*ARCIA* 1897, 329)

This, he felt would allow teachers to connect the new knowledge they were teaching with the children's previous experiences. Hailmann worked with Theodore Roosevelt to make the Civil Service examination for Indian Office employees more relevant to their jobs, but because his position was not under the Civil Service he was replaced in 1898 when President William McKinley assumed office. When the new *Rules for Indian Schools* was issued in 1898, rule 198 stated, "All instruction shall be in the English language. Pupils shall be required to converse with employees and each other in English. All school employees must be able to speak English fluently (25). Requiring all employees to speak English was a slap at immigrant Catholic nuns and priests who had not yet learned to speak English.

Civil Service and the Merit System

In 1889 Gen. Henry Heth, a former Indian Service inspector, reported
to the Board of Indian Commissioners:

> The Indian Bureau has been made the dumping-ground for the sweepings
> of the political party that is in power. I have found an abandoned woman
> in charge of an Indian school. I found a discharged lunatic in charge of
> another, and he was still there a year after I reported that fact. He would
> lock himself into a room with the children, and light his pipe. As soon as a
> report that is derogatory to these people goes to Washington, their friends
> rush to the Interior Department and say that these reports are wrong, and
> that another trial must be given, and they are kept on and on. . . . If you go
> to an Indian school or an agency, and stay only a day or two, everything
> will seem to run smoothly. But if you stay there a month, and get behind the
> scenes, into the arcanum, you will find two or three who are physically,
> mentally, or morally incapacitated. You find good, earnest people among
> them, but they are the exception. You find people who are there only to
> draw their pay. You will find cliques, wrangles, quarrels going on that are
> a disgrace to any institution. (*ARBIC* 1889, 139)

Laurence Schmeckebier, in his 1927 study of the Office of Indian Affairs,
included descriptions of "fearful" conditions in Indian schools in the
1880s, among them incompetent teachers and deplorable facilities.

The assassination of President James A. Garfield in 1881 by a disgruntled office seeker and the continued barrage of criticism led to
Civil Service reform, which was introduced to Indian schools in the
1890s. However, the Civil Service examination in the 1890s, like the
National Teachers Examination of the 1990s, tested for general knowledge rather than for competencies specific to the job. Estelle Brown
(1952, 48) took the Civil Service examination in about 1901, expecting
"to be tested on [her] fitness to teach children of a savage race to whom
the word education was unknown and who were without knowledge
of a written language. No such test was given." She had expected
questions on tribal history and reservation conditions; she was not even
told which tribe she was to teach. In effect, the Civil Service examination, like the teacher competency tests of today, was designed, at best,

for teachers of mainstream students. This cultural bias excluded many potential Indian teachers as well as a few "incompetent" white teachers while letting through teachers with little or no knowledge of Indians and Indian education. Low government salaries plus the isolation (from white communities) of many Indian schools meant that the Indian Service was often the last resort for teachers who could not find employment elsewhere.

Former Carlisle student and agency teacher Luther Standing Bear complained that the Civil Service examination was not necessary for primary teachers and that his students did better than the students of white teachers who obtained all their knowledge from books "but outside of that, . . . knew nothing."

> The Indian children should have been taught how to translate the Sioux tongue into English properly; but the English teachers only taught them the English language, like a bunch of parrots. While they could read all the words placed before them, they did not know the proper use of them; their meaning was a puzzle. (Standing Bear 1928, 239)

Alfred Riggs, who learned Dakota as a child and was the first principal of the successful Santee High School, noted that "the Indian was a great deal more effective as a preacher and teacher among his own people than any white man could be" (Howard 1958, 180).

In 1892 the merit system was applied to physicians, school superintendents, teachers, and matrons. In 1896 all agency and school employees except for the Indian agent were put under the civil service. Although this led to general improvement in the quality of personnel, Pratt found that it made it more difficult for him to staff Carlisle Indian School with the people he wanted (see chap. 6). Pratt desired the freedom to choose teachers based on something more than an examination, and he became a vocal opponent of the Civil Service. In 1893 Theodore Roosevelt personally investigated Pratt's complaints and his request for exemption from Civil Service rules. Pratt continued his attack in the Carlisle school newspaper in 1897. These repeated confrontations led, after Roosevelt became president, to his dismissal, first from the army and then from his post at Carlisle Indian Industrial School.

Estelle Reel

Estelle Reel (1862–1959) served as superintendent of Indian schools from 1898 to 1910, when Congress eliminated funds for her position and she married a rancher in Washington State. As a young woman, Reel moved from the Midwest to Cheyenne, Wyoming, where her brother was mayor. As a teacher there she told the school board they had no right to tell her where she should go to church, buy her clothes, or live. In 1894 she was elected Wyoming state superintendent of public instruction and promoted equal pay for equal work for women. As a reward for her assistance in William McKinley's presidential election campaign, she was nominated to a federal position requiring Senate ratification—the first woman to receive such a nomination. Starting as superintendent of Indian schools, she went on a 65,900-mile inspection tour of the Indian educational system that consisted of two hundred fifty schools stretching from Carlisle, Pennsylvania, to Salem, Oregon, two thousand teachers, and twenty thousand students (Lomawaima 1996).

According to the historian K. Tsianina Lomawaima (1966, 6), it was during Reel's tenure that "the Indian Office's education division was professionalized, and national Indian policy turned from conquest and relocation to bureaucratic control." Federal traveling inspectors started to visit agencies in 1873, but formal government inspection of schools for other than political purposes was much slower in coming. Summer teaching institutes started in 1884. In 1894 five summer institutes were held, and in 1895 the Indian Office held three one-week institutes in Tacoma, Sioux City, and El Reno with five hundred Indian school employees attending, representing more than one-third of the Indian school staff (ARCIA 1895). Reel expanded on and improved these institutes, and by 1903 there were ten a year. In 1906 there were four "well attended" summer institutes, at which experienced teachers gave demonstration lessons. The San Francisco earthquake forced the cancellation of a planned institute there (ARCIA 1906, 75).

One of the four institutes in 1900 was held in conjunction with the annual meeting of the NEA. Reel got Indian educators recognized as a department of the NEA, and they met at the organization's annual meetings from 1900 to 1909. Reel served as the secretary of this group from 1901 to 1909. Pratt served as the first president of the department, followed by the Reverend H. B. Frissell, principal of the Hampton

Normal and Industrial Institute, and he was followed by administrators from Chilocco and Haskell boarding schools. During Reel's tenure as superintendent, leading educators, Indian office administrators, and teachers exchanged ideas at the NEA's annual meetings.

In Frissell's 1901 keynote address, "Learning by Doing," to the NEA Indian educators in Detroit, he declared, "There is an increased endeavor on the part of the heads of our Indian schools to study the conditions from which students come and to which they must return, and to adapt their work and study while in school to their needs at home" (894). G. Stanley Hall, president of Clark University, stated in his 1903 address to the Indian educators:

> Now, my simple proposition today is that the lower races should first be understood, their customs studied, their language made familiar, their feelings, views of the world and life, their traditions, myths, institutions, sympathetically by appreciated; and all attempted reconstruction of their lives, thoughts, and emotions should be guided by this knowledge. . . . Instead of trying to make good Indians, we try to make a wretched third-class white man. (1903, 1054)

At the 1908 NEA meeting in Cleveland, Ohio, Hall called for providing primary education for Indian students in their Native language.

In 1901 Reel led the development of the *Uniform Course of Study (UCS)* for Indian schools. The influence of the government's assimilationist policies and the educational ideas of Froebel, Rousseau, Pestalozzi, and Comenius is apparent:

> The aim of the course is to give the Indian child a knowledge of the English language and to equip him with the ability to become self-supporting as soon as possible. . . .
>
> The value of education must be measured by its contribution to life interests, and it is our purpose to fit the Indian pupil for life.
>
> The child learns to speak the English language through doing the work that must be accomplished in any well regulated home, and, at the same time is being trained in habits of industry, cleanliness and system. He learns to read by telling of his daily interests and work with the chalk on the blackboard. In keeping count of his poultry and in measuring his garden, he becomes familiar with numbers in such a practical way he

knows how to use them in daily life, as well as on the blackboard in the schoolroom. . . .

All theoretical and experimental work must be discarded by the [government] farmer. The boy has but a few years to go to school and it is highly necessary that he be taught the practical work necessary to become self-supporting while in school.

Do not attempt much memorization of rules. Where principles are understood, the rule will be of little practical use. All teaching should be of such a nature as will best fit the child to cope with his environment. (Quoted in Morris 1954, 99–100)

Reel's *UCS* reflected her limited view of Indian capabilities in its concentration on domestic and manual labor training, and it received widespread praise, from Charles F. Lummis and George Bird Grinnell, among others. However, former Commissioner of Indian Affairs T. J. Morgan condemned it: "Now why should the national government offer to its wards so much less in the way of schooling than is offered by the States to the pupils in the public schools" (quoted in Prucha 1984, 828).

Three thousand copies of the *UCS* were printed for Indian schools and then another six thousand copies for the Philippines and Puerto Rico. Lomawaima (1996, 13) maintains that "the UCS was a blueprint for total control of Indian people—mental, physical, and moral—in excruciating detail." However, Robert Valentine, Leupp's private secretary, who succeeded Leupp as Commissioner of Indian Affairs in 1909, reported in 1911 that the *UCS* had "not been in general use for some time" (Prucha 1984, 829). A 1905 news release reported:

[Reel] does not believe in making a white man of the Indian but thinks it best to educate him and let him remain an Indian. . . . She believes in what Booker T. Washington is doing for the negro, and has adopted may of the Tuskegee methods [which were a development of the Hampton Institute practices were Washington attended] for Indian schools. (Quoted in Lomawaima 1996, 14)

This replication of the methods used at Hampton and Tuskegee included the building of "practical cottages" at the large off-reservation boarding schools "where senior girls lived a facsimile of some idealized Victorian domestic idyll on the princely budget of $4.50 per week" (Lomawaima 1996, 14-15). Students liked the cottages, which were an escape from the dormitories and regimentation (Lomawaima 1996).

Reel was echoing the ideas of her new boss in 1905, writing that while English was the cornerstone of education, "the commissioner [Leupp] urges us to see that no child shall be forced to drop out or forget the language of his ancestors. The child's natural love for his mother-tongue must be respected" (*Addresses* 1900–1909, 932).

An interesting educational approach supported by Reel was sand tables for primary school children, which were used extensively in one-room BIA day schools on the Pine Ridge and Rosebud Reservations in South Dakota at the turn of the century (see fig. 3). The 1903 *Annual Report of the Commissioner of Indian Affairs* contained a description and photograph of the sand table, a waist-high sandbox. Older students used it to teach the younger ones: "The table is arranged like a home with irrigating ditch, ridge, fence posts made out of clothespins, house, etc. The pupil teacher says to the class, say 'the horse,' then 'the horse runs,' etc." (376–77). The table was changed to suit the seasons of the year. In her 1904 annual report Reel again said the "sand table" and "teaching objectively" (using objects) worked well and called for teachers to find out about their students' homes and home life, interests, and individual characteristics. This description of using objects is remark-ably similar to the "realia" Edwina Hoffman endorsed in *Teaching American Indian Students* (Reyhner 1992, 132–42).

At the 1902 NEA meeting, Claude C. Covey, a teacher at Pine Ridge, called for textbooks "especially adapted to Indian children": "In the Indian school—especially the lower grades—some of the best results obtained are from home-made text-books; that is, lessons worked out by the teacher and pupils" (*Addresses* 1900–1909, 874–75). He noted the importance of nature study and teaching words "that actually occur in the everyday life of the child" and suggested "lessons should be talked over, written, read, and preserved" (875). However, he also noted that it was hard for teachers to make their own textbooks and that ones were needed that were appropriate to the *Uniform Course of Study*.

Reel's 1905 report described setting up the print shop in the Albu-querque Indian School as a means of getting students to learn to write. The Chilocco Boarding School was described as having the most exten-sive print shop in the Indian Service:

Students using a sand table, Pine Ridge Day School No. 27. Photograph from the 1903 *Annual Report of the Commissioner of Indian Affairs*.

A new plan for teaching language has been put into practice the past year. . . . The teacher of language and her class are constituted the staff—editors and reporters—of a weekly journal. They gather news all about the school and bring it to the classroom, where it is itemized and paragraphed. Criticisms are made. The paragraphs are boiled down to make them concise and simple [and] sent to [the] print shop edited and corrected. (*ARCIA* 1905, 428)

Although Reel advocated a child-centered approach to teaching that is still popular today, recent historians (e.g., Ellis 1996; Lomawaima 1996; Ryan 1962) find that her policies were motivated by the racist notion that Indians had limited abilities. Reel's view contrasts with that of her contemporaries, such as Carlisle Superintendent Richard H. Pratt and Elaine Eastman, who believed Indians could be the white man's equal. She wrote in her 1900 annual report, "[T]he overshadowing importance of industrial training in our work of Indian education becomes more clearly recognized as time passes. The theory of cramming the Indian child with mere book knowledge has been and for generations will be a failure" (quoted in Prucha 1984, 826). The Indian child was to learn English while receiving "practical training." This training even included

Native industries, Phoenix Indian School. Photograph from the 1903 *Annual Report of the Commissioner of Indian Affairs*.

Indian arts and crafts (see fig. 4); however, by the 1920s the arts and crafts efforts had faded in Indian schools (Lomawaima 1996).

Johann Heinrich Pestalozzi

Of particular interest to educators trying to teach Indians English were the ideas of the Swiss educator and writer Johann Heinrich Pestalozzi (1747–1827). Pestalozzi rejected the classical approach to learning of his time, which stressed discipline and memorization, and instead stressed the use of the natural environment as a source of educational opportunities and the use of children's senses, beginning with objects found in their immediate environment (Gutek 1968).

Educators who read Pestalozzi's writings and visited his schools spread his ideas across Europe and to America. The American educator Henry Barnard (1811-1900) published a collection of his essays,

Pestalozzi and Pestalozzianism, in 1859, and Edward A. Sheldon (1823-97) popularized "the narrow English conception of the formal object lesson into teacher education" at the Oswego (New York) Normal School (Gutek 1968, 163). According to Gerald Gutek (1968, 162), a biographer of Pestalozzi, "The basic operating principle at Oswego was that all knowledge derived from sense perception and that all instruction should be based on real objects."

The Quaker Samuel M. Janney described "object-teaching" in 1873:

> They have in their schools diagrams representing various objects—cow, lamp, boy, horse, &c.—with the Indian name of the object underneath. The scholars are told the name of the object in English, and the way to spell it. The class spell that word over and over again till they get it thoroughly. . . . Books are used afterwards. I have learned in some cases where the scholars learned to read English in six months. We endeavor to avoid teaching them to repeat parrot-like. (*ARBIC* 1873, 181)

This use of real objects to teach second languages provides what modern experts of teaching English as a second language such as Stephen Krashen (1996) call "comprehensible input." Indian Commissioner Morgan (1889, 45), in his *Studies in Pedagogy*, wrote that object lessons were part of the training of senses and that "things, objects, must be measured, counted, weighed." He was against rote learning and thought that observation needed to precede books and that physics and chemistry could not be taught outside the laboratory. He declared, "[T]he first stages of all education should be experimental. When the child has acquired the power of gaining knowledge readily and accurately without help, then objects hinder instead of aid" (294). According to Reel in her 1904 annual report,

> It was found that the most successful teachers worked objectively altogether, using articles with which the pupils were familiar and gradually bringing them to associate the English name of the object, spoken and written, with the object itself; many teachers were adhering too closely to text-books. (*ARCIA* 1904, 397)

Her office distributed sample lessons to teachers to improve instruction. Reel's boss, Commissioner of Indian Affairs Francis Leupp, later wrote:

[T]he more intelligent teachers in the Indian Service are ignoring books as far as they can in the earlier stages of their work. They are teaching elementary mathematics with feathers, or pebbles, or grains of corn; then the relations of numbers to certain symbols on the blackboard are made clear, and thus the pupils are led along almost unconsciously from point to point. Had a system like this been in vogue twenty years ago, an Indian who became a bank teller would have been spared a confession he once made to me, that he had reached a full man's estate before he understood why he multiplied four by five in order to find out how much four pounds of sugar would cost at five cents a pound! Throughout his school life he had been an expert mathematician, yet figures meant nothing to him but so many pure abstractions which could be put through sundry operations mechanically; they bore no relation in his mind to any concrete object in nature. (Leupp 1910, 127–28)

In 1905 Reuben Perry, superintendent of the Navajo Indian School, told the Indian department of the NEA:

The natural method of giving a child English lies in a presentation of objects and the English names to represent them. This should be done in a manner to command his interest and attention. The names of the objects and the simple sentences *given by the child* should be repeatedly written on the board, until a correct mental picture of the written word or sentence is formed. (*Addresses* 1905, 935; emphasis added)

Using the object method with Indian children was an improvement over using words without anything to give those words meaning, which led to the "parroting" described by Luther Standing Bear and others. However, the rejection of the importance of what Pestalozzi called the "home circle," which he credited as "the origin of all education," in most boarding school education made reference to Pestalozzi a travesty. Gutek maintains that Pestalozzi would have hardly recognized the formalized object lessons used in England and America that he was credited with inspiring. For example, Don Talayesva, a Hopi, described his first experience with a BIA school in 1899: "The first thing I learned in school was 'nail,' a hard word to remember. Every day when we entered the classroom a nail lay on the desk. The teacher would take it up and say, 'What is this?' Finally I answered 'nail' ahead of the other boys and was called 'bright'" (1942, 90). Another Hopi, Helen Seka-quaptewa (1969, 12–13), who attended the Keams Canyon Boarding School in the first decade of the twentieth century remembered liking school and recalled, "Our teacher was Miss Stanley. She began by teaching us the names of objects about the room. We read a little from big charts on the wall later on, but I don't remember ever using any books."

John Fire, a Lakota born in about 1903, recalled his day school experiences on the Rosebud Reservation. His teacher told him, "'Stand,' 'sit down! . . . again and again until we caught on. 'Sit, stand, sit, stand. Go and stop. Yes and no.' All without spelling, just by sound" (Fire and Erdoes 1972, 33). Another teacher would "hold up one stick and say, 'One.' then she'd hold up two sticks and say, 'Two,' over and over again. For many weeks she showed us pictures of animals and said 'dog' or 'cat.' It took me three years to learn to say 'I want this'" (Fire and Erdoes 1972, 23). He recalled spending six years in third grade, the highest grade at the day school. "In all those years at the day school," he recalled, "they never taught me to speak English or to write and read. I learned these things only many years later, in saloons, in the Army or in jail" (Fire and Erdoes 1972, 24).

In 1908 Ella Flagg Young, principal of the Chicago Normal School, addressed the NEA's Indian department and described the new Progressive education being promoted by her colleague John Dewey and others:

> The old education assumes that the teacher knows first what the learner needs to know and that the soul of the learner is nourished and developed by the acquisition of that knowledge. The new education acts on the assumption that a teacher makes such an environment in school that the mind of the learner is stimulated to use its own experience to acquire and capitalize knowledge, and that the soul is nurtured thru that activity and by its fruits. (*Addresses* 1908, 1157)

Gertrude Golden (1954, 209), who taught in Indian schools in the early twentieth century, strongly defended having "the child use his hands in the learning process, or providing a half-day of useful work to offset the half-day devoted to the formal studies." She stated that teachers "had to make their own" course of study before the one put in effect about 1912.

In 1912 Congress authorized fifteen days of paid educational leave for teachers to attend training sessions, and in 1922 this was increased to thirty days. The Indian Office's 1915 course of study recommended interest in home reading, creating a love for good literature, and adding two new words a day to a child's vocabulary. In 1916 the government schools started to use nearby public school curricula (Morris 1954). There was an effort to provide job-related academic coursework, and most schools "followed a curriculum divided into four levels—primary (the first three grades), prevocational (grades 4–6), junior vocational, and senior vocational—with students at the last tier taking such courses as shop mathematics, agricultural botany, and rural economics" (Adams 1995, 315). The junior and senior vocational courses were offered in off-reservation industrial schools, and uniform final examinations were introduced. The great diversity of reservation conditions hampered the use of a uniform curriculum (Fischbacher 1967). Golden (1954, 209) remembered being required to read one "up-to-date" book per year on general education and having to write a report on it: "Promotion and salary increases were based upon the grade thus obtained [on the written report] and upon the quality of work done in the classroom." In the early years of the twentieth century, according to Evelyn C. Adams,

> [t]he uniform examinations accompanying the uniform course of study made it impossible to raise or lower grades arbitrarily, and further regimented instruction. The co-operation of the teachers in a speed program of passing the largest possible number of pupils was rewarded by promotion if at least seventy percent of the students made a satisfactory rating. Uniform examinations were suspended in 1917 but were soon resumed and they remained in effect until 1928. (1946, 63)

In 1926 the half-work, half-study boarding school program was changed to one-half academic classroom instruction, one-fourth vocational instruction, and one-fourth schoolwork detail (Prucha 1984, 832).

By 1905 the Indian Office's educational system had seven supervisors, 118 school superintendents (1 Indian), 15 assistant superintendents (1 Indian), 64 clerks (18 Indian), 20 doctors (1 Indian), 500 teachers (50 Indian), and 42 kindergarten teachers (1 Indian). Indian Affairs Commissioner Leupp (1910) reported that one of the large off-reservation boarding schools had sixty-nine employees, including teachers plus instructors of tailoring, harness-making, shoemaking, tinsmithing, painting, blacksmithing, and carpentry, along with a librarian, florist, teamster, and laundresses. Leupp (1910, 141) complained, "[At boarding schools] a pupil grows up amid surroundings which he will never see duplicated in his own home. Steam-heating, electric lighting, mechanical apparatus for doing everything—these cultivate in him a contempt for the primitive contrivances which must make up his environment as a poor settler in a frontier country."

In 1920, as a cost-saving measure, Congress required the closure of all nonreservation boarding schools with fewer than eighty students, reservation boarding schools with fewer than forty-five students, and day schools with fewer than eight students. This led to the closing of twelve boarding schools and some day schools (Fischbacher 1967).

Leupp supported day schools over boarding schools, especially those that were located off reservations. Leupp even experimented with open-air schools called "bird cages" in the warm, dry Southwest (Prucha 1984). In his first annual report he described day schools as "outposts of civilization":

Situated near the homes of the old people, they are centers from which radiate some measure of better living, better morals, and better habits generally. There are 139 of these schools. . . . During the last year they had an enrolment of 4,399 and an average attendance of 3,271. (*ARCIA* 1905, 43)

In his 1910 report, he wrote:

[Day schools teach children] to read and write English and to cipher a little; the boys learn also how to raise vegetables, and perhaps to harness a horse and milk a cow, to build and mend a fence, and the like; the girls learn sewing, cooking, washing and ironing, how to set a table and make a bed, and in some cases the care of poultry and the rudiments of dairy work. This variety of instruction presupposes the presence of instructors of both sexes, so provision is always made at such schools for a man and wife, one acting as the teacher and the other as housekeeper or farmer as the case may be. (*ARCIA* 1910, 128)

A day school of this period, before school buses and paved roads, often had just one or two rooms along with a cottage for the teacher to live in and a kitchen garden. The teacher was also expected to work with parents. Students were provided with a simple lunch. In 1923 the typical day school was reported to have from forty to fifty students (Fischbacher 1967).

In his 1917 Declaration of Policy, Indian Commissioner Cato Sells (1913-1921) declared that all students whose parents could pay for their education or who lived near public schools should be removed from Indian schools, leading to the closing of boarding schools in eight states as well as some day schools (Prucha 1984). Despite this push for assimilation, Frederick Hoxie (1984) documented a change in attitude toward the potential success of Indian education between the last two decades of the nineteenth century and the first two decades of the twentieth century. Politicians and the public underwent a period of initial optimism, spurred by success stories at Carlisle Indian School, during which they believed that Indians could be quickly and completely assimilated. After two decades of experience, many were disillusioned. In about 1900, many people reached the conclusion that Indians, like blacks, would remain a permanent underclass and therefore needed an appropriate vocational, rather than academic, education. Yet this lowering of expectations had little real effect on Indian education, because education at Carlisle and other Indian schools had always been largely at an elementary level with a vocational, manual labor emphasis. Missionaries and other educators like Hampton's General Armstrong feared that too much education could lead to religious skepticism, as it had done among many whites.

INDIAN RENAISSANCE

The era of government control sought to save the Indians from vanishing by substituting a policy of cultural genocide for the old policies of removal and actual genocide. Genocide was embodied in the slogan, "The only good Indian is a deadIndian," which in several cases extended to the killing of women and children as happened at the massacres at Sand Creek and Wounded Knee (Brown 1970). The new policy as enunciated by the assimilationists was to kill the Indian but save the man. Wrapped in the popular belief that the dominant society represented the pinnacle of civilization, the average American could see no good in Indian culture. But despite the offer of civilization, many Indians stubbornly resisted attempts by the government to control their thinking in the same way it now controlled their lives, and they clung to their tribal languages and traditions.

The general lowering of educational expectations for Indians had an unintended side effect for Indians who had resisted assimilation in that if they could not be educated to be like whites, maybe it was all right for them to remain Indians. In addition, according to Prucha (1985, 58), "[t]he old view that Indian cultures had nothing to offer American society, that the sooner they were destroyed and replaced the better, gave way little by little to an interest in Indian ways and then to a positive appreciation of Indian art and other contributions." This change in attitude could be attributed in part to the new scientific outlook that went beyond the ethnocentric view that all cultures were inferior to the dominant culture and in part to books such as Helen Hunt Jackson's *A Century of Dishonor*, first published in 1881, which described the mistreatment of American Indians.

Jackson became interested in Indians whenThomas Henry Tibbles, an itinerant preacher and associate of the abolitionist John Brown, brought Standing Bear and Suzette La Flesche (Bright Eyes) to Boston on a speaking tour to raise money for Indian causes. Tibbles helped Standing Bear to win his release from army custody in the 1879 legal battle *Standing Bear* v. *Crook* (Tibbles [1905] 1957). Jackson hoped her book would publicize the plight of the Indians in the way Uncle Tom's Cabin had publicized the evils of slavery. It emphasized broken treaties, stolen land, and the fact that Indians lacked legal rights in state courts because they were not citizens. Not all were convinced by Jackson, including future President Theodore Roosevelt. In his 1889 *Winning of the West*, he called her book a "spiteful diatribe against various army officers" and wrote off Jackson and like-minded people as "foolish sentimentalists" (334–35).

The explorer of the Grand Canyon, John Wesley Powell, and the anthropologist Franz Boas exemplify a new scientific way of looking at Indians. In 1877 Powell published *An Introduction to the Study of Indian Languages* and in 1879 took over the new U.S. Government Bureau of Ethnology. In an 1896 speech titled "The Need of Studying the Indian in Order to Teach Him," Powell emphasized the need to meet Indians as equals and to have teachers first learn about Indians and win over the elders. He noted the importance of understanding Indian customs before interfering with them and remarked that too often teachers began by affronting Indians and "unintelligently opposing the tribal beliefs and usages" (110). In regard to religion, Powell declared:

> [S]o few Americans yet realize that of all the people on this continent, including even ourselves, the most profoundly religious, if by religion is meant fidelity to teachings and observations that are regard as sacred, are the American Indians, especially wherever still unchanged from their early condition, and this deeply religious feeling of theirs might, if properly appreciated, be made use of, not weakened or destroyed by premature opposition. (112–13)

In his 1903 NEA speech to the Indian department, G. Stanley Hall noted that "Miss [Alice C.] Fletcher and [Frank Hamilton] Cushing have taught us that to know the real Indian is to love him, and suggest that we teach that our own religion is only another form of theirs" (*Addresses*, 1055). However, despite the fact that he advocated a sympathetic understanding of Indians, Hall referred to them in his speech as a "lower race." The anthropologist Franz Boas, who studied the Kwakiutl, wrote in 1911:

> It is somewhat difficult for us to recognize that the value which we attribute to our own civilization is due to the fact that we participate in this civilization, and that it has been controlling all our actions since the time of our birth; but it is certainly conceivable that there may be other civilizations, based perhaps on different traditions and on a different equilibrium of emotion and reason, which are of no less value than ours, although it may be impossible for us to appreciate their values without having grown up under their influence. (208)

Leupp reported to the House of Representatives in 1905:

> The Indian is a natural warrior, a natural logician, a natural artist. We have room for all three in our highly organized social system. Let us not make the mistake, in the process of absorbing them, of washing out of them

whatever is distinctly Indian. Our aboriginal brother brings, as his contribution to the common store of character, a great deal that is admirable
and which needs only to be developed along the right line. Our proper
work with him is improvement, not transformation. (Quoted in Prucha
1985, 58-59)

Estelle Reel, who continued as superintendent of Indian schools under
Leupp, reported to the NEA that the new commissioner "wishes the
schools to preserve and develop along the right lines the best of the
children's inherited traits and attributes, and not attempt to make the
Indian over and transform him into a white man. . . . He wishes to
preserve their natural filial affection (*Addresses* 1905, 931). Although
learning English was the "cornerstone" of Indian education, Leupp did
not want the Indian student "to drop or forget the language of his
ancestors" (*Addresses* 1905, 932). He also favored preserving Indian
music in the schools.

Leupp's predecessor as Commissioner of Indian Affairs, W. A. Jones,
wrote in his last annual report that Indians were "far superior to
thousands of foreign immigrants who annually throng our ports"
(*ARCIA* 1904, 30). He felt the number of nonreservation schools was
excessive. Further:

Some schools industriously taught that all Indian reservations were bad,
and pursued a line of instruction and formation of character which it was
fondly believed would keep the Indian in the East. Time has shown that
such a course could not and did not settle the Indian graduate in the
East. . . .

It is a waste of public money to bring the average Indian to an eastern
school, educate him for years upon the theory that his reservation home is
a hell on earth, when inevitably he must and does return to his home. It is
not only a waste of money, but an injustice to the Indian. (*ARCIA* 1904, 32)

At the same time that Jones and Leupp were changing the way of
thinking about Indian education at the top, the writer George Wharton
James could report in 1908:

Again and again when I have visited Indian schools the thoughtful youths
and maidens have come to me with complaints about the American history

they were compelled to study[:] . . . "When we read in the United States history of white men fighting to defend their females, their homes, their corn-fields, their towns, and their hunting-grounds, they are always called 'patriots,' and the children are urged to follow the example of these brave, noble, and gallant men. But when Indians—our ancestors, even our own parents—have fought to defend us and our homes, cornfields, and hunting grounds they are called vindictive and merciless savages, bloody murderers, and everything else that is vile." (1908, 25)

CHAPTER FIVE

MISSION SCHOOLS

The contract school system that the government began in 1869 provided direct support to schools run by missionary groups. In annoucing his Peace Policy to Congress in 1870, President Grant said, "Indian agencies being civil offices, I determine to give all the agencies to such religious denominations as had heretofore established missionaries among the Indians; and perhaps to some other denominations who might undertake work on the same terms" (quoted in Sievers 1952, 136).

The various religious groups that sent missionaries to reservations competed with one another for Indian souls and with the government for Indian students. The 1890 *Annual Report of the Commissioner of Indian Affairs* describes the competition:

> It frequently happens that upon setting out to procure a certain number of children to maintain the average the [non–reservation school] superintendent . . . is dismayed upon entering a village to find the field already occupied, and a brisk competition for pupils going on between a superintendent of a Presbyterian Mission School, a priest who is working for a Catholic school, and the local teacher of a day school who is trying to prevent the others from taking children from the village, thereby affecting her interests. . . . The effect on the Indian mind can only be damaging to the [Indian] service, and always confirms the Indian parent in his opposition to education. This competition for pupils should not be permitted, nor is it at all necessary. There are enough children to fill all the schools now in operation. (*ARCIA* 1890, 300)

Actually, the competition worked to the advantage of the Indians because, without a monopoly, schools needed to be attentive to the interests of their students and parents.

THE BOARD OF FOREIGN MISSIONS

From 1837 to 1893 the Presbyterian Church's Board of Foreign Missions (BFM) sent more than four hundred fifty missionaries to nineteen tribes. Michael C. Coleman concluded,

> With a heavy emphasis on rote learning and recitation the [BFM] schools at their best provided an impressively wide academic curriculum: English, arithmetic, algebra, history, geography, chemistry, botany, physiology, natural philosophy (the sciences), natural history (geology and biology), Latin and Greek, and sometimes—for pragmatic reasons—literacy in tribal languages. (1987, 475)

Often missions had farms for vocational instruction. In the BFM records Coleman found students were more interested in the vocational, musical, and academic aspects of the instruction than in religious instruction. One missionary noted that students did their best academic work in arithmetic, which he noted had its own universal language. In 1861 the school for the Omaha was using *McGuffey's Fourth Eclectic Reader* for the most advanced students, and in 1863 the *Fifth Eclectic Reader* was added (Baerreis 1963). Francis La Flesche, an Omaha, described in his work *The Middle Five* ([1900] 1963) his experiences at a BFM mission school. And in 1911, in a book cowritten with Alice C. Fletcher, he wrote, "One great difficulty besets the efforts of the missionary teachers; this was the influence exerted on the native mind by the contradiction between the principles taught as belonging to Christianity and the conduct of most of the white people with whom the Indian came into contact" (Fletcher and La Flesche 1911, 628). Fletcher noted, "[T]he mission work comes in and strikes down everything in the way of amusement for the Indians, and gives nothing in its place. I mean nothing in the way of recreation, and all work and no play is not better for Indians than for anyone else" (*ARBIC* 1886, 119).

THE CHURCH MISSIONARY SOCIETY

Not all missionaries were taught to dismiss the value of Native cultures. Henry Venn, clerical secretary of the Church of England's Church Missionary Society (CMS) from 1843 to 1872, was in favor of having the Society's missionaries set up locally controlled Native churches as quickly as possible. In the words of David Nock:

> Venn's policy was the "euthanasia" of missions. The missionary, far from being a big white father, was to be a temporary and intermediate figure aided by the local people. He was to build up the necessary institutions for a native church. When his task was finished, he would be free to go on to some new field of endeavor. (1988, 34)

Venn had practical concerns: there was an inadequate number of missionaries available to convert the whole world, and new Christian congregations needed to be protected from being labeled foreign and thus liable to expulsion.

The CMS sent Edward Francis Wilson to Canada in 1868, where he ran an Indian mission school for twenty-five years. While Wilson began, despite Venn's teachings, with a policy of cultural replacement, according to his biographer David Nock, he became disillusioned, especially with the idea that Indians could be assimilated rapidly. In a series of articles written in 1891 that are attributed to Wilson, a policy of letting Indians be Indians was put forward. Wilson made a trip through the United States in 1888, visiting Carlisle Indian School and a number of tribes, including the Cherokee. In an article based on his trip, Wilson reported a discussion with "a well-educated Cherokee lawyer" about why the Cherokee opposed allotment. The lawyer said:

1. By holding it [land] in common, they are better able to resist the aggression of the whites;
2. Their present social system has never developed a mendicant or a tramp;
3. Although poor, yet they have no paupers, none suffering from the oppression of the rich. With the whites, everyone is scrambling to live, but not so with them;

4. They do not believe that the whites have any better conditions to offer them, therefore they prefer to remain as they are. (Quoted in Nock 1988, 114)

Wilson was often "forced to accept children who were a burden to their parents, because of either physical or behavioral defects. . . . Those children who seemed to be successes in their own society were kept at home by the parents" (Nock, 1988, 89).

HAMPTON INSTITUTE

Unlike Wilson, Gen. Samuel Chapman Armstrong (1839-93) never wavered from his assimilationist ideology. A Congregationalist minister and the son of a prominent Hawaiian missionary, Armstrong started Hampton Institute in 1868 as a nondenominational private school for former slaves that was based on an industrial (vocational) model to give black children a practical "education for life." Armstrong remained principal at Hampton until his death in 1893. His successor, the Reverend H. B. Frissell, shared Armstrong's view of education. Students usually spent three years at Hampton (Ahern 1983). The school received government funding, as well as private donations for the support of individual students. Armstrong's goal was to instill a Christian work ethic. The academic curriculum was limited because Armstrong believed that too much education would draw students away from both Christianity and hard work. The historian Donal F. Lindsey (1995, xii) concluded from his study of Indians at Hampton that "independent thinking by blacks and Indians was usually unwanted." The feeling at the school was, "Religion without other training has brought success, but there has been, so far, no case where training without religion has proved either strong or reliable" (Folsom 1893, 393). Of course, "religion" meant Christianity.

In 1878 Lt. Richard Henry Pratt proposed bringing Indian prisoners of war to Hampton, and Armstrong agreed. Each of the seventeen young adults whom Pratt brought from St. Augustine was paired with a black student, who reportedly were fearful of the Indians at first (Adams 1995). Both Armstrong and Pratt had commanded black troops in the army. While Pratt quickly set out to start his own school, the famous Carlisle Indian Industrial School (see chap. 6), Hampton continued as a contract boarding school for Indians until 1912, when Congress refused to reauthorize its $167 per student funding because of fears surrounding racial mixing. With the loss of government funding, Indian enrollment at Hampton declined until in 1923 there were none left (Adams 1995). During the period of its operation, 1,388 Indians from sixty-five tribes attended Hampton, but only 160 graduated (Lindsey 1995). At Hampton, Indian students were allowed to help each other using their tribal languages, despite Indian Office policy to the contrary. Unlike Pratt, who wanted his students at Carlisle to melt into the eastern white population, Armstrong wanted his students to return to their home communities and become advocates of Christianity and progress.

Local whites and blacks objected to Indians at Hampton, but it brought the school valuable publicity and political support, including mention in the four annual messages of President Rutherford Hayes. Hampton depended on charity for its funding of black education, and so it needed support from wealthy and influential people who tended to be more interested in Indians than blacks, especially as the Civil War receded in people's memory (Lindsey 1995).

An 1880 article in *Harper's New Monthly Magazine*, "Indian Education at Hampton and Carlisle," reported:

> The effort has been for a natural, all-around growth rather than a rapid one. Books, of course, are for a long time of no avail, and object-teaching, pictures, and blackboards take their place, with every other device that ingenuity is equal to, often on the spur of the moment, to keep up the interest and attention of the undisciplined minds that, with the best intentions and a strong desire to know English, have small patience for preliminary steps. A peripatetic class was thus devised to relieve the tedium of the school-room, and had, to speak literally and figuratively, quite a run. It usually began with leap-frog, and then went gaily on to find its "books in the running brooks, sermons in stones," etc. Geography is taught with moulding sand and iron raised dissecting maps; arithmetic at first with blocks. (*Indian Education* [1880] 1972, 41)

The article noted that "phonics exercises are found useful" and "that Indian children are, on the whole, very much like other children, some bright and some stupid, some good and some perverse, all exceedingly human" (42, 49).

Ruth Spack (2002), in *America's Second Tongue*, conducted an extensive examination of how English was taught at Hampton. Out of necessity, teachers were forced to experiment and draw on sources such as the *Workman's Modern Language Series* for teaching French and Spanish, which was based on the "natural method" derived from the work of Pestalozzi. Teachers learned to begin by asking students to perform actions: "[B]odies became useful resources for learning. Students were taught to match action to word, for example by following directions to 'stand up,' 'sit down,' 'walk softly,' 'speak louder,' or 'march out'" (60). Later, students drew pictures of actions in stories, role-played, and performed scenes from books. A debating society was started in 1886. Spack concludes, "[G]iven the special linguistic circumstances of the Hampton classroom, the Pestalozzian method proved invaluable, inasmuch as it called for dealing first with observation and direct participation rather than definitions and abstract rules" (61).

Hampton teachers used objects to make what they were talking about comprehensible. However, the use of twelve objects at a time, as recommended by Isaac Lewis Peet's *Language Lessons* [for] *Deaf Mutes and Foreigners*, was too many. The current Berlitz method uses only a few students and three objects (Reyhner and Tennant 1995). The use of objects worked up to a point, but how did one learn the meaning of a word such as "had"? Francis Parker's "student-centered approach" was used, and objects such as live and stuffed animals, globes, pictures, and sand tables were found effective teaching aides. Teachers there recognized that it was extremely hard for students to make English sounds that did not exist in their own language and that the use of choral rather than individual recitation decreased students' worries about being singled out for their mistakes (Spack 2002).

Indian students did not get books until they had learned to speak English, and they resented the fact that black students were able to begin their studies using books. Cora Folsom, a teacher at Hampton, noted that "to read well with an Indian means that he must be *interested*, and to be interested he must have something [to] think about and study over out of school" (quoted in Spack 2002, 68; original emphasis). Teachers found that "when the texts to be memorized grow out of the students' direct participation, the students were more likely to comprehend" (63). But Appleton's second reader, which was used at Hampton, had a larger and different vocabulary than the students had. In addition, the books used at Hampton were designed for much younger students. In the 1985 *Annual Report of the Commissioner of Indian Affairs* section on Hampton, Harriet Holbrook noted:

> Working day after day at their reading, repeating, "See the cat," "I see the dog," and like sentiments, makes one long for a set of readers written especially for the Indians, giving facts worth remembering, and with stories which they can comprehend and which interest them. Books written for ordinary school use are either too hard, or else so childish as to make it dull work for pupils as old as many of them. (*ARCIA* 1895, 240)

Indian students at Hampton showed a special interest in their past experiences, geography, and natural history. They were taught handwriting from "Spencerian copybooks," and they wrote letters home and to their patrons who were helping to pay for their school expenses. Student letters were also published in the school's magazine, the *Southern Workman*, which was a propaganda tool to gain political and financial support for Hampton.

Hampton, like most other Indian schools, did little to support students' Indian languages, though it was noted by Folsom that being literate in their own language helped them to learn English, and being able to translate an English word into their own language was even more helpful (Spach 2002). An Oneida student at Hampton declared, "I was put to work in the machine shop handling a sledge hammer. I worked ten hours a day, and after supper I went to school. At 9 o'clock, the close of school, I had to go to the Indian boys' quarters and report whether I had been speaking English or Indian through the day" (*ARBIC* 1892, 51).

ST. LABRE INDIAN SCHOOL

The history of St. Labre Indian School on the Northern Cheyenne Reservation in Montana is illustrative of Catholic mission schools generally. The St. Labre Mission was founded in 1884 among the Northern Cheyenne in the same year they were granted a reservation in Montana and only eight years after they had fought Custer nearby at the Battle of the Little Big Horn. Gen. Nelson A. Miles asked George Yoakam, a former soldier and Catholic convert, to help the Cheyenne obtain land under the Indian Homestead Act of 1875. Four masked cowboys beat up Yoakam for this effort, and the frontier newspaper, the *Miles City Daily Journal*, applauded the cowboys' efforts. It was Yoakam's suggestion that the "Catholic Sisters could do as much for the good of the Cheyennes as a regiment," and in 1884 four Catholic nuns founded a school on the Tongue River supported under contract with the U.S. government. It did not entirely lose funding from tribal moneys held in trust by the government until the 1940s (Kraman 1984).

In 1885 a Dutch Jesuit arrived and began learning Cheyenne. He remained until all Jesuits were withdrawn in 1897. While their international outlook made it acceptable for Catholics to learn and use Native languages, they found nothing to value in Native cultures (Harrod 1971). St. Labre was almost closed in 1892 because of Indian indifference and the controversial Ghost Dance movement. However, when the government started recruiting Cheyenne children to go several hundred miles north to the off-reservation boarding school at Fort Shaw, the Cheyenne decided a Catholic school closer to home was better. In 1897, when a white sheepherder was killed near St. Labre, Cheyennes were jailed for the crime. There was a rumor that five hundred white cowboys were waiting in Sheridan, Wyoming, ready to "clean up the Indians" (Kraman 1984, 50). The mission priest helped to calm the Cheyenne and defuse the situation.

Over the years, the St. Labre Mission opened schools on the Northern Cheyenne and Crow Reservations at Birney, Busby, St. Xavier, and Pryor. The purpose of the Ursuline sisters who staffed the St. Labre Mission schools was to take charge of "poor debased" children, remove them from a "beastly life and raise them up to the path of virtue and civilization" (quoted in Watembach 1983, 9). Father Barcelo wrote in 1880, "From the very beginning, I declared to them that I could not teach them properly, if they were to be all the time roaming about, that it was necessary for them to settle themselves in a fixed place, and there to cultivate the ground, to build a large and nice church and to do all the rest for their civilization" (quoted in Watembach 1983, 10).

Father Palladino wrote in 1894 that "the Indian has a great, deep, natural aversion to work and manual exercise of any kind" (93).

Furthermore: "A plain, common, English education, spelling, reading and writing, with the rudiments of arithmetic, will be for the Indian at large, book-learning enough for all the purposes of his civilized life and social intercourse" (113). According to Palladino, one could not educate Indians without Christianity, and after Christianity, work and manual labor were most important for civilizing the Indian. He also opposed day schools and felt it an advantage that some Catholic schoolteachers spoke their students' Native language. He served as president of Gonzaga College in Spokane, Washington, from 1894 to 1897 and had not changed his mind about Indian education when a revised version of his *Indian and White in the Northwest* came out in 1922.

From 1885 to 1947 the students at St. Labre only saw their parents on Sunday after Mass and went home only for Christmas vacation. A runaway was whipped and put in a dark room for nine days. The scribe of house diaries at St. Xavier wrote in 1893 that if the students "had no Crows for parents—how much better would they be" (quoted in Watembach 1983, 72). To convert the Crow, Catholics had to teach about sin first, since there was no need for grace without sin, and the concept of sin did not exist in their traditional culture. The Crow preferred day schools over boarding schools, and many voted with their feet when the Baptists opened day schools. To compete for students, the Catholics opened their own day schools, despite thinking that they were a "farce." Catholics translated catechisms, sermons, Bible stories, and hymns, but not the Bible itself, into Crow (Watembach 1983).

The removal of Northern Cheyenne children from their homes was of course not without regret. Wooden Leg, a Northern Cheyenne leader, described in his autobiography how he built his house on a hill overlooking the mission so that he could see his children during the week, as he was only permitted to visit them on Sunday (Marquis 1931).

Over the years, the school suffered from a chronic lack of funds. In 1924 the Bureau of Catholic Indian Missions provided a list of five thousand potential donors, and fifteen hundred letters were sent out. In about 1927 Indian men were invited to wear their traditional costumes when they served in the honor guard in the Corpus Christi procession. This became a reservation tradition that symbolizes a significant change in attitude toward Cheyenne culture.

In 1931 the mission started a high school, and the U.S. government insisted that it admit whites. The high school closed in 1938 for financial reasons. By 1943 there were only forty-one students in eight grades. Farther north, Holy Family Mission on the Blackfeet Reservation closed in 1940 after the onset of World War II crippled fund-raising efforts. In 1947 Father Marion Roessler came to the St. Labre Mission to serve as superintendent. According to Sister Carla Kraman,

[Father Marion] sent a memo to all the teachers urging them to treat their pupils as the Cheyennes treated their children—with respect for their individuality. It is not the Cheyenne way to force a person to do anything against his/her will. The Cheyennes do not scold or threaten their children nor do they make decisions for them. Many of the teachers complained that the Indian children were undisciplined and according to white culture this was probably true. Father Marion, however, saw the difference and appreciated the way the Cheyennes love and respect their children. (1984, 59)

The high school was reopened and a bus purchased to make it possible for more day students to attend. For the first time, students who boarded at the school could go home on weekends. By 1969 enrollment had climbed to 529 students.

In 1962 a factory was built to provide employment for local Cheyennes and to make plastic figures that were used in a direct mail fund-raising campaign. In 1967 the mission added the Cheyenne Home for Homeless Children. In 1970, after the Second Vatican Council (1962-65) encouraged the use of vernacular languages and a variety of forms of worship that reflected the local cultures of Catholics, Cheyenne-language classes were added to the elementary school curriculum. In 1977 new postal regulations hurt the direct mail fund-raising campaign. This campaign was also criticized for spending too much money on fund-raising and too little on Northern Cheyenne children (Burnette and Koster 1974). In 1978 the school went under contract as a BIA-funded school, and its name became simply Labre School—this time funded by Public Law 93-638. Students had released time to attend religious classes. However, after 1984 the school stopped contracting and again became a mission school.

James Spear, a Northern Cheyenne, wrote in the school newsletter in 1972:

A mechanized world can rob the unaware man of his vision—of who he is and where he comes from. But the Indian has found a new self-awareness in the heritage he knows is his own. Today, the Indian speaks for himself, knowing that all America must listen, for all people in this country are bound together in a common destiny. . . .

We are striving for the same goals as other races of people—to strengthen our social and economic position. In order to do this we must become educated and encourage education for our children . . . but this does not mean we have to discard our culture. . . . We need only to follow the example of other Indian tribes and ethnic groups who are educating their children according to their own heritage and culture, while at the same time enabling their children to become educated for whatever role or profession they happen to choose in life. (Quoted in Kraman 1984, 26)

Several of Sister Carla's conclusions in her official history of St. Labre School are interesting. For example: "Many of the early missionaries to the Cheyennes found them hard to convert but the simple fact was that they had their own belief in God, their own religion which was integral to their daily life and not restricted to worship on Sundays" (Kraman 1984, 49).

While admitting that the purpose of religious boarding schools was to Christianize through conversion and to civilize through education, she writes, "But the needs of the Cheyennes who came to Saint Labre became priorities at times even more important than conversion and education" (1984, 76). Here she is referring to starvation, among other things.

TEACHERS AND STUDENTS

A teacher at a mission school on the Warm Springs Reservation in Oregon reported in 1862:

Indian children, situated as these are on this reservation, in commencing an education, are placed at a great disadvantage as compared with white children. They are unable to enunciate many of the sounds represented by the letters of the English alphabet, and being ignorant of the meaning of the words which they learn and the sentences they read, the exercises do not naturally possess an equal interest to them as to white children. (*ARCIA* 1862, 295)

This teacher also declared that the textbooks he had were for "advanced scholars" and that more elementary ones were needed (*ARCIA* 1862, 296). A Catholic teacher on the Tulalip Reservation in Washington reported, "My scholars complain that they do not understand what they read in English, and, in order to aid them, I am compiling a Snohomish-English and English-Snohomish Dictionary. . . . [They] must become as orphans, that is, they must forget their parents as far as possible in order to abandon the habits of the Indians with less difficulty" (*ARCIA* 1862, 406).

Students, especially girls, were given a limited education. Corabelle Fellows, who started teaching for Alfred Riggs in 1884, was set to work teaching sewing to five- to eight-year-olds who spoke no English. She reported a high rate of teacher turnover and was sent out to a field station after learning some Dakota. There she held a night school every weekday for adults, teaching numbers and reading. However, when one of the students, Yellow Hat, began to keep the children and teach them what he had learned in night school, she threatened him with the guardhouse (Duncan [1938] 1990).

Some Indian students fondly remembered contract mission schools; others had bitter memories. Mary Ground, a Blackfeet, remembered attending Fort Shaw, St. Peters Mission, and the Holy Family Mission, which was built from money donated by Katherine Drexel in the late nineteenth century,

You went to school in the morning until 4:00 p.m. in the afternoon. You started with the ABCs, learning to write and speak English at the same time. School was from grade one through grade five. There was no such thing as graduation. A lot of children quit, some to get married, a very few went to college or away to school. Schools were good. You didn't waste time. They took care of the children. You had three good meals a day and a clean place to sleep. I worked in the kitchen and bakery. The children didn't mind working. They would have had to work at home. The boys brought in the wood and the vegeables [sic]. They milked the cows and brought the milk to the girls who strained it. It was churned by hand to make butter. You had to obey. The good students were never punished. If you were bad you

were locked up and given bread and water. Your hands were paddled. The
girls and boys couldn't play together. The girls' building had a high fence.
The boys and girls had to sit on different sides of the church. Boys and girls
were always on opposite sides of the room, no mingling at all. Families
brought their children to school of their own free will. You could talk
Indian, but not much. I had plenty to eat. They were the happiest days of
my life. (Parsons 1980, 9)

Other Blackfeet echo Mary Ground's memories. James Little Dog
remembered that he "begged to go to school" (Parsons 1980, 11).
Gertrude Lynch, a student at St. Michael's Indian School in Arizona,
wrote to Father Anselm in 1915 to thank him for "all you are doing for
our people." She also mentioned that she was in a "literacy society."
"[E]very month we have a little play that is to help us learn the English
language better, as we talk in English every day, but it is quite hard"
(Iverson 2002b, 88).

Emotions still run high. Tim Giago, an award-winning Lakota newspaper columnist and the editor of the largest Indian-owned weekly
newspaper of the period, wrote many columns criticizing the treatment
that he and his classmates received in a Catholic mission boarding
school. He was born in 1934 and went to elementary and high school
at the Holy Rosary Indian Mission on the Pine Ridge Reservation, where
his father had also gone to school. During Giago's time there, students
were punished by being forbidden to attend Sunday evening movies,
among other ways. He recalls a fellow student saying,

One time I was given enough demerits so I had to miss two movies in a
row for speaking my native Lakota language. What upset me is the prefect
who gave me the demerits was studying the Lakota language at this time,
and he would spend many hours questioning the elders who stopped by
the mission but would never ask any of the kids who knew the language
because, like other Jesuits, he was trying to destroy our knowledge of the
language.

Missing two movies was bad enough, but this prefect also made me bite
down on a large rubber band, and then he stretched the rubber band to its
limit, and let it snap back against my lips. It was very painful. All of this
punishment for speaking my Lakota language. (Giago 1984, 125–26)

Giago writes:

> There are thousands of us who can recall with vivid clarity, attending
> church services seven days a week at the Indian missions. We can recall
> kneeling in hardwood pews until our young knees ached with pain, knowing
> that anything less than our reverent attention to the services would bring
> us a rap on the head with a key ring or knuckle.
>
> We can recall attending classes in American history and being taught
> that our ancestors were blood-thirsty savages with no higher ambition than
> to rage, pillage, and kill the white settlers. We were taught that the religions
> of these heathens were paganistic. The clear implication was that if we did
> not embrace Catholicism, we would be doomed to the same destruction as
> our ancestors. (Giago 1984, 367)

Florence Kenney (1995, 36), an Inupiat who was brought to a Catholic
mission school by her alcoholic parents, recalled that in the 1940s, "We
didn't have names, we were called by numbers—like I was Miss 14."

Reuben Snake, a Winnebago who went on to become a national
leader of the American Indian Movement and president of National
Congress of American Indians from 1985 to 1987, attended a United
Church of Christ mission school in the 1940s in Neillsville, Wisconsin.
The school's founder and his children spoke Winnebago, but students
could not. Runaways were brought back by local law enforcement
officers. Snake (1996, 53) remembered good and bad teachers: "Our
teachers were puritanical. We could only have fun in a Christian way.
For them, having a good time meant singing hymns. We had vespers
every evening." He recalled, "[M]y favorite subject was reading. I
developed a love for reading in that school. I'd pick up anything and
read it. I enjoyed reading *Treasure Island* and all of Jack London's book
about Alaska. And oh, *The Black Stallion*. That kind of storytelling was
really interesting to me" (54).

> The Winnebago language and culture were suppressed at the mission
> school because anything Indian was considered to be inferior. For us to be
> "saved" we had to forfeit our Indianness. We had to adopt European values
> and the European life style. We could not practice our culture, speak our
> language, or sing our music. If we wanted to truly be children of God and
> followers of Christ we had to give up all our Indian ways.

We had to have our hair cut regularly. We couldn't go to school with long hair. We weren't allowed to wear anything Indian. We had to wear White man's clothing. It was all right to wear the White man's jewelry but not the Indian jewelry. . . . Not a trace of our culture was allowed in the school. (61–62)

In 1950, when he was thirteen years old, Snake went to Haskell for two and a half years. Life was regimented there, and he was encouraged to but did not go to church. By this time he was already involved in the Native American Church.

Not all was work, study, and prayer at mission schools. Thomas Riggs, Stephen Riggs's son, told his niece about life at the Santee Sioux mission school:

[A] favorite sport was "broncho busting" and lassoing. The boys would divide into two groups, bronchos and cowboys, and the result was lively. They like to play ranch, too. Their "ranch" was enclosed with a make-believe fence and had a well, gates and cattle. . . . The little girls played with dolls, but they like best to make a tipi with ten poles properly tied, build a fire in the middle of it, gather in a dog or two to make it homelike and serve food Indian style. (Howard 1958, 194)

DR. CHARLES EASTMAN

One of the most famous mission school students was Ohiyesa, or Charles A. Eastman, a Santee Sioux. Eastman's father was involved in the Minnesota Sioux uprising, which led to his being condemned to hang. His mother fled with Ohiyesa to Canada, where he was unaware for a time that his father was one of the uprising participants who was spared from hanging through the intervention of President Abraham Lincoln. After learning of his father's survival, Ohiyesa returned to the United States and was encouraged by his father to go to school.

In 1872, at fifteen and speaking no English, Ohiyesa entered school. In 1874 he went to the Santee Agency and was one of the first five students at Alfred L. Riggs's Santee Normal Training School. This bilingual school grew out of the Santee Mission, which was started in 1870 once the missionaries were convinced the Santee Sioux would not undergo removal farther west. Although it was described by the Santee Indian agent as "one of the best conducted schools in the service," by 1893 its enrollment dropped from 150 to 60 students because of the loss of government funding (*ARCIA* 1894, 194).

At Santee, Eastman was given books in both English and Dakota. His father wrote him encouraging letters in Dakota. Eastman went on to attend Beloit College in Wisconsin from 1876 to 1879 and graduated from Dartmouth College in 1887. He received his medical degree from the Boston University School of Medicine in 1890 at the age of thirty-two (Eastman [1916] 1977). He is most famous for his autobiography, *From the Deep Words to Civilization* ([1916] 1977), and his work with the YMCA and the Boy Scouts of America. He also spent seven years working on a project to give the Sioux names that fit the English system so their allotments could be recorded and protected.

Eastman became convinced after observing the materialism of late-nineteenth-century America that "Christianity and modern civilization are opposed and irreconcilable and that the spirit of Christianity and of our ancient [Sioux] religion is essentially the same" (Wilson 1983, 87). Eastman recalled an elder at one of his Bible study meetings remarking,

> I have come to the conclusion that this Jesus was an Indian. He was opposed to material acquirement and to great possessions. He was inclined to peace. He was as unpractical as any Indian and set no price upon his labor of love. These are not the principles upon which the white man has founded his civilization. (Eastman [1916] 1977, 143)

He went on to note in his autobiography that it appeared that white men were "anxious to pass on their religion to all races of men, but keep very little of it themselves" (193). This sentiment is echoed by Episcopal Bishop Walker of North Dakota: "[A] converted Indian is generally a truer Christian than the average white man. I speak from practical knowledge. I find they are willing to make sacrifices for their faith that the white man is not" (quoted in Folsom 1893, 490).

While serving as the Pine Ridge Agency physician, Eastman married Elaine Goodale shortly after she was appointed the first field super-visor of Indian schools in 1890. She had taught at Hampton and was supervising schools on the Sioux reservation during the tragedy of Wounded Knee. Eastman was the first physician on the scene when the

Seventh Calvary massacred Big Foot's band of Sioux at Wounded Knee in 1890 during the hysteria engendered by the Ghost Dance movement. He treated wounded soldiers and Indians alike.

The intermingling of Christian missionary work and the government effort of civilization through schooling can be seen in Elaine Goodale Eastman's *Christian Century* article, "Does Uncle Sam Foster Paganism," in which she attacked Commissioner of Indian Affairs John Collier's 1934 directive, "No interference with Indian religious life or ceremonial expression will hereafter be tolerated." Writing late in her life after years of work with Indians, she accused Collier of promoting a "Bastard Religion" (the Native American Church), witchcraft, and death ceremonies (Eastman 1934). In the same issue, Collier defended the regulation that forbade compulsory religious exercises in government schools and defended constitutional liberties for Indians.

In a book on their Navajo and Zuni missions, the Christian Reformed Board of Missions found:

> [L]ike a cold blast . . . came the Collier administration. Mr. Collier, the new Commissioner of Indian Affairs, asserted that he wanted to leave it to the Indians whether they wished to become Christians or not. The fact is that he openly encouraged the Indians to cling to their "beautiful" religion. The Navaho council was told: "We white people have nothing to give to you Indians. . . . Our culture is a disintegrating thing. Yours is an integrated culture. You must do your best to preserve it." We always tried to keep our Christian Indians away from the pagan ceremonials, now they were brought there in government trucks. (DeKorne 1947, 111)

THE MISSION SCHOOL LEGACY

At the close of the nineteenth century Protestant missionaries threw their support behind government schools and their nondenominational religious training and closed most of their mission schools. Catholics, who felt nondenominational religious training was really Protestant religious instruction and that public schools were essentially godless, fought to keep their schools open. From 1894 to 1900 direct federal funding for contract schools was phased out completely as Congress insisted on enforcing the constitutional separation between church and state. Mission schools won the right in court to continue to get tribal funds held in trust by the U.S. government, but with the end of direct federal funding, the number of mission schools gradually declined (Prucha 1979a).

The old missionaries often had no sympathy for traditional Indian culture, and some still do not in the twenty-first century. But American society and mainstream churches generally became more tolerant. In 1904–5, at the chapel built at Zuni, the Christian Reformed missionary Andrew Vander Wagen "preached hell and damnation for those who followed" traditional religious practices. When he was summoned before the tribal council "a government man, appointed to add emphasis to the council's decree, pointedly suggested, 'Young fellow, you know no one believes these old-fogy ideas about hell anymore[.]' [T]he young missionary looked him squarely in the eye and said, 'Maybe you don't, but God does'" (DeKorne 1947, 53).

The best-selling American novelist of his time, Zane Grey, characterized the product of the ethnocentric missionary in several of his novels. In his 1915 *The Rainbow Trail*, the sequel to his tremendously popular *Riders of the Purple Sage*, he has his wise trading post proprietor declare, "Most missionaries are good men. . . . There have been missionaries and other interested fools who have given Indians a white man's education. In all the instances I know of, these educated Indians returned to their tribes, repudiating the white man's knowledge, habits, life, and religion" (57).

In 1925, in *The Vanishing American*, Grey has his character Withers say that missionaries should emphasize sanitary laws and how to farm and raise sheep better rather than religion. A missionary, after telling the students that their parents are doomed to hell, draws aside an Indian girl and tells her, "Love me—the white man of God!" (171). At the book's government school, the children's milk and fruit are stolen by government agents and a child is kicked for running across a porch. The missionary is asked, "How can you lie to the Indian, cheat them in money deals, steal their water and land, and expect to convert them to Christianity?" (108). The Indian hero tells the missionary, "We have no desire to get to your heaven. . . . If there is such a paradise as you preach about, all the land will be owned by missionaries" (129).

In his 1928 novel, *Wild Horse Mesa*, Grey described a Navajo girl who had spent nine years in a government school:

The religion of the Indians had been schooled and missionaried out of her. Then when she had advanced as far as possible she was given a choice of becoming a servant or returning to her own people. . . . Her people believed the white education had made her think she was above them. She could no longer accept the religion of the Indian tribe and she would not believe in the white man's. (261–62)

Even Peter Bourgade, Catholic archbishop of Santa Fe, noted in 1906 that "stuffing these little Indians with an endless number of pious practices [in boarding school] is simply calculated to give them a lasting aversion for practicing their religion later on" (quoted in Wilken 1955, 124).

In 1928 the Meriam Report found the Indian missionary "only too likely to be a person who, however honest his intentions and earnest his zeal[,] . . . put most of his energies into non-essentials. One finds him fighting tribal ceremonials without really knowing if they are good or bad" (Meriam 1928, 398). This insistence on cultural as well as religious conversion gave missionaries individual successes such as Charles Eastman, but many Indians continued to think of Christianity as a foreign religion. For every Thomas Mayhew Jr. who allowed Indians to become theologically Christian and remain culturally Indian, there was a host of missionaries, Protestant and Catholic, who insisted that their converts become assimilated into the dominant white culture.

However, some Christian missionaries continued to work to preserve Indian languages and cultures by researching and publishing dictionaries and other books. One of many examples is the Catholic Franciscan Fathers' *Ethnologic Dictionary of the Navajo Language*, printed at their St. Michael's Mission in 1910. The dictionary's main writer was the Franciscan Berard Haile, who came to Navajoland in 1900 and began studying the Navajo. From 1935 to 1937 the U.S. government hired him to teach reading and writing to the Navajo at the Charles Burke Indian School at Fort Wingate, New Mexico, and at Fort Defiance, Arizona. In 1948, after many years of mission work, Father Berard wrote:

It seemed to me one had to study their [Navajo] customs, their outlook on life, on the universe, natural phenomena, their concepts on the origin of man, vegetation and animals, before one could approach them on religious matters. Here were human beings, intelligent, ingenious, industrious, religious, enormously so; why then approach them on a "you're all wrong, listen to me" basis? Traditions of such long standing cannot be uprooted by such matter-of-fact statements as we are accustomed to, owing to our training.

I did not convert from theology to anthropology on this score. But I did feel that theology needed some anthropology to help mission work along. Why evangelize any people unless you know something of their background, their ideology? Some of my conferees and others laughed at this idea. They thought of a simple people, primitive perhaps, who could be persuaded to your viewpoint by nicknacks, candies, a noon meal, and toys. (Haile [1948] 1998, 138)

Father Anselm Weber, who served the same mission from 1898 until his death in 1921, promoted tribal ownership, opposed allotment, and worked to get the Navajo more land (Wilken 1955). According to the historian Peter Iverson (2002a, 104), Weber wrote "thousands of letters to the Office of Indian Affairs, individual superintendents . . . , the Land Office, the Board of Indian Commissioners, members of the U.S. House of Representatives and the U.S. Senate, the Santa Fe Railway, and the Bureau of Catholic Indian Missions." When Weber went to St. Michael's, he contacted Dr. Washington Matthews and others who had worked among the Navajo for advice. Matthews told him, "[I]f you want to reach the *hearts* of the people and gain a permanent influence over them, you cannot too soon begin to learn the Navajo language . . . one and all of you" (Wilken 1955, 38; original emphasis). St. Michael's became a high school in 1946. It continued to educate Navajo children into the twenty-first century, and dictionaries compiled by missionaries continue to serve as basic sources of information on some Indian languages. Wycliffe Bible translators are still active on a number of reservations with tribal permission and have freely provided help to some school bilingual programs.

A 1958 survey found that only 22 percent of Protestant missions were using Native leadership, as compared to 50 percent of the Catholic missions. However, 14 percent of the Protestants, as compared to 6 percent of Catholics, could speak the local dialect. Only about 10 percent saw value in Native American values and lifestyles (Bowden 1981).

CHAPTER SIX

GOVERNMENT BOARDING SCHOOLS

The Indian Office boarding schools were sometimes located in old forts and were run like military organizations, which meant there could be fewer staff members and less expense. In 1881 Rhode Island spent $600,000 educating 49,000 students; the Indian office, in contrast, spend $215,000 on the same number of Indian children (Prucha 1976). There was one-half day of academic instruction and one-half day of vocational instruction. The academic curriculum consisted mainly of elementary subjects. The vocational curriculum entailed having the students maintain the school. This included growing and cooking their own food, making and mending their clothes and shoes, and cleaning and maintaining school buildings.

RICHARD HENRY PRATT AT ST. AUGUSTINE AND HAMPTON INSTITUTE

Richard Henry Pratt (1840-1924) started the first off-reservation, government-run boarding school. Pratt, who had only a common school education that ended when he was thirteen, enlisted in the army as a private at the beginning of the Civil War and rose to the rank of captain. When he returned to civilian life he was unsuccessful in business, as was his commander, General Grant. He reenlisted as a second lieutenant in 1867 and commanded black Tenth Calvary troops, the "buffalo soldiers," as well as Indian scouts in Indian Territory until 1875. His army career was not without its ups and downs. He was court-martialed in

1872 and received a light punishment. He may have volunteered to go to Fort Marion in St. Augustine, Florida, in 1875 with seventy-two Indians charged with murder and rapine to get away from his commanding officer (Ryan 1962). The Indians were sent in irons to Fort Leavenworth and then traveled by railroad. One Cheyenne chief was shot and killed trying to escape en route. Crowds gathered at the rail stations to see the "wild Indians" (Morton 1962).

Pratt is described as being friendly to his prisoners. Three weeks after arriving at Fort Marion, he interceded with the War Department to ask for clemency and passed on the words of the Kiowa chief Mah Mante:

> We want to learn the ways of the white men. First we want our wives and children and then we will go any place and settle down and learn to support ourselves as white men do. . . . We want to learn how to make corn and work the ground so we can make our living and we want to live in a house just as a white man. (Quoted in Morton 1962, 59).

Pratt found work for the prisoners with the souvenir dealers in town and persuaded the townspeople to let his charges work at odd jobs without guards. Townspeople complained to Washington, D.C., that the Indians were taking the jobs of local residents. Not having funds, he persuaded local ladies to come to the fort to teach his prisoners English. Within three months he was using prisoners as guards. Pratt's work drew considerable attention. Episcopal Bishop Henry B. Whipple preached at the prison and Harriet Beecher Stowe wrote about his work in the magazine *Outlook*.

In 1876 Pratt wrote to his commanding officer, General Sheridan:

> There is nothing of note to report regarding these prisoners, unless that fact is of itself important. They are simply under good discipline; quite well behaved, doing the work I can find for them to do cheerfully and industriously. They have abandoned about all the appearances and characteristics of the savage and are as neat and clean in their dress and persons as the men of a disciplined company. My 1st Sgt is about as competent as the average of those we get in the colored troops. I have a two hours school daily with an average of fifty pupils divided into four classes with a good teacher for each. The teachers work from the purest and best motives of

Christian charity and as a consequence successfully and there is no cost to the Government. . . . I try offenses by a Jury of their own number which works well and the few cases I have had have been awarded ample punishment. (Quoted in Morton 1962, 62)

Pratt was so successful that in 1878 he reported that twenty-two of the younger adult prisoners refused to return to their tribes. He convinced Gen. Samuel C. Armstrong to establish an Indian department at Hampton Institute for these and other Indians. Hampton Institute, in Hampton, Virginia, was established after the Civil War by Armstrong for freed slaves. Pratt was unable to recruit any children from Chief Joseph's defeated Nez Perce to join his recruits from St. Augustine, but he was able to recruit another forty boys and nine girls from Dakota Territory.

PRATT AT CARLISLE INDIAN INDUSTRIAL SCHOOL

Pratt did not like being Armstrong's subordinate and was unhappy with the segregation of Indians from blacks at Hampton. If Indians were not to associate with and learn from the more assimilated black students, then it did not make much sense to have Indian students become associated with black students in the public mind by attending school together because of the widespread prejudice against blacks (Lindsey 1995).

Encouraged by the success of the students at Hampton but discouraged because he was forced to play second fiddle to Armstrong, Pratt set out to start a school exclusively for Indians. Pratt's choice of the abandoned army barracks at Carlisle was no accident. Carlisle was far enough from the frontier that the locals lacked the "border prejudice" against Indians, and among the Pennsylvania Mennonites and Quakers there was perhaps the greatest racial tolerance in the nation (Pratt 1964; Marriott and Rachlin 1969).

Lieutenant Pratt was able to convince the townspeople to petition Washington to establish a school for Indians. The townspeople had complained about the troops' effect on the morals of the community, but merchants were unhappy when the garrison was removed and

Sioux boys on arrival at Carlisle Indian Industrial School, 1879. Photograph courtesy of the National Archives, NWDNS-75-IP-1-4A.

Omaha boys in cadet uniforms at Carlisle, 1880. Photograph courtesy of the National Archives, NWDNS-75-IP-1-10.

petitioned to have the barracks reactivated. Pratt obtained special congressionally approved detached duty from the army to become Carlisle Indian Industrial School's first superintendent. Like Armstrong, Pratt knew the value of public relations. To get support for his school, he had incoming students photographed in their traditional dress (see fig. 5) and then later had them photographed in "civilized" clothes (see fig. 6) to demonstrate the transformation students at Carlisle were undergoing.

Getting the support of the townspeople and the government was easier than getting the Indians' support. When Pratt presented his plan to the Sioux chiefs assembled in council, Spotted Tail stood up and declared, "The white people are all thieves and liars; we don't want our children to learn such things" (quoted in Morton 1962, 69). Pratt responded that if the Sioux had been able to read and write English, they would have been better able to deal with white men.

He recruited women teachers who were open to innovation. Instruction was started with English-language books, but this was not successful. Students did a "nightly confessional" on their English use and were required to write their parents once a week. Advanced students attended nearby Dickinson College (Ryan 1962). On Saturday evenings students were entertained professionally. Among the performances were concerts by the New York Philharmonic and the Boston Symphony.

Carlisle opened its doors in 1879 with 136 students. Luther Standing Bear (1928) claimed to be the first Indian boy to enter the Carlisle Indian Industrial School grounds. He reported no beds in the dormitories, bread and water for breakfast, and no practical use for the trade he learned. Pratt quickly worked to get proper clothing and beds for his students, and he was disturbed by the small food allowance provided by the Indian Bureau. He insisted that his students have the same food allowance as soldiers. However, other Indian boarding schools did not benefit from the higher rations that Pratt was able to get for his Carlisle students.

Standing Bear complained that being forced to speak English made it hard to get along. He remembered "how hard it had been . . . to forgo the consolation of speech," and he could "never forget the confusion and pain" caused when his teacher made him compete with other students (Standing Bear 1933, 16, 242). He recalled that one of the teachers asked him to read aloud the same paragraph eleven times in front of his classmates to the point that he was "thoroughly cowed and humiliated in front of them (17). He wrote:

> So we went to school to copy, to imitate; not to exchange languages and ideas, and not to develop the best traits that had come out of uncountable experiences of hundreds and thousands of years living upon this continent. So, while the white people had much to teach us, we had much to teach them, and what a school could have been established upon that idea! However, this was not the attitude of the day, though the teachers were sympathetic and kind, and some came to be my lifelong friends. (237)

Pratt used a student court of older students to maintain discipline. He believed in having as few rules as possible, but those that existed were rigidly enforced (Ryan 1962).

No textbooks were used with entering students who could not speak English. The first principal of Carlisle's education department, Miss Carrie M. Semple, described this approach in an article published in the Dakota Mission's bilingual newspaper, *IAPI OAYE:*

Almost from the first, by the use of slate and blackboard, the pupils were taught to write and read the names of objects, or short sentences—using script—describing actions. "Harry ran," "Mathew ran," "Lena ran," written upon the slate, at first almost illegibly. . . .

No criticism was made, however awkward the attempt at imitation. . . . This is substantially the method pursued in the institution for the deaf mutes at Hartford, Conn., under the superintendency of Dr. Keep, and fully explained in his book—"First Lessons for the Deaf and Dumb." . . . The phonic method is employed to aid in the pronunciation and discovery of new words. The combination of the phonic and word-method we find especially adapted to our Indian pupils. . . . It is often necessary to show the Indian pupil the proper position of the teeth, tongue and lips, and insist upon his imitation. . . . We believe it is a great mistake to use books at the first. . . . [A]lso[,] . . . time spent in teaching the alphabet is lost. (Semple 1882, 23)

Students taught the alphabet would "parrot" it, and if they were found "stupidly droning over a reading book," the book was thrown aside and objects were taken up. Objects were also used to teach math and some classes kept diaries (Semple 1882, 23).

In 1887 Carlisle had a total enrollment of 617 students, with 106 children of Apache prisoners at Fort Marion in Florida, including seven married couples (*ARCIA* 1887). Its enrollment was a third of the enrollment of the off-reservation boarding schools, and the average age of new students at Carlisle was fifteen (Eastman 1935). The *Annual Report of the Commissioner of Indian Affairs* in 1888 noted that 21 out of 637 students had died the past year at Carlisle. A normal, or teacher training, department was added to the school in 1889, consisting of a three-year course following graduation from the eighth grade. Under the supervision of the normal teacher, eight or ten of the most advanced students taught the youngest students one-half day, including some of the Apache students who had never been in school before. They received academic instruction the other half day (*ARCIA* 1893). By 1895 normal departments had been added to the schools at Haskell, Hampton, and Santa Fe. That year President Cleveland amended Civil Service rules to allow graduates of Indian normal schools to be assistants or day school teachers without additional examination (*ARCIA* 1895).

Over the twenty-four years of Pratt's direction, Carlisle graduated only 158 students (Eastman 1935). The school had no graduates until 1889, and in 1893 only six students graduated (*ARCIA* 1893). The school provided an elementary education to older Indian students, who usually remained away from their families for three years. Students were placed with area families under the Outing System during the year. They were to be paid for their work and in the winter attended local public schools. The 1887 report of the Commissioner of Indian Affairs described the Outing System:

> [I]n placing out for a series of months among the families of farmers in that part of Pennsylvania, boys and girls who have had a year or so of training at Carlisle . . . can make the most of the advantages thus afforded them for learning practical farming, the use of tools, and thrifty housekeeping. In addition to their board they receive fair wages for their labor—from $5 to $8 per month for farm work—and as members of the household are admitted to the privileges enjoyed by the sons and daughters of the family. In some cases they remain a year at these places, attending district school in the winter. Such a training upon a farm is the best possible way of fitting them for the ownership and cultivation of the lands which are being allotted them by the Government. This experience, taken in connection with their training and education at school, places them beyond all reasonable doubt upon a footing of self-support. Under this system 299 Carlisle pupils have spent more or less time in private families during the past year. (*ARCIA* 1887, xvii–xviii)

In 1893, 200 students were placed out during the winter and attended public schools. In 1900, 1,880 Carlisle students participated in the Outing System, each with his or her own bank account (*ARCIA* 1900). Pratt complained when in 1894 the Indian Office halted the practice of allowing students to be paid for some of their work at school (*ARCIA* 1895). While Pratt's idea of the Outing was to place Indian children in white homes as another son or daughter, in the West it quickly became a way for white families to obtain cheap servants. Boarding schools such as Phoenix Indian School became, in effect, employment agencies for white households, with field matrons to monitor the children's performance (Trennert 1988).

However, Carlisle's fame does not rest on either its academic program or the Outing System. Like many well-known universities today,

Carlisle achieved its most lasting fame from extracurricular programs, especially its football team, which played Ivy League universities under the coaching of Pop Warner, who was hired by Pratt in 1899. Pratt was ambivalent about football: he liked the publicity and boost to school spirit, but he was concerned about the lack of sportsmanship and the sport's violence (Bloom 2000). The Carlisle school band was also used to publicize the school (see fig. 7).

The Carlisle football team provided the school with valuable publicity and income. By 1914 Warner was making four times the salary of lead teachers and double the salary of the school's superintendent, and he was reportedly virtually running the school. Colleges bid against each other to play Carlisle, and the athletic fund took in $33,275 in 1912. Players were paid some money and received special, more lenient treatment when caught drinking or disobeying other school rules (Ryan 1962). Famous Carlisle athletes included 1912 Olympic medalists Jim Thorpe, a Sauk-Fox; Louis Tewanima, a Hopi sent to the school as a prisoner (he set a U.S. Olympic record in 1912, which was not broken until 1964, by an Oglala Sioux, Billy Mills); and Charles A. Bender, a Chippewa (later, a World Series pitcher and major league coach).

English at Carlisle

A student newspaper, the *School News*, was started at Carlisle soon after its founding. The paper was used to get students to exhort their peers to speak only English, though it was admitted that after two years only two students spoke English well (*School News*, October 1881, 2). Sophie Rachel wrote to her brother:

> I want you to try to talk English every day and I want talk now I must try try hard to talk this time and when we go home we must teach our own people. I want to talk English every day not to talk old Sioux. Now I don't want to talk Indian anymore because I like English every day every boy and girl must try to talk English not to talk Sioux. I always hear the boys and girls talk Sioux. Now let us stop that this time if you do not know how to talk just try. (*School News*, October 1881, 3)

An editorial in November 1881 stated that a few students "talk their own language all the time" but that students should "speak the English

Carlisle school band, 1915. Photograph courtesy of the National Archives, NWDNS-75-EXEC-7.

language to everybody and don't be afraid of mistakes" (2). Also in that issue, students wrote one-paragraph essays about what they saw in a picture. Luther Standing Bear wrote a letter to his father in the April 1882 issue reiterating the Carlisle message: "I wont you must give up Indian way. . . . [Y]ou must believe in God, obey him and pray to Him. He will help you in the right path and He will give you what you want if you ask Him. . . . Then you will be always happy. . . . I have been speaking only English about 14 weeks now" (4).

The June 1882 issue contained similar exhortations to "Speak Only English" but with the admission, "I hear everybody talking Indian" (4). The same issue stated, "Books in Indian languages are of no account in this school. Out west where the Indian can read the Indian language may be of some good. English is what every Indian child should learn" (2). Pratt's biographer, Elaine Eastman (1935), stated that students were constantly encouraged to speak only English but were not punished when they did not. However, Luther Standing Bear (1928) reported that students were not allowed to speak English.

In 1893 the school, using student help in an elaborate print shop (fig. 8), was printing two publications: the monthly *Red Man* with a circulation of 2,000 to 3,000 and the weekly *Indian Helper* with a circulation of

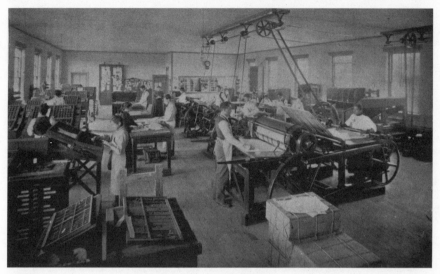

Carlisle print shop. Photograph from the 1903 *Annual Report of the Commissioner of Indian Affairs.*

9,000 (*ARCIA* 1893, 449). Both periodicals were used to publicize Carlisle and Pratt's message of assimilation. In 1894 the school had 818 students from fifty-three tribes, including 101 Chippewa (Ojibway), 93 Oneida, 76 Sioux, 70 Apache, 49 Seneca, 38 Ottawa, 37 Pueblo, 36 Piegan (Blackfeet), 34 Cherokee, 34 Assiniboine, 29 Osage, 24 Nez Perce, 20 Umatilla, and 19 Crow students. Only one death was reported during the previous year. At that time Carlisle was the only Indian school with electricity, and it was paid for from private donations (*ARCIA* 1894).

Pratt complained in 1895 that his "greatest difficulty is with those [students] who have previously made some progress with reading some Indian vernacular (*ARCIA* 1895, 399). In the 1890s Pratt also complained to the Commissioner of Indian Affairs about the difficulty of recruiting students and being sent sick children and children with discipline problems (*ARCIA* 1893).

Pratt's Legacy

Pratt himself had only two years of formal education. The only thing he was qualified to teach at his school was tinsmithing, which he had taken up at age thirteen after his father was murdered returning from the California goldfields. Lindsey (1995, 22) wrote that Pratt "showed the supreme confidence generally born from a healthy ignorance of one's own shortcomings." For Pratt, the purpose of Indian boarding schools was to take the "Indian" out of his students, and he was agreeable to intermarriage with whites. His goal was "a multiracial society where everyone acted like Anglo-Saxons of the Judeo-Christian persuasion" (Lindsey 1995, 26). Pratt (1964, 335) told a Baptist group, "In Indian civilization I am a Baptist, because I believe in immersing Indians in our civilization and when we get them under holding them there until they are thoroughly soaked." Carlisle's slogan was, "To civilize the Indian, get him into civilization. To keep him civilized, let him stay" (283). Thus Pratt's goal was first to break down the students' fear through love and second to get students to "long" for civilization through, among other things, having the experience of joining the white community at its fairs, festivals, and picnics. As a result, Indian students would learn to speak English, work hard, get a common school education, and become moral Christians (Lippincott 1882).

In 1899 Commissioner of Indian Affairs W. A. Jones memorialized Pratt:

> When Pratt began his work, it was understood that unless the Indian youth be educated and assimilated with our population, the tribes would stand as a menace to the peace of the government and require a large army to keep them within bounds. By his strong individuality and labors he has done as much, or more, to remove the need of an army for this work as any other man ever did, or ever could do. (Quoted in Eastman 1935, 259)

Pratt's strong individualism led him to speak out on many issues. He saw the Indian Bureau as having a vested interest in keeping the Indian uncivilized and thought the new Bureau of Ethnology, staffed by anthropologists, encouraged interest in traditional ways that were best forgotten by Indians. He also argued with missionaries who, he felt, did not "advocate the disintegration of the tribes and the giving to individual Indians rights and opportunities among civilized people" (Eastman 1935, 113) and opposed Buffalo Bill Cody's Wild West shows because they glorified Indian culture. Pratt told Indian Commissioner T. J. Morgan, who shared his views, "Pandering to the tribe and its socialism as most of our Government and mission plans do is the principle reason why the Indians have not advanced more and are not advancing as rapidly as they ought" (*ARCIA* 1890, 313).

Pratt received increased criticism as time went on, and by 1901 wrote in his report to the Commissioner of Indian Affairs, "I feel that I am becoming more and more extraneous to about all that is being done for the Indians" (*ARCIA* 1901, 565). In a 1903 article in the magazine *Out West*, its editor, Charles Lummis ([1903] 1968, 34), an unofficial adviser to President Theodore Roosevelt, wrote, "[Pratt] broke up more Indian homes and broke more Indian hearts of fathers and mothers. . . . He tried to Make his Indians White People. . . . His pupils learned to despise their parents and their native industries—the blanket-making and the basketry and the pottery, which are the admiration of scholars the world over."

That year Pratt was promoted to colonel and summarily retired from the army at age sixty-two for disagreeing publicly with Roosevelt. In 1904 he was advanced to the rank of brigadier-general and dismissed from his position at Carlisle when he again called for the abolition of the Indian Bureau on the grounds that its bureaucrats sought to maintain the reservation system in order to keep their jobs (Eastman 1935).

Based on interviews with former Carlisle students, Alice Marriott and Carol K. Rachlin (1969, 193) described Pratt as a "rigid disciplinarian," as might be expected from his military background, who "was basically a kind and fair man, with a great human warmth." Chauncey Yellow Robe, a grand nephew of Sitting Bull, was one of the students who at fifteen, against his wishes, was "given" to Pratt to take to school in the "far east." Yellow Robe (1926, 12) later wrote, "Never had I experienced such homesickness as I did then. How many times I have watched the western sky and cried with a broken heart—wishing to see my father and mother again and be free on the plains." However, after the experience, he wrote of the "fatherly care" of General Pratt and stated, "I owe to him and the inspiration received from him all that I am" (1926, 12). Yellow Robe spent his summers while at Carlisle harvesting fields under the Outing System and attending a Moody Bible Institute school. He went on to become the disciplinarian and athletic director at the Indian boarding school in Rapid City, South Dakota.

The Arapaho artist Carl Sweezy, who attended Carlisle for two years, brought away memories of "good teachers" and two summers under the Outing System. He also brought away Pratt's belief that the Indian could learn anything white people could. He went home early to recover from illness brought on by the cold, damp Pennsylvania winters and enrolled at the Chilocco boarding school when he recovered (Bass 1966). Gertrude Golden (1954) recalled working with the disciplinarian Joe Tyndall and his wife, the assistant matron, at the Fort Yuma Boarding School at the time of Pratt's dismissal. According to Golden (1954, 70), Tyndall was a "fierce champion" of Pratt and was angered by any criticism of him. Tyndall was antagonized by the "young lady employees [sic] . . . open and constant adverse criticism of the Indians, and he retaliated by giving them poor help for the laundry and janitor work when he detailed boys for those tasks." The Indian employees at Fort Yuma ate at a separate table.

In 1913 Pratt wrote a long letter to Indian Commissioner Cato Sells and later sent a copy in 1921 to Commissioner Burke. He declared:

> Every church effort . . . and all government education except . . . by a very few non-reservation schools, had the same tendency—to strengthen and build up the tribes, as such. When the resources of their old nomadic life were passing, they would, with little encouragement, have individually sought and readily entered the activities of our civilized life to obtain a living. . . . High loyalty to United States citizenship is impossible when loyalty to the tribe predominates. The Bureau itself, when non-reservation schools were beginning to turn out young Indians equal to taking up the responsibilities of American life, began at once the system of persuading and even hiring them to go back to tribal associations. (Quoted in Eastman 1935, 268)

Despite his ethnocentrism, which prevented him from seeing any good in Indian cultures, Pratt was credited both in his own time and by later historians for his role in convincing both the federal government and the American public that Indians could and should be educated. In a speech to the NEA's Indian department in 1909, he objected to the limited view of Indian capabilities that was prevalent at the turn of the century and the use of terms such as "child races" to refer to Indians. However, he went on to state in the same speech:

> The mass of children of primitive races are not well developed in the power of abstract reason and personal initiative. Vocational training, therefore,

rather than higher education is their need, allowing full scope for those of
exceptional ability to pursue college, professional, or technical training.
(*Addresses* 1909, 732)

Carlisle after Pratt

After Pratt was fired in 1904, things began to change. The Indian agent
who replaced him was reported to know nothing about how to administer a large school. However, he was a good friend of the new Commissioner of Indian Affairs and was related to the secretary of the
interior through his wife. He allowed weekly dances, expanded the
football program, and increased the amount of military training for
students. The Apache Carlos Montezuma who served as the football
team's doctor in the 1890s changed his attitude after Pratt left, even
writing a nationally syndicated column detailing corruption in the
school's athletic program. A former Carlisle administrator wrote him
in 1907, "The school has degenerated into a school of professional
athletes where everything—the welfare of the individual as well as
that of the community—must step aside to gratify the desire of . . .
'Pop' Warner" (quoted in Bloom 1996, 37). In 1906 a Native Indian Arts
program was started that offered rug weaving and beadwork, and the
age of admittance was raised to fourteen. After 1900 salaries failed to
keep up with inflation, and the quality and morale of the staff declined
(Ryan 1962).

A new superintendent in 1908 showed more interest in the buildings
than in the students. Students did not respect the superintendent.
Drinking, immorality, and running away increased, and the expulsion
of pregnant girls was commonplace (Ryan 1962). A 1914 congressional
investigation of the school found that with the exception of the superintendent "all witnesses agreed that complete lack of discipline, overemphasis on sports, incompetent administration, and generally bad
management were responsible for the sad state of affairs at the Indian
school" (quoted in Ryan 1962, 221). The superintendent was fired, and
the chief clerk, a former Carlisle student, was found guilty of financial
irregularities. A new superintendent, one of the four supervisors of
Indian schools, had the three worst girls sent to reform school and
reinstituted Pratt's approach to discipline. He turned the special dorm

for athletes into an honor dorm. One problem Carlisle faced was its use by reservation schools as a dumping ground for unruly students, a practice that continued for the remaining off-reservation boarding schools after Carlisle closed. The need for more army facilities brought on by World War I was used as an excuse to close Carlisle in 1918. The scandals at the school were becoming an embarrassment to the government, and congressmen from the West wanted schools, and the money they brought, in their own electoral districts. The idea of permanently removing Indians from the West by educating them was no longer seen as a workable solution to the "Indian problem."

Carlisle's Legacy

The historian Robert M. Utley (1964) concluded that most of the Carlisle students could make their way in Pennsylvania, but they were sent home to their reservations where there were few jobs. However, in 1911, 209 of Carlisle's 574 living graduates were employed by the government and 300 had nongovernment jobs (Ryan 1962). Francis E. Leupp, former Commissioner of Indian Affairs and Pratt's longtime enemy, painted a dim future for the educated Indian in his 1910 book, *The Indian and His Problem*. According to Leupp, the Indian doctor, lawyer, and missionary were not well accepted in the East or the West. Leupp found only the Outing System admirable among Pratt's educational innovations. He concluded it was better to carry civilization to the Indian than to carry the Indian to civilization via the off-reservation boarding school. Of course, his most convincing argument was that reservation day schools were cheaper to run.

Lewis Meriam reported in 1932, "[During our extensive study of the Indian Office,] we met in their homes returned students from the widely advertised Carlisle Indian College, renowned for its college football team, who had only completed the fourth grade. Scholastically Carlisle was never even a first class high school, it was only an elementary school" (83). In fact, none of the off-reservation schools in 1927 were equivalent to a first-class high school, according to Meriam. However, some students at these schools were prepared in normal departments to be elementary school teachers, and at Carlisle some students even took physics (see fig. 9).

Physics class, Carlisle, 1915. Photograph courtesy of the National Archives NWDNS-75-EX-6D.

Meriam asked returned students what trades they had learned at school: "[T]he answer 'printing,' when the Indians rarely read and have no paper; shoemaking, when most of them wear moccasins made by the women; painting, when the houses are made of logs, adobe or brush; carpentering, where there is almost no carpentering to do" (26). He concluded, "The Indian children taken away from families and communities got no training in Indian family life, and many of them never had any experience in white family life. Thus the moral force of traditional community opinion was seriously weakened if not destroyed" (129).

Zane Grey portrayed the "Carlisle Indian" Lo Blandy in his serialized novel, *The Vanishing American*, in 1922. After returning home, Lo Blandy is caught between two worlds. His rejection of what he learned at Carlisle is symbolized by his rejection of Christianity, but neither can he return to his old way of life:

> I am an Infidel! I cannot believe in the Indian's God; I will not believe in the white man's God. . . .

The Indian's religion is best for him. The white preacher kills the Indian's simple faith in his own God, makes him an infidel, then tries to make him over. It cannot be done. There is not one real Christian Indian on the reservation. (199)

In one notorious incident, in 1891 Plenty Horses killed Lt. Edward Casey to cleanse himself of the effects of attending Carlisle (Utley 1964). The Navajo had a simpler means, the Enemy Way ceremony, to cleanse their children after contact with whites.

OTHER GOVERNMENT BOARDING SCHOOLS

After the publicity generated by Carlisle convinced many people that off-reservation boarding schools could effectively educate Indian students, Congress funded twenty-three more schools over the next twenty years. Unlike Carlisle, they were nearer the reservations from which they drew their students. Table 1 provides a list of off-reservation boarding schools started between 1879 and 1905. Off-reservation boarding schools competed with each other and with reservation boarding and day schools for students. This led to attendance boundaries and restrictions regarding how schools could recruit students. In 1894 and 1895 Congress stipulated that parental permission was required before Indian students could be sent out of state to boarding schools; in 1896, this permission needed to be in writing.

Reservation schools became feeder elementary schools for off-reservation boarding schools. The off-reservation schools that remained open changed from teaching only elementary subjects in the nineteenth century to teaching only secondary subjects in the latter part of the twentieth century. Table 2 shows the increase in number of Indian schools and Indian school enrollment from 1880 to 1930.

When Carlisle closed, Haskell Institute, patterned after Carlisle, became the Indian Bureau's flagship boarding school. Charles Lummis described it in a letter shortly after it opened near Lawrence, Kansas, in 1884:

The grounds are a half-mile wide, and one and a quarter miles long, mostly devoted to farming purposes, and admirably adapted thereto. The buildings

TABLE 1
Location, date of opening, capacity, attendance, etc., of non-reservation boarding schools during the fiscal year ending June 30, 1905

Location of School	Date Opened	Number of Staff	Capacity	Enrollment	Average Attendance
Carlisle, Pa.	1879	90	1000[a]	948	898
Chemawa, Ore. (Salem)	1880	52	550	566	435
Chilocco, Okla.	1884	72	600	866	741
Genoa, Neb.	1884	31	300	391	302
Albuquerque, New Mex.	1884	30	300	369	344
Lawrence, Kans. (Haskell)	1884	70	700	1,127	781
Grand Junction, Colo.	1886	19	200	216	192
Santa Fe, New Mex.	1890	33	300	376	321
Fort Mojave, Aris.	1890	22	200	228	210
Carson, Nev. (Stewart)	1890	25	250	307	272
Pierre, S. Dak.	1891	16	150	163	146
Phoenix, Ariz.	1891	60	700	781	717
Durango, Colo.	1892	21	300	198	180
Fort Shaw, Mont.	1892	33	300	329	286
Flandreau, S. Dak. (Riggs)	1893	36	350	435	401
Pipestone, Minn.	1893	16	200	181	162
Mount Pleasant, Mich.	1893	33	300	361	324
Tomah, Wisc.	1893	25	250	264	225
Wittenberg, Wisc.	1895[b]	13	100	118	106
Greenville, Calif.	1895[b]	9	90	94	75
Morris, Minn.	1897	19	160	174	165
Chamberlain, S. Dak.	1898	19	200	184	169
Fort Bidwell, Calif.	1898	9	100	79	62
Rapid City, S. Dak.	1898	21	250	259	230
Riverside, Calif. (Sherman)	1902	45	400	722	492
Total		822	8,250	9,736	8,236

SOURCE: ARCIA 1905, 41
[a]1,500 with outing pupils
[b]previously a contract school

are of stone, three in number, and generous in size and equipment. The dormitory is 100 x 60 feet and four stories high, with large, well-ventilated rooms, in each of which are from six to a dozen comfortable beds. The Superintendent also has his office and apartments in this building. Next stands the school-building, two stories high, and about 100 x 40 feet in dimensions. It is a model school-house, inside and out. . . .

TABLE 2

Numbers of Indian Schools and Enrollments of Indian Students
by Type of School and Year, 1880–1930

Year	Number of Schools[1] Day	Boarding	Total	Federal School Enrollment[2] Day	Boarding	Total	Mission and Private[3]	Public School[4]	All Schools
1880	109	60	160	N/A	N/A	7000+	N/A	N/A	7000+
1890	106	140	206	3,967	12,410	16,377	N/A	N/A	16,377
1900	154	153	307	5,120	19,810	24,930	1,275	246	26,451
1911[5]	227	156	383	6,121	19,912	26,033	2,739	10,265	39,397
1920	204	143	347	5,765	21,659	27,424	3,518	30,858	61,800
1930	150	136	286	3,983	28,333	32,316	3,358	34,775	70,449

SOURCE: *Report on BIA Education* 1988, 15

1 Federally administered schools plus mission and private Indian schools, with and without federal contracts.

2 Federally administered plus mission and private schools with federal contracts.

3 Mission and private Indian schools without federal contracts.

4 Indian students attending public schools and living within the administrative jurisdictions of the Bureau of Indian Affairs.

5 Data for 1911 used because comparable 1910 data were unavailable.

The pupils range in age from 8 to 23 years and are of both sexes. . . . There are now 131 young Indians here, of whom half work upon the farm and about the buildings while the others go to school, the two divisions changing places every week. . . .

The school-room instruction is at present of the kindergarten sort, as the pupils understand but few words of English. (Lummis [1884] 1989, 19-20)

John Charles, one of only four Navajos attending Haskell in 1915, wrote to the Crownpoint Indian agent about working in the carpenter shop, having a big Thanksgiving dinner, the football team (fig. 10), drilling in the morning, going to town on Saturday afternoons, the kindness of his teacher, other boys running away, and writing home every month and sending his report card (Iverson 2002b, 89). Like Carlisle, Haskell was run like a military school. Esther Horne (Horne and McBeth 1998) went to Haskell in 1924 along with two younger siblings after her white father died and her family sank into poverty. To ease the cultural shock of attending boarding school, younger siblings were sometimes enrolled, and students from the same tribe were paired

Football team, Haskell Institute, 1914. Photograph courtesy of the National Archives NWDNS-75-L-3D.

(Parker 1996). Horne (Horne and McBeth 1998) gives an interesting description of Haskell. Not all her classmates were poor like she was. An Osage roommate, benefiting from oil money, had Saks Fifth Avenue clothes, which she lent to Horne. At Haskell, high school girls could study nursing, home economics (fig. 11), teacher training, or business (fig. 12). Boys were assigned to the paint shop, blacksmith shop, dairy, bakery, masonry, power plant training, business, or normal training.

Horne rose to the rank of major in her years at Haskell and had generally happy memories. In her memoirs, she wrote that she received "a very good education" there that benefited her "all through her life" (Horne and McBeth 1998, 36, 39). She mentioned the "missionary zeal" of her teachers and was especially thankful for two outstanding Indian

Girls learning to cook, Haskell Institute, 1903. Photograph from the 1903 *Annual Report of the Commissioner of Indian Affairs*.

Shorthand class, Haskell Institute, 1910. Photograph courtesy of the National Archives NWDNS-75-EX-1D.

teachers: Ella Deloria, a Dakota Sioux graduate of Columbia University's Teachers College, and Ruth Muskrat Bronson, a Cherokee graduate of Mount Holyoke. They had a sense of humor and "taught us not to believe that everything we learned was the truth" (41). In 1927 Horne starred as Hermia in the school's production of Shakespeare's *A Midsummer Night's Dream*. She remembered that Haskell had a good library and up-to-date textbooks. Her teacher training included methods and psychology classes, and she did practice teaching to the lower grades. Students stayed at Haskell year-round, and those over sixteen participated in the school's Outing Program, which she remembered as a good experience. She remembered meals of meat, potatoes, bread, and gravy, with some World War I surplus food, and rats infesting the school.

A boarding school menu from the 1910s included oatmeal, milk, fried potatoes, syrup, bread, and coffee for breakfast, boiled meat, gravy, potatoes, cabbage, bread, and water for dinner, and roast meat, gravy, potatoes, beans, prunes, bread, and water for supper. A 1929 menu included corn flakes, bacon gravy, and cocoa for breakfast, swiss steak, mashed potatoes, gravy, cabbage and pineapple salad, fig and tapioca pudding, bread, and milk for dinner, and beans, bread, peach sauce, and cake for supper (Riney 1999).

George A. Boyce (1974, 17), who started work in 1938 as a curriculum specialist and textbook writer stationed at Haskell, noted, "The quality of equipment and teaching was unimpressive. The students were largely light skinned. Some were blond, some redheaded. They were well-behaved, presentable, intelligent. Upon closer acquaintance they revealed they were more culturally Indian than appearances would indicate."

The historian Scott Riney (1999) gives a good description of the Rapid City Indian School, which was one of the small off-reservation boarding schools. It had about three hundred students and was open from 1898 to 1932, when it was converted to a tuberculosis sanitarium. Rapid City had to compete with other schools for students and issued catalogs as a recruiting tool. The 1916-17 catalog was thirty pages long and included pictures. That school year eight students attended Rapid City's public high school from the dorm, and one became captain of its football team and senior class president. A few other students attended the Rapid City Business College. Competition for students forced school administrators to make their programs more attractive for students.

In 1909 two Rapid City runaways lost their lower legs to frostbite. In 1920, 38 boys and 12 girls ran away. In 1921 there were five teachers for about 290 students. By then, according to Riney (1999, 73), "boarding schools had become welfare providers of last resort for Indian families." The worst aspect of schools like that at Rapid City was that they were breeding grounds for trachoma (an eye infection that could lead to blindness), measles, tuberculosis, and other diseases. Students could also be permanently injured operating the schools heavy machinery. Two girls at Rapid City lost fingers using the school laundry's "mangle" (Riney 1999).

Teachers at Rapid City had to pledge to abstain from alcohol and narcotics and worked long hours, including evenings and teaching Sunday school. They received thirty days of vacation in the summer (Riney 1999).

Carl H. Skinner, superintendent of Phoenix Indian School from 1931 to 1937, started his new job at Phoenix with no experience in Indian education. He also served as a Sunday School teacher for fifty Protestant boys and as the superintendent of the Salt River Pima, Fort McDowell Apache, and Camp Verde Yavapai Reservations. He remembered the school having four dorms, 100 employees (10 percent Indian), 900 students from more than thirty-five tribes, a new 60-bed hospital, 100 hogs, 50 cows, 1,000 hens, and 3 swimming pools. He recalled most students going home summers and wanting students "to learn the English language not because it is a better language than their own but rather because [it] is more nearly universal," and Hopi students were recruited without soldiers or policemen (29). Indian students had to sit in the balcony when they went to the movies in Phoenix.

One of the premier off-reservation boarding schools, Phoenix Indian School had some advanced courses, as did Carlisle and Haskell, including art (fig. 13). In the 1930s it had literary societies, home economics clubs, Boy Scouts, Campfire Girls, band, choral groups, athletic teams, lettermen's clubs, and a National Guard unit. Company F of the Arizona National Guard was drawn from Phoenix Indian School students and alumni from 1924 on. The most popular sport was football, but boxing was also popular. In 1937 there was a deemphasis on sports, with boxing and wrestling eliminated, and more emphasis on academics. Seniors lived in cottages. Students in the Outing System had the right to refuse to participate and the right to refuse particular employers. In 1934 sixty boys hired out to build the Salt River Day School. Phoenix Indian School also provided bookmobile service to twenty-three day schools (Parker 1996). Phoenix, Haskell, and Chilocco developed modern print shops that printed "almost all of the printed material used by the Indian Bureau" (Parker 1996, 23).

The boarding schools system was not entirely imposed on Indians. The Navajo political leader Chee Dodge wrote to the secretary of the interior in 1914:

> The tribe is uneducated. Aside from this [sic] children in the different schools there are not even 400 members of the whole tribe of about 25,000 who understand and speak the English language. Ten years ago they had but one Government boarding school for the whole tribe and, before that time, the children were not kept long enough in school to be benefited. . . .
>
> We are pleased that the Government has begun building more schools for our children, but we have no trade school, and such a school is very urgent necessity for our large tribe. A trade school would furnish efficient journeymen for the tribe who are necessary for the advancement of the Navajos, to build better homes, etc., and it would also enable them to compete with their white neighbors. (Iverson 2002b, 4–5)

Art class, Phoenix Indian School, 1900. Photograph courtesy of the National Archives NWDNS-75-EXP-1D.

Dodge also wrote in the same letter that it would hurt the Navajo to be put under the jurisdiction of state governments and that the reservation should not be allotted but kept intact. Dodge went on to serve as tribal chairman from 1923 to 1928 and from 1942 to 1946 and as vice-chairman from 1946 until his death in 1947.

In 1926 twelve Navajo Tribal Council members unanimously adopted a resolution stating,

> We are glad the Chas. H. Burke school at Ft. Wingate is being built for the Navajos. We will be glad to send our children to that school. We hope and ask that the school be made, as far as it can be, a industrial school where our children can be taught trades which will be useful to them and help them to make a living as workmen, and also help them in the raising of stock and the making of homes and farms. (Iverson 2002b, 8)

In 1932 the Navajo chapter officers for Greasewood petitioned the Commissioner of Indian Affairs to build them a boarding school, stating, "Here in Grease Wood Valley alone, there are two hundred children of school age who are not in school" (Iverson 2002b, 52). While in sympathy with the government's desire for more day schools, they did not think day schools would work in Greasewood. In 1939 some Navajo residents of Rock Point petitioned for a day school (Iverson 2002b). In 1941 Sam Gorman, a Navajo Tribal Council delegate, expressed his regret at not having received more education: "The man who does not have education is one who cannot get anywhere, like his wing is cut off and he cannot fly around. It is the man who had an education who can get about freely like a free bird" (quoted in Iverson 2002b, 95).

While most of the off-reservation boarding schools have closed over the years, including Phoenix Indian School (in 1989), Chemawa (see fig. 14), Flandreau, and Sherman remained open at the beginning of the twenty-first century as secondary boarding schools. Haskell Institute started accepting only high school graduates in 1965 and became Haskell Indian Junior College in 1970 and then Haskell Indian Nations University in 1993. In 1968 it was serving students reporting membership in seventy tribes, one-third from English-speaking homes, one-third from Indian-language homes, and one-third from bilingual homes, with many students coming from the Southwest (Goodner, Woods, and Harkins 1970).

Among the reasons that most of the off-reservation boarding schools were closed over the years were their high cost of operation in comparison to day schools, their alleged ineffectiveness, parental opposition, and the growing desire to integrate Indians into the public schools. Indian Commissioner Leupp, in his 1907 report to the secretary of the interior, characterized the off-reservation boarding schools as "educational almshouses" (*ARCIA* 1907, 22). At one time Indian parents were jailed or refused government rations if they did not send their children to boarding schools. Today these schools have Indian school boards that exercise real control, and Indian parents lobby to keep the remaining schools open. However, over the years, the enrollment of children from dysfunctional families rose, creating increased discipline problems.

TEACHERS

Indian Service teachers were not required to have a four-year degree until the 1930s. Teachers choosing to work for the relatively low pay and isolation of the Indian Service seemed to be seeking either adventure or

Indian Training School (Chemawa), Forest Grove, Oregon, 1882. Photograph courtesy of the National Archives, NWDNS-75-IP-1-20.

escape. Lucy Gage, a longtime professor of elementary education who moved to Oklahoma in 1901 and visited Indian schools there, noted that the teachers' "most telling characteristic . . . was some physical defect caused by birth, accident or circumstance. . . . Out here they seem to have been able to shake off their shackles to gain both freedom and self-respect." She noted, however, that the teachers "were for the most part refined and well-prepared" (Gage 1951, 297). The autobiographical accounts of turn-of-the-century Indian Service employees describe mixed experiences, but they tended to portray Indians in a favorable light and often criticized fellow employees and government policy.

Many teachers could not adjust to the isolation and cultural differences on reservations. Estelle Brown started teaching at Crow Creek Indian School in South Dakota in 1897. While on her way to the school twenty-four miles in an open wagon, her driver told her, "[T]eaching Injun brats is throwin' away good money. All them old Injuns is too lazy to work. They'd ruther starve or let the gov'ment feed 'em. Brats grow up the same way" (Brown 1952, 25). Living conditions for teachers were primitive:

> The discolored, plastered walls had known neither paper nor paint. In a corner stood a single, black iron bed, in the center a potbellied coal stove with lengths of rusted pipe supported by a tangle of wires nailed to the ceiling. Against one wall was a scabrous bureau, its mirror blotched where the quicksilver had flaked off. An upended packing case served as a table to hold an oil lamp; beside it was a wooden rocking chair. . . . In another corner stood a washstand with a chipped white enamel bowl and pitcher and a cake of yellow laundry soap. Familiar with washstands, I knew that somewhere in its recess there would be a chamber pot. Beside it stood an old galvanized slop bucket. (30).

The bed had no springs, and she concluded that a "tepee would have been more cosy" (30). She recalled another teacher who came from Boston in September, took one look at the school, and caught the next stage home.

Soon after Brown started teaching at Crow Creek, a fellow employee told her, "[T]here ain't nobody here who could earn a living anywhere else. They're the only kind of people who ever come into this dirty Indian Service" (43). There were only three teachers for two hundred students. She found her students systematically underfed, forever scrubbing the school, and housed in unheated dormitories. Conditions were harsh, crude, and discouraging. Her pay was $600 a year. She described the Indian Service as the "unloved and unwanted stepchild of Congress" and "instinctively felt that, in teaching Indian children to like and want the things we liked and wanted, we were headed in the wrong direction" (19, 42). Teaching her students required "unlimited patience" and "a belief in the necessity for recreating primitive children in my own image," a belief she did not acquire during her sixteen years in the Indian Service (42). She found the Indian Service bureaucracy preoccupied with paperwork and staff morals rather than responsive to the firsthand advice of their field-workers or the Indians they were there to serve. "A knowledge of the pupils' home environment was not considered necessary since their education aimed to make that environment unsuitable to them" (204). She never heard any of her fellow employees express an interest in improving reservation conditions. Corporal punishment was discouraged in favor of depriving students of play time or making them work longer hours. Brown quotes another teacher who pointed out that they were being told to teach Indians "sex equality" and Christianity, but white girls were not treated equally, for example, not being able to vote, and "we ain't ever acted like Christians to" the Indians (63). Although there was a yearly supply of textbooks, she recalled "no newspapers, books, or magazines" being furnished to the school (68).

Minnie Braithwaite Jenkins started her Indian Service teaching career a century ago in an isolated school in Blue Canyon, Arizona, near present-day Tuba City. Before even arriving at her job, she was told by an Indian school employee on the train out to go back home, because "most of the employees in those schools live on jealousy and intrigue" (Jenkins 1951, 6). She found herself teaching sixty "listless & bored" Navajo and Hopi children in four two-hour shifts plus an hour in the evening with the entire group. They were in ragged clothes and most had no shoes, could only say their names in English, and one was blind. Luckily, she had thought in advance about teaching children who did not know English and used what is now called Total Physical Response (Asher 1977), that is, having them "stand up," "sit down," and touch various parts of their bodies in response to her English commands. Her students sang and drew pictures on slates "of animals in the most intimate of corral animal life" (Jenkins 1951, 39). She reported that many parents visited, that there were no discipline problems, and that students who "were happy and learned quickly." "Out of the schoolroom they would repeat over and over the lessons they had had in school" (Jenkins 1951, 53). She attended an Indian School Summer Institute nearby in Keams Canyon at the Hopi Agency headquarters. One of the teachers was a Carlisle graduate. She reported that Indian Service employees were discouraged about being able to "Christianize these Indians" (Jenkins 1951, 122).

When school started again in fall 1901, Jenkins had one hundred students and was forced to use rigid discipline to keep control: "My future usefulness as a teacher depended upon my ability to enforce an order, once it was given" (1951, 166). When a smallpox epidemic hit, the fact that the children had been vaccinated previously prevented any deaths. At the end of the school year, with 117 students, she resigned to escape from the teacher in charge and the matron, his wife. However, she then asked for reinstatement and was sent to Fort Mohave, where temperatures reached 129 degrees in the summer and there was no air conditioning. She reported that the employees there had "in the main . . . a real interest in Indians and were desirous of giving their best effort to help them" (265). She gave parties for her students who spoke only English, with the result that all her students were able to attend. She also reported that "many kindergartners were in jail for running away" but that they broke the door down and escaped (283). Kindergarten students were spanked for speaking Mohave.

Janette Woodruff (1939, 26), hired as a matron, found Crow children she worked with in Montana in 1900 "restrained and orderly and never given to outbursts of any kind." "Everything [in the school] was routinized until it moved with the precision of clockwork." She found that to teach the children, "[t]here always had to be a concrete, an objective way of presenting an idea" (65). Teachers who did not demonstrate their lessons found attempts to teach "utterly futile." She felt that nonsectarian religious teaching was "a vital part" of the school training, and she reported that fellow Indian Service employees feared an Indian attack in 1903.

Gertrude Golden entered the Indian Service in 1901 and served seventeen years as a teacher in Oregon, Arizona, Oklahoma, Montana, and

South Dakota. She found the bureaucracy excessively hierarchical, permitting little criticism from the lower ranks. When she tried to tell Estelle Reel, chief supervisor of Indian schools, about her principal, Reel told Golden, "[A]bsolute, unquestioned obedience to superior officers is necessary in the Indian service. If Commissioner [of Indian Affairs] Jones should order me to *black his boots*, I should do so immediately" (Golden 1954, 50; original emphasis).

About her students in Oregon in 1901, Golden wrote:

[They] excelled in those subjects which required observation, imitation and memory and were more backward in those demanding reasoning and imagination. Indians excelled the whites in interest, appreciation and obedience to rules. They were affectionate to those who loved them and who had a sincere interest in their welfare. Unerring intuition on the part of the small red child told him who were his real friends.

These Indian children had great pride in race. They were brave and patient and, in the main, honest. (1954, 8)

She recalled that principals and inspectors were more interested in the attractiveness of the bulletin boards than in the quality of teaching. She reported that "all too frequently" her fellow employees had no respect for the "lousy Indians" they taught and worked only for the money (1954, 10). Similarly, when Estelle Brown (1952, 153) was transferred to Arizona, she observed that "no employee was here because of an interest in Indians and their welfare. We were here to make a living." Teachers with students who sat quietly with shoes shined and noses wiped received good reports that were sent on to Washington.

In one school where Golden (1954) worked she found the educated Indian employees segregated from the white staff. The tribes she worked with had "a universal and decided aversion to using the English language" (Golden 1954, 83). It was "the tongue of their despised conquerors" (10). Albert H. Kneale, looking back on a thirty-six-year career with the Indian Bureau that began in 1899, wrote,

Every tribe with which I have associated is imbued with the idea that it is superior to all other peoples. Its members are thoroughly convinced of their superiority not alone over members of all other tribes but over the whites as well. . . . I have never known an Indian who would consent to being changed into a white man even were he convinced that such a change could readily be accomplished. (1950, 105)

When he started teaching in 1899, Kneale found "the Indian Bureau, at that time, always went on the assumption that any Indian custom was, per se, objectionable, whereas the customs of whites were the ways of civilization" (41). He found inept Indian agents but not dishonest ones. On being transferred to a school in Oklahoma with "notoriously bad" discipline, Kneale found the windows barred and the doors padlocked to keep students from running away. A "hard-bitten army sergeant" attempting to restore discipline by force was beaten up by the students and hospitalized (85). Against advice to maintain the old repressive policies, Kneale, through interpreters, got the Cheyenne and Arapaho boys' cooperation by organizing them into companies and letting them choose their own officers: "These officers, with myself, formed a group to enact such rules and regulations as it was deemed wise to enforce, to pass judgment on all infractions of these rules and to outline proper punishments for infractions. Every boy in school pledged obedience to the rule of this group. It worked!" (86). He gave the students the satisfaction of removing the bars and padlocks.

Kneale went on to write that things ran smoothly, but he and his wife did not like the life: "Our every action of every day was prescribed by a bell, and the bell was controlled by a clock—there was the rising bell, the breakfast bell, the work bell, the school bell, the recall bell, the dinner bell, and again the work bell, the school bell, the recall bell, the supper bell, the night school bell, the retiring bell. It was a drab life" (89-90). At the Navajo boarding school at Fort Defiance, Arizona, in 1903, the schedule listed twenty-three bells, starting with a rising bell at 6:00 A.M. and ending with a retiring bell at 8:00 P.M. (Mitchell 1978, 74).

Flora Greg Iliff, who taught from 1900 to 1901 in a small boarding school on the Hualapai Reservation and in a day school on the Havasupai Reservation, reported that these tribes felt themselves superior to all other races. She recalled an old Walapai man counseling Indian women who were excited about clothes sent from the East, "[T]he white man gives you what he does not want. You forget the old-time things" (Iliff 1954, 18). She remembered that "when a teacher's attention was diverted, the children made a game of slipping about, exchanging seats or leaping through the nearest window" (26). She violated the English-only rules and used older students as translators so that she could teach the younger children. She found that "the duties of too many other positions had been assigned to the teachers to permit efficient work" (89). One visiting supervisor of education for Indian schools was able to get the girls a more varied diet and attractive prints for dresses. As the Indians realized "that the boarding school provided good food, warm clothing and comfortable surroundings for the children," they brought their children in willingly (228).

Zitkala-Sa (1985, 95), a Sioux teacher, found her white coworkers around 1900 as interested in "self-preservation quite as much as Indian education." When she questioned why an opium-addicted teacher was allowed to continue working, she was told it was because she had a "feeble mother" to support. School inspectors from Washington saw special sample work rather than students' everyday work. Golden (1954), when she taught in Oklahoma around 1905-6, worked with a staff who were prejudiced against Indians one year and a morphine-addicted teacher.

The Shoshone Esther Horne (Horne and McBeth 1998) received her high school diploma from Haskell in 1928 and returned there for junior college but started teaching first and second grades at the Eufaula (Oklahoma) Boarding School in February 1929, when she was just nineteen years old, because of a teacher shortage. She taught thirty-five Creek students, some of whom were overage, some of whom were native speakers of Creek, and some of whom were Black Creek Freedmen. She used peer tutoring and allowed students with good English-language skills to translate for those students whose English was poor. According to Horne, both in Haskell's Outing System, which she liked, and at Eufaula she was discouraged from socializing with black cooks and servants.

All female employees at Eufaula had to sign in and out to leave campus, and she was the only Indian teacher. She secretly attended Creek Stomp Dances, saying, "[T]hrough the tribal network at Haskell, we learned each other's culture" (Horne and McBeth 1998, 57). She soon married her Haskell sweetheart and transferred in 1930 to Wahpeton Indian School in North Dakota, where her husband worked in the school's power plant. There she taught thirty-six fourth-graders, many of whom were teenagers, and later taught classes with as many as fifty-two students. At Wahpeton, students attended class all day, and they no longer had to march and wear uniforms.

Horne recounts that conditions for Indian students improved at Wahpeton between 1930 and her retirement in 1965. Over time, discipline was relaxed and students were allowed more freedom regarding how they dressed. Boys and girls were able to socialize and leave campus more frequently, and they ate better. She was encouraged by the Indian Office to take summer courses in Progressive Education (see chap. 8) and Indian studies, formed an Indian club, and went on to demonstrate to other teachers how to integrate Indian studies into their classrooms. In 1982, long after her retirement, she testified before a congressional committee against closing Wahpeton and two other boarding schools, stating that most boarding schools were a refuge for students from dysfunctional families.

Horne's long tenure at Wahpeton was an exception. The best and the worst teachers were frequently transferred. It was difficult to fire the former under Civil Service regulations, and it was required that the latter be transferred on receiving a promotion. Kneale (1950) felt that the frequent change in school personnel hurt the quality of Indian education. In his attack on the spoils system, Superintendent of Indian Schools Daniel Dorchester wrote years earlier:

> Frequent changes in the personnel of the Indian Bureau at Washington, at the agencies, and also in the schools is one of the serious obstacles in the way of systematizing and making effectual the work of Indian school education. . . . It takes not a little time for new comers to gain the confidence of the Indians, old or young; and when gained it is no small loss to sacrifice this confidence. Indeed, frequent changes are the bane of the Indian Service. (*ARCIA* 1890, 269-70)

THE BOARDING SCHOOL LEGACY

Government boarding schools had their successes and failures. Successful students, urged on by Pratt and others to speak out, were the ones who were mostly heard by whites, but the failures provided a core of resistance to both assimilation and education. The ethnocentric approach of the Indian Bureau can be criticized from the viewpoint of cultural relativism at the end of the twentieth century, but it is hard to imagine how any more enlightened policy could have been followed in the nineteenth century. Even the mission schools that used Indian languages sought total assimilation.

Even today, as more Indian schools are indigenized with the hiring of Indian teachers and contextualized with the use of culturally appropriate curriculum under local control, problems remain. Based on his one-year observation in an Indian-controlled boarding school for Pueblo students that met New Mexico state standards, the educational psychologist Alan Peshkin (1997) tackled the persistent question of why American Indian students' academic achievement is still below average. Peshkin found that the poor academic performance at the "Indian High School" he studied could not be attributed to "savage inequalities" (Kozol 1991) in the funding of education in the United States that prevents schools from hiring good teachers and having adequate facilities and instructional materials. The school received a combination of BIA funding and various federal grants, and it was staffed with well-educated teachers. The school had the highest percentage of Indian teachers of any high school in New Mexico. In addition, he found that the students' parents valued education.

The goal of the school was to prepare students for college. But its success was limited. Students would participate with sustained effort and enthusiasm in basketball, but Peshkin (1997, 5) "regrettably . . . saw no academic counterpart to this stellar athletic performance."

> In class, students generally were well-behaved and respectful. They were not rude, loud, or disruptive. More often they were indifferent. . . . [T]eachers could not get students to work hard consistently, to turn in assignments, to participate in class, or to take seriously . . . their classroom performance. (Peshkin 1997, 5)

To explain why these students did not enthusiastically embrace education, Peshkin enlarges on the cultural discontinuity (two worlds) theory of academic failure. He makes a good argument for the "student malaise" he describes and for its sources in the ambivalent attitude of the Pueblo toward schooling. After hundreds of years of contact with

European immigrants, Indians have good reason to be suspicious of anything European, and schools, even Indian-controlled ones with Indian administrators and Indian teachers, as Peshkin points out, are alien institutions as far as Indian cultures are concerned.

Many Indians, under cultural attack from all the forces of the majority society, are obsessed with cultural survival. Pueblo culture emphasizes fitting into the group and participating in the life of the village— "standing in" versus "standing out"—in contrast to the individualism found outside the Pueblo. "Schooling is necessary to become competent in the very world that Pueblo people perceive as rejecting them"; school is a place of "becoming white" (Peshkin 1997, 107, 117).

According to Peshkin, "imbued with the ideal of harmony in their community life, Pueblo parents send their children to schools that promote cultural jangle" (117). The sounds in the school are not particularly discordant. The discordance is between what the Pueblo communities teach their young and what the schools teach, and this discordance goes far beyond just the matter of teaching Pueblo languages in the home and English in schools.

The Pueblo have resisted literacy in their own languages as something "white." This resistance has probably been strengthened because the initial proponents of Native language literacy were missionaries who used reading and writing to more quickly introduce Indians to the Bible, catechisms, hymns, and other materials in order to promote conversion to Christianity.

Federal and state governments continue to use schools to foster the assimilation of Indian children into the dominant culture. Today, we call this a "subtractive" or "submersion" educational process. Thus, while education is ostensibly supported by parents, "because the school is fundamentally an ambiguous institution [an Indian-controlled school with an essentially non-Indian curriculum], ambivalence runs deep" (Peshkin 1997, 112). Ambivalence is a poor motivator for academic success.

CHAPTER SEVEN

STUDENTS AND PARENTS

Upon enrolling, boarding and day school Indian students were reclothed, regroomed, and renamed. They found it difficult to adjust to schools that devalued their families' way of life and were taught in an alien tongue. Some were eager to learn and, despite hardships, adjusted well to their new settings. Others resisted by running away or by refusing to cooperate. Some began to identify with their captors and to despise their own upbringing.

Hoke Denetsosie, a Navajo, described his boarding school experiences at Leupp, Arizona, in the early twentieth century:

Conditions at the school were terrible. . . . Food and other supplies were not too plentiful. We were underfed; so we were constantly hungry. Clothing was not good, and, in winter months, there were epidemics of sickness. Sometimes students died, and the school would close the rest of the term.

It was run in a military fashion, and rules were very strict. A typical day went like this: Early in the morning at 6 o'clock we rose at the sound of bugles. We washed and dressed; then we lined up in military formation and drilled in the yard. For breakfast, companies formed, and we marched to the dining room, where we all stood at attention with long tables before us. We recited grace aloud, and, after being seated, we proceeded with our meal. . . .

Some teachers and other workers weren't very friendly. When students made mistakes they often were slapped or whipped by the disciplinarian who usually carried a piece of rope in his hip pocket.

At the end of the term in May parents and other visitors would come to the school. (Johnson 1977, 83–85)

At the Tuba City Boarding School north of Leupp, Paul Blatchford was exhorted, "Speak English! Speak English!" and learned to sing "Ten Little Indian Boys." After Christmas in second grade the students could understand English and start learning to read books, including *Little Black Sambo* (Johnson 1977, 180).

STARTING SCHOOLS AND SCHOOL

While parents sometimes voluntarily sent their children to Indian schools and a few students even ran away to school, the process was traumatic for most Indian children. An example the government's efforts is the history of Hopi schooling. The government started to show interest in providing schools for the Hopi in Arizona Territory in 1884. Twenty Hopi leaders petitioned Indian Commissioner J. D. C. Atkins in 1887 for a school, pledging to "gladly send [their] children." However, it is likely that they did not fully understand the import of the document they were signing, and many Hopis quickly became disenchanted with schooling when they found that Christian religious holidays, Sunday included, were recognized by the schools but not important Hopi ceremonies, which their children were forbidden to attend (James 1974).

A boarding school opened at Keams Canyon in 1887. Edmund Nequatewa who attended this school in the late 1890s recalled that usually students were able to complete only the third grade and learned little English (Seaman 1993). Nequatewa's grandfather told him,

The white man said that if the school should be established and the children go to school and learn to speak and write the English language, they will become our leaders, that they will be able to compete with the white man. At that time it was decided that every clan among the Hopi people must be represented by a child from his group at the school. . . .

Whatever you do here at school, try to learn all you can, because you have only a limited time. It has been agreed upon that every child must only come four years. (Seaman 1993, 96–97)

Nequatewa could not remember a rule that forbade speaking Hopi and said all the students spoke their language. After four years he could not carry on a conversation in English: "The only thing they were learning in the classes was reading and arithmetic. I could read all right, but many times I really won't understand what I was reading about. I could pronounce the words, that's all. . . . If a child could count up to one hundred, they will pass a grade" (Seaman 1993, 95).

In 1899, after four years at Keams Canyon, Nequatewa went to Phoenix Indian School. This time his grandfather told him,

> Whatever you do when you get down there, do the best you can. See what you can learn, but first of all my advice is to choose that book of knowledge which holds the truth of what I have been telling. The book that holds the truth is a black book, and it is about that thick. The white people keep it at the bottom of the pile, where Hopis cannot see it. If we ever learn the truth of this book, then we can compete with the white man. This is why he is afraid to teach us right now. This is the truth that I want to know. . . .
>
> [Missionaries] told me that it was the true knowledge that they had brought to us. They said that when you are baptized into this religion you are not going to hell. They said that you are going to heaven, but I doubt it. They said that hell is a firepit where the bad people be thrown in.
>
> Hearing all this, I wanted to go further into it, that I might understand and find out the truth. But how will I ever do it? You have to go, and be sure to choose this book and find out all you can about the truth. But one thing you must never do: don't ever get baptized into this thing until you bring me back the truth. . . . [T]here is a lot of bait thrown out, I find. A lot of sweet talk. Don't ever believe it! (Seaman 1993, 111–12)

However, his grandfather added that if he was convinced by the information Nequatewa brought back, then they would both be baptized. Since Christianity was actively promoted and taught in all government Indian schools, Nequatewa would certainly have learned about the "book" (see fig. 15). He and six girls went by wagon and then train to Phoenix. At one point he was nearly left behind because no one had told him there was a washroom on the train. The heat and salty water at Phoenix Indian School was a real strain for him, but an uncle took him around. The uncle, who was also a student but a grade ahead,

Girls praying, Phoenix Indian School, 1900. Photograph courtesy of the National Archives NWDNS-75-EXP-2B.

told him that learning to smoke and chew tobacco was the only way for him to become a man.

In 1899 the Keams Canyon superintendent called on troops to enforce a smallpox quarantine at his school. Troops were used to overcome the Hopi's resistance to vaccination (Wilken 1955). Charles E. Burton was appointed the new superintendent of Keams Canyon school in July 1899 at the age of twenty-seven. His efforts to put Hopi children in school produced considerable resistance. Burton was shocked by what he described as the "revolting and immoral and heathenish uncivilized exposure of human forms" in Hopi dances (quoted in Whiteley 1988, 93–94). Over the protest of missionaries, Burton ordered all Hopi men to have their hair cut. Another smallpox scare led to all Hopis being quarantined and vaccinated. The Oraibi villagers resisted and were forced to be vaccinated.

To back the government's policy of cultural genocide, the Indian Bureau set out to break up Indian tribalism through the allotment of communal lands. Even more than schooling, the Hopi disliked the government's allotment policy, which started in 1887. The purpose of allotment was to break up the tribe's communal landholdings and give individual Indians small landholdings. The Hopis protested by pulling up the surveyors' stakes (Whiteley 1988).

Schooling was a major issue in the factional division among the Hopi, especially in the village of Oraibi, a majority of whose residents did not want their children to go to the white man's school. These residents became known as the Hostiles; those who supported schooling were called Friendlies. The Hostiles practiced a strategy of delay, saying they would send children, but they did not. Loololma, an Oraibi leader, was sent to Washington, D.C., in 1890. Seeing this bustling modern city changed his attitude about the Hopi needing education. However, a company of Tenth Calvary troops was sent out during winter 1890–91 and again in summer 1891 from Fort Wingate near Gallup, New Mexico, to force Hopi parents in Oraibi to send their children to school. A small detachment sent in June 1891 was met with barricades, and the lieutenant in command called for reinforcements and Hotchkiss guns. Four companies were sent the following month armed with two Hotchkiss guns, which were fired to intimidate the Hostiles. Nine leaders of the Hostiles were arrested and taken to Fort Wingate. The Indian agent requested that the troops destroy part of Oraibi with their guns, but the colonel declined (Whiteley 1988).

A day school was built below Oraibi in 1892, but it enrolled only the children of Friendlies. The government gave up attempting to enforce allotment of Hopi lands in 1894. The acting Indian agent, Capt. Constant Williams, held a meeting in Oraibi in November 1894 and reported:

> [The Hostiles said that] they do not want to follow the Washington path; that they do not want their children to go to school; that they do not want to wear white man's clothes; that they do not want to eat white man's food; that they do want the white man to let them alone and allow them to follow the Oraibi path; and they totally denounced the Friendlies for departing from the Oraibi path. (Quoted in Whiteley 1988, 86)

Williams brought two cavalry troops in November 1894 and arrested nineteen Hostiles and shipped them to the military prison on Alcatraz Island in San Francisco Bay, where they remained at hard labor until their release in August 1895. Indian agent Leo Crane (1929) called for troops to search houses for Hopi children as late as 1911. A number of young married Hopi men were arrested and shipped to Carlisle Indian school. Their wives got remarried in order to survive (Kabotie 1977).

Belle Axtell Kolp, who taught for a short time at Oraibi Day School in 1903, testified to the Sequoyah League about all that was done "in the name of the 'Big Chief at Washington'" and that "[w]henever a punishment was threatened or carried out, it was represented to the Indians that it was by 'Washington's' orders" (quoted in Lummis [1903] 1968, 43). She stated:

When I began work at Oraibi, the daily attendance at the school was about 125 children. There were two schoolrooms and two teachers. When I left, there were 174 children in school, and still two teachers—one of them having in her charge 96 children, whose ages ranged from less than four years to others who were 18 or 20. One of the latter—a girl—was said to have been married. The school age is from 5 to 18. There were, when I left, at least a dozen little ones in school who were not more than four years of age. They were not strong enough to walk the mile which lay between the village where the Indians live and the schoolhouse. These children, with others, were taken forcibly from their homes by an armed body of Government employees and Navajo Indians, under leadership of C. E. Burton [the Hopi Indian agent]. . . .

About 10 o'clock on the night of Feb. 2, 1903, the raiding party . . . arrived at the school grounds from Government headquarters at Keam's Cañon. The Navajos, armed with rifles, were sent to surround the Hopi village in the night. The next morning . . . snow thickly covered the ground, and was still falling. Those children who could be found, who were not already enrolled in the school, were sent down to the school under guard. (Quoted in Lummis [1903] 1968, 43–44)

A second raid took place on February 5. According to Kolp,

Men, women and children were dragged almost naked from their beds and houses. Under the eyes and the guns of the invaders they were allowed to put on a few articles of clothing, and then—many of them barefooted and without any breakfast, the parents and grandparents were forced to take upon their backs such children as were unable to walk the distance (some of the little ones entirely nude) and go down to the school building, through the ice and snow in front of the guns of the dreaded Navajos. They were kept there all day, until after six in the evening, while clothing could be made or found for them. (Quoted in Lummis [1903] 1968, 45)

Kolp reported that the real reason for increasing the school's enrollment was to justify the establishment of a boarding school at Oraibi, which would mean higher salaries for the staff. Whereas Kolp thought there were not enough rations for the enlarged school, Helen Sekaquaptewa (1969, 12), who was born in 1898, recalled going weeks without enough food in her village and that "tradition required that it appear that [she] was forced into school." She also reported that the Friendlies' children threw rocks at and teased the Hostiles' children (14, 91). Overall, she liked school because it was "pleasant and warm inside" (14). During her four years at Keams Canyon, she saw her father return from prison, and her mother visited twice. Her success in school caused her to be "razzed" by the other students. In 1915 she completed sixth grade and needed her parents' consent to leave the reservation to further her education. She "begged" the Indian agent, Leo Crane, to allow her to go to Phoenix Indian School (Sekaquaptewa (1969).

Another Hopi, Polingaysi Qöyawayma (1964), remembered good times and bad times, feast and famine, bountiful rains and searing droughts in her Hopi village of Oraibi in the 1890s. There were times "people clawed through refuse piles looking for kernels of corn they had discarded in more prosperous times" (8). "From earliest childhood she had been taught to pray. Getting up at dawn and going to the mesa's edge to voice one's thankfulness for life and all good was part of the established Hopi pattern" (15). Into this life came H. R. Voth, a Mennonite missionary, who hired her father as a laborer. Despite her father's employment by missionaries, when a schoolhouse was built, Polingaysi's mother hid her from Navajo policemen "carrying guns and clubs" who gathered up children to enroll in school. Sometime after her sister was caught and enrolled in a Indian Office day school below Third Mesa, Polingaysi became curious and followed her sister to school. At the school her teacher gave her a new name, Bessie, and did not allow her to speak the only language she knew, Hopi. In her autobiography, Polingaysi describes students being booted and slapped and one student having an eraser shoved in her mouth for not behaving the way the teachers wished. Polingaysi, reflecting the even-tempered nature of her people, became very cautious and seems to have avoided such punishments. Many years later, after a thirty-year teaching career, Polingaysi concluded that "[s]he and her companions had been treated like dumb little animals because they did not speak the language of the school authorities" (174).

In 1906 the pressures exerted on her village led to a split whereby the progressive faction, the Friendlies, literally pushed the conservative antischool faction, the Hostiles, out of town. Her grandfather proposed this less violent solution to the bitter dispute. On the day of the shoving match, Polingaysi's parents sent her to stay for the day with a Mennonite missionary. That same year she met a wagonload of students going to "the land of oranges." She wanted to go but found out that her parents needed to provide written permission. Told at first that she could not go, she hid in the wagon and was caught. But she then managed to convince her parents to let her go. She rode by wagon to Winslow, Arizona, and boarded a train to Sherman Institute in Riverside, California, where she spent four years without returning home. There, "little ones and teenagers attended classes and worked wherever they were assigned" (63). The school had a farm where students worked, and food was plentiful.

The Hopi were not the only Indians who opposed their children going to school. In 1892 Navajo Indian agent David L. Shipley, described as "profane and given to drinking more heavily than an Indian agent should," took a small party of Navajo policemen to Round Rock to get children for the Fort Defiance Boarding School (McNitt 1962, 278). He had a quota to meet of thirty-four children from the area. He and a policeman were dragged from a trading post co-owned by a Navajo, Chee Dodge, and beaten. Shipley sustained a broken nose. Dodge helped to rescue and defend him in the trading post until a party of eleven soldiers came to the rescue from Fort Defiance. Shipley returned to Fort Defiance without any children (McNitt 1962).

Frank Mitchell (1881–1967), a Navajo who started school in Fort Defiance when he was about thirteen years old, recalled that Navajo leaders tried to persuade the people to send their children to school; in return, the leaders were given wagons, farm equipment, and other benefits. However, families were rarely convinced:

> One of the main objections to enrolling the children was that white people were not Navajos. They are foreign people, people of another race. The

People were suspicious; they thought that if they put their children in school, the white people would take the children away from them and either kill them or do something so they would never be seen again. Even if they remained alive, the children would just go further and further from their homes, and before the People knew it, they would never come back. That's what they used to say. (Mitchell 1978, 55–56)

When forced, the Navajos sent to school their least useful children. Earlier, in 1886, the Mescalero Apache Indian agent had reported:

Everything in the way of persuasion and argument having failed, it became necessary to visit the camps unexpectedly with a detachment of police, and seize such children as were proper and take them away to school, willing or unwilling. Some hurried their children off to the mountains or hid them away in camp, and the police had to chase and capture them like so many wild rabbits. This unusual proceeding created quite an outcry. The men were sullen and muttering, the women loud in their lamentations and the children almost out of their wits with fright. (Quoted in Adams 1995, 211)

In his 1910 book, *The Indian and His Problem*, former Commissioner of Indian Affairs Francis Leupp declared:

The competition between the schools [to recruit students] had become so intense that sometimes two canvassers would lay hold of one child and each would devise schemes to steal it away from the other. The parents, in many cases, had to be entrapped into consenting, as they had had so sad experiences in the past with children whom they had been lured into letting go, only to have them sent home in the last stages of consumption. (146)

Leupp had issued circulars in 1908 to prevent the coercion of parents and the sending of very young children away to boarding schools, but sometimes parents wanted younger children to attend schools with their older siblings.

Much later, Willard Beatty, director of BIA education from 1936 to 1952, recounted a story told by Clyde Blair, the first director of Navajo Education Programs and former superintendent of Albuquerque Indian School, about how he "recruited" Navajo students for his school on "orders from Congress":

He and a Navajo policeman had started out in a buckboard drawn by two horses and went from hogan to hogan looking for children. As they got in sight of a hogan and the Indians recognized who they were and guessed at their purpose, the children could be seen darting out of the hogan and running into the brush. Whereupon the Navajo policeman stood up in the buckboard and fired a shotgun into the air to scare the children and make them stop running—if possible. Then he jumped out of the wagon and ran after the children. If he caught them (and many times he didn't), he wrestled them to the ground, tied their legs and arms, and with the help of Mr. Blair put them in the back part of the wagon, where they lay until Blair had gathered in the quota for the day. Then they returned to the Albuquerque school and enrolled the children they had captured. (Beatty 1961, 12)

These children spoke no English and could not understand what was happening. Furthermore, according to Beatty, there were no Navajo matrons or teachers who could speak Navajo at the Albuquerque Indian School to explain to the children what was happening. He also noted, "The average Navajo parents felt a school education was a relatively useless thing, so far as they could see," and they sent their children to school in rotation, keeping some at home to herd sheep (1961, 14).

Testimony by Dana Coolidge before the Senate Subcommittee of the Committee on Indian Affairs in 1932 included the following:

I am making a brief statement of my experience with what I consider the greatest shame of the Indian Service—the rounding up of Indian children to be sent away to government boarding schools. This business of "kid catching," as it is called, is rarely discussed with outsiders, either by the Indians or by the government employees, but during my numerous visits to the Navajo Reservation I have picked up the knowledge of its working.

In the fall the government stockmen, farmers, and other employees go out into the back country with trucks and bring in the children to school. Many apparently come willingly and gladly; but the wild Navajos, far back in the mountains, hide their children at the sound of a truck. So stockmen, Indian police, and other mounted men are sent ahead to round them up. The children are caught, often roped like cattle, and taken away from their parents, many times never to return. They are transferred from school to school, given white people's names, forbidden to speak their own tongue, and when sent to distant schools are not taken home for three years. (Quoted in DeJong 1993, 117–18)

Frank Mitchell (1978), who began to attend school in about 1894, recalled having to learn to button and unbutton his pants and use silverware to eat. On Saturdays he got to shower, put on clean clothes, and loaf around. On Sundays the children were preached to by various ministers and priests but with no translation: "They talked about God, and most of us did not understand it. So I guess they were just talking to themselves" (65). The teachers, who also knew no Navajo, accomplished little more. Elders ridiculed Mitchell and other students when they returned home because their hair had been cut short. Mitchell, who only had a few years of schooling, went on to become a Navajo Blessingway singer and tribal councilman.

Irene Stewart (1980), a Navajo born in 1907, recalled traveling on horseback with a policeman to school. She found school "a shocking experience," starting with "a huge bathtub full of water." She "screamed and fought" but had to reconcile herself to "a strange place with strange people, food, clothing." She said, "I was homeless. No one cared for me as my old home folks had. I feared everything" (15). She remembered having a kind teacher who taught using colored balls. Later teachers were "mean and strict," and her studies were very hard. She recalled standing and ironing for hours until her "legs ached far into the night." "We were too tired to study," she said (17). But she also missed the fun she had at school.

James McCarthy (1985), a Tohono O'odham, described how he and the other boys were too ashamed to eat after getting their hair cut on entering Phoenix Indian School in 1906. Jim Whitewolf (1969), a Kiowa Apache, recalled that when he started school in 1891 in Oklahoma, he played with blocks while the teacher taught the other students because he could not understand English. The Hopi artist Fred Kabotie (1977) recalled the common practice of being assigned a new "Christian" name when he started school, often because the non-Indian teachers could not pronounce students' tribal names.

Often, students, especially elementary students, who were sent to boarding schools were orphans, even in the early 1920s and 1930s, as Lomawaima (1994) found at the Chilocco boarding school. In the 1990s students in the few remaining boarding schools tended to be from dysfunctional families or Navajos living in remote areas of their reservation where roads became impassable for weeks during the winter.

VOCATIONAL CURRICULUM

Once students got to boarding school, they received half-day instruction in vocational education in order to learn good work habits, maintain the school, and prepare for a career once they finished school. Lomawaima (1994, 68), in her history of Chilocco, reported that in 1927 twelve boys at the school bakery produced "2,000 loaves, 2,000 buns, 900 cinnamon rolls, 220 pies, 900 cookies, 900 slices of gingerbread and cake, and 1,800 pieces of cornbread" weekly. In 1931 the school's laundry was processing annually "475,000 towels; 98,000 sheets; 35,000 shirts; and tens of thousands of nightgowns, pillowcases, bloomers, and long underwear" (68). She concluded from her study of Chilocco, "Much of the work subsumed under 'trades training' could fairly be called drudge work, with little or no educational value," but it did lower the cost of running the school (68–69). A Chilocco student recalled being paid 25 cents a day for cutting grass all day during the summer.

A student in the 1920s remembered his vocational training as follows:

I'll never know whether I volunteered or was assigned the Dairy Barn. . . . I found out later that was probably the least desired assignment as far as vocational was concerned. Really it wasn't that bad. . . . [I]t was a lot of fun, but it was a lot of hard work. . . . We milked forty-five cows, I believe, twice a day. We also fed 'em, put up feed and mended the fences, separated the cream, they had automatic milkers incidentally, and I guess the prize job down there was being a milker. . . . They put us in a dormitory of our own, and the night watchman would wake us up at 3:30 in the morning and we'd milk the cows. (Lomawaima 1994, 74)

In the early 1920s the Chilocco school superintendent described the girls' vocational training:

Half of the vocational girls are detailed to the sewing room. Of the remaining half, five-eighths are assigned to the laundry, the balance divided among

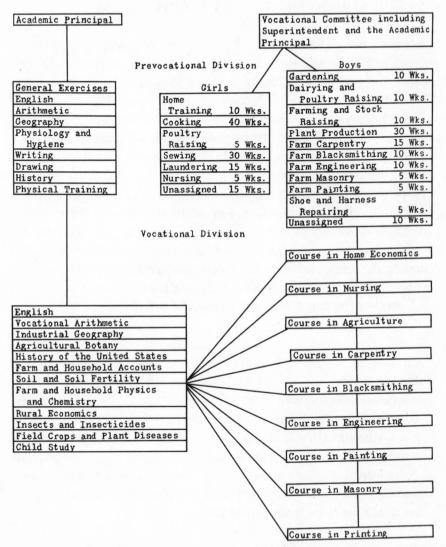

Diagrammatic Representation
of the
Course of Study

Superintendent

Academic Principal

Vocational Committee including
Superintendent and the Academic
Principal

Prevocational Division

Boys	
Gardening	10 Wks.
Dairying and Poultry Raising	10 Wks.
Farming and Stock Raising	10 Wks.
Plant Production	30 Wks.
Farm Carpentry	15 Wks.
Farm Blacksmithing	10 Wks.
Farm Engineering	10 Wks.
Farm Masonry	5 Wks.
Farm Painting	5 Wks.
Shoe and Harness Repairing	5 Wks.
Unassigned	10 Wks.

General Exercises
English
Arithmetic
Geography
Physiology and
  Hygiene
Writing
Drawing
History
Physical Training

Girls	
Home Training	10 Wks.
Cooking	40 Wks.
Poultry Raising	5 Wks.
Sewing	30 Wks.
Laundering	15 Wks.
Nursing	5 Wks.
Unassigned	15 Wks.

Vocational Division

English
Vocational Arithmetic
Industrial Geography
Agricultural Botany
History of the United States
Farm and Household Accounts
Soil and Soil Fertility
Farm and Household Physics
  and Chemistry
Rural Economics
Insects and Insecticides
Field Crops and Plant Diseases
Child Study

Course in Home Economics

Course in Nursing

Course in Agriculture

Course in Carpentry

Course in Blacksmithing

Course in Engineering

Course in Painting

Course in Masonry

Course in Printing

Diagrammatic representation of the Course of Study. From the 1917 *Annual Report of the Commissioner of Indian Affairs*, 10.

kitchen, dining room and homes. Not more than one-fourth of the kitchen detail is vocational so that at all times there are enough prevocational girls to keep the work going. As a result, we have a large detail of vocational and a small detail of prevocational girls in the sewing room and laundry. . . . Prevocational girls entering Chilocco are always assigned to the kitchen/ dining room if they are large enough. A double detail of kitchen/dining room girls work before breakfast, after breakfast and after supper. (Lomawaima 1994, 84)

Lomawaima's interviews of Chilocco alumni in her book, *They Called in Prairie Light*, reveal that they valued the school as a place where they "learned to work" (1994, 71). The extent of the vocational curriculum in the larger boarding schools can be seen in figure 16. Vocational education continued to be an important part of Indian education into the 1950s (see figs. 17, 18).

Daisy Pino, Acoma, doing on-the-job training at Brown's Cafe in Albuquerque, New Mexico, 1951. Photograph courtesy of the National Archives NWDNS-75-N-ALB-6.

Mary Parker, Seminole, at Brighton Day School on the Glades County Reservation in Florida, 1941. Photograph courtesy of the National Archives NWDNS-75-N-SEM-60.

INAPPROPRIATENESS OF THE CURRICULUM

Superintendent Leo Crane reported that Hopi parents "know a thousand times more than the white instructor for agriculture, and have demonstrated it to his discomfiture; and therefore they are suspicious or contemptuous of all other white instructors" (RSS #24, pt. 4, 1917, 66). Parents were not the only ones who thought the curriculum in Indian schools was inappropriate. Agency superintendents found that the equipment, such as steam presses that the students were trained to operate in off-reservation boarding schools, was not available at home. Furthermore, the knowledge "of Shakespeare, and the higher arts" they gained in these schools did not compensate for their lack "of the homely art of physical labor" (RSS #24, pt. 4, 1917, 61). In addition, the individual craftsmanship in harness making, blacksmithing (see fig. 19), printing, carpentry, masonry, and other trades offered in Indian schools were rapidly becoming outmoded by mass-production in factories. Luther Standing Bear (1928, 1933) had wanted to learn to be a carpenter

Blacksmithing class, Indian Training School (Chemawa), Forest Grove, Oregon, 1882. Photograph courtesy of the National Archives NWDNS-75-IP-1-23.

or take academics all day at Carlisle Indian Industrial School but was assigned to tinsmithing, which was Pratt's trade. Returning home, he found that there was no demand for tinware because of all the tinware supplied by Carlisle. For example, the May 10, 1889, issue of Carlisle's *Indian Helper* reported, "Six thousand articles of tin-ware have been packed and will be sent this month to the Utes, Wichitas, Sioux, Blackfeet, Gros Ventres, Cheyenne and Arapahoes and Assinaboines. The balance of the tin-ware will be shipped this fall. The wagon shop has eight wagons ready to ship with the harness and tin-ware."

Lomawaima quotes from a letter written by one of the first graduates from Chilocco who went on to become a teacher:

Yes, I graduated from Chilocco after completing about seventh grade work. There had to be a *first graduating* class, and unfortunately mine was the one. . . . Chilocco has my gratitude for her training in sewing-room, assistant matron's work and about three years of good, solid class-room work; and this out of eight years attendance. Five years of important foundation work were practically lost—due to incompetent primary teachers. . . . [T]he Arkansas City public schools, Carlisle, Chicago, Colorado Springs and Los Angeles summer schools and the Philadelphia Training School (for Kindergarten and Primary Teachers), deserve much credit for rendering me excellent instruction in Literary work. (1994, 25; original emphasis)

The superintendent of the Taholah, Washington, Agency reported a student commenting, "I graduated in scrubbing and they teach nothing else" (RSS #24, pt. 5, 1917, 157). The superintendent of the Yakima, Washington, Agency commented that most returned students had not completed the BIA course of study, and the Omaha (Nebraska) Agency superintendent noted that the course of study was not always appropriate.

Anne Phelps Kopta, who taught at Phoenix Indian School from 1908 to 1918, wrote in her introduction to the autobiography of one of her Pima students:

> Her experience with academic subjects was extremely satisfactory. The courses of study at the school were not designed to make whites of Indians, as is sometimes charged, but to give young Indian students a basic education in the three R's, to acquaint them with the rudiments of many different trades, and to introduce them to the world off the Indian reservation. (Shaw 1974, xiii)

However, that Pima student noted, "Most of us spent two years in each grade in order to master the difficult English language along with the subject matter," so that students were often eighteen to twenty-two years old when they graduated from eighth grade (Shaw 1974, 137).

REGIMENTATION

The superintendent at Towaco, Colorado, thought that life was too easy at boarding schools and that the schools were too large for students to receive individual attention:

> [Students are] herded together . . . like so many sheep. They get up by the bell. They eat by the bell. They go to classes by the bell. They go to bed by the bell. Their individuality is crushed to the Earth. Their teachers must think of them as classes. There are so many of them that individual thought can not be given.
>
> After three or four years of herding of this kind during the formative period of a boy's life, how can any intelligent man expect a boy to be anything but a machine. (RSS #24, pt. 5, 1917, 119)

At Chilocco the bugle was blown twenty-two times a day. Older students were chosen by school matrons and disciplinarians to help enforce the rules. A student who attended there in the late 1920s recalled, "It was just like in the Army. We had old World War I uniforms, wrap leggins, and high-button collars, and if you can imagine a nine-year-old kid carrying a big Enfield rifle in close order drill, that was all part of it" (Lomawaima 1994, 101). Other alumni recalled being marched everywhere and having to suffer through white glove inspections of their dormitory areas. Coed alumni complained about the drab uniforms they were required to wear. Two Chilocco alumni became so used to being told what to do that in 1904 they wrote the school superintendent for advice. One letter contained a request for permission to date a "well brought-up" young man; the other was a request for advice about getting a divorce (Lomawaima 1994).

In response to continued criticism of off-reservation boarding schools and the adjustment problems faced by returned students, a survey of Indian agency superintendents was conducted in 1917 to determine how well students did after they left the off-reservation boarding schools. A number of superintendents commented that the close supervision at boarding schools failed to prepare students for the independent decision making they would have to do once they left school. The Salt River Agency superintendent declared, "[T]oo much thinking and planning for them has been the practice, and it is with the Indian as in our own case: when a problem has been worked out without assistance, we are stronger and better able to tackle and work out a harder problem" (RSS #24, pt. 5, 1917, 99). Other superintendents in the Indian Office's Returned Student Surveys of 1917 commented on the lack of initiative of returned students.

DISCIPLINE

Frank Mitchell recalled that many boys ran away from school and were punished by having to do chores or getting a whipping. Girls would have to stand in the corner all day. "If you were disobedient in the classroom, they used to hit you on the palm or the back of your hand, and then make you stand in the corner" (Mitchell 1978, 67). Big boys would have to carry a big log on their shoulders and walk back and forth. Thomas Clani, a Navajo, recalled:

> When a student was naughty or did something wrong he was punished immediately. The boys' disciplinarian usually kept a strap, and he used it on the boys when they got out of hand—even just slightly. He also used such punishment as marching us back and forth in front of the boys' dorm for at least five hours on Saturday afternoons while we were supposed to be free to play, carrying signs saying, "I am a bad boy." At that time the parents could do nothing about it when they were told these things by the boys. . . . We were afraid of punishment. We kept our dormitories spotless, and we made our beds. Some of us had to clean the classrooms, too, because there were no custodians to pick up after us. The older boys got odd jobs such as mowing the lawns and weeding the flower gardens to earn a little spending money. (Johnson 1977, 244)

Edmund Nequatewa attended Phoenix Indian School in the first years of the twentieth century. He recalled being hit with a ruler across his face by the principal because he left class hurriedly to find a restroom when he was sick. He broke the ruler, and when the principal picked up another one, he picked up a chair. He broke the window with the chair and jumped out. Nequatewa headed for the superintendent's office to explain what happened, and the superintendent told the principal:

> Now, Miss Harvey, I would do the same thing if I was as sick as he was. You should have asked him the reason, and he could have explained for himself why he had to do that. But you just got all upset and lost your mind. Now, we can't have things going on like this. You would be in more trouble if you had put his eye out. Now, don't ever hit any child in the building anymore. Whipping a child is just using an iron hand. You must realize that there are a lot of other ways you can punish the pupils. (Seaman 1993, 127)

Fred Kabotie (1977), a Hopi born in about 1900 whose father was arrested for not sending his kids to school, recalled being paddled for being late and was told by the other boys to cry in order to get the teacher to stop. He reported having "mean" teachers; even a Hopi teacher he had was mean. Irene Stewart (1980, 18), a Navajo born in 1907, was warned never to run away; runaways "were spanked, and either locked up in a room or made to walk back and forth in front of the girls' and boys' dormitories. If a boy, he was dressed in girl's clothing; if a girl, in boy's clothing" (see also Johnson 1977, 240). Jim Whitewolf (1969) ran away from school three times and was given a choice of punishment: he could spend all Saturday in chapel, or he could be whipped on the palm of his hand. He remembered a fistfight between a school superintendent and a workman who would not strap a student, which led to the firing of the school superintendent. James McCarthy (1985), who attended Phoenix Indian School just before World War I, recalled runaway students being caught and put in the school jail. He reported in his autobiography, "The boys were laid on an empty barrel and whipped with a long leather strap. After that they had to work hard on a long tunnel under the mess hall. Sometimes they were put on a ball and chain. The school's rules were strict, and punishment was hard" (1985, 30). Not liking the school, McCarthy ran away after a year and was not caught.

Helen Sekaquaptewa (1969, 136–37), who started attending Phoenix Indian School in 1915, recalled, "Student life was obnoxious to many students, and discipline was military style. Corporal punishment was given as a matter of course, whipping with a harness strap was administered in an upstairs room to the most unruly. . . . Repeaters [chronic runaways] had their heads shaved and had to wear a dress to school."

In 1925 Chilocco Indian School reported 80 "deserters" in three months; 35 were caught and returned. From January 1 to April 21, 1927, 18 girls and 111 boys AWOL out of a total of 813 students were AWOL at Chilocco. A reward of $3 to $5 was offered for help locating runaways (Lomawaima 1994). In 1906 a visiting officer from the German Imperial Army visited Chilocco to "study methods of discipline and military tactics." "He was very much pleased with his visit, and like other foreigners, did not hesitate to say that he was greatly enlightened and surprised at the thorough manner in which Uncle Sam is training his Red children" (Lomawaima 1994, 20–21).

Despite the strictness at Chilocco, according to the students interviewed by Lomawaima (1994), some of them still secretly made home brew and drank vanilla extract, and some openly went hunting in the surrounding countryside on weekends.

It was reported in 1908 that Chilocco's "school guardhouse" was torn down, but each home (dormitory) retained a small room called a "lock-up" or "jail" for isolating runaways and misbehaving students. These lock-ups "had iron bars on the window and big steel doors" (Lomawaima 1994, 111). Students being punished were given a bread-and-water diet. The use of lock-ups continued at Chilocco until the early 1930s, when, according to Lomawaima, their demise was brought about by the Meriam Report. At Chilocco corporal punishment was the exception rather than the rule, but students recalled being put on the "rock pile" for punishment: "They had this thing, put big rocks in it and it'd grind 'em up and make little ones" (Lomawaima 1994, 110). Another student recalled the use of a "beltline" at Chilocco in the late 1920s. A student with a lot of demerits would have to run a gauntlet of students who would thrash him with their belts. Students who did not behave properly could not graduate at Chilocco even if they had satisfactorily completed their academic and vocational requirements (Lomawaima 1994).

When Esther Horne (Horne and McBeth 1998) enrolled at Haskell Institute in 1924 a demerit system was in place that was enforced by student officers. Students who broke the rules received demerits, which they had to work off by doing menial chores such as cleaning toilets. She also described the use of a "belt line," but she did not know of any students who had been hurt in this process. She felt that "much of the student-to-student discipline was in the form of guidance and coun-seling" (36). By the time Horne arrived at Haskell, runaways were no longer being locked up. Later, in the 1930s, she reported that the prin-cipal at Wahpeton Indian School was fired when he brought back three older AWOL eighth-grade girls roped in a string trotting behind his car. Elaine Salinas (1995) recalled witnessing an eighteen-year-old boy at Wahpeton going through the "belt line." She noted, "That caused a lot of hostility within the student body, which I think is what the staff intended. There was a divide-and-conquer mentality" (81).

Navajo Tribal Council delegate Roger Davis spoke in favor of com-pulsory education in 1947:

> When I ran away [from school] they sent a policeman after me to bring me back and gave me whipping like that. That knocked some sense into me and I did not have the desire to run away. The Government says it cannot

whip children, cannot punish them. How can we get somewhere? I blame the Government. . . . I sent my boy to school at Bacone College. I realize that education is the only salvation for the Navajo tribe. (Iverson 2002b, 102)

Davis's comments need to be interpreted in light of the dramatic increase in the Navajo population, which made it increasingly difficult for the Navajo to make a living in traditional ways.

Another Navajo Tribal Council delegate, Hoskie Cronemeyer, declared in 1952 that he was glad that a policeman had been sent to return him to school during Collier's administration, that there were separate dormitories for boys and girls, and that the students were forced to speak only English so they could learn it. Now, he said, "[v]ery often girls come home [from boarding school] with babies who are supposed to be in school" (Iverson 2002b, 107).

PHYSICAL AND MENTAL HEALTH

Poor nutrition and sanitation, crowding, dilapidated buildings that lacked adequate heat in winter, and other conditions led to health problems among students. At the Rosebud camp schools, a policeman was assigned to each school, and the midday lunch was coffee and hard bread (*ARCIA* 1893). At an on-reservation boarding school where she worked, Estelle Brown (1952, 72) recalled that the "children drank coffee three times daily. For it there was neither sugar nor milk. Butter, cheese, fresh fruit, and vegetables were never seen in that dining room." It was a "daily diet of bread and molasses, coffee, meat and gravy," with eggs on rare occasions. Students "dressed in a frigid room, washed in icy water in an unheated washroom" (73). She recalled that in another school the students were locked overnight in dormitories with just two iron-barred windows and no toilets, resulting in "slop buckets" running over with urine in the morning (114–15). Edmund Nequatewa remembered similar conditions at the school at Keams Canyon:

During the day we would look around on the floor, which was just built out of one-by-twelve boards. It was poor lumber with lots of knots. Those that can't get up to the windows to urinate crawl around the floor at night and urinate through these holes. . . .

It wasn't very long before the warm weather comes around, and the whole place just stunk. Later on, these larger boys couldn't stand it any longer. . . . [They] decided that they will just crap all over the floor, which they did. (Seaman 1993, 91)

When the disciplinarian asked them to clean up the mess, they told him to take the padlock off the door. The upshot was that buckets were provided. However, the bars on the windows of this dormitory were not enough to keep the boys from sneaking out at night to visit the girls dorm.

Lakota John Fire (Fire and Erdoes 1972, 35) recalled the "terrific shock" of going from the "warm womb" of an Indian home "to a strange, cold place," a boarding school, around 1917 when he was fourteen. While writing his memoirs, which were published in 1972, he admitted that school facilities had become better and teachers a little more understanding:

[I]n these fine new buildings Indian children still commit suicide, because they are lonely among all that noise and activity. I know a ten-year-old who hanged herself. These schools are just boxes filled with homesick children. The schools leave a scar. We enter them confused and bewildered and we leave them the same way. When we enter the school we at least know that we are Indians. We come out half red and half white, not knowing what we are. (Fire and Erdoes 1972, 35)

In 1921 Brown (1952) reported that food and clothing appropriations to all Indian schools were cut by 25 percent. Ernest Nelson went to boarding school at Tuba City, Arizona, in the 1920s. He recalled, "Food was scarce. Breakfast was only a bowl of oatmeal, plus one slice of bread and a glass of milk. At noon it was about the same, except that there were two slices of bread" (Johnson 1977, 233). The milk came from the school's own dairy herd. He remembered that the only meat was "boiled pork rind cut into beans" and that "half of the time [the students] were hungry" (Johnson 1977, 233).

Former Indian Commissioner Leupp (1910, 144) noted that large boarding schools, with "their herding practice and their institutional routine, their steam-heated buildings and their physical confinement, furnish ideal conditions for the development of germ diseases." In

1912, 22.7 percent of Indians and 29.8 percent of students were reported
to have trachoma. Attempts to improve conditions in Indian schools
were hampered by new government priorities caused by World War I.
After the war, at the request of Commissioner of Indian Affairs Charles
Burke, an experienced Red Cross public health nurse, Florence Paterson,
spent nine months in the Southwest reporting on Indian health
conditions. Burke buried her scathing criticism of the conditions for
four years. She found that 50 percent of students in the Pima and
Mescalero Apache schools had contracted trachoma. She found health
conditions deplorable:

> This [boarding school] program, combined with the strain of bells, bugles,
> and horns, forming in line five or six lines each day, and the mental struggle
> to combat physical fatigue, could not fail to be exhausting, and the effects
> were apparent in every group of boarding school pupils and in marked
> contrast to the freedom and alertness of pupils in the day schools. One
> gained the impression that the boarding school child must endure real
> torture by being continually "bottled up" and that he somehow never
> enjoyed the freedom of being a perfectly natural child. (Quoted in Adams
> 1995, 135)

Students who spent long years in boarding schools often did not
learn parenting skills that they would have learned had they stayed at
home. A Mormon from Ramah, New Mexico, noted:

> Perhaps the greatest tragedy of the Navajo people was the school system.
> The treaty with the Navajo required education, and the Government
> thought this should be done at boarding schools, most of them quite distant
> from the reservation. Despite rigorous discipline at home, Navajo parents
> have very tender feelings for their children, and the separation of children
> of very young age from their parents was devastating. This was never
> considered. (Quoted in Manuelito 2001, 98)

Estelle Brown (1952, 94) recalled that her school was quarantined during
a measles epidemic at Crow Creek and that "from the dormitory windows we could see blanketed figures squatting in the snow, waiting for
someone to bring them word of their children." Minnie Braithwaite
Jenkins met a teacher at Keams Canyon a few years later who asked her,

"Don't you hate the Navahoes? They are such devils! . . . You can punish and punish them, and still they won't obey." . . .

She told lurid tales of how Navahoes had besieged the Fort Defiance school and had taken the children away by force. She admitted that the children were ill, and that when the parents went to the school to see them the nurses would not allow them to come in. The nurses said *the parents were not clean!* This caused the Navajoes to besiege the school, and they had removed the children by force. (1951, 123; original emphasis)

Braithwaite (1951, 213) recalled telling this teacher, "Why, I have never had to so much as slap a little Navaho. . . . Their parents never have to punish them, either."

In 1931 Frank Mitchell (1978) wrote to the superintendent of Albuquerque Indian School, whom he had known for thirty-one years, to express his grief that his daughter Mary had been sent home from Haskell Institute to die. He was especially disappointed that he was told nothing of her illness during her two years there and that by the time she reached home "she was entirely out of her mind" (303). He called on the schools to notify parents when their children became seriously ill. Lucy Gage (1951, 297) observed the devotion of Indian parents to their children when they could visit them at school: "They came often to the government school, always with them some token of affection for their child, an apple, an orange, some nuts. Evidences of a shared confidence could be seen when a father and his child were in close conversation out on the grounds under a tree. A loving companionship was thus kept alive."

OTHER PROBLEMS

The Ute Mountain Indian School superintendent found that too many Indian school employees were lazy "clock watchers" and accused labor unions of keeping students out of trades (RSS #24, pt. 6, 1917). The superintendent of the Cheyenne and Arapaho Agency in Oklahoma found that students learned in school "that they have been robbed and plundered by the whites," with the result when they came home they felt "white people owe them a living" (RSS #24, pt. 5, 1917, 88). He got three returned students to write their own responses to the Indian

Bureau Returned Students Survey. One, a bureau clerk, indicated that he left school broke and was forced to return home. The trades he had learned in school were out of date and not in demand. The students who baked bread for the schools never learned the extra skills a professional baker would need. School musicians did not learn the popular music that would be in demand, and the pervasive prejudice against anyone looking like an Indian prevented success. Other superintendents gave examples of that prejudice, such as not being allowed to eat in a restaurant.

An Arizona Indian school superintendent criticized the overemphasis on athletics in off-reservation schools, stating that the football team members did not do regular schoolwork and never graduated (RSS #24, pt. 4, 1917, 76). The superintendent of the Winnebago Indian School in Nebraska felt that the schools taught students "a selfish viewpoint rather than a broad one. The question in every case is what will benefit the individual rather than society at large" (RSS #24, pt. 10, 1917, 225). Many of the superintendents indicated that students would be better off in on-reservation schools, where the teachers and the curriculum would be more responsive to the conditions that students would actually face when they finished school. A few recommended the public schools.

RETURNED STUDENTS

The problems faced by students when reintegrating into Indian society after long periods of off-reservation education have a long history. The Six Nations of the Iroquois Confederacy, as reported by Benjamin Franklin, rejected an offer from colonial officials to send their sons to the College of William and Mary in 1745:

> [B]ut you, who are wise must know that different Nations have different conceptions of things; and you will therefore not take it amiss, if our ideas of this kind of education happen not to be the same with yours. We have had some experience of it; Several of our young people were formerly brought up at the colleges of the Northern Provinces; they were instructed in all your Sciences; but, when they came back to us, they were bad runners, ignorant of every means of living in the woods, unable to bear either cold

or hunger, knew neither how to build a cabin, take a deer, or kill an enemy, spoke our language imperfectly, were therefore neither fit for hunters, warriors, nor counsellors; they were totally good for nothing. We are however not the less obliged by your kind Offer, though we decline accepting it: And to show our grateful sense of it, if the Gentlemen of Virginia will send us a dozen of their sons, we will take great care of their Education, instruct them in all we know, and make *Men* of them. (Franklin 1784, 21–22; original emphasis)

Indian Commissioner T. J. Morgan, in his 1890 annual report, quoted an "acute observer" who stated there was "little employment for educated Indians, and there is a general prejudice, among both Indian and white employees, against the young men who have returned from Eastern schools" (*ARCIA* 1890, 265). John H. Seger was critical of the returned students who wore neckties but who had only "a smattering of very poor English" and an inadequate education to make their way in the world (*ARCIA* 1894, 403). In 1893, Cora M. Folsom, the Hampton Institute Indian graduates' correspondent, followed up the lives of 460 former Hampton students, 37 of whom had graduated. Ninety-eight were reported as doing excellent, 219 good, 91 fair, 35 poor, and 17 bad. The poor and bad had either resumed traditional tribal ways ("gone back to the blanket") or taken to drinking and other vices. Of the successful students,

nine had become teachers, nine other school employees, 22 were attending other schools, 15 were missionaries or catechists, and 45 were Indian agency employees, including two medical doctors. Henry H. Lyman (Sioux) was attending Yale Law School. Annie R. Dawsen (Arickaree) graduated from the State Normal School in Framington, Massachusetts, and was teaching under Alfred Riggs at Santee, Nebraska. Susan La Flesche (Omaha) had graduated from the Woman's Medical College in Philadelphia. Thomas Miles (Sac & Fox Agency) wrote back to Hampton, "I am disgusted with *some* of the people who have been sent out here to educate the Indians; in some ways the savage can educate them." (Folsom 1893, 232; emphasis in original)

Of the 460 former Hampton students, 163 had voluntarily stayed in school after their initial enrollment had expired, 56 returned for a second term, and 70 went to other schools after leaving Hampton. Folsom also reported that former Hampton students often showed more interest in their children's education than their own. Survival itself was a major problem for students who had returned to their tribes; out of 640, 110 had died within thirteen years. The successful returned student had to come to terms with traditional tribal values of hospitality and generosity:

> No sooner does a young man, or woman, get a good salary than all his relations, and step-relations and relations-in-law and relations by adoption, immediately spring up in poverty and distress, and are really so needy that it requires a strong heart to turn away from them. Those who have needy families to help or who cannot bear to be called "stingy" and "mean," impoverish themselves, while the absolutely frugal are apt to make enemies and lose a certain amount of influence. There are many who succeed in striking a happy mean and these must command our respect. (Folsom 1893, 322)

Episcopal Bishop William H. Hare of South Dakota wrote a letter of support for the Hampton Institute in which he gave his own explanation for some of the criticisms of the eastern boarding schools:

> Indian youth, like white young people, when they come back to their homes from school or college, are apt to have an exaggerated sense of their own importance and want to have their way. They have ideas of their own, and are harder to manage than ignorant Indians: a disagreeable thing to incompetent guides. They know too much to be easily cheated, and they have too much independence to submit to being treated like dogs. To some this is inconvenient. (Folsom 1893, 490)

Other than one former student who was Sitting Bull's secretary, returned students from Hampton were reported to have resisted the Ghost Dance movement on the Sioux Reservation.

Albert Kneale (1950, 169), who served as a teacher, principal, and Indian agent, wrote that boarding schools did not erase the Indianness of the vast majority of students, although "they were taught to despise every custom of their forefathers, including religion, language, songs, dress, ideas, methods of living." In his autobiography he wrote a vivid description of the homecoming of the returned student after five or more years away at boarding school:

> The Indian agent would receive notice from a distant school advising that a group of returning students was to reach his railway station on a named date. Many times have I met these young people. Full of life, bubbling over with enthusiasm, they came, wearing their hair in the mode of the moment, dressed in the latest creations—on the girls, high-heeled shoes, silken hose, hats and dresses aping the latest style—the boys with patent leather shoes and silk socks, their clothing modishly cut and carefully pressed, and with hats of the latest design on their heads.
>
> I have seen these girls, when they first cast eyes upon their parents, stare in abject horror, then, as the truth dawned upon them, burst into tears. . . . With the girls . . . adjustment came in one of two ways. If their home reservation was located in reasonably close proximity to white settlements, they might seek employment in white homes as cooks, maids, and so forth. Those that failed in this search and those that chose the other alternative . . . in the course of a week or ten days appeared . . . looking not materially different from girls that had never been absent from the reservation. . . .
>
> Those that succeeded in obtaining employment were not so fortunate. . . . After a year or possibly two, these returned to the reservation pregnant or with a baby in their arms, and again the agency school became a haven from which they gravitated back to their homes as had those following the more direct route. Some may say "Were these girls, then, so immoral?" Surely not. It was that, in their simplicity, they had taken for granted that a promise of marriage meant a wedding and a home. (Kneale 1950, 170–72)

Gertrude Golden wrote:

> Short-sighted people have a great deal to say in condemnation of the "return to the blanket" of the educated Indians, little realizing the hardships and disillusionment which await these youths upon leaving their boarding schools. They are trained for a job which cannot be found. They face competition with the whites as well as race prejudice wherever they go. Further, there is the powerful influence of parents and reservation friends who taunt the returning student with charges that he is aping the dress, manners and customs of his white conquerors. (1954, 88)

The anthropologists Clyde Kluckhohn and Dorothea Leighton ([1946] 1962, 141) concluded that 95 percent of Navajo children "went home rather than to white communities, after leaving school, only to find themselves handicapped for taking part in Navajo life because they did not know the techniques and customs of their own people."

Edmund Nequatewa had been told by his grandfather when he went off to school to learn the secrets of the white man's black book. He went to Phoenix Indian School in 1899, and soon after a new superintendent started requiring Bible class every afternoon, which Edmund thought overmuch. Returning home in 1904 after several attempts at running away from school, he told a missionary:

> The only thing you have done for these people whom you have supposedly converted is to take them out of one superstition and get them into another. . . . You have been telling these people that if they miss on Sunday and do not come to church, they are condemned. Now is that not superstition? (Seaman 1993, 166)

The missionary burst into tears. He concluded, "I do not believe that no one really knows what is going to happen hereafter, but this has never been brought out in any publication of any one church or denomination" (Seaman 1993,167).

When Polingaysi Qöyawayma returned home, the poverty of the Hopi land made her heartsick, and she could not return to the old life. She criticized her parents for not buying a white man's bed and table and was unwilling to get married. She tried to turn her parents into white people, and the Hopi elders laughed at her. She quotes her mother as saying, "What shall I do with my daughter, who is now my mother" (Qöyawayma 1964, 69). It was only later she came to realize that her white teachers "had no conception of the true needs of Indian people" (73). Her father traveled forty miles to speak to the new Mennonite missionary, Jacob Frey, about his daughter's problems, and the missionary took her in and gave her a new name, Elizabeth Ruth.

Missionaries saw traditional Hopi beliefs as "utter foolish and abysmal sinfulness" (Qöyawayma 1964, 30). Unable to fit in as a missionary, Polingaysi took advantage of an opportunity to live with a missionary in Newton, Kansas, and to further her education at Bethel Academy from 1912 to 1914. In Kansas she was refused service in a restaurant for being "colored," and again on a rail trip to Pennsylvania she was discriminated against. When she returned home again in summer 1913 an uncle scolded her,

> You proud and stubborn girl! Why are you straying from the Hopi way of life? Don't you know it is not good for a Hopi to be proud? Haven't I told you a Hopi must not pretend to hold himself above his people? Why do you keep trying to be a white man? You are a Hopi. Go Home. Marry in the Hopi way. Have children. . . . Leave these white people who are leading you away from your own beliefs. (90)

She found her parents "unkempt" and saw "women stripped and marched through a dipping vat like so many cattle" to be deloused (106). Again, unable to adjust, she returned to Kansas to further her missionary education. She eventually became an Indian school teacher.

The superintendent of the Western Shoshone Agency in Nevada described how parents and other family members would "ridicule the English tongue, and the dress of civilization brought into the home by the returned member" (RSS #24, pt. 4, 1917, 60). The Cass Lake, Minnesota, superintendent wrote:

> [T]he longer the student has been away from his home in attendance at a non-reservation school the more worthless he is. . . . [T]hose who have spent from one to three years away from home do not lose that love for home and the home people, and when they return are still able to content themselves with conditions and go to work and be fairly good citizens. On the other hand those returning after having spent from six to perhaps fifteen years away find that everything has changed and find themselves an utter stranger, if not an outcast. And there is not much chance for them even if they were inclined to do well. (RSS #24, pt. 5, 1917, 94)

Other superintendents in the 1917 Returned Student Survey reported that returned students were doing well. The feeling of failure experienced by both students and educators was attributed in part to the fact that the value of an off-reservation education was oversold so as to entice students to enroll.

Luther Standing Bear (1933, 236), on returning to his reservation from Carlisle Indian Industrial School, said, "[I began] the battle of my life—the battle with agents to retain my individuality and my life as a Lakota." Returned students were ordered by the agent not to attend traditional gatherings, but Standing Bear, like many others, resisted these efforts.

THE PAN-INDIAN MOVEMENT

An unintended result of the large off-reservation boarding school was the breaking down of barriers between Indian tribes. In the words of Colonel Dodge (1882, 44–45), "[Each tribe had] with vanity not entirely aboriginal, believed in its own infinite superiority, and disdained to learn even a few words of its enemy's language. . . . There were no intermarriages, no social intercourse, no intermingling of any kind, except that of mortal strife."

Although Dodge exaggerated greatly, there was an element of truth in what he said about the divisions between tribes. Boarding schools— by concentrating youth from different tribes for years away from their parents and requiring them to speak English—helped to create a pan-Indian movement, an intertribal identity that finally gave Columbus's inaccurate term "Indian" some semblance of meaning. That the boarding schools were coeducational also led to tribal intermarriage. Another bond that united boarding school Indians was the prejudice they faced within and beyond their school boundaries.

James McCarthy's (1985) account of his schooling illustrates the development of an Indian rather than a tribal identity. He started mission school in 1900 after a tribal policeman told his parents he had to go to school. He did not remember learning anything during the first year. When he transferred to Phoenix Indian School, he recalled riding "on top of the boxcars" to get there. He ran away but later entered Santa Fe Indian School, which did not have the military organization of most BIA boarding schools of the time. By 1911, he recalled, "like most Indian boys, I had forgotten about my home and family" (42). In the summer he went to Colorado to hoe beets. In 1912, when he was seventeen, he wrote:

Kids from all the tribes were like brothers. . . . Those who came here to school with me in 1909 forgot about their parents at home in Arizona. Our parents were poor and could not send us money. Sometimes I thought about my parents and felt badly. However, during the six years I was at school, I never wrote them a letter and I never got one from them. (45)

Esther Horne reported:

We students nurtured a sense of community among ourselves, and we learned so much from one another. Traditional values, such as sharing and cooperation, helped us to survive culturally at Haskell, even though the schools were designed to erase our Indian culture, values, and identities. (Horne and McBeth 1998, 33)

Horne, a part Shoshone from Wyoming, married a Hoopa from California whom she met at Haskell Institute. Boarding schools, which were established to destroy tribal identity, ended up helping to create an Indian identity. Haskell especially took on the role of schooling a pan-Indian leadership, and as more and more graduates from the various Indian schools were employed by the Indian Service and worked with other tribes, it also became a promoter of a pan-Indian identity (Hertzberg 1971).

THE RESULTS

Albert Yava, a Hopi, who started school around 1893–94, wrote in his autobiography:

You have to remember that this school business was new not only to the children but also to most of the people in the villages. There had been a big commotion when the Government gave the order that all the children would have to attend school. There was a lot of resistance. . . . The conservatives—you can call them that or Hostiles—felt very strongly that the white man was cramming his ways down our throats. Many people felt that the Government was trying to obliterate our culture by making the children attend school. And if you want to be honest about it, the schooling the children have been getting over the past seventy-five or eighty years has educated them to the white man's ways but made them less knowledgeable about the traditional ways of their own people. A lot of what they have been taught is good. It makes them able to understand the way the white man thinks, and to compete in the outside world. But at the same time, they aren't getting as much of their own traditions as they should. Something important is being gained, but something important is being lost.

In the years just before I appeared on the scene, the [Hopi] villages were split down the middle over whether to allow the children to be sent to the day schools or boarding schools. (1978, 10)

Another Hopi, Fred Kabotie, recalled:

I've found the more outside education I receive, the more I appreciate the true Hopi way. When the missionaries would come into the village and try to convert us, I used to wonder why anyone would want to be a Christian if it meant becoming like those people. (1977, 12)

However, not all the effects of education were necessarily lost on returned students who went "back to the blanket." Unlike the bitter returned student Slim Girl in Oliver La Farge's Pulitzer Prize–winning novel, *Laughing Boy*, who told the hero, "If ever they come to take a child of ours to school, kill her" ([1929] 1971, 58), Flora Greg Iliff (1954) recalls a Hualapai girl returned from Carlisle who went back to the tribal way of life under family pressure but who was then the first to enroll her children when a mission day school was opened. The supervisor in charge of the Rosebud Agency in South Dakota reported in 1917 that when returned students reached the age of thirty to forty-five they started to take up leadership positions and their schooling showed itself as a definite advantage:

Among these are to be numbered many of the first pupils to Carlisle. These men and woman retain all the staunchness of character of their race and tribe and are putting into operation much of their education and traits acquired in their schooling. They are now the bulwark of all school, church, and temperance work. (RSS #24, pt. 7, 1917, 140)

Returned students acted as intermediaries between tribal and white society. This could often be an uncomfortable position, but it was a very necessary one. Vern Dusenberry (1962, 166) studied the Montana Cree and concluded that the Cree wanted their children educated in white ways but also to know Cree values: "The young people themselves are caught in a trap. On the one hand, they hear the virtues of the white man's education extolled; on the other they listen to their parents reminding them that they are not and can never be white."

Hopi Indian agent Leo Crane (1929, 98) described his Navajo interpreter as "one of those half-educated, half sullen returned students[,] . . . a part of the economic system aimed at cheaply teaching grandfather through his unrespected grandson." The historian Wilbert Ahern (1983) concluded that returned students used their education to become "defenders of community interests" more often than advocates of government policies.

The Crow Agency, Montana, superintendent reported that a Carlisle graduate advised him "that her mother constantly nagged her about wearing white clothes and aping the ways of a white woman, and that when her mother was completely worn out and exhausted her vocabulary along these lines, she invited the neighbors to come in and take up the task, which they did" (RSS #24, pt. 9, 1917, 220). The superintendent of the Ponca Agency in Oklahoma reported, "An old Ponca Indian, now dead, once said that it takes Chilocco three years to make a White man out of an Indian boy, but that when the boy comes home and the tribe has a feast, it takes but three days for the tribe to make the boy an Indian again" (RSS #24, pt. 5, 1917, 88).

James McCarthy (1985) commented on the differences in the schools he attended between 1906 and 1917. He noted in his autobiography that the Phoenix Indian School was much more like the army than either the Santa Fe or Albuquerque schools he attended. Boarding schools varied from place to place as well as over time, and the students varied as well. For example, after 1931 military uniforms at Phoenix Indian School were no longer required and merits and demerits replaced promotion in the ranks for discipline, with demerits meaning extra work maintaining the school. Demerits were given for speaking tribal languages.

Some students adjusted to and even thrived in the boarding school environment, while others could not wait to get away from it. Students who were part white and knew how to speak English before coming to school generally adjusted better than non-English-speaking full-bloods. The mixed reaction to boarding schools can be seen in the recollections of the American Indian Movement leader Dennis Banks (1994), whose teacher in the fourth grade at Wahpeton Boarding School was Esther Horne. Banks wrote,

> My memories are rooted in the military boarding schools I attended in Minnesota, North Dakota, and South Dakota during the 30s and 40s. Even now, the varied faces of my friends stay with me. . . . [D]uring the eleven years I spent in government boarding schools, smiling was always far from my mind. . . . What days those were! But somehow, despite the difficulties, those were the glory days. . . .
>
> I say "glory days" because those are the fondest memories of my early childhood. It was in this phase of my life that I met other kids who became my friends for life. . . .
>
> We went through the forced haircuts during which we'd be shaven bald, the slaps on the wrists by wooden rulers when we spoke Indian languages, the mouth washing if we said "damn" or other bad words. And we all learned how to march; in cadence we marched to the dining room, to the school building and to the gym. Yes, we marched—until we learned to run.
>
> We all ran away from those schools from time to time, not really knowing where we were running to. In a way it was our own survival instinct telling us to go, and so we went. But the price for getting caught was the "hot line." That was when the older boys would form two lines facing each other—ten boys on either side—and they would hit you with belts, sticks, and straps as you ran through the "line." Can you imagine? A government policy that encouraged kids to punish other kids. But we all survived, though at times the Indianness was almost beaten out of us.
>
> Then there were the books we had to learn from. Books about white people. White heroes. White presidents. All the stories were about how the white settlers settled this land among savage Indians, or how Indians came marauding, stealing, scalping, and killing innocent babies. All our teachers were white. (1994, viii–ix)

However, Horne specifically remembers teaching Banks and her other students about Indian contributions to America (Horne and McBeth 1988).

Criticism of boarding schools mounted at the beginning of the twentieth century because some students were abused and because the schools were not producing the rapid cultural assimilation promised by Richard H. Pratt and other boarding school advocates. The stage was set after World War I for the concerted attack on both the Indian Office and the boarding schools. This attack is described in the next chapter.

CHAPTER EIGHT

A New Deal, 1924–1944

In his 1922 serialized novel, *The Vanishing American*, Zane Grey writes, "[P]erhaps ninety-nine out of one hundred students returned to the old life, the hogan and the sheep [and his heroine] inclined more and more to the conviction that the whole government school and reservation system was wrong" (178–79). The publishers delayed the book version because religious groups were offended by its portrayal of missionaries raping Indian girls and stealing Indian land. Grey was forced to kill off his Navajo hero rather than have him marry the white heroine and to tone down his indictment of missionaries. In the movie version the missionaries were eliminated (Grey 1982). Even into the 1950s twenty-six states had antimiscegenation laws (Beatty 1951).

Mounting criticism after World War I forced the government to rethink federal Indian policy. In 1923 the secretary of the interior convened the Committee of One Hundred to recommend changes in Indian policy. The group elected Arthur C. Parker, a Seneca author, anthropologist, and great-nephew of the Civil War general and Commissioner of Indian Affairs Ely S. Parker, as their chair. Other Indian delegates included the Reverend Sherman Coolidge, Charles Eastman, Thomas L. Sloan, the Reverend Henry Roe Cloud, Dennison Wheelock, and Father Philip Gordon. The Committee's final report called for adequate school facilities, higher salaries to attract more qualified teachers, more schools with a special regard for day schools and meeting the needs of Navajo children, an increased number of Indian students in public schools, and high school and college scholarships. Their recommendations helped to bring about reservation day schools that offered a sixth-grade education and off-reservation boarding schools that offered an eighth-grade education. The final report stated that there had been "400 years of debauchery at the hands of the white man" and that the "the white man has shamefully mistreated the red race" (Otis 1924, 6, 17). The general idea was that more funding would improve education so that Indians would assimilate faster and the government could close the Indian Office in twenty-five years. The Committee reported that in the ten large nonreservation boarding schools, all students wear uniforms when not working and that there is "a real college atmosphere in these schools" (Otis 1924, 34). Only John Collier and one other delegate spoke out against William Jennings Bryan's resolution commending the government's support of missionary activities (Fischbacher 1967; *Report on Indian Education* 1976; Kelly 1983).

JOHN COLLIER, THE EARLY YEARS

John Collier (1884–1968) spent eleven years in settlement house and community work in New York City. There he met Mabel Granson Dodge at her famous Thursday salons. Later, Dodge obtained a divorce and moved to Taos, New Mexico, where she met and later married Tony Lujan, a Taos Pueblo politician. She invited Collier, who had moved to California, to visit her and become involved in the Pueblo Indians' struggle for land and water rights. He finally gave in to her urgings and rode the stagecoach to Taos in December 1920 and stayed most of the year. There he observed the Taos Red Deer Dance:

> If our modern world should be able to recapture [this power for living] the earth's natural resources and web of life would not be irrevocably wasted within the twentieth century which is the prospect now. True democracy, founded in neighborhoods and reaching over the world, would become the realized heaven on earth. . . . [Modern society has] lost that passion and reverence for human personality and for the web of life and the earth which the American Indians have tended as a central sacred fire. (Collier 1947, 16, 17).

In his memoirs Collier (1963, 128) declared that by the start of 1922 it was clear that Secretary of the Interior Albert Fall "was out to loot the

Indians of every bit of land and resources they still had." Fall's efforts failed. He was forced to resign and ultimately sent to prison for his role in the looting of U.S. Navy oil reserves in Wyoming, known as the Teapot Dome Scandal. In 1923 Collier, supported by Mabel Dodge Luhan and the General Federation of Women's Clubs' Division of Indian Welfare, organized the American Indian Defense Association and, as its executive secretary, wrote a series of articles critical of the Indian Bureau. In an introductory heading to a *Current History* article, "America's Treatment of Her Indians," he declared: *"The administration of Indian affairs [is] a national disgrace—A policy designed to rob Indians of their property, destroy their culture and eventually exterminate them"* (1923a, 771; original emphasis). In *Sunset Magazine* he wrote, "The Indian problem embodies a world-wide problem, whether material civilization— machinery and the dictates of machinery—and selfish individualism shall dominate man or whether man shall dominate them, subordinate them and use them," and he contrasted the United States with Canada, where "Indians are subjugated, but there is no record of shame" (1923b, 13). For its efforts, the Indian Office branded the Indian Defense Association a "Soviet [Communist] tool" (Collier 1963).

THE MERIAM REPORT

In 1926 Secretary of the Interior Hubert Work asked the Institute for Government Research (also called the Brookings Institute) at Johns Hopkins University to conduct a nonpolitical investigation of Indian affairs. His goal was to prevent a partisan investigation by Collier and other Indian Office critics (Kelly 1983). The results of this privately financed study were published in 1928 as *The Problem of Indian Administration*, popularly known as the Meriam Report after Louis Meriam, who headed the investigation. The report condemned the allotment policy and the poor quality of services provided by the Department of the Interior's Indian Office, urged protection for Indian property, and recommended Indians be allowed more freedom to manage their own affairs. Dr. W. Carson Ryan Jr., a prominent figure in the Progressive Education movement, wrote most of the education section of the Meriam Report with help from the Reverend Henry Roe Cloud, a Winnebago who had graduated from the Santee Normal Training School. The education section was influenced by the teachings of John Dewey and other progressive educators, and it documented the lack of correlation between the curriculum of Indian schools and the realities of reservation life. In addition, the care of Indian children in boarding schools was found shockingly inadequate. The report concluded that elementary age children did not belong in boarding schools and that there was a need for more day schools:

> The philosophy underlying the establishment of Indian boarding schools, that the way to "civilize" the Indian is to take Indian children, even very young children, as completely as possible away from their home and family life, is at variance with modern views of education and social work, which regard the home and family as essential social institutions from which it is generally undesirable to uproot children. (Meriam 1928, 403)

The report also emphasized the need for preservice training of Indian Service employees and that the course of study "should be mainly suggestive rather than prescriptive (Meriam 1928, 371).

The underfunding of Indian schools that had begun in 1921, when their appropriations for food and clothing were cut 25 percent (Brown 1952), continued. Students at Rice Boarding School in Arizona, an extreme case, were found by a Red Cross investigator to be subsisting on a diet of bread, black coffee, and syrup for breakfast and bread and boiled potatoes for dinner and supper and a quarter cup of milk with each meal (Meriam 1928). In general, the Meriam Report found the food in boarding schools "deficient in quantity, quality and variety" (11). The poor food made Indian students more susceptible to tuberculosis and trachoma, which were endemic in Indian communities and boarding schools. Further, the Meriam Report commented on using students as laborers: "The question may very properly be raised as to whether much of the work of Indian children in boarding schools would not be prohibited in many states by child labor laws, notably the work in the machine laundries" (13).

To quell the growing criticism of the government's Indian policy, in 1929 President Herbert Hoover appointed a fellow Quaker and president of the Indian Rights Association, Charles J. Rhoads, Commissioner of Indian Affairs. In 1930 W. Carson Ryan Jr. became director of Indian education and served until 1935. Ryan had a three-point program: to develop community schools, to support federal-state contracts to put Indian children in public schools, and gradually to phase out boarding schools. Rhoads and Ryan also sought to increase boarding school budgets, to hire education professionals to administer the education department, and to secure the other reforms recommended in the Meriam Report, including an end to a uniform Indian Service curriculum that stressed only the cultural values of whites (Szasz 1977). In 1932 Jennings Wise's *The Red Man in the New World Drama* (1931) was sent to Indian Service teachers. One teacher on the isolated Havasupai Indian Reservation described it as "a gripping story of the red man's part in the rise of the world out of the dark ages. It puts the Indians in a much different [positive] light than any story or history I've ever came in contact with" (Knobloch 1988, 44–45). Ryan's lack of faith in the old assimilationist policy was underlined in 1935 when he wrote that "native life itself has values that urgently need to be maintained" (quoted in Prucha 1984, 977).

While the number of boarding schools decreased from 77 to 65 between 1928 and 1933, the number of students increased. Congress resisted closing boarding schools because they constituted a significant boost to the economies of the communities in which they were located. A persistent problem of BIA schools remained discipline. While the type and severity of discipline varied from school to school, depending on its superintendent, flogging and other severe forms of punishment continued at some schools. The Meriam Report found that almost all schools had locked rooms or isolated buildings that were used as "jails," and in some schools children were forced to "maintain a pathetic degree of quietness" (329, 332) that might also be attributed to poor diet.

The criticism of U.S. Indian policy in the Meriam Report provided justification for major change when the Great Depression caused considerable rethinking about whether the United States was progressing toward a future of wealth and plenty. Some people, including John Collier, looked to the close-knit, nonmaterialistic world of the American Indians for an alternative to what they saw as wrong with modern society.

The American people expressed their dissatisfaction with the way things were going by electing Franklin D. Roosevelt president in 1933. Roosevelt appointed Harold Ickes secretary of the interior. Ickes's wife spoke Navajo and had written a popular book on southwestern Indians

(Deloria and Lytle 1984). Collier had met Ickes years before in Chicago and interested him in Indian welfare. Ickes asked Collier to be his Commissioner of Indian Affairs. As Commissioner, Collier immediately sought to end allotment of Indian lands and to further implement the recommendations of the Meriam Report. In his memoirs Collier indicated that he entered his new office in 1933 with three policies: "the economic rehabilitation of the Indians, principally on the land," "organization of the Indian tribes for managing their own affairs," and "civil and cultural freedom and opportunity for the Indians" (1963, 173). His efforts resulted in the Indian Reorganization (Wheeler-Howard) Act (IRA) of 1934 that ended allotment of Indian lands and provided for Indian religious freedom, a measure of tribal self-government, and Indian preference in hiring Indian Service employees. However, Vine Deloria Jr. and Clifford Lytle (1984) concluded that the act was a defeat for Collier because of the major changes that were made in it by Senator Burton K. Wheeler of Montana and others in the process of negotiating its passage.

In his testimony to Congress on the IRA, Collier emphasized "removing the bureaucratic stranglehold of the Indian Bureau from Indian communities" and the lack of Indian employees in the Bureau (Deloria and Lytle 1984, 85). The continuous upgrading of the Civil Service examination meant that less Indians were employed in the Indian Bureau in 1934 than were employed in 1900. In a first for Indian legislation, ten Indian congresses were held around the country to discuss the bill before its passage. After its passage, elections held by each tribe led to 181 tribes choosing to come under the provisions of the IRA and 77 tribes rejecting reorganization (Deloria and Lytle 1984). In addition to the greater self-government Collier promoted, he saw the educational reforms of the Progressive Education movement as a solution to the problems of Indian education.

PROGRESSIVE EDUCATION

The president of the Progressive Education Association said in 1930 that "the child rather than what he studies should be the centre of all educational effort and that a scientific attitude toward new educational ideas is the best guarantee of progress" (Fowler 1930, 159). Like Whole

Language advocates of the 1990s, advocates of Progressive Education maintained that it "could not be defined, that it was a 'spirit,' a 'method,' an 'outlook,' a 'matter of emphasis'" (Cremin 1961, 258). John Dewey, considered the father of Progressive Education, saw it as an alternative to traditional education that was academic in orientation and divorced from the realities students faced. He founded the first laboratory school at the University of Chicago to test his theories. The problems he faced are illustrated by a story he tells about trying to furnish his new school. All the desks at the school supply houses were designed for students to sit passively listening and studying, whereas Dewey was interested in getting furniture that would allow students to be active learners (Dewey 1900). Dewey is most famous for his dictum "learning by doing," which fits in with much modern constructivist research about learning.

In 1929 Charles Rhodes, the new Commissioner of Indian Affairs, echoed the Meriam Report, emphasizing local material and the use of Indian daily experiences in teaching students, and he explicitly mentioned the Progressive Education movement in his 1930 annual report: "Emphasis is being placed upon the importance of basing all early primary reading on words that already have a place in the children's speaking vocabulary" (*ARCIA* 1930, 9). He declared, "All Navajo schools now have native weavers who teach blanket weaving to girls" (11). The next year Rhodes encouraged elementary teachers to urge their students "to write about their own Indian life, and to depict their own customs, their own legends, their own economic and social activities (*ARCIA* 1931, 7).

The February 1932 issue of the journal *Progressive Education* was devoted to Indian education, and the lead article was written by W. Carson Ryan Jr. and Rose K. Brandt, respectively the director of education and the supervisor of elementary education for the Indian Service. They declared that summer school training for Indian service teachers should include:

1. Environmental experiences of children as a basis for school procedure and curriculum content.
2. Philosophy of progressive education, basing school work on activities and at the same time recognizing and providing opportunities for various learning outcomes rather than beginning and ending teaching procedures mainly with subject matter. (Ryan and Brandt 1932, 83)

In the same issue Nancy Heger, a teacher at Eastern Navajo School in Crownpoint, New Mexico, published an article, "Before Books in an Indian School." In her view, the school lunch was the place to start teaching English, with students learning names for utensils and different kinds of food. She recommended using games to learn vocabulary and also commended the use of sand tables (see chap. 4):

> The sand table provides another center of never-failing interest an opportunity for vocabulary building. Here are constructed houses such as we live in, barns, schoolhouse, sidewalks, windmill, stores, chicken houses, pens, fences, troughs, trees, tanks, church, garages, trucks, cars—all illustrative of the school and agency or the home community.
>
> Usually, the first sand-table scene consists of the school village. (1932, 143)

Helen Lawhead, a first grade teacher at the Theodore Roosevelt Boarding School at Fort Apache, Arizona, wrote about teaching reading to Navajo students. She noted that Navajo students should not be expected to learn to read English without first developing some oral English vocabulary. Students would often read aloud well, yet not comprehend what they were reading. She (1932, 133) recommended that reading materials should be based on the children's own experiences and that the books should have "simple sentences" and "plenty of action." In her classes students did drawings to illustrate their favorite stories and dramatized scenes from them. She also used a sand table to "make the story."

In a section titled "Language Experiments of Children" contributed by Rose Brandt, the 1932 special issue had the following description of what is now called the Language Experience approach to teaching reading:

> The children talk over their experiences in group discussion, the teacher keeping a written record on the blackboard of their comments. These are later presented to the children to be read on large charts or in the form of booklets which have been hektographed or written on typewriters having Primer type faces. (Language 1932, 154)

Two examples of first-grade stories from Toadlena, New Mexico, were given:

Navajo Father

Navajo father wears a shirt and pants. Navajo father wears a green head band. He wears red kil'chi on his feet. He wears a blanket to keep him warm. Navajo father wears blue ear rings. He wears beads on his neck.

Navajo father works. He plows the ground. He plants corn and watermelons. He makes the hogan. He chops the tree. He chops wood. He takes care of goats and sheep. He rides the horse.

Navajo Mother

Navajo mother wears a Navajo dress. A Navajo dress is a long dress. She wears beads on her neck. She wears shoes on her feet. Sometimes she wears kil'chi on her feet. She wears ear rings in her ears. She wears stockings. Navajo mother wears no head band. Navajo mother wears long hair. She ties it with a string.

Navajo mother works. She makes bread. She cooks corn, meat, potatoes, coffee, and pumpkins. The Navajos eat it. She makes the blanket. She makes kil'chi and a cradle. She makes a dress and shirt for father. She rides the horse. (Language 1932, 154)

In a 1935 article in the Indian Service publication *Indians at Work*, Brandt described how older students wrote books for the younger ones so that they would be learning words that were familiar to them. She described a book written by fourth graders at Todalena that had chapters on home life, history, customs, ceremonials, and legends.

A 1943 *Indian Education* article emphasized the need for students to speak English before reading it (Experience Reading 1943, 8). The article called for "first the experience or activity, then the written record, then the reading" (5). Stories, including group-made reading material, were to be made into mimeographed books for the children. The following year an *Indian Education* article, "Writing for Pleasure," called for starting with "one sentence diaries." Teachers were told, "The secret of creative writing with children is simple. . . . [F]irst . . . let the child pick his own subject. . . . [S]econd take the good, praise it, save it and ignore the bad" (Writing 1944, 6). A few months later, Robert Young (1944, 2) wrote: "On the Navajo Reservation . . . the vast majority of the people were either illiterate, or read the English language after the fashion of parrots—pronouncing the words without understanding the meaning." Young was of the opinion that many Navajos felt that the "acquisition of the White Man's language is tantamount to taking on his civilization" (3). To overcome this resistance to assimilation, Young promoted teaching reading and writing in the children's Native language. A month later an article in the same publication called for giving students "a real, lifelike opportunity to" learn a foreign language quickly and delaying learning to read from books as well as writing for a year or two until the child became a fluent speaker (Learning 1944, 7).

In a 1950 article on choosing schoolbooks, Ryan's successor as director of education, Willard Beatty, warned against "word calling" wherein students read without comprehension and noted that "beginning reading only makes sense when the things that the child reads about are things with which he is familiar and which he understands. One of the important attitudes toward reading, which a child should gain in the early grades, is that it is fun to read" (Beatty 1950, 2). He further noted that "modern trends in education are directed toward students working in small groups, as opposed to the older method of teaching enmasse" (4).

Esther Horne (Horne and McBeth 1998) describes receiving an Indian Service directive encouraging teachers to take Progressive Education courses at Milwaukee State Teachers College in 1933, a welcome break for her from sanding student desks in the summer. There she was encouraged to integrate various subjects into thematic units. She describes a farm unit:

> Children might begin by making and decorating the farm buildings out of cardboard boxes. We then might study concepts associated with farm life, like keeping records of the sale of produce. . . . I found this method of teaching interesting and challenging but also difficult to use in teaching my students enough of the basics. I felt that sometimes the students were shortchanged by the use of this method alone, and I supplemented it with materials correlated to the state course of study. (Horne and McBeth 1998, 76–77)

In summer 1935, with the help of the Albuquerque Indian School superintendent, Horne took two anthropology classes at the University of New Mexico and Indian art classes at the Albuquerque Indian School. After her retirement, Horne spoke highly of Beatty, a Progressive Education proponent. Beatty, she said, "had a deep respect for Native

American culture" (Horne and McBeth 1998, 69). The next summer Horne was asked to demonstrate how to incorporate Native American materials into the classroom to other Indian Service teachers at Pine Ridge. There, she was also able to take an ethnology course from the well-known anthropologist Ruth Underhill, who had taught a similar summer institute for Indian school teachers at Santa Fe in 1934 (Heyer 1990). Horne taught at Wahpeton Indian School throughout Beatty's long tenure as the Indian Service's director of Indian education.

The Studio at Santa Fe Indian School

In 1926 Pueblo day school teachers were told not to let children draw pictures with Indian themes. Two years later the Meriam Report recommended that the Indian Service encourage Indian art, and the Santa Fe Indian School became a focus of these efforts. When Dorothy Dunn, who had left teaching at the Santo Domingo Pueblo Day School to attend the Chicago Art Institute, returned to the Southwest in 1932, she opened up "The Studio" at Santa Fe Indian School under the job description "laborer." She told her students she was a "guide" rather than a teacher and is reported to have been "well-liked" by her students (Heyer 1990, 44). Things looked bad at the end of the first year because the bureaucracy could not come up with a Civil Service position for Dunn, but Rose K. Brandt, supervisor of elementary education for the Indian Office, personally intervened after visiting Dunn's program (Bernstein and Rushing 1995). She was even able to start a two-year post–high school arts program that lasted until World War II led to cutbacks in the school's programs (Heyer 1990). In 1933 Indian Commissioner Collier discussed with the Pueblo governors at an All-Pueblo Council meeting the closing of Santa Fe Indian School, but they wanted to keep the school open so that their children could become acquainted with other Pueblo groups and tribes and receive vocational training (Heyer 1990).

Dunn did not find things easy during her five years at The Studio and had to battle the Indian Office professional staff. She did not find Beatty as supportive as Brandt, and she resigned in 1937. Her position was taken by one of her students, Geronima Cruz Montoya, who directed the art program until 1962, when the buildings were used for the establishment of the Institute of American Indian Art as an accredited high school (Bernstein and Rushing 1995; Dunn 1968). According to J. J. Brody in *Indian Painters and White Patrons:*

> Through the Santa Fe Studio, Miss Dunn became the single most influential individual for an entire generation of Indian painters. The Studio became the model for art departments at other Indian Schools. . . . Virtually all the important Indian painters of her generation came under her guidance or were taught by her students, and in turn they taught most Indian artists of the succeeding generation. (1971, 128)

Willard Beatty as Director of Indian Education

Willard Beatty had been president of the Progressive Education Association since 1933 when Collier appointed him education director for the Indian Service. Before his involvement in Indian activism, Collier himself had a home school in New York for his own and his neighbors' kids based on the teachings of John Dewey, of whom he was a "devotee" (Palmer 1976, 174). Collier had a rather unconfined childhood growing up in Atlanta, Georgia, where his father had been mayor, among other things, before committing suicide. Collier had found teaching in the Atlanta high schools "wretched" (Collier 1963).

Like Collier, Beatty, who served as the Indian Service's education director until 1952, felt that whites put material values ahead of human values. Under the Collier-Beatty administration, more day schools were built on reservations, allowing Indian children to go to school and remain within their home areas. In addition, some boarding schools were closed, and for the first time, a few Native-language textbooks were written, and there was more emphasis on teaching Indian cultures and languages in Indian schools. A 1938 survey of boarding school graduates by the anthropologist Gordon MacGregor found that the majority of boys did not use their industrial training in their jobs, one-half of them worked for the government (primarily in relief work), most girls became housewives, in California and Oklahoma the majority of boys did not go back home, and the industrial and home economics training did not seem to promote assimilation (Fischbacher 1967).

One of the most interesting experiments of the Collier and Beatty administrations was the hiring of anthropologists and other experts and using them as educational consultants. For example, Gladys Reichard from Barnard College was commissioned by Collier to run a summer institute near Ganado, Arizona, to teach Navajo writing to eighteen Navajo interpreters ranging in age from twenty-two to fifty-five (Lockard 1995). She fictionalized an account of her experience in *Dezba: Woman of the Desert:*

> The school was held in a hogan during the summer months and consisted only of a teacher and adult Navajo students with pencils, paper and a blackboard. . . . {I]ts purpose was to deal with educational problems with equipment available to even the most isolated Navajo. . . .
>
> As the Hogan School continued it became clear that the students most needed education in subjects which were taught only in colleges and universities, although only two of them had the equivalent of a high school training and that was vocational, not academic. Students were interested in the history of Indians, botany, forestry, agronomy, zoology, animal husbandry, geology, law, linguistics and the like. (Reichard 1939, 130, 136)

Another experiment involved fifty young Navajos chosen in October 1934 to receive training at Red Rock Cove to become teachers. Their classes stressed land use, community relations, health, and tribal culture, but both the Navajo cultural preference for older teachers and the lack of formal college training ended up relegating them to supportive rather than leadership roles in the new schools (Parman 1976). According to Katherine Jensen (1983, 53), Collier repeatedly "urged that Navajos with at least three years of formal schooling be hired in a hogan-based program of primary education" (1983, 53). The former Navajo Indian agent Albert Kneale (1950, 376) recalled that Navajos were critical of hogan schools, which had "earthen floors, smoke holes, sheep-pelt divans, low roofs, and entrances carefully placed to the east" and were "manned by a single 'teacher,' a Navajo child who had but recently completed the eighth grade." The schools had a "complete absence of anything remotely resembling discipline" along with an "absence of plan, of books, or [sic] furniture, of equipment" (376).

The radical change from the assimilationist goals of the allotment period that Collier and Beatty attempted is shown in the 1938 introduction to the Civil Service examination for positions in the Indian Service:

> The primary objectives of Indian schools are:
> 1. To give students an understanding and appreciation of their tribal lore, art, music, and community organization;
> 2. To teach students, through their own participation in school and local governments, to become constructive citizens of their communities;
> 3. To aid students in analyzing the economic resources of their reservation and in planning more effective ways of utilizing these resources for the improvement of standards of living;
> 4. To teach, through actual demonstration, intelligent conservation of natural resources:
> 5. To give students first-hand experience in livestock management, use of native materials in housing and clothing, in subsistence gardening, cooperative marketing, farm mechanics, and whatever other vocational skills are needed to earn a livelihood in the region.
> 6. To develop better health habits, improved sanitation, and higher standards of diet with a view to prevention of trachoma, tuberculosis, and infant diseases;
> 7. To give students an understanding of the social and economic world immediately about them and to aid them in achieving some mastery over their environment;
> 8. To serve as a community center in meeting the social and economic needs of the community;
> 9. To provide the training necessary to obtain and hold a job away from the reservation area for those students who desire or need such training. (Beatty 1951, 13)

A conservationist, Beatty (1942, 134) promoted the revival in Indian schools of interest in native fruit-bearing shrubs and trees, including "wild plum, choke cherry, June berries, buffalo berries, and currant." He praised the Oraibi high school for having a graduation requirement that students plant new fruit trees on their families' lands.

Beatty also continued the practice of holding summer institutes to give teachers special training in teaching Indian students. Soon after his appointment as education director, he began publishing a bimonthly bulletin, *Indian Education*, to disseminate the new policies and new educational methods to Indian Service employees. Beatty's *Indian Education* articles noted that elements of white culture needed to be identified and deliberately taught to Indian students, that white teachers needed to learn something about Indian cultures and languages, and that intelligence tests measured cultural experience rather than "native ability" (Beatty 1951). Both Beatty and Collier were aware of other countries' educational approaches to aboriginal education, especially Mexico's, and foreign criticism of U.S. treatment of its Native population. Their efforts led to the publication by the Indian Service of Young and Morgan's *Navaho Language: The Elements of Navaho Grammar with a Dictionary in Two Parts Containing Vocabularies of Navaho and English* (1943) and the *Indian Life Series* of bilingual booklets for children, including *Little Man's Family* (fig. 20). However, efforts to teach Navajo in schools were not always appreciated. Lilly J. Neil, the first Navajo woman tribal council delegate, complained in 1947,

> To be sure our White instructors are trying to get our Native language taught in school along with English, and confusing our little children, but will this fulfill their part in our treaty, even if they do succeed in getting our little ones to speak Navajo the broken White Mans way, Will this qualify our children to compete with their White Brothers? The answer is *Positively No*, it only confuses them, and holds them back so they will have to be wards of the Government, and have to hire high paid white men to help them to get a mere existence our [sic] of this country we live in. (Iverson 2002b, 105).

In his memoirs, Collier (1963) was appreciative of the environmental and conservation curriculum that Beatty introduced into the schools. Collier noted that the two silent crisis of his day were the destruction of the environment and overpopulation. He also noted that he and Beatty "intended that school life become bilingual, and that the schools should serve adult and child alike" (1963, 196). According to Collier, Beatty "scoured" the Navajo reservation recruiting Navajo teachers, Navajo assistants, and translators. However, Collier's educational policies, which included religious freedom, antagonized missionaries and their students, especially on the Navajo Reservation. There, Jacob Morgan (1879–1950) became one of his major opponents.

Morgan graduated from Hampton Institute in 1990 and then returned there for two years of additional education in business, bookkeeping,

Little Man's family

diné yázhí ba'áłchíní

Reader

by

J. B. Enochs

illustrated by

Gerald Nailor

A Publication of the Education Division—U. S. Office of Indian Affairs

Cover of one of the eight bilingual (Navajo/English) readers developed by the U.S. Office of Indian Affairs and printed at Phoenix Indian School in 1940. In his foreword, Willard Beatty, Director of Indian Education, wrote, "These bilingual texts are frankly experimental, being an attempt to speed up Indian understanding of modern life. Use of native languages is a new departure in Indian policy made possible by the liberal viewpoints of Harold Ickes, Secretary of the Interior, and John Collier, Commissioner of Indian Affairs." In a revised foreword to the 1950 printing, Beatty dropped the reference to Ickes and Collier, who had left the office, and stated that "the new departure . . . has proved very successful" and that its purpose was "to speed up acquisition of English."

and advanced carpentry. He also edited the school newspaper. He went on to become a Protestant missionary, served as his tribe's first elected chairman from 1938 to 1942, and led the opposition to Collier's policies (Parman 1972; Boyce 1974; Philp 1986). Morgan, who served briefly as an Indian Service teacher before going into missionary work and politics, is described by the historian Donald Parman (1976) as a "moralistic fundamentalist" who hated day schools and opposed bilingual education. He hated Catholics and warned Navajos repeatedly not to become Catholic because then "they would be shipped overseas to fight the Pope's wars" (Parman 1976, 19). Morgan's local attack on Collier was an echo of a nationwide attack, but for Navajos like Morgan, the dislike of Collier was aggravated by the latter's support for livestock reduction on the Navajo Reservation (Iverson 2002a).

Unlike Morgan, the Hopi educator Polingaysi Qöyawayma (1964) found that things got better under the administration of Collier and Beatty. When she started teaching in an Indian school before the Meriam Report was published, she was nervous, but she felt that she at least knew the language her students spoke. However, her supervisors soon reminded her she was forbidden to speak Hopi to her students. She questioned her supervisors' directives and the English curriculum she was required to teach: "What do these white-man stories mean to a Hopi child? What is a "choo-choo" to these little ones who have never seen a train? No! I will not begin with the outside world of which they have no knowledge. I shall begin with the familiar. The everyday things. The things of home and family" (1964, 125).

In defiance of her supervisors she continued to substitute familiar Hopi legends, songs, and stories for "Little Red Riding Hood." She found that her students loved these stories translated into English, but parents questioned what she was teaching, saying, "We send them [our children] to school to learn the white man's way, not Hopi. They can learn the Hopi way at home" (126). Despite these complaints she persevered in trying to help her children "blend the best of the Hopi tradition with the best of the white culture, retaining the essence of good, whatever its source" (127). When Indian Commissioner Collier changed Indian Service policies in 1934, she found "overnight" her teaching methods supported, to the "consternation" of the older teachers.

In 1941 Qöyawayma was chosen to demonstrate her teaching methods to other Indian Service educators at a summer training institute. She had found that her method of educating children starting "from what they already know, not from a totally new, strange field of experience" reduced the chance her students would withdraw into a shell (1964, 151, 174). She wrote to a friend the same year:

> If the teachers to the Hopi or other tribes would come to them [their students] with human interest and love and take them for what they are and where they are and begin from their world with them results would be success. There should be less teacher dominance and theories. . . . [T]eacher and child should meet on mutual ground. (Qöyawayma 1941, 51)

Florence Little, one of the first Navajo "college graduate" teachers, took a similar approach. She used words such as "yucca," "piñon," and "hogan" as the initial English vocabulary for her beginning students rather than "post office," "bank," and "skyscraper" (Boyce 1974).

The Project Method

The educational psychologist William Heard Kilpatrick wrote in Columbia University's *Teachers College Record* in 1918 about the "project method," which was to involve students in "purposeful acts." According to Kilpatrick (1918, 18), "Whole hearted purposeful activity in a social situation as the typical unit of school procedure is the best guarantee of the utilization of the child's native capacities now too often frequently wasted." But he also warned against foolishly humoring childish whims. Mendel Branom, in his *Project Method in Education* (1919), wrote that projects had to be related to students' interests and needs.

John Dewey added a short chapter on projects in the 1933 edition of his classic book, *How We Think*. He wrote that "constructive occupations" or "projects" are characterized by the following conditions:

1. Engage interest: "Unless the activity lays hold on the emotions and desires, unless it offers an outlet for energy that means something to the individual himself, his mind will turn in aversion from it, even though externally he keeps at it."
2. Intrinsic worth: "the activity must be worth while intrinsically." Projects must "stand for something valuable in life itself."

3. Awaken curiosity: The project must "awaken new curiosity and create a demand for information."

4. Time span: "the project must involve a considerable time span for its adequate execution. The plan and the object to be gained must be capable of development, one thing leading on naturally to another. It is not a succession of unrelated acts, but is a consecutively ordered activity in which one step prepares the need for the next one and that one adds to, and carries further in a cumulative way, what has already been done." (218–19)

Katherine Jenson (1983) recalled that Indian Service teachers were advised to use the project method. In a 1944 article, Ruth Underhill declared that Papago children traditionally "learned through activity, in a system surprisingly like our modern project method" (5). A 1948 article on day school methods for Sioux students by the Indian Service's associate supervisor of education, Gordon MacGregor, noted:

The educational method is based on class projects or activities which are centered around the home, pet animals, and health. Garden projects create an early interest in farming and the production of food—an interest not highly developed in the older Dakota. . . .

The project method is exceptionally well suited to educating the Dakota because it follows their own method of learning by doing and following the example of others. By bringing the children to participate and to share in the work and the responsibility for completion of a project, this method also reinforces the training for cooperative work already begun in the family.

The project method has a special value for many reservation children who know little or no English when they enter school. Working with bilingual children who can translate for them and help them build up English vocabularies is a great help to the shy Indian-speaking children. Projects are immensely successful in diverting the timid new child's attention from the strange school situation, which often terrifies him at first, and in getting him to enter into school life. By working and playing with others, he makes new friends and has a good time. Projects are also a basis by which the teacher can establish herself as a friendly and kindly person, interested in the child's welfare and happiness. (6–7)

He noted that this method had been used very successfully for seven or eight years at Pine Ridge schools, and that the competition between students fostered by traditional American teaching methods was difficult for young Sioux children to understand, as they were taught at home to work cooperatively and not to outshine their peers (MacGregor 1964). In the 1990s the project method—now called explorer curriculum, enterprises, and the like—was still recommended for Indian students (McCarty and Schaffer 1992).

New Day and Hogan Schools

During Collier's administration a great many Americans were unemployed as a result of the depression. Collier was able to use Public Works Administration (PWA) moneys to hire unemployed Indians to build day schools. PWA money was supposed to be spent quickly in the hope that it would stimulate the U.S. economy. In 1935 only 15 percent of Navajo children were in school, and $1.5 million of PWA money was spent to build forty day schools (Parman 1976). Collier's plan was as follows:

> The new "day schools" are to be real community centers, primarily concerned with the fundamental economic and social problems of the Navajos. Child education will not be their dominant function, but rather the creation and focusing of group thought and group activity on the pressing problems of erosion control, stock reduction, grazing management, public health, social organization, relations to white culture and the intensifying and widening of Navajo economic activities in such enterprises as subsistence farming and arts and crafts, as well as the maintenance of the native Navajo culture. (Shepard 1934, 9)

As an educational experiment, four of the new day schools were built in a hogan design at Mariana Lake, Cove, Navajo Mountain, and Shonto (Parman 1976). The wife of the trading post operator at Shonto described the hogan schools built there in 1934:

> The hogan-type rooms were grouped in twos and threes connected by covered cement walks, and modern windows let in the bright sunshine and

plenty of fresh air. The children smiled when they looked up at the juniper ceilings and felt at ease, it was not so frightening to be in school after all. The first resident teachers liked the layout of these rooms and found the living quarters very comfortable. (Hegemann 1963, 380)

Hogan classrooms of similar design were still being used for classes at the beginning of the twenty-first century at Crystal Boarding School north of Window Rock, Arizona. Hogan schools were one solution to the problem of finding classroom space for the 50 percent of Navajo school-age children not currently in school. In addition, the cost of educating a Navajo child in a day school was estimated by Collier (1934, 74) to be one-third of what it cost to keep the same child in a boarding school.

Despite the best intentions, day school enrollments never reached capacity, owing to the Navajo's dispersed population and the reservation's dirt roads. In addition, the schools' modern equipment and buses were difficult to keep running because of the distance to a city where knowledgeable specialists could be found to make repairs. Kneale (1950) found that Navajo children were unable to get to the new day schools because of muddy roads and that the schools had all the modern conveniences but no trained staff to operate them. Furthermore, in the interest of economy and authenticity, adobe had been used instead of cement to construct the day schools, and, over time, the adobe washed out, causing major difficulties. In the day schools students "took naps after lunch and, in Navajo logic, were being taught to be lazy" (Boyce 1974, 97). After ten years of experience, Willard Beatty (1951) eventually concluded that day schools were not feasible on the Navajo Reservation.

THE NEW DEAL

The Johnson-O'Malley (JOM) Act of 1934 authorized the secretary of the interior to enter for the first time into contracts with states or territories to pay them for providing services to Indians rather than having to deal with each school district individually, as had been done since 1891. By 1934 this could mean thousands of separate contracts. The Act allowed the federal government to pay states for educating

Indians in public schools. California, Washington, Minnesota, and Arizona were the first states to sign contracts between 1934 and 1941. However, things did not always run smoothly: state educational administrators worked to be independent, and BIA officials worked to control how JOM funds were spent, with many bureau officials doubtful of the ability of public schools to provide a quality education for Indians. Originally, JOM money went into the general operating fund of the school districts and was used to support the education of non-Indian as well as Indian students (NAACP 1971; Szasz 1977). The increased federal-state cooperation is evidenced by the fact that during the 1940s all BIA high schools became state accredited (Fischbacher 1967).

Indian students faced many problems in public schools. For example, in Nevada several communities resisted having Indian students in their public schools (Haglund 1966). In the words of Szasz (1977, 101), "Rural teachers who had to conform to the attitudes of the local populace often found it difficult to regard their Indian pupils with even ordinary civility and kindness." In addition, public schools were in financial crisis because of the Great Depression and were eliminating health, physical education, shop, and other courses that Collier and others thought were essential for Indian students. The BIA was able to introduce vocational programs in some public schools that served Indian students and to provide textbooks, school supplies, and clothing, but it had little success in convincing the schools to offer Indian culture courses (Szasz 1977). Agnes Yellowtail Deernose recalled:

> Even in the thirties and forties Crow children entered school without any real background in English. They didn't have interpreters in the classroom then, and interpreters were no longer used in churches either. By the time the Indians were in fourth grade in public school, most of them were too far behind to keep up with the White kids in reading. Because of this, they became more and more bashful when called on to recite, especially if they had ewatkusua, or joking relatives, in class who would tease them later if they made a mistake. . . .
>
> In class, boys and girls retreated behind the safety of their reading books and often drew pictures of camping, horses, deer, buffalo, and tipis. They knew they were different from White kids, who could beat them at reading, spelling, and arithmetic. Books were a part of the White nature, but Indian kids learned from the old people and from the medicine fathers.

Besides, there wasn't much chance to study in a one- or two-room log cabin crowded with several kids, a mother and father, and probably a brother or sister of the mother or father. Usually there was a lot going on at the house in the evening, and we had only candlelight, kerosene, or Coleman lanterns to study by until we got rural electrification in the thirties under Roosevelt.

Basketball was the one thing about school that we all liked. (Voget 1995, 100–101)

Mark Monroe, a Sioux who attended the Alliance, Nebraska, public schools, recalled that "all Indian children regardless of age" were put in an "Opportunity Room" where "they weren't taught anything."

They weren't given a report card. They weren't advanced from one grade to another. They just stayed in this room, drew pictures, and marked on the blackboard. My wife was in this room for seven years. When she started school, she was in the fifth grade. When she got out, she was still in the fifth grade. There was no advancement. . . .

I suppose this was the white school system's way of obeying the state law to keep Indian children in school without teaching them. (1994, 19)

Monroe refused to go to the "Opportunity Room" and attended regular classes. He remembered that Indians were at the bottom of the pecking order, below Mexicans and blacks. Stores in the town had signs saying, "No Indians or dogs allowed" (1994, 20). A 1976 study of public schools in Arizona found the following:

While increasingly, Indian parents are encouraging their children to attend and complete the public school program, the students apparently feel an estrangement between their homes and schools. Most Indian parents are reported to feel rejected by the schools. Having less education than their children, they are in awe of school administrators and are hesitant to become involved in school policy or programs. This attitude contributes to the lack of communication between Indian parents and teachers. (Arizona Department of Education 1976, 10)

In addition to the effects of what was called the Indian New Deal, Indians benefited from the many other mainstream New Deal employment programs such as the Works Progress Administration (WPA) and the Civilian Conservation Corps (CCC). Public works projects built many Indian day schools and gave many Indians their first introduction to wage labor, which began a cash economy that led gradually to the end of reservation trading posts.

JOHN COLLIER'S LEGACY

Collier (1963) was proud that he had helped to increase the number of Indian staff in the Indian Bureau from about 30 percent in 1933 to about 65 percent in 1945. He concluded, "*Assimilation*, not into our culture but into modern life, and *preservation and intensification of heritage* are not hostile choices, excluding one another, but are interdependent through and through. . . . It is the ancient tribal, village, communal organization which must conquer the modern world" (Collier 1963, 203; original emphasis). In contrast to traditional Indian societies, Collier found Western industrial society "manipulative, exploitive, and imposed" (235).

While new teachers were recruited with Collier's new goals in mind, many old Indian Service employees resisted the radical changes Collier sought and continued to administer schools and teach the way they had always done. One of these older employees, Albert Kneale, who had risen in the Indian Service from teacher to agency superintendent and had criticized the regimentation of the old government boarding schools, gives an interesting account of going from one extreme to the other. In his autobiography he scathingly criticizes the progressive idealists who wrote the Meriam Report:

> Under no circumstances should a pupil in an Indian school be punished. . . .
> Truant officers must go; children must not be compelled to attend school;
> the school would be made so pleasant, the instructress would be so
> talented, work would be so completely eliminated, play would have such
> a prominent part, as to transform the school into a fairy land, a place of
> enchantment. No labor either physical or mental would be required, in fact,
> nothing would be required; everyone would do precisely as he or she
> wished and, all in all, it would be such a paradise that the children would
> flock to it. (Kneale 1950, 130–31)

According to Kneale (1950, 376), "a new form of education was being catapulted into the reservations. The child must be unrepressed, free from rules, free from plans, unhampered in directing its own development."

George A. Boyce supervised schools on the Navajo Reservation for the BIA throughout the 1940s and described his experiences in his book *When Navajos Had Too Many Sheep*. Boyce (1974, 109) found Collier "a man of mysticism and paradox. He had a great reluctance about building roads in Indian country, or providing universal education, or providing other services that he felt would destroy 'Indian culture.'" Boyce was particularly upset about a budgeting error in 1937 that omitted funding for textbooks, library books, paper, pencils, playground equipment, soap, transportation, bus operation, and the like. In fact, the Navajo day schools were being run on the same amount per student that Pratt had received back in 1879, not adjusting for inflation. Boyce (1974, 94) found that "[a]ll of the Navajo boarding school plants were out of date and in poor repair," and students were still doing "farm work under the guise of its being 'vocational training.'" Even the recently built day schools were run-down, and many had water problems. Boyce thought that Collier's and some anthropologists' ideas for "hogan schools" were unrealistic, and he accused Collier of refusing to increase funding of Navajo schools despite the fact that fifteen thousand school-age Navajos were not in school because he thought that better roads and more schools would destroy Navajo culture. Collier opposed publicizing the financial problems of Navajo schools, but a publicity campaign that started in Gallup, New Mexico, and involved civic clubs, church groups, and newspaper editors publicized the plight of the Navajo in much the way Collier had done for the Pueblo in the 1920s. After leaving office, Collier opposed the passage of the Navajo-Hopi Rehabilitation Bill in 1949, which resulted from the publicity about Navajo poverty and lack of schools. This bill was supported by the Navajo tribe, and it provided $88,570,000 to improve the Navajo economy and education.

In *Indian Self-Rule*, Kenneth R. Philp (1986) presents the contradictory views on Collier's efforts. In that book, Floyd O'Neil notes that missionary teachers tended to despise Collier and to think he was in league with the devil. Boyce noted that missionaries to the Navajo were especially opposed to bilingual education. Collier himself attended a Catholic boarding school after the death of his mother and declared, "[W]ithin Catholicism, I experienced nothing except wisdom and great human kindness" (1963, 24). When he successfully helped to stop the use of tribal trust funds to support Protestant home missions in 1933, he was backed by the Bureau of Catholic Missions. The California Indian activist Rupert Costo, who felt the Indian Reorganization Act was imposed on tribes, labeled Collier's efforts the "Indian Raw Deal." In sharp contrast, Wilcomb E. Washburn, director of the American Studies Program at the Smithsonian Institution, expressed the opposite view— that Indian tribes only survived because of John Collier's efforts (Philp 1986, 48, 104). That real progress in Indian education had been made under Collier is indicated by the results of a three-year study of Indian students in federal, public, and mission schools. It showed that in 1928 only 6 percent of students were performing academically at the age-appropriate grade level, whereas in 1946 the figure was 36 percent (Peterson 1948). Indian education still had a long way to go. A 1948 article titled "No Place for Censors" in *Indian Education* indicated that long-term practices such as censoring boarding school students' letters home were still being practiced and should be stopped.

THE END OF PROGRESSIVE EDUCATION

As time went on, Progressive Education came under more and more criticism. Even Willard Beatty became disenchanted with the movement as it traveled on the road to advocating "life adjustment" classes and a deemphasis on academics. In a 1946 pamphlet Mrs. Charles Dietrich, president of the New Mexico Association on Indian Affairs, wrote:

> [Navajo leaders] ask for the same system of education as provided for white children. They are not satisfied with Progressive Education as it has been demonstrated on the reservation during the past ten years. Progressive Education demands specially gifted or trained teachers not always available for isolated spots on the reservation. (Quoted in Boyce 1974, 164)

The historian Donald Palmer (1976, 208, 215) concluded that "in the hands of an imaginative teacher, Dewey's methodology worked well in reaching the younger students" but "the goal of creating day schools which would become community centers failed because Navajo society lacked the [needed] cohesiveness and structure." Unlike the more assimilated Indians of the time and the sedentary Pueblo Indians, the still prevalent nomadic nature of the sheep-grazing Navajo economy worked against fixed-site day schools.

The conservative historian and critic of Progressive Education Diane Ravitch (2000, 244) concluded, "When used by teachers who saw activities as a better way of teaching subject matter rather than as a way of avoiding it—as means to an end rather than ends in themselves—the activity program was valuable. But in the hands of teachers who lacked subject matter knowledge, the activities became ends in themselves." Further, Ravitch found that "an educational philosophy of 'do your own thing' was the worst possible prescription for poor children" (393).

World War II quickly wiped out most of the New Deal gains in Indian education as funding was shifted from domestic programs to the war effort. Yet education lost in the schools owing to funding cuts was more than made up for in the field. More than twenty-four thousand Indians served in the armed forces. The most famous of these were the Navajo code talkers who served in the South Pacific providing a communications code based on their Native language that the Japanese could not break, though the original Navajo code talkers did not receive Congressional Medals of Honor until 2001. Thousands of other Native Americans, including women, found work in cities. Some of the returned veterans took advantage of the G.I. Bill after the war to get a college education, most majoring in education, and later took up leadership positions (Sando 1998). According to Szasz (1977, 107), World War II, "given the comparatively short time span of the conflict[,] . . . affected some tribes more than any other major event in the four centuries of Indian-white relations."

CHAPTER NINE

TERMINATION AND RELOCATION, 1944–1969

At the end of World War II, there was a renewed call to "set the American Indian free." In 1945 O. K. Armstrong maintained in an article in the popular magazine *Reader's Digest* that "tribal control and governmental regulations constantly remind the Indian of his inferior status" (Armstrong 1945, 49, 51). Indian Office attorney Felix S. Cohen (1945, 2) responded that what Armstrong was calling restrictions were actually privileges and that "all history shows that plunder, to be successful in a large scale, must be able to point to a high moral motivation." Later the same year Cohen declared that the denial of voting privileges to Indians in Arizona and New Mexico was a violation of the U.S. Constitution. Indian education director Willard Beatty noted in a 1947 article that in a number of states Indians were not welcome in "better" hotels, restaurants, and stores, but these same states were not able to suppress illegal bootlegging. In 1948 the Supreme Court struck down the legal barrier to Indians voting in Arizona and New Mexico and the following year barred religious instruction during the school day.

It was Armstrong's rather than Cohen's thinking that was accepted in a conservative U.S. Congress, which now found that the Indian Reorganization Act was forcing on the Indians a collectivist system with bigger doses of paternalism and regimentation. Testifying before the Indian Affairs Committee of the U.S. House of Representatives, Joseph Bruner, president of the American Indian Federation, which had been formed to fight the Indian Reorganization Act ten years before, declared:

[The Act] provided for communistic and un-American activities and government policies that were in principle communistic, subversive, and dangerous to our Nation, not only among the Indians, but all other Americans.

The Wheeler-Howard Act was conceived and sponsored by American Civil Liberties Union, a communistic organization with headquarters in New York City. . . . [W]e have continued to oppose the Indian Bureau program authorized by this act of Congress. We believe the same to be a dangerous, Christmocking, communistic aiding, subversive set up. (Quoted in Taylor 1973, 142)

Conservatives also wanted to reduce "big government." The relative political powerlessness of Indians made cutting the budgets for Indian programs easier than cutting other programs supported by powerful political constituencies (Fischbacher 1967).

However, the conservatives' assimilationist beliefs could actually push their efforts in the opposite direction from supporting cheaper educational programs such as day schools. The House Select Committee to Investigate Indian Affairs and Conditions criticized community day schools in 1944, saying day school students suffered the "handicap of having to spend their out of school hours in tepees, in shacks with dirt floors and no windows, in tents, in wickiups, in hogans where English is never spoken . . . and where there is sometimes an active antagonism or an abysmal indifference to the virtues of education" (quoted in Szasz 1977, 109).

The Committee found the answer to this problem in the old off-reservation boarding schools. This change in attitude received some support from Indians. The respected Navajo leader Chee Dodge sent a letter in September 1944 to the House Committee stating, "All day schools should be eliminated and more boarding schools established. Eliminate any effort to teach Navajo language in the schools in that Navajos have to learn English to compete with other people in employment" (quoted in Niethammer 2001, 65). Dodge also called for more trade schools, and in 1946, testifying in Washington, he called for making education compulsory again (Iverson 2002b). George L. Sánchez (1948) of the University of Texas was commissioned in 1946 to study the Indian Service's Navajo schools. He concluded that they could not function on the Navajo Reservation because the students' home life did not support education.

Chee Dodge's daughter, Annie Wauneka, was elected to the Navajo Tribal Council in 1951, and in a round-table discussion she lobbied for more boarding schools. Having been a boarding school student herself, she called for all Navajo children to be taught in state-accredited reservation boarding schools:

> The day schools were a failure from the start. . . . Scattered families and hogans many miles apart makes it hard for the children to attend classes. To attend a day school is very hard for the child. He learns how to keep clean, is told to learn the white man's language during the day. But he returns home to his hogan, he finds no conveniences, his parents are still clinging to the old way of living and the child is caught between the Indian way and the white way.
>
> Boarding schools are best for the Navajo children because they attend school nine months of the year. They learn fast, can keep clean, have suf-ficient diet, good sleeping quarters and a good recreation. When every child of school age is actually in school, we will know we have begun to solve our problems. Once we have education, the other problems will be taken care of. Lack of education has caused many of our young men and women as well as the old people to pass their time drinking, bootlegging, and using peyote. (Quoted in Niethammer 2001, 161)

However, at a 1968 congressional hearing on the Kennedy Report she called for smaller community schools for younger children (Neithammer 2001).

Tribal council delegate Hoskie Cronemeyer also criticized the poor quality of day school education in a speech in 1952. He called for a return to the "very good" boarding schools of "thirty or forty years ago," compulsory education, and speaking only English on the school compound. He declared, "The teaching of Navajo customs should be done away with so that only school work will be carried on for our children. We ask that this be carried on instead of customs we already know" (Iverson 2002b, 107–8).

The use of Native languages in schools of the Bureau of Indian Affairs (the new name of the U.S. Indian Service as of 1947) decreased under this conservative onslaught, but it was not totally eliminated as under the old policy of the late nineteenth century. The 1951 *BIA Manual* stated:

> It is self-evident that the first step in any program of instruction must be to develop in the children the ability to speak, understand, and think in the English language. Every effort shall be made to provide activities and other forms of encouragement for children to use English in their daily association in the classroom, in the dormitories, and on the playgrounds. However, as language expression is essential to the development of thought, the use of native languages by Indian children *may not be forbidden*. In fact, it has been determined experimentally that the use of teacher-interpreters to clarify English meaning in the early grades greatly speeds up the acquisition of English. (Task Force 1976, 122; original emphasis)

Some continued concern for cultural sensitivity is indicated by a one-month summer workshop held in 1953 at the newly opened Inter-mountain Boarding School in Brigham City, Utah, for five hundred BIA school employees on the topic "the problems of cultural exchange" (Fischbacher 1967).

The "final solution" Congress came up with for the "Indian problem" was to let the Indians become "free" by terminating their reservations. With termination, the federal trust status of the reservation would be ended and the tribe's land and other assets would be divided up and distributed to the tribal members. Congress abolished its standing committees on Indian Affairs in 1946 and transferred their work to committees on public lands dominated by westerners. In 1953, as part of the relaxation of controls, Indians were allowed to buy liquor (over the objections of tribal governments) and firearms, and the House passed Concurrent Resolution 108, which declared:

> [It is] the policy of Congress, as rapidly as possible, to make the Indians within the territorial limits of the United States subject to the same laws and entitled to the same privileges and responsibilities as are applicable to other citizens of the United States, to end their status as wards of the United States and to grant them all the rights and prerogatives pertaining to American citizenship. (Quoted in Prucha 1984, 1044)

The same year Congress passed six termination bills. States were to assume responsibility for the education of all Indian children in public schools. The reservation of the Menominee in Wisconsin was terminated by Congress in 1954. Indians were slow to oppose termination, and some even testified in favor of the policy before Congress. Early termination legislation went through Congress under unanimous consent procedures, meaning that a single legislator could have stopped it.

However, educated Indians were organizing to defend their rights. In 1944 they founded the National Congress of American Indians. Unlike older organizations such as the Indian Rights Association and the American Indian Defense Association, the National Congress of American Indians was an Indian- rather than white-run advocacy group. With the help of Indian opposition, Congress judged the termination policy of the 1950s a failure much faster than the old allotment policy it resembled. In 1973 Congress put back into federal trust status land still owned by the Menominee tribe. Other terminated tribes such as the Klamath in Oregon were not so lucky.

Dillon S. Meyer became Commissioner of Indian Affairs in 1950. He had directed the War Relocation Authority in charge of releasing West Coast Japanese who were interned during World War II in concentration camps, some located on Indian reservations. Perhaps that is the origin of the idea for another termination program involving the relocation of Indians off reservations and into the cities. These relocated Indians often had great difficulty adjusting to urban life and frequently returned home. Philleo Nash, Commissioner of Indian Affairs from 1961 to 1966, described relocation as "essentially a one-way bus ticket from rural to urban poverty" (Philp 1986, 165). Nash had recommended Meyer for the post of Commissioner and then later asked President Harry Truman to fire him. Nash continued the relocation policy with $4,000 in support, but the need to spread out Indians in urban areas to prevent segregated enclaves gained little community support.

Wilma Mankiller's experiences give an indication of what happened to thousands of Indians. When she was about eleven years old her family was relocated to San Francisco, where they discovered "'the better life' the BIA had promised all of us was, in reality, life in a tough, urban ghetto" (Mankiller and Wallis 1993, 73). They spent the first couple of weeks in 1956 in the city's tough Tenderloin District. Living in areas like Hunters Point, she rubbed shoulders with other minorities, and the San Francisco Indian Center became her second home. She was radicalized in this urban environment and participated in the takeover of Alcatraz Island with her brother and was director of the Native American Youth Center in East Oakland for a time. Later she would return home to become the first female principal chief of the Cherokee, serving from 1985 to 1995 (Mankiller and Wallis 1993).

THE SPECIAL NAVAJO FIVE-YEAR PROGRAM AND LONG RANGE ACT

Progress in Indian education was reversed not just at the congressional level. Because of the disruptions of World War II, there were more Indian students out of school in 1946 than in 1928, most of them Navajo (Szasz 1977). Chee Dodge estimated that there were fourteen thousand Navajo children without any school facilities available to them in 1946. While most tribes underwent allotment of their reservations in the nineteenth century and experienced nearly one hundred years of close contact with whites, the Navajo Reservation was a vast isolated exception (Iverson 2002a, 2002b). A national publicity campaign supported by service organizations, newspaper editors, and churches was started in Gallup, New Mexico, to publicize nationally the lack of schools for Navajo children. Supporters cited the contributions of the Navajo code talkers in World War II and the Navajo Treaty of 1868, which promised a teacher for every thirty children, as evidence to support the federal responsibility for providing more schools (Boyce 1974).

In 1900 it was estimated that only one out of nine school-aged Navajo children was in school. By 1930 an estimated 46 percent were attending school, but World War II resulted in the closing of nineteen day schools on the reservation. As staff went to war, Navajo assistants took over. The Civil Service Commission temporarily abolished teacher examinations and allowed schools to hire locally. Ruth Werner (1972) started teaching at Red Rock Day School in 1941 and found, "The whole instructional program appeared to be an insurmountable mountain with no course of study, few texts and no training for teaching English as a second language" (52). She reported having students ranging in age from six to thirteen in her classroom.

Selective Service during World War II classified 88 percent of male Navajos screened for military service as illiterate; 9 percent had tuberculosis. The Bureau of the Budget would not approve new Navajo school construction until existing off-reservation schools were filled (Boyce 1974). Rather than send elementary age students to faraway boarding schools, a Special Navajo Five-Year Program was started under the direction of Hildegarde Thompson (1975) in September 1946 to fill those schools with adolescent Navajos who had never been in school. This program solved two major problems for the BIA. It helped the large number of teenage Navajo children who had never attended school, and it helped to fill the off-reservation boarding schools that were experiencing declining enrollments as more Indian children from other areas attended public schools. The use of underenrolled existing schools allowed the government to save money by not having to build new schools on the Navajo Reservation.

Although many of the students in the Navajo program had never been in school, they were teenagers. They needed to learn to speak English to get jobs, they needed both academic and vocational training, and they needed to learn something about the "major culture." According to the Navajo Tribal Council member Sam Gorman, who supported relocation in 1953, there was "no hope of making a decent living under any conditions" on the reservation: "The students of today, even if they only finished third or fourth grade, so long as they have some English, so long as they have a little knowledge of how to read and write, they have the opportunity through Placement and Relocation to go out and find a good world in time" (Iverson 2002b, 97–98).

The Special Navajo Five-Year Program taught in the Navajo language in the initial years so that students could immediately begin basic studies. Books were written in Navajo using a special beginners' vocabulary. The first principle of the program was that it was bilingual. Teachers worked under the following guidelines:

1. Their teaching, so far as possible, should be based on first-hand experiences.
2. Instruction should be individualized by organizing the classroom into smaller flexible groupings.
3. Pupils' misbehavior should be analyzed as to its causes and dealt with by eliminating the causes, not by punishment. (Thompson 1975, 94)

During the first three years of the program, classes were limited to twenty-five students and were staffed by a teacher with experience on the Navajo Reservation and a bilingual Navajo-English-speaking teacher's aide, called a teacher-interpreter. In addition, the program employed Navajo-speaking shop and home economics teachers. The last two years of the five-year program emphasized vocational instruction. Students were taught white ways, but they were also encouraged to maintain their traditional culture:

> The pupils also were taught to keep their deep respect for their parents and their Navajo way of life. They were cautioned, now that they were being given formal schooling, that they should not look down on their parents and Navajo friends on the reservation who had no such opportunities and who could not speak English. They were taught that their parents, even though many never had been to school a day in their lives, still were well educated and wise in their Navajo culture. The teaching of respect for the Navajo way of life, and regard for parental authority, was important because the staff recognized that any lessening of this esteem for parents was the dangerous beginning of possible destruction of respect for other types of authority. (Thompson 1975, 104)

The program started with two hundred students, all of them over twelve years old, at Sherman Institute in Riverside, California, which was facing closure because the state of California agreed to educate Indian children, and immediately was viewed by the BIA as an overwhelming success. A second group of more than one hundred students was sent to Sherman a few weeks after school started (Boyce 1974). In fall 1947 the program was expanded to ten more boarding schools, and it served fifty thousand students over a period of twelve years. The five-year program was expanded to an eight-year program, which was eventually replaced with a full high school program. The last Special Navajo Program student graduated in 1963 (Parker 1996).

In 1950 the Long Range Act was passed by Congress "to further the purposes of existing treaties with the Navajo Indians, to provide facilities, employment, and services essential in combating hunger, disease, poverty, and demoralization among the members of the Navajo and Hopi Tribes" (Young 1961, 1). The Act authorized the appropriation of $88,570,000, including $25 million for education. Various efforts were made to provide more schools for Navajo students. The Bushnell Army Hospital in Brigham City, Utah, was converted into the Intermountain Boarding School for several thousand students and opened in 1950. However, over time the Navajo objected more and more to having their children so far from home, and in 1974 students from twenty-seven tribes were admitted. However, some of these tribes had a history of hostility, and in February 1975 rioting erupted. Over three days students "injured three officers and destroyed several police cars [and] [t]wenty students were arrested" (Hodgkinson 2002, n.p.). Subsequently, enrollment declined and Intermountain was closed in 1984.

Another approach to finding classroom space for Navajo students was the building of dormitories in towns bordering the reservation from which students would attend public schools. In 1954 a twenty-year agreement was signed with school boards in Arizona, New Mexico, and Utah (Young 1957). Although intended for older students, in fact, many younger children were boarded in these dormitories (see table 3). According to Robert Roessel (1967, 49), under the Navajo Emergency Education Program, "more was accomplished during the year 1954–1955 to get all Navaho children in school than in all previous years put together. By the close of that school year, 8,000 additional children were in school." In addition, twenty-five mission and parochial schools enrolled another 1,483 Navajo students (Young 1957). According to Thompson (1975, 147), "Only six federal schools on the [Navajo] reservation in 1960 were large enough to permit children in accordance with policy to continue through grades 6; 53 provided instruction through grade 3, and 16 could not accommodate children beyond grade 1 or 2."

Additional space for primary students was also found by establishing trailer schools in isolated areas (fig. 21). First reported having been used in 1953, trailer schools consisted of "'quonset hut' buildings for the classrooms and kitchen, trailers for quarters for employees, and toilet trailers for the boys and girls" (Roessel 1967, 49). There were twenty-eight schools in 1957 and eleven in 1965 (serving 383 Navajo students) to supplement the central boarding schools, community boarding schools, and regular day schools. The idea was that in areas where trailer schools were successful, permanent schools would be built.

TABLE 3
Bordertown Dormitory Enrollment, 1957–1963

Year	Total	Ages 6–12	Percent Ages 6–12
1957	1460	515	35
1959	1755	714	41
1961	2332	1064	41
1963	2300	838	35

Source: Thompson 1975, 148.

Whipporwill Trailer School, 1961. Photograph by Edward C. Hinckley.

INTRODUCTION OF ESL AND
BILINGUAL EDUCATION

The use of special educational programs for Indian students was not just criticized by non-Indians who thought American Indians should be treated like everyone else. The Navajo questioned whether their children were receiving the same education as white children. Thompson describes her appearance before the Navajo Tribal Council to explain the BIA's teaching methods:

Once, an entire day was spent with the Navajo Tribal Council explaining the methods used in teaching English to non-English-speaking Navajo beginners. Many Navajos at that time were critical of methods used in federal schools. Teachers provided a variety of first-hand experiences, much of which was in the form of play, to make oral English meaningful to small Navajo-speaking beginners. This did not look like good teaching to some Navajos. I used a pictorial chart showing the early experiences and language learning of two children—one learning in Navajo, the other in English. After sketching the learning experiences of each child to age six, I put the picture of the Navajo child beside the picture of the English-speaking child, each shown with a speaking vocabulary of 2,000 words, and I simultaneously removed from the mouth of the Navajo child all of the Navajo vocabulary in which he had learned to converse. Then I explained that both children entered school and that the child had to learn to talk in the language of the school—English—but that the English-speaking child was six years ahead of him in English language. I then showed some of the materials and toys which Barbara Henderson, a Navajo who taught at Beclabito, used to help overcome the English language deficit of Navajo beginners; and I explained how she used the materials. "This might seem that she was letting children play," I pointed out, "but she uses the children's play to teach them enough English so that they can begin their primary grade work." (Thompson 1975, 13)

HILDEGARD THOMPSON
AS DIRECTOR OF BIA EDUCATION

After Hildegard Thompson ran the Navajo Special Program, she was put in charge of all Navajo education programs starting in 1949 and then took over from Willard Beatty in Washington, D.C. Beatty resigned in 1952 in frustration when the BIA was decentralized and he lost direct authority over its educational system to the area directors, who reported directly to the Commissioner of Indian Affairs. The BIA had been reorganized in 1949 into eleven area offices: Juneau, Alaska; Phoenix and Window Rock, Arizona; Sacramento, California; Minneapolis, Minnesota; Billings, Montana; Albuquerque, New Mexico; Anadarko and Muskogee, Oklahoma; Portland, Oregon, and Aberdeen, South Dakota.

Szasz (1977) marks Thompson's accession to the directorship as the start of a decline in BIA educational programs. With reduced authority, Thompson was forced to make a number of compromises. Beatty is reported to have remarked that Thompson could "bend farther without breaking than anyone I have ever seen" (Szasz 1977, 124). However, not all was bad. In the 1950s BIA teachers got more cultural orientation, students got more opportunities to leave campus and visit local homes, and family-style dining was added to the school cafeteria (Horne and McBeth 1998). Thompson also worked to make BIA high school curricula more suitable for college preparation, but this hurt the vocational programs (Parker 1996). In 1957 the BIA held thirty workshops that were attended by more than two thousand teachers. Special summer programs for Indian students were started in 1960, and by 1963 some 20,444 students participated. Programs like this one were designed to stem the estimated 60 percent Indian high school dropout rate in the late 1950s. A BIA Master Teacher program was started in 1962.

Thompson continued the publication of the BIA newsletter, *Indian Education*, which was started in 1936, but publication ceased with issue 441 the year after she left office (Fischbacher 1967). Underhill's *Here Come the Navaho!* was published by Haskell Institute in 1953 for use in Indian schools. It was one of eight books about the Paiute, Papago, Pueblo, Blackfeet, and other Indians published by the BIA for use in Indian schools. There were also seven Indian handcraft books; and the bilingual *Indian Life Readers*, which included a Navajo series, a Sioux series, and a Pueblo series illustrated by Indian artists, was reprinted.

When Thompson left the BIA in 1965 its educational programs declined precipitously. The position of Commissioner of Indian Affairs was eliminated and replaced by assistant secretary of the Department of the Interior for Indian affairs in 1977. That new position and the position of director of the Office of Indian Education Programs became revolving doors, with each appointee staying in office for at most a few years. The central office curriculum support staff was reduced and then moved to a regional center in Albuquerque. Later, with budget cuts, what remained was for all practical purposes eliminated, leaving no real curricular support for BIA-funded schools other than that provided by Chapter 1 of the Elementary and Secondary Education Act and Special Education staff.

THE "NEW FRONTIER" OF
INDIAN EDUCATION

When John F. Kennedy became president in 1961, there were still five thousand Indian and Eskimo children without available schools. Kennedy set up a task force whose members were W. W. Keeler, a Cherokee and high official in the Phillips Petroleum Company; Philleo Nash, former lieutenant governor of Wisconsin; James E. Officor, a professor at the University of Arizona; and William Zimmerman Jr., former Assistant Commissioner of Indian Affairs. The task force called for a new independent study of Indian education. Under the Kennedy administration, the BIA increased classroom square footage, added libraries, and developed a standard list of supplies and equipment. For the first time money for equipment and supplies was provided with new school construction money. New schools were built based on population trends and available water. These site considerations made for large regional schools rather than small community schools.

The original 1965 Elementary and Secondary Education Act (Public Law [P.L.] 89–10) that provided funds for disadvantaged students under Title I did not include BIA schools, even though Congress allocated funds to states based partly on Indian student populations. A year later, Title I funds were made available to BIA schools. Kindergarten and special education programs became common in the early 1970s.

As more and more Indian students attended public schools, BIA schools increasingly served the most isolated children and children from broken or disrupted homes. In 1952 it was estimated that there were 127,957 Indian children between the ages of six and eighteen. Almost 37,000 were attending BIA schools; a little over half of these students were still in boarding schools, and the rest were in 233 day schools in fourteen states and Alaska. Two hundred forty-four students were in health sanatoria. There were almost 52,000 Indian students in public schools, 60 percent of whom were supported with Johnson-O'Malley funds for a cost of over $2.5 million a year. Almost 10,000 students were attending mission schools, and 21,435 were not in school (Fischbacher 1967). By 1965, 20 percent of the children in BIA schools were dropouts or failures from other schools. Another postwar change was a move to the old idea that "English language capability is fundamental to Indian progress" (Thompson 1975, 227). A high school education was now seen as the minimum necessary for gaining employment.

SCHOOLS AND CURRICULA

The typical reservation school of the termination era, Bureau, mission, or public operated, has been described by the anthropologist Murray L. Wax:

> The situation almost appears colonial, or at the least caste-like: between Indian community and schools there is a strong social barrier, typified by the fences which surround the [school] compound. Parents rarely visit the schools; teachers rarely visit the homes; each side finds interaction with the other uncomfortable.
>
> The consequence of this barrier [between the school and the community] is that by the intermediate grades Indian children have begun to develop a closed and solidary peer society within the walls of the school. (1971, 83)

There was little parental participation in school management at the beginning of the 1960s. Since the 1930s school boards had existed in some communities, but these boards, where they existed, were selected, not elected. They could only advise and lacked real power (Thompson 1975).

Ralph Nader testified before the Special Subcommittee on Indian Education:

> In any school with Indian students, BIA or public, cultural conflict is inevitable. The student, bringing with him all the values, attitudes, and beliefs that constitute his "Indianness," is expected to subordinate that Indianness to the general American standards of the school. The fact that he, the student, must do all the modifying, all the compromising, seems to say something to him about the relative value of his own culture as opposed to that of the school. . . .
>
> It has been estimated that for half of the Indians enrolled in Federal schools English is not the first language learned. Yet, when the child enters school he is expected to function in a totally English-speaking environment. He muddles along in this educational void until he learns to assign meaning to the sounds the teacher makes. By the time he has begun to understand

English, he has already fallen well behind in all the basic skill areas. In fact, it appears that his language handicap increases as he moves through school. And although it is no longer official BIA policy to discourage use of native languages, many reports in the hearings indicate the contrary in practice. (Nader 1969, 49, 51)

As in the past, most beginning teachers of Native students were not receiving special training or curricula appropriate to their students' needs. Nancy and Gary Brooks accepted positions to teach Aleut students on St. George Island in Alaska in 1962. They missed the July 27 sailing from Seattle owing to poor advice and had to borrow money to fly to Alaska to catch up with their ship. They found that the Bureau of Commercial Fisheries (BCF) was in charge of operating their school. According to the BCF, "[Students] just needed to be able to fish, kill the fur seals and do the work in the village, under BCF's directions." They had all the latest equipment and supplies but no curriculum guides. They were amazed that they were given no advice or guidance about teaching the children. They were there simply to fill the vacant positions. They also found that the Aleuts were being mistreated, and like many other teachers in similar isolated communities, they only lasted one year (pers. comm., March 4, 2003).

Pamela J. Cook, who was recruited to teach on the Navajo Reservation in 1967, recalled:

The children were brought into the boarding schools at age six and taught to line up. None of them spoke English. It was constantly drilled into us that the students were not allowed to speak Navajo. Wednesdays were religious release days. The teachers gave up their classrooms early and missionaries would give religious instruction. When the parents registered the students they were required to sign up for a religion—traditional Navajo was not a choice. The parents rarely entered the school compounded [sic] area. It was fenced in against sheep and cattle. They dropped their children outside the fence at the back of the school. Very few families had vehicles. Children rarely went home all school year. They ran away from boarding school. We always had a tracker on staff. (Pers. comm., January 29, 2003)

Teachers who allowed students to speak Navajo were reprimanded by school administrators.

The books used in Indian schools in this period reflected all-white middle-class culture. Joseph H. Suina described their effect on one Indian child from Cochiti Pueblo:

> The Dick and Jane reading series in the primary grades presented me with pictures of a home with a pitched roof, straight walls, and sidewalks. I could not identify with these from my Pueblo world. However, it was clear I didn't have these things and what I did have did not measure up. At night, long after grandmother went to sleep, I would lay awake staring at our crooked adobe walls casting uneven shadows from the light of the fireplace. The walls were no longer just right for me. My life was no longer just right. I was ashamed of being who I was and I wanted to change right then and there. Somehow it became so important to have straight walls, clean hair and teeth, and a spotted dog to chase after. I even became critical and hateful toward my bony, fleabag of a dog. I loved the familiar and cozy surroundings of my grandmother's house but now I imagined it could be a heck of a lot better if only I had a white man's house with a bed, a nice couch, and a clock. In school books, all the child characters ever did was run around chasing their dog or a kite. They were always happy. As for me, all I seemed to do at home was go back and forth with buckets of water and cut up sticks for a lousy fire. "Didn't the teacher say that drinking coffee would stunt my growth?" "Why couldn't I have nice tall glasses of milk so I could have strong bones and white teeth like those kids in the books?" "Did my grandmother really care about my well-being?" (1988, 298)

The psychologist Otto Klineberg examined fifteen widely used basal reading textbooks used in U.S. schools and published between 1957 and 1962. He found only one example of a nonwhite American in them. The white Americans were "almost exclusively North European in origin and appearance" and blond (Klineberg 1963, 75–76). In 1970 the American Indian Historical Society based in San Francisco published *Textbooks and the American Indian* by Jeannette Henry criticizing the inaccurate portrayal of Indians in textbooks.

Naomi Hand, a BIA education specialist, reported in *Indian Education* on changes in the BIA secondary curriculum:

> Emphasis is now placed on academic training in grades 7, 8, and 9, with some practical arts courses (home economics and basic shop) required in all

ninth and tenth grades. Although vocational courses may be taken as electives in grades 11 and 12, high school graduates are encouraged to continue education beyond the high school, either in vocational or technical schools, or in college or universities. (Quoted in Fischbacher 1967, 433)

This shift to a more academic focus in BIA schools had both positive and negative consequences (see chap. 10). Other changes that were taking place in BIA schools involved the age of students: in 1936 the average ninth-grader was twenty years old; in 1959, fifteen years old. In 1965 Haskell Institute discontinued high school classes and became a postsecondary vocational school. That same year the BIA offered scholarships to approximately seventeen hundred postsecondary students. Adult education programs were started in 1956 for five tribes and expanded to 107 Indian communities in 1961. According to the historian Theodore Fischbacher (1967, 442), "By the end of 1962 some 6,700 adult Indians had participated in the programs and 51 had completed the required course, then representing the equivalent of high school graduation." By 1966 there were programs in 302 communities.

POSITIVE STEPS FORWARD

One bright spot in the otherwise bleak picture for Indian tribes in the termination era was the passage in 1946 of the Federal Indian Claims Commission Act. This Act allowed Indians to file claims against the United States for lands illegally taken over the years. Millions of dollars have been paid out under this act; however, money cannot replace land and the traditional way of life that use of that land represented.

The effort to get Indians into public schools showed rapid progress after World War II. In 1953 fifteen states and the Territory of Alaska, along with individual school districts in other states, had Johnson-O'Malley contracts. These contracts provided funding for educating fifty-one thousand Indian children in public schools. This effort got another boost through Impact Aid. Public Laws 874 and 815, first passed in 1950, authorized funds for public schools in federally impacted areas.

These laws were designed to ensure that children living on tax-exempt land such as military bases did not pose a financial burden to public schools. In 1953 Congress amended the Impact Aid laws to include Indians living or working on reservations or other federal trust land. Public Law (P.L.) 874 provides a large part of the operating expenses of many reservation public schools today, and P.L. 815 funds were used to build many of them (Szasz 1977). With the new funds available to support Indian students in public schools, JOM funds were reduced and shifted from schools' general operating funds to providing special services to Indian students. This could mean anything from Indian counselors to school supplies that parents could not afford. In 1956 P.L. 959 was passed by Congress to provide vocational training to primarily rural Indians ages eighteen to thirty-five (Fischbacher 1967). In 1965 there were 48,000 Indian students in BIA schools and 4,200 in BIA dorms attending public schools (*Indian Affairs* 1968).

In 1966 President Lyndon B. Johnson appointed Haskell graduate Robert L. Bennett Commissioner of Indian Affairs. A member of the Oneida Nation, Bennett was the first Indian appointed Commissioner since Ely Parker. Bennett was a veteran BIA employee who, in contrast to some other BIA employees, "believed that the job of the commissioner was to advocate Indian desires rather than to promote government policies to Indians" (Ellis 1979, 326). President Johnson, in a special message delivered to Congress in 1968 on "the forgotten American" called for Indian self-determination ("that erases old attitudes of paternalism and promotes a partnership self-help"), an equal standard of living for Indians and non-Indians, freedom of choice, and their full participation in modern America—"a policy of self-help, self-development, self-determination" (quoted in Taylor 1973, 200). That year more than half the BIA budget, more than $125 million, went to education, kindergartens were reintroduced to some BIA schools, five thousand Indian high school graduates entered college, and the Instructional Service Center was started for the BIA, housed at Intermountain Boarding School in Utah (*Indian Affairs* 1968).

There was also some university interest in Indian education. In 1959 Arizona State University established the Center for Indian Education under the direction of Robert A. Roessel Jr. and began publishing the *Journal of American Indian Education* in 1961. Along with the *Journal of*

Navajo Education, published from about 1981 to 1997, and the *Canadian Journal of Native Education*, published since 1973, it is among the few journals exclusively devoted to providing information on American Indian education. In 1969 Indian educators meeting in Minneapolis formed the National Indian Education Association.

CHAPTER TEN

SELF-DETERMINATION, 1969–1989

Over the years, through education, federal programs, and deeper involvement with mainstream America, Indian tribes developed a core of leadership capable of telling the federal government what they wanted. This leadership was almost unanimous in it opposition to termination. The alternative put forward was self-determination: letting Indian people determine their own destiny through their tribal governments. The drive for Indian self-determination must be viewed in the larger context of American minority groups seeking equal rights after World War II. Blacks, through the National Association for the Advancement of Colored People (NAACP), pursued a civil rights agenda through litigation and nonviolent civil disobedience. Radical leaders such as Malcolm X and more moderate leaders such as Martin Luther King Jr. kept the struggle for equal rights in the news. Especially important were the graphic images of racism broadcast on television, which was just being introduced into America's living rooms.

The 1954 Supreme Court decision *Brown* v. *Board of Education* outlawed "separate but equal" schools for blacks. The treatment of all minorities in the United States received increased attention throughout the 1960s. The raised consciousness of some educators resulting from the renewed interest in culturally appropriate education is demonstrated in the words of the new director of the BIA's Office of Education Programs, James E. Hawkins:

> Culture shock at any age can be a grueling ordeal. In a child it is heart-rending. What is encouraging about the new thrust of bilingual education

for the Indian children who need it is that it will go a long way in making these children feel at home in their early classroom years. If these children are able to work in their own frame of reference, with their own familiar language and customs, there is every reason to hope that their early experience in school will be a happy and fruitful endeavor. (1971, ii)

Hawkins came from the Peace Corps and got a fellow Peace Corps alumnus, Robert Rebert, to head up the BIA's Language Arts Branch. Rebert was instrumental in changing the Bilingual Education Act to include Indian programs and then helped several BIA schools to obtain bilingual funding. However, the push for Indian preference in hiring gutted the key Language Arts Branch staff in 1973.

At the end of the 1960s there were two major studies of Indian education. Robert J. Havighurst of the University of Chicago directed the National Study of American Indian Education from 1967 to 1971. The 1972 book, *To Live on This Earth*, by Estelle Fuchs and Havighurst, summarized the results of that study. In their introduction they wrote:

With minor exceptions the history of Indian education had been primarily the transmission of white American education, little altered, to the Indian child as a one-way process. The institution of the school is one that was imposed by and controlled by the non-Indian society, its pedagogy and curriculum little changed for the Indian children, its goals primarily aimed at removing the child from his aboriginal culture and assimilating him into the dominant white culture. Whether coercive or persuasive, this assimilationist goal of schooling has been minimally effective with Indian children, as indicated by their record of absenteeism, retardation, and high dropout rates. (1972, 19)

The second study was by the Special Senate Subcommittee on Indian Education. Testimony from hearings held by this committee fill seven volumes, with a 1969 summary report titled *Indian Education: A National Tragedy, a National Challenge*, also known as the Kennedy Report. The title of this report says it all.

Fuchs and Havighurst reported that most Indian students and parents approved of their schools but that Indian community leaders were "overwhelmingly in favor of the school doing something to help Indian students learn about their tribal culture" (1972, 181, 187) and that the most common parental suggestion was that "schools should pay more attention to the Indian heritage" (1972, 170). Rosalie Wax and Murray Wax's (1968) research on the Pine Ridge Reservation showed that tribal elders and the students' extended families were forces for keeping students in school and that the forces causing students to drop out of school were those of cultural disintegration, forces similar to those that cause dropouts in all schools.

One of the most interesting parts of the National Study was a film analysis of cultural confrontation in Alaskan schools done by John Collier Jr. (1973), son of the former Commissioner of Indian Affairs. Collier filmed and taped isolated Alaskan village schools, the schools at Bethel, and Native students in the Anchorage public schools. He found that formal education was designed to get Eskimo children to leave their village life and enter the white world, with no teaching of English as a second language or culturally relevant education. Collier used movie film and tapes of actual classrooms to study verbal and nonverbal interaction. Too often he found only teacher-to-student com-munication rather than the instructional conversation between and among teachers and students that Roland Tharp and other researchers identified in the 1990s as needed for effective instruction (Tharp and Yamauchi 1994). Collier also found teaching in the schools run by the BIA, missionaries, the state of Alaska, and the Anchorage public school system much the same.

Senator Edward Kennedy, chair of the Special Senate Subcommittee on Indian Education after the assassination of his brother Robert, was even more critical than Havighurst of Indian education in his foreword to *Indian Education:*

1. Drop-out rates are twice the national average in both public and Federal schools. Some school districts have dropout rates approaching 100 percent
2. Achievement levels of Indian children are 2 to 3 years below those of white students; and the Indian child falls progressively further behind the longer he stays in school
3. Only 1 percent of Indian children in elementary schools have Indian teachers or principals
4. One-fourth of elementary and secondary school teachers—by their own admission—would prefer not to teach Indian children; and

Indian children more than any other minority group, believe themselves to be "below average" in intelligence. (Special Subcommittee
on Indian Education 1969, ix)

While Havighurst's study showed that some of these claims were
exaggerated, the situation was still intolerable, and in a special message
to Congress on Indian affairs in 1970, President Richard Nixon wrote:

The story of the Indian in America is something more than the record of
the white man's frequent aggression, broken agreements, intermittent
remorse and prolonged failure. It is a record also of endurance, of survival,
of adaptation and creativity in the face of overwhelming obstacles. It is a
record of enormous contributions to this country—to its art and culture, to
its strength and spirit, to its sense of history and its sense of purpose.

It is long past time that the Indian policies of the Federal government
began to recognize and build upon the capacities and insights of the Indian
people. Both as a matter of justice and as a matter of enlightened social
policy, we must begin to act on the basis of what the Indians themselves
have long been telling us. The time has come to break decisively with the
past and to create the conditions for a new era in which the Indian future
is determined by Indian acts and Indian decisions. (Nixon 1971, 565)

Nixon appointed Louis Bruce, a Mohawk-Sioux who was a founder
and executive director of the National Congress of American Indians,
his Commissioner of Indian Affairs. The first major legislative victory
for this new policy of self-determination was the passage of the Indian
Education Act, Title IV of P.L. 92-318 (86 Stat., 334–45) in 1972. The act
provided funds for supplemental programs for Indian children in
public schools on and off Indian reservations. It was an attempt to
remedy some of the problems in Indian education identified in the
National Study of American Indian Education and the Kennedy Report.
All public schools with ten or more Indian students were eligible to
receive funding for supplemental programs designed to meet the
special needs of Indian students, including the use of culturally
relevant and bilingual curriculum materials. Schools were required to
involve Indian parents and communities in designing these programs.
It also established the Office of Indian Education in the Office of
Education (which became the U.S. Department of Education in 1980)

and the National Advisory Council on Indian Education with fifteen members to be appointed by the president from nominees provided by Indian tribes and organizations. The Council was to report annually to Congress on the state of Indian education. There were also sections providing competitive grants to public schools, adult education programs, and colleges and universities for training teachers for BIA schools, with preference given to Indians. A key feature of the act was its recognition of the special needs of Indian students who did not live on Indian reservations.

In 1974 new JOM regulations were drawn up by representatives of nearly forty Indian organizations. JOM funds were to be used for supplementary programs designed to meet the special needs of Indian students. Parent advisory committees were required for JOM programs, and progress was made to shift the flow of JOM money from states to Indian groups. Also in 1974, the BIA "published regulations and due process procedures " for its schools, which included "the right to freedom of religion and culture [and] speech and expression" (Prucha 1984, 1144). The Indian Education Amendments of 1978 (P.L. 95–561) established standards for BIA schools, institutionalized BIA school boards, required formula funding of BIA schools, and provided for increased Indian involvement in the spending of Impact Aid funds (Szasz 1977).

BOARDING SCHOOLS IN THE ERA OF SELF-DETERMINATION

In the 1960s the BIA started a large building program. For example, extensive construction was done at Phoenix Indian School in the 1950s and 1960s to improve the school facilities. In 1960 it became Phoenix Indian High School (PIHS), and it received regional North Central accreditation for its programs. The school superintendent and principal earned master's degrees from Arizona State University. In 1966 students were found to average three grade levels behind mainstream students, and "many still had severe language problems" (Parker 1996, 49). Between 1968 and 1973 male students began to wear long hair. In 1979 PIHS staff was weakened by the "Honky Out Bill" that caused experienced non-Indian BIA employees to take early retirement. This new federal law mandating absolute Indian preference in hiring and promotion helped to create a hostile working environment and ended the chances of non-Indians for professional advancement within the BIA (Parker 1996; Feraca 1990).

The director of the Indian Studies Program at the University of California spoke to PIHS students about "Red Power," and they started to demand their "rights." The student body also changed as more students came from dysfunctional homes, with schools closer to the reservations getting better students. "Student elections had become nothing more than popularity contests. . . . [F]ew of the winners served out their terms" (Parker 1996, 55). In 1986, at the request of the school board, the principal was removed for his failure to maintain discipline and to communicate with parents. Alcohol abuse became epidemic at the school, and during the 1984–85 school year, 256 of 700 students were expelled. Students had unstructured time every day, and the library was not open during the late afternoon and evening hours. In 1998 only 108 students were enrolled. The last 19 students graduated from the school and it was closed in 1990. Dorothy Parker (1996) attributes the decline of PIHS to the demolition of old buildings on campus that led to teachers moving off campus, changes in the makeup of the student body, the reduced emphasis on vocational training, poorly prepared students coming from reservation schools having to cope with an academic curriculum, and a new sense of Indian identity that empowered students. She concluded, "Undoubtedly there were some students for whom the school was an unhappy experience, but most have recalled Phoenix Indian School as a place where doors were opened to opportunities in the world beyond the reservation" (1996, 5).

Ben Chavis's (1999) study of former students who attended Intermountain, Phoenix Indian, Sherman, and Stewart Indian High Schools between 1976 and 1986 found that the students appreciated having other Indian students to interact with and some Indian teachers. A Pima who attended Intermountain Boarding School in the 1970s after having problems in the public school system stated, "We had some good times in school and got to meet other Indians from all over the United States. I didn't realize there were so many different Indian tribes. The most difficult part was not being able to see my family" (Chavis 1999, 17). In her senior year at Intermountain she met a Seminole from Florida whom she later married. A Washoe student who was attending Stewart Indian School in Nevada when it closed stated:

It was difficult when we heard they were closing the school. It was like losing a part of our family. We didn't want to lose our schools. Because they meant so much to us. It's hard for some people to understand the family environment we had together in those boarding schools. I remember the rallies and protest we held to try and keep them going. At the rallies I got a chance to meet other Indians who had gone to the boarding schools. We had some good times in the B.I.A. schools! (Chavis 1999, 44)

INDIAN ACTIVISM

Indian educators became increasingly active during the 1960s. In 1971 they established the Coalition of Indian Controlled School Boards. While the more mainstream Indian leadership such as the Coalition testified before congressional committees and lobbied Congress, the more radical young urban Indians followed the lead of the Black Panthers. In 1968 the American Indian Movement (AIM) was formed in Minneapolis to fight civil rights violations. In 1969 a group calling itself "Indians of All Tribes" seized Alcatraz Island in San Francisco Bay and demanded that the former prison on the island be turned into an Indian cultural and educational center. Three years later AIM took over the BIA headquarters building in Washington, D.C. and trashed it. AIM was paid $66,500 to leave Washington, D.C, and Louis Bruce was forced to resign as Commissioner of Indian Affairs. A year later, AIM took over the village of Wounded Knee on the Pine Ridge Reservation in South Dakota. On the local level, AIM organized a number of high school sit-ins and walkouts with the purpose of getting more classes in Indian culture and history and more Indian involvement in school administration.

AIM was controversial on reservations as it coalesced "the out-groups" and attacked "the incumbent tribal governments as stooges of the bureau [BIA]" (Smith 1979, 344). At Pine Ridge, AIM opposed the mixed-blood elected tribal government in what became essentially a local civil war. John C. Rainer of Taos Pueblo, who served as chairman of the All Pueblo Council, was accused by AIM of being an "apple," red on the outside and white on the inside. According to his biographer, Joe S. Sando (1998, 126), he responded, "AIM discriminated against Indian people who were not in favor of the type of activism they engaged in. . . . [I] was initiated as a young boy. . . . By contrast, many of the AIM members during that period of controversy where "born again Indians" from the urban communities."

In 1973 the United States Commission on Civil Rights held hearings on the Navajo Reservation that were reported in *The Navajo Nation: An American Colony*. The report concluded:

> Regardless of the school system they are in, Navajo students find them-selves in an environment controlled and dominated by non-Indians. Most of the teachers and administrators in reservation schools are Anglo [white]. Public school boards of education are dominated by non-Indians and those few Indians who do serve wield little authority. Parent advisory boards are the BIA school equivalent of a board of education; while these are all Indian, their function is only advisory and they are essentially powerless.
>
> Navajos, in fact, have been excluded from the decision-making process in these school systems. The result has been a variety of education policies unrelated to the Navajo community. The Navajo language and culture have been largely ignored in the curriculum offered to Navajo students. (U.S. Commission on Civil Rights 1975, 126–27)

The Commission found that only 188 of 2,800 teachers on the Navajo Reservation were Navajo. A Navajo Arizona public school kinder-garten teacher was written up in her teacher evaluation in 1973 for "on several occasions actually having taught 'Navajo Words' over the objection of the school's administration" (U.S. Commission on Civil Rights 1975, 205). Arizona law at that time required all instruction to be in English. Student witnesses expressed concern about biased textbooks. During the 1972–73 academic year, four public school districts on the Navajo Reservation experienced student movements with some AIM involvement. In response to the demands of students and parents, some white school board members, often operators of trading posts and BIA employees, lost their positions and were replaced by Indians. In addition, some white school administrators were replaced by Indians, and more classes in Navajo history, culture, and language were offered.

One problem created by the growth of public schools was that, unlike the BIA school attendance areas, their boundaries tended to be straight lines on a map that showed no regard to local geography or the tribal units of government. This disregard weakened community control and involvement in the public schools.

In general, the new tribal leadership did not find schools, whether public or BIA, responsive to their demands for greater local control and a local, Indian curriculum. In 1964 Congress passed the Economic Opportunity Act setting up the Office of Economic Opportunity (OEO) and authorizing programs such as Head Start, Upward Bound, Job Corp, and Vista. In 1975 the Indian Self-Determination and Education Assistance Act (P.L. 93–638) required the BIA to contract as many of its services to tribes as those tribes desired. The purpose of the act was "to promote maximum Indian participation in the government and education of Indian people" and "to support the right of Indians to control their own educational activities" (*Indian Education* 1982, 120). Two of the first P.L. 638 contract schools were Rough Rock Demonstration School and Rock Point Community School on the Navajo Reservation in the northeastern corner of Arizona. The histories of Rough Rock and Rock Point, only twenty-five miles apart on the map, illustrate some similarities and differences among the new contract schools.

ROUGH ROCK DEMONSTRATION SCHOOL

Rough Rock Demonstration School (RRDS) was established in 1966 as a War on Poverty experimental project, a joint effort of the OEO and the BIA. Starting with 220 students, almost all of whom lived on campus in dorms, its bold mission was, according to John Collier's son, to "correct a hundred years of Native American mis-education" (Collier 1988, 253). An initial yearlong attempt to establish the OEO experiment at an existing BIA school at Lukachukai was handicapped by having to work with an existing staff, dual administration, and Civil Service regulations. To avoid these handicaps, a newly built and unstaffed school at Rough Rock in the remote center of the Navajo Nation was chosen as the place to restart the experiment. According to Gary Witherspoon, RRDS's assistant director for community services, there was no Rough Rock "community" at the time the school was started; rather, it was the trading area for the trading post and the attendance area for the school, which was made up of sixty dispersed "camps" with an average of twelve people each (RRDS 14th Monthly Report 1967, 204; Dahlberg 1968).

The Navajo tribal chairman, Raymond Nakai, declared in November 1967:

The Rough Rock Demonstration School is the nation's most unique and exciting experiment in the field of Indian education. It is proving conclusively that Navajo parents do care and are able to provide both leadership and control over the education of their children. It is thrilling to witness the involvement of Navajo parents in all aspects of the school and its program. This is what we want for the Navajo people throughout the reservation. (Quoted in Johnson 1968, 21)

Robert Roessel Jr.

Robert Roessel Jr. (1926–), RRSD's first director, was a non-Indian former BIA employee and director of the Center for Indian Education at Arizona State University. According to John Collier Jr. (1988, 259), Roessel was an "essential presence who drew the loosely related Navajo population into a supportive community." Former Commissioner of Indian Affairs Phileo Nash expressed the opinion that RRDS "was the single-handed creation of Bob Roessel, a charismatic educator of great energy, imagination, creativity, and determination" (Allen 1970, 105).

Roessel came as a young teacher to the Navajo Reservation. As a boy, he had "read every account he could find on American Indian people" (McCarty 2002, 74). He taught for one year at the Crownpoint BIA school and then at Round Rock from 1952 to 1955, where he attended 103 Navajo ceremonies in twenty months and married into the tribe (Roessel 1960). From Round Rock he went to the even more isolated community of Low Mountain, where he was the lead teacher from 1955 to 1958. He, his wife, and a "colored" person were the sole teachers at the trailer school at Low Mountain and taught one hundred day students, beginners through third grade. Students were transported to the school in two buses (one-ton Chevrolet carryalls) over very poor roads (Roessel 1967). The trailer school was replaced in 1957 with a five-teacher boarding school. Roessel was reassigned in April 1957 against his will and received a letter of reprimand from the Deputy Commissioner of Indian Affairs over a dispute about feeding volunteer adult workers using BIA funds. He responded with a letter to the Commissioner of Indian Affairs stating that he was "disillusioned with the Bureau" (Roessel 1967, 110). He later declared that "all that had been done [in regard to community building] at Low Mountain was destroyed" by the BIA's action (Roessel 1967, 111).

Roessel left the BIA to pursue doctoral work at Arizona State University (ASU). His 1960 dissertation was titled "An Analysis of Select Navaho Needs with Implications for Navaho Education." One of the basic assumptions of his dissertation was that "Navahos should have a major role in determining the educational objectives and the educational program(s) for Navaho children" (Roessel 1960, 13–14). At ASU, he became the first director of the Center for Indian Education and coeditor of the *Journal of American Indian Education*, which was launched in June 1961. His work focused on the process of community building. In his *Handbook for Indian Education*, published in 1962, he called for a more Indian-oriented curriculum. He declared that "many schools enrolling Indians fail to have even [a] single Indian unit" and "a subject taught in school is a subject which is considered 'worthy' and 'important'" (Roessel 1962, 82–83). Thus the omission of anything about Indian life and the students' tribe in the curriculum devalued their Indian heritage and attacked their identity.

The negotiations that allowed the opening of Rough Rock as a locally controlled school were hurried and frantic, with a nonprofit DINE corporation being set up to receive OEO and BIA moneys just a few days before the deadline. Before the school opened in July 1996 and again in August, Roessel spent two weeks giving daily morning lectures on the history and present state of the Navajo to the education staff (RRDS 2d Monthly Report 1966). Roessel's Navajo wife started out as the school's arts and crafts coordinator but soon became the assistant director for dormitory services when all the dorm's professional staff quit in the first few months of the school's operation.

Roessel believed in a "two-fold Navaho History Program" that included "(1) teaching the part covering the early beginnings of the tribe, including myths, religious beliefs, stories and traditions, and (2) the part, starting with recorded history, including the earliest records and coming down to the present." "Such a program," he wrote, "would do much to stabilize and strengthen Navajo society in these times of increased disintegration and cultural crises. A people with no traditions are a beaten people" (Roessel 1967, 51). Such a curriculum could bring together the educated progressive and uneducated conservative Navajo. The school board minutes report that Roessel wrote that he opened the 1967–68 school year staff orientation with a prayer "inasmuch as the school exists as a result of faith." The school was "a Mission" needing "fervent zeal" (RRDS 14th Monthly Report 1967, 117). In his self-published autobiography titled *"He Leadeth Me": An Account of How God/Jesus/Holy People Have Led Me Throughout My Life*, Roessel noted repeatedly the religious force behind his work and declared that he had a polarizing effect so that people were either for or against him.

Goals, Staff, and Curriculum

Roessel (1968a, 2) saw the distinguishing features of RRDS as "local control" and "cultural identification." The intensity of the effort for local control can be seen in the fact that the school board met every Monday for the whole day (Roessel 1977). The goals of Rough Rock School were:

1. The school should be an economic center for the community.
2. Children should learn in two languages, Navajo and English, so they could fend successfully in both cultures and see the Navajo way as part of a universal system of values.
3. Navajo children should learn to manage their own survival, and education should be built on extreme individual competence. (Collier 1988, 261)

According to Roessel (1968a, 3), "The first policy developed [at Rough Rock] was that the child belongs to the family and parents, and not to the schools." He reported that "the second area in which the board is blazing trails is in the sphere of cultural identification. This is what we call the 'both-and' approach to Indian Education—taking the best of the dominant culture and the best of the Indian culture and putting these together in the classroom so the child grows up with a positive sense of well-being, a positive self-image, with pride in his heritage" (1968a, 5).

RRDS was advantaged in achieving its goals in that it got more than double the funding of BIA schools with similar enrollments. On top of the regular funding of $307,000 received from the BIA for running an elementary boarding school, RRDS got $329,000 from the OEO. The school's goals as stated in the OEO proposal were that students should feel "better about themselves and their culture," "the community should be stronger, more capable, more cohesive, more aggressive, more independent," and pupils should be able to succeed "in both worlds" (Erickson 1969, 1.3). The extra OEO funding was used for school-community relations and parental involvement, cultural identification, home and school visitation, language development and teaching English as a second language (ESL), Navajo language learning, in-service training and staff orientation, adult education, dormitory living, guidance and counseling, and auxiliary services, such as evaluation, recreation, art, finances, social work, and a school library (Roessel 1968b, 4).

In its first year the school had 91 employees, including 45 Navajos of whom 38 were local, plus 15 Vista volunteers and 8 dorm parents (McCarty 2002). Board member John Dick reported at the June 18, 1967, school board meeting that "people from this immediate area do not like the idea of having other people from other areas working at the school" (RRDS 13th Monthly Report 1967, 112). In April 1967 the staff included 10 teachers with 20 aides (RRDS 10th Monthly Report 1977). In its second year the BIA provided $346,000 and the OEO granted $447,000. The funds were used to educate 370 children and 250 regularly scheduled adults (Roessel 1968b). In its second year the school moved to an ungraded ability-grouped "continuous progress program" with a primary Phase 1 and an upper-grade Phase II. At the beginning of the second year students were reported as having each week 2 1/2 hours of Reading/TESL (teaching English as a second language), Navajo Language, and Navajo Social Studies; 3 3/4 hours of math and science, 3 1/2 hours of social studies, 3 hours of art, 3 hours of home economics, and 3 hours of industrial arts. The school board had asked that home economics be offered (RRDS 14th Monthly Report 1967). Some teachers would not teach for a whole week because of the "difficulty in scheduling and finding time for all the subjects in the school" (RRDS 15th Monthly Report 1967, 114). The math teacher complained about the "lack of time for teaching" in his November 1967 report, and daily math and science classes were reintroduced (RRDS 17th Monthly Report 1967, 28, 61). In September 1968 it was reported that the third year of the school "began in a state of confusion" because of problems with the elective system (RRDS 27th Annual Report 1968, 36).

The school was a media showcase and claimed to have fifteen thousand visitors in its first two years. Visitors included the influential U.S. senators Robert Kennedy, Edward Kennedy, and Walter Mondale (Roessel 1968b; McCarty 2002). A full-time information officer was employed to publicize the school. In addition, Roessel (1968a, 2) reported one hundred parents a day "visiting the school to see what's happening: visiting the classrooms, taking part in school programs, working in the dormitories, eating in the cafeteria, really participating in the school." One of Rough Rock's early achievements was the production of a number of books focusing on Navajos, including *Black Mountain Boy, Denetsosie, Coyote Stories, Rough Rock History, Grandfather Stories, Navaho Biographies*, and *Navaho History*.

The 1969 Erickson Evaluation

The much-publicized success of RRDS was not without controversy. The OEO required an external evaluation, which was led by Donald A. Erickson of the University of Chicago. As part of the evaluation, Henrietta Schwartz spent thirty days living in the girls' dorm at Rough Rock, eleven days at Rock Point, and fourteen days at Chinle Boarding School. Despite Roessel's claims of openness, Erickson found that school board meetings were held in the director's inner office and were not generally known to be open to the public. While Roessel trumpeted the board's willingness to meet weekly, Erickson noted that the payment for attending those meetings made the board members wealthy overnight by local standards and that the board members used their position to "blatantly" favor their close relatives (Erickson 1970).

The school had "no prescribed curriculum," with the result that "teachers had to start from scratch each year, not knowing what the child had mastered before" with "much random behavior, boredom, and disruption" observed in Phase II classrooms (Erickson 1969, 5.7, 5.12, 5.14). Schwartz concluded that the Navajo teachers were doing a better job. The anthropologist Oswald Werner reported that "the principal had failed to create a non-threatening atmosphere of give and take and sharing of materials" (Erickson 1969, 5.35). Part of the reason for the tremendous turnover of the "Navajo Social Living" teachers was the assumption at Rough Rock that if you were Navajo you could teach Navajo social studies without any special preparation (Erickson 1969).

Erickson (1969, 5.41) concluded that Rough Rock classrooms were "basically conventional" and that "inservice training was deficient," especially in regard to teaching reading and how to use instructional aides. This was especially important because of the youth and inexperience of Rough Rock teachers. Erickson's report noted that aides, who were in every classroom, were used as clerks and messengers and that the teachers needed training in how to use them better. Teachers reported that they received "negligible" assistance from the Navajo Curriculum Center and that they could not get readable materials copied for their students. The school's routine was described by a student as follows:

> In the morning a bell rings at 6:00 to get up. At 7:00 a bell rings for roll call and breakfast. At 8:30 a bell rings to get to school. At 11:30, a bell rings to go back to the dorm to get fixed for lunch. At 12:00 a bell rings for lunch [which] you get free and all the same thing. At 3:30 a bell rings to go to the dorm; at 6:00 one rings for dinner. At 9:00 all the girls go to bed. (Erickson 1969, 4.12)

The students were escorted in double lines to meals and classrooms. "A higher proportion of children mentioned punishment by aides at Rough Rock than at Chinle or Rock Point" (Erickson 1969, 4.50). Based on interviews, Erickson (1969, 4.55) reported that Roessel "would tolerate no criticisms of the dormitories" while his wife was in charge.

Despite Roessel's claims of school board involvement in decision making, Erickson found that the board complained about not being consulted, that teachers were fired without school board approval, and that large sums of money were spent for purposes not originally budgeted. In a July 1968 board meeting the president of the school board opposed group meetings, saying, "The Navaho people are suspicious of one another and don't trust their fellows," and there was general opposition to group meetings (RRDS 25th Monthly Report 1968, 162). In the following month at another board meeting, "Ashkie Tsosie, a school board member, declared that the supervision of the dormitories has improved tremendously since the hiring of an

Anglo to head the Dormitories Services Department" (RRDS 26th Monthly Report 1968, 72).

While Roessel and the school publicized the importance of local control, all the funding for the school was external. When the initial OEO funding was cut back at the end of the first two years of operation, board member Yazzie Begay complained, "We have clearly stated our wishes to continue the existing programs. We are told we are in charge of this program and we are, and yet they tell us our funds might be cut. I wonder who really is in charge?" (RRDS 18th Monthly Report 1967, 158).

According to Erickson, the Navajo school board wanted stringent attendance rules, but Roessel considered such "coercion" an affront to Navajo culture. In fact, he found that Roessel supported an "ultra-traditional Navajo culture, at the expense of preparation to compete in more modern contexts" (Erickson 1969, 83). Gloria Emerson (1970, 97), a Navajo graduate of Harvard University and Office of Navajo Educational Opportunity education specialist, visited Rough Rock in 1967 and 1968. She declared, "[The school is] bent on selling an image to whites, to Navajo communities, to bureaucrats, and, most important, to funding sources. I felt then that the discrepancies between the puff pieces and the reality at Rough Rock were probably due to administrative weaknesses." She described Rough Rock as an "'ego-tripping' showcase" and its administration as "chaotic." She felt it was demeaning to condone "administrative deficiencies" at Rough Rock as "Navajo 'cultural' ways" (94–95).

Erickson (1969) concluded in his more than three-hundred-page report that the priorities of the school were first, publicity and funding; second, hiring local Navajos with 50 percent or more of family breadwinners employed in school programs; and third, everything else such as curriculum. He concluded that OEO development projects, which included a greenhouse, poultry farm, and furniture factory, were chosen for their public relations value, that is, to be "big, flashy, attention-getting" projects, and that they quickly failed (3.43). But he did not view the school's problems as owing to local control. He thought that "too many aims were pursued simultaneously at Rough Rock to be achieved conclusively in less than three years" (1.3).

Erickson's evaluation team was accused of "culture shock" by a team of researchers, including two nationally prominent anthropologists, before it was officially released (Bergman 1969). The rebuttal to Erickson's evaluation report claimed it was influenced by disgruntled non-Navajos who could not adjust to Navajos and by assimilated dormitory aides unsympathetic to the goals of the demonstration school:

> The dormitory aides are the lost souls of the Indian education system. They bring with them the dormitory culture of their youth, which often cruelly controlled children and their affiliation with Navajo language and culture. All people who have gone through the dormitory experience in the past have horror stories to tell about the stupidity and callousness of some of the dormitory aides. They are lost souls because no one pays attention to them. They are (except for the children) on the bottom of the academic totem pole. Considering their role and importance as parent surrogates, they receive minimal training and instruction. It seems there is a belief operating that any able-bodied Navajo, by simply applying, becomes an ideal dormitory parent. It is rather common knowledge on the reservation that many dormitory aides hold traditional Navajos in contempt. In a way, the aides have made it in the white man's world. They qualified for civil service with a limited education. Because of their low status, the only way they can feel their importance is to despise everybody and everything that is truly Navajo. They have passed the baptism by fire of the English language, and they can show the "primitive" children and their parents a thing or two. Dormitory parents have been known to deny knowledge of the Navajo language, in spite of the fact that their Navajo should be one of the key bridges to children and parents. Some who have tried to act in a more human manner have often been severely reprimanded by an unfeeling administration. (Bergman 1969, 15–16)

Despite the coordinated campaign to discredit Erickson's report, it also had its defenders. A prominent anthropologist, Murray Wax (1970, 67), who had extensively studied Indian education and visited Rough Rock as a consultant, found Erickson's report "honest and accurate." A Northwestern University anthropologist, Oswald Werner, put his name on the "cultural shock report," but the section he provided for Erickson's evaluation is not any different in tone from the rest of the report. Internal criticism at Rough Rock was suppressed and external criticism was not taken with grace. The fifth RRDS monthly report for November

1966 contained a dispute over the director censoring the school newspaper and being questioned as to whether it was a newspaper or a
publicity sheet.

After the Roessel Years

Roessel stepped down as the school's director in 1968 and moved on
to become the founding president of Navajo Community College. He
was replaced by Dillon Platero, a Navajo, who served as director until
1973 when he became the first director of the Navajo tribe's new Division of Education. He was replaced as director by another Navajo,
Ethelou Yazzie. Roessel noted in his 1977 book about the school that
while he and Dillon focused on community involvement and economic
development, Yazzie focused on the school's curriculum. Roessel (1977,
34) wrote that prior to Yazzie's efforts, "many students complained that
they may learn the same area in twelve years under the old system of
laissez faire." He complained in 1977 that changes in BIA leadership
caused the school to lose support and that the Navajo tribal government's bureaucracy was seeking to replace the Washington, D.C.,
bureaucracy, which hampered the operation of the school.

The economic impact of schools such as Rough Rock on reservations
with high unemployment can overshadow educational concerns.
Because school jobs provided the major source of family income in the
Rough Rock community, McCarty (1987, 105), not surprisingly, found
that the Rough Rock School Board's involvement in academics was
"minimal." ... [O]over a third of the school board's discussion between
1966 to 1983 concerned personnel issues, specifically the hiring and
firing of local people." And this discussion was often as a result of
alcohol use, sometimes by the children of board members who worked
at the school. McCarty (1987, 105) concluded that school "board members' concerns related to their position as community rather than educational leaders." At an October 31, 1966, community meeting complaints
about the school focused on who was being hired (4th Monthly Report
1966, 82). The board also spent considerable time discussing issues such
as purchasing water troughs and hay for community sheep and the
various OEO-funded saddle and moccasin making, silversmithing, and
medicine man training. Erickson (1969) concluded that these projects

served more to provide rotating employment for locals than to develop skills that could be used later on.

Much of the energy of school administrators was taken up with fund-raisingy, which often involved key administrators spending time away from the school meeting with government and foundation officials in Washington and elsewhere. For example, in April 1969 Dillon Platero visited Salt Lake City, San Antonio, Albuquerque, Washington, D.C., and New York City (RRDS 34th Monthly Report). Basic contract money often arrived late, and federal grant money varied greatly from year to year. Ethelou Yazzie testified before the American Indian Policy Review Commission:

> It is June:
>
> The BIA contract is not signed. We have no idea what our budget for fall will be. No teacher is certain that his/her job will be funded. No money has yet arrived to fund the clinic, our arts and crafts co-op is locked. The curriculum center will stay open half-time because there is no money. There is no capital to produce its product, or to train apprentices in writing, editing, and printing. Our summer school is severely limited in its offerings and staff size, relying heavily on volunteers.
>
> This is the way it is at Rough Rock. We expect a crisis a month, and we are never disappointed. . . .
>
> The system is a monumental fake and hoax. It is a political game in which the community or school that refuses to lie down and not die wins just enough to stand up for the next punch. (Task Force 1976, 259)

These problems, which included late paychecks for staff, led to a high annual turnover in teaching staff. McCarty (1987, 105) found that "between 1966 and 1983, an average of 50% of the Navajo language and culture faculty and about 33% of the elementary faculty was new each year." In addition, "between 1968 and 1983 students attended, on average, less than three-quarters of the school year, or about 130 days" (McCarty 1987, 105). This absenteeism was in part a result of the school's philosophy that the children belong to their parents, not to the school. Parents checked students out of school to help with chores and ceremonies at home, and unimproved roads often made it difficult to get them back to school (McCarty 1987). Anita Pfeiffer, RRDS assistant director for educational services, reported in November 1967 that "absenteeism became a habitual thing for a number of our student population' (RRDS 17th Monthly Report, 21).

Rough Rock relied primarily on non-Navajo proposal writers to seek supplemental funding. Over the years more than a dozen different programs resulted, many with different objectives and funding guidelines, and they were not well integrated with each other or with the regular program. By 1983, though school leaders still sought ways to remedy these discontinuities, an English basic skills program competed for time on teachers' daily schedules with two bilingual-bicultural programs, both of them very different (McCarty 1987). Meanwhile, funding for the production of Rough Rock's bilingual-bicultural texts, which were in use in schools throughout the reservation, became increasingly limited. While the school's Navajo Curriculum Center, which has produced some fine books, remained in operation, its budget—and its future—are tenuous.

Rough Rock's Legacy

Rough Rock was a failure as a "Demonstration School" in the sense that other schools could replicate its programs, both because of its chaotic curriculum and because of the impossibility of providing other schools with the additional funding Rough Rock received. Roessel's (1969) focus on using athletics, especially basketball and rodeo, served a valuable purpose in bringing together dispersed Navajo camps and providing recreation for young Navajos, but it also helped to develop a trend still seen in many Indian schools and communities whereby athletics are more highly valued than academics (see, e.g., Peshkin 1997; Colton 2000). Another questionable trend that Rough Rock helped to establish is local school board priorities that put local hiring above concerns about classroom practices. A future Navajo tribal president, Peterson Zah, noted in his comments on Roessel's community building at Low Mountain, a community Zah came from, that community factionalism can be exacerbated by one group getting control of the school board (Roessel 1969). In a 1983 speech, Zah supported community control but warned that "*Parents should vote against, and campaign against those candidates who are only interested in the income they receive as board members, or in handing out jobs to their* relatives, political supporters, and friends" (Zah 1983; original emphasis). At Rough Rock, in the early days, the large amount of funding and the many adult education projects allowed the board to hire a large segment of the community, but this is not possible for schools faced with typical BIA or public school funding. While the rotation of jobs at Rough Rock allowed more community members to be employed, this practice militated against having well-trained employees, especially in the dorms.

Guy B. Senese (1991, x), who worked at Rough Rock in the early 1980s, concluded, "Rough Rock is an institution of great vision and promise, but frequently unfulfilled ambition." He described the school's climate as "fraught with crisis planning and overreaction" (xi). It can be argued that Rough Rock put Indian education in the national spotlight more than any effort since Pratt's at Carlisle, and for all its faults, it forced politicians in Washington, D.C., to pay more attention to Indian education. Rough Rock broke new ground so that other Indian educators could experiment with their curricula, including developing comprehensive bilingual education programs such as was done at Rock Point Community School.

ROCK POINT COMMUNITY SCHOOL

In contrast to Rough Rock, Rock Point Community School had a more gradual transition to local community control. Wayne Holm, a non-Navajo married to a Navajo, worked in the school as a BIA employee and continued there until 1986, with a break to obtain a Ph.D. in Navajo linguistics at the University of New Mexico. He was the school's director and then its assistant director for academic programs. ESL instruction was started at Rock Point in 1960 and bilingual instruction in 1967. In 1960, when Holm first came to Rock Point, it was one of the most isolated of eight Chinle Agency BIA schools, and it "ranked at the bottom in student achievement as measured by standardized tests" (Vorih and Rosier 1978, 263). An intensive TESL program that was started in 1963 resulted in its scores moving to the top of the Agency, but they were still two years behind national norms at the sixth-grade level in reading and math. Holm (1964, 6–7) argued in a *Journal of American Indian Education* article, "In most grade-level Bureau classrooms

American English, as a spoken language, is not taught. . . . *Too many Navaho children struggle daily to read and comprehend a language—American English—which they neither speak nor 'hear' well"* (original emphasis).

Hildegard Thompson wrote that the experiments at Rock Point affirmed the basic principles and premises of the BIA's primary grade English-language program:

1. The development of spoken English precedes the development of English reading and writing skills. The Bureau sets aside the first year of school for the development of oral English, and oral English is emphasized throughout the grades. . . .
2. Spoken English in the early elementary grades should be developed in association with classroom, home, and community experiences. This practice recognizes that language learning accrues from experience, and in the beginning from concrete experiences.
3. Experiences provide the meaning content of language. Oral English expression should be welded to meaning since expression and meaning are inseparable in the communication of thought. Patterned drill is important to establish English patterns of expression, but patterned drill is undertaken in close association with meaning.

   To summarize, oral language development requires that the individual learn to recognize and then to produce the complete sound system of English, to make the correct association between meaning and expression, and to make English patterns of expression a matter of habit. (1965, 3)

Thompson (1965, 3) asked teachers to ask themselves these questions: "Am I relating my oral English teaching to firsthand experiences? Do I make use of the everyday things children do at school, and do I provide children with a wealth of experiences to enrich their background?"

Because of the continued lag in student achievement, Rock Point started a bilingual education program in 1967 using Elementary and Secondary Education Act (ESEA) Title I funds. But the bilingual program remained limited until 1971, when ESEA Title VII Bilingual Education Act funds were received. Rock Point Navajo aides were trained as teachers, spending their summers taking courses at Northern Arizona University. "In 1977 15 Navajo staff at Rock Point received their BA degrees," and they "adapted, translate[d], or wrote their own materials" in Navajo (Vorih and Rosier 1978, 268).

In 1972, in order to provide "quality Navajo education through local community control," the community elected a school board, and in 1973 it contracted to operate the school so as to have more control over hiring and curriculum (Holm 1975, 185). Originally an elementary school, starting in 1976, one grade a year was added until in 1982 the first high school seniors graduated.

Forty-three percent of Rock Point students in 1988 were dominant Navajo speakers; only 5 percent were dominant English speakers. Under the Rock Point bilingual curriculum instituted in 1967, kindergarten students were taught reading in Navajo. In kindergarten two-thirds of the instruction was in Navajo, in grades one through three about one-half of the instruction was in Navajo, and in grades four through six about one-fourth of the instruction was in Navajo. Students received English reading instruction starting in second grade. The approach used at Rock Point has been described as both a coordinate and a maintenance bilingual program. Instruction in the two languages was separate but complementary. Instruction was not repeated in each language, but concepts introduced in Navajo were reviewed in English. Some teachers taught only in English and others only in Navajo.

In the primary grades, mathematics was taught first in Navajo, and the specialized English vocabulary was taught later (Rosier and Holm 1980). Since content area subjects were taught in the early grades in Navajo, Rock Point students were not held back in those subjects until they learned English, as was often the case in neighboring BIA and public schools. The nontextbook, hands-on nature of *Stern Mathematics*, emphasizing manipulatives, and *Science: A Process Approach*, emphasizing experiments, made them adaptable to both Navajo and ESL instruction. Concepts learned by students in Navajo transferred and were usable later in either language, and almost all basic reading skills learned in the Navajo reading program transferred into the English reading program (see Thonis 1981 for evidence of a similar transfer of reading skills from Spanish to English). Seventh- and eighth-grade students had one period of Navajo studies plus one quarter of Navajo writing each year. High school students received a half year of Navajo studies plus one quarter of Navajo writing each year (Reyhner 1990).

Another important aspect of the Rock Point bilingual program was that the Navajo portion of the curriculum did not depend on supplemental funding, although Title VII bilingual funding was first received in 1971 and other funding helped out. Navajo-language teachers in grades K–12 were paid from the same main contract funds as most of the English-language teachers. Other federal programs such as Chapter 1 were also integrated into the regular school program.

To get enough Navajo-speaking teachers, most of the Rock Point elementary school teachers were hired locally without college degrees. The school board and administration concluded that the only way an isolated Navajo community could get a stable teaching staff would be to hire and train local people. An on-site training program brought college-level courses to Rock Point. By 1989 an estimated forty-five Navajos working at Rock Point had earned degrees, and twenty-one of the fifty teachers on staff had worked at the school ten years or more. Nondegreed teachers were required to take twelve semester credits each year leading to an appropriate education degree as a condition of their employment contract. All but one teacher in the elementary school during the 1988–89 school year were Navajo (Reyhner 1990).

Teachers at Rock Point produced many of their own materials to teach in Navajo. Bernard Spolsky (1973b, 31) found in 1973 a "good bit" of Navajo-language material but not enough "to fill out a first grade year of reading." The Navajo Reading Studies Project, which produced a considerable amount of Navajo material for the whole reservation, ceased operation, and funding for similar projects is no longer available. Although there is now considerably more material, schools still must use some materials produced by teachers and students.

In 1983, by eighth grade, Rock Point students outperformed Navajo students in neighboring public schools, other Navajo-speaking students throughout the reservation, and other Arizona Indian students in reading on the California Achievement Test. On the grammar (written English) portion of the test the results were much the same. In mathematics the Rock Point students did even better, outperforming the comparison groups and approaching and sometimes exceeding national averages (Holm 1985).

On the 1987–88 school evaluation, Rock Point students scored on the English language California Test of Basic Skills (CTBS) equal to or better than students at surrounding BIA schools at almost all grade levels in reading, language arts, and math. At the same time, Rock Point students were improving their Navajo-language skills. Thus at Rock Point, it was found by standardized testing what the Riggses had found by observation at the Santee Indian school in the nineteenth century—that instruction in the students' Native language helped rather than hurt Indian students academically. In addition to test scores, the success of bilingual education at Rock Point was shown by student attendance rates and parent conference attendance rates, above 94 percent and above 80 percent, respectively. Parent involvement at Rock Point was a high priority. Parent activities included quarterly parent-teacher conferences, a yearly public meeting held in November, an eight-member elected parent advisory committee that formally observed the school several times a year, school-sponsored cultural events, and community dinners (Reyhner 1990; Rock Point 1988).

Community involvement was enhanced by the fact that, unlike surrounding public school districts with arbitrary straight-line boundaries and schools that draw students from many communities, Rock Point Community School draws its students from a single community represented by the Rock Point Chapter, a division of the tribal government. The Rock Point Chapter House and the Rock Point Trading Post are all centrally located within the Chapter near the school.

Spolsky summed up the results of the Rock Point Community School's educational program:

> In a community that respects its own language but wishes its children to learn another, a good bilingual program that starts with the bulk of instruction in the child's native language and moves systematically toward the standard language will achieve better results in standard language competence than a program that refuses to recognize the existence of the native language. (Rosier and Holm 1980, vi)

Navajo Tribal Chairman Peterson Zah noted the importance of teaching Navajo in schools in 1983. He declared, "No-one can fully participate in the affairs of the Navajo people without speaking Navajo."

The increase in the number of tribal schools, from twelve in 1973 to sixty in 1988, shows the continued interest among Indians in self-determination. Yet, as T. L. McCarty (1989) notes, the problems in curriculum, staffing, and program stability are endemic in federally funded

Indian schools and are largely the consequence of their necessary reliance on various short-term federal contracts and grants that change from year to year in funding level and purpose depending on the current thinking of Washington officials in the BIA, the Department of Education, and Congress.

To avoid the cumbersome contracting procedure, in 1988 Congress allowed P.L. 638 schools to apply for direct grants in 1988. Despite the problems of Rough Rock and other tribally operated schools, they have played an active role in community development and the maintenance of tribal culture. The coursework they have offered in Indian history and culture has been their unique contribution to Indian education.

TEACHING ENGLISH AS SECOND LANGUAGE

In 1963 Commissioner of Indian Affairs Philleo Nash, who held a Ph.D. in anthropology and was appointed by President John F. Kennedy, reported, "Because more than 80 percent of students enrolled in BIA schools come from homes where an Indian language is spoken regularly, development of facility in speaking and understanding English is one of the most important primary tasks of the Bureau's school system" (quoted in Fischbacher 1967, 430). Most public schools, especially those serving the rural West, were not set up to teach non-English-speaking students. In 1967 one thousand BIA teachers attended an ESL workshop at Fort Wingate, New Mexico, and the BIA issued a booklet titled *ESL for Navajos: An Overview of Certain Cultural and Linguistic Features*, by the linguist Robert Young, which was revised and enlarged in 1968 (New Curriculum 1970; Young 1968). The booklet described the implications for teaching of cultural differences and provided a contrastive analysis of Navajo and English.

In fall 1969 approximately two hundred new teachers were hired to serve Navajo BIA schools, and their reaction to being told they were required to teach ESL was, "What is it?" (Harvey 1970, 23). The then current focus of ESL was on oral practice and pattern drill in primary grades. In June 1969 the BIA held a workshop Brigham City, Utah, for its teachers to look at "all commercially available materials for teaching ESL at the intermediate and secondary levels" (Harvey 1970, 25). Starting in November of that year, Gina Cantoni spent one or more days each week in seventeen Navajo Area BIA schools observing, demonstrating, and offering encouragement, help, and advice for teaching ESL to Navajo students. The same year, the BIA published the monograph *Teaching English to Speakers of Choctaw, Navajo and Papago: A Contrastive Approach* (Ohannessian and Gage 1969) that compared and contrasted the grammar and sounds of English with three Indian languages. During the 1970–71 school year, the BIA was offering bilingual-bicultural kindergarten and first-grade instruction in four BIA schools (Saville 1970). Cantoni directed annual Navajo Summer Institutes in Linguistics and ESL for Teachers from 1971 to 1975 and codirected national seminars on Indian education from 1972 to 1975.

At Albuquerque Indian School students were one year behind in third grade and three years behind in seventh grade. Annabelle R. Scoon (1971, 268) wrote in the *TESOL Quarterly*, "[T]he results of TESL efforts have not been especially successful. Drills and pattern practice improve certain surface aspects of the students' language, but higher level abilities still do not develop." She continued,

> If the students find that they can learn about the really important things in their lives just by making the effort to express themselves in English, we will find them talking. This has been demonstrated in classrooms that I have visited repeatedly. The quiet, monosyllabic Indian students will soon be interrupting each other to get a chance to talk, if the discussion concerns things they really want to know. Whenever they feel that they can learn something they want to learn, the language will grow to meet the demand. A student will work hard to find a means of expression for an idea he wants to express. Perhaps the area of affect is one of the first places we would seek for the content of lessons that will motivate the student to improve his English. (290–91)

Gina Cantoni-Harvey (1977, 230) wrote that the common practice in Round Robin reading instruction of "interrupting a child's oral reading to point out his deviant rendition of a word does not help his understanding of the text." She advised that teachers should model standard English but not constantly correct students' nonstandard English:

> The respect for the learner's home dialect, which is so important in the early grades, should not be set aside when the need arises for instruction in

Standard English. Red [Indian] English may be encouraged to develop its fullest range of expressive power and flexibility in creative writing, where the freedom from certain grammatical restrictions, the slightly different connotations of lexical items, as well as some direct translation from the Indian language, along with the rich content of Indian tradition, may result in poetry and prose more exciting than the correct but cliché-ridden out put of the Standard speakers. (Cantoni-Harvey 1977, 232)

Later, she wrote:

I proposed that English-as-a-Second-Language be taught not as a separate subject but as an integral component of each content area; in other words, I felt that the particular needs of the student population would be served more effectively by an ESP (English for specific purposes) approach than by the more general ESL. (1983, 178)

Early on, researchers such as Spolsky (1973b) recognized that ESL should be part of a total bilingual program. He estimated that in 1972 there were 50,000 Navajo students and that 98 percent of the Navajo students entering BIA schools and 90 percent entering public schools were Navajo speakers. In the beginning there was little public school participation in these initiatives. For example, there were no Arizona public school representatives at the Navajo Bilingual-Bicultural Materials Conference held in Albuquerque in 1972 (Kari 1973).

Spolsky found that Navajo ESL programs were ineffective and that teachers needed to be bilingual. In 1973 he wrote in the lead article in a BIA publication, "Bilingual education has become a pressing need for Navajo schools; without it, Navajo students are doomed to inferior education" (1973b, 1, 2).

BILINGUAL EDUCATION

In response to pressure from Hispanics and other groups for bilingual education, Congress passed the Bilingual Education Act as Title VII of the ESEA of 1968. In 1969 there were five public school Indian-language programs: two Cherokee programs, one in Gentry, Arkansas, and one in Tahlequah, Oklahoma; a Poma program in Ukiah, California; a Navajo and Keresan program in Grants, New Mexico; and a Navajo program in Blanding, Utah. In 1970 BIA schools became eligible for Title VII funding, and Rough Rock got the first program that year. By 1971 there were sixteen Indian-language Title VII programs (Tennant 1971). The BIA had already started with some of its own initiatives, including the Navajo Reading Study Program funded in 1969 that printed fifty Navajo-language reading books over the next four years (Spolsky, Holm, and Murphy 1970; Spolsky 1976).

In the 1974 case *Lau* v. *Nichols*, the Supreme Court found that the historically common practice of "submersing" students in a regular classroom did not give non-English-speaking students an equal education opportunity compared to English-speaking students as required by the Civil Rights Act of 1964. This case involved Chinese-speaking students in the San Francisco public schools who received no special educational program though they spoke no English—an experience shared over the years by many Indian students. The Supreme Court mandated that they receive some form of special bilingual or ESL instruction until they could speak English well enough to be put into a regular classroom.

The Bilingual Education Act was amended in 1984 to fund maintenance ("developmental"), transitional, and immersion ("special alternative") bilingual programs. "Maintenance" and "transitional" referred to the long-term role of the first language in the school's educational program, while "immersion" referred to the way in which the second language was taught. In the United States, immersion programs tended to become specifically designed, English-only programs for non-English-speaking students. All three types of bilingual programs use various ESL teaching methods for the English-language portion (Reyhner 1992b).

Maintenance bilingual programs, such as the one at Rock Point, developed children's Native- as well as English-language abilities. Transitional bilingual programs are designed to teach English to language minority students as quickly as possible. While children are taught extensively in their native language during their first year of school, instruction in English is quickly phased in so that by about fourth grade all instruction is in English. Transitional programs do little to promote native language skills. Though they were the most common form of bilingual programs for Indians in the United States, Cummins (1981) found that there was no educational justification for transitional bilingual programs and that quick exiting of students from transitional programs had negative effects. In immersion bilingual programs, teachers only speak the language to be learned to the children. This type of program is very effective in teaching French and Spanish to middle-class English-speaking students and has no long-term negative effects on children's skills in English (Ovando and Collier 1985).

In his review of the research, Cummins (1981) concluded that the decision as to whether a child should learn a second language by a maintenance, transitional, or immersion bilingual program depended on the socioeconomic background of the child, the social status of the child's native language, and the language preferences of the child, the parents, and the community. Students who come from middle- and upper-class backgrounds and are members of the dominant society (language majority students) do well in immersion programs. However, these programs do not replace the home language, which is either spoken in the home or is brought back for instructional purposes after an initial period of all second-language instruction (Studies 1984). American Indian students, whose families often have below average incomes, tend to lose their first-language skills in immersion programs.

For Indians, both the old "submersion," which taught Indian students to "parrot" English words without comprehension (Standing Bear 1928) and the new English "immersion" often reinforced feelings of inferiority and worthlessness by ignoring the home language and culture of the child. Subtractive educational programs that sought to replace Native language and culture with the English language and culture cause minority students to fail, whereas additive educational programs teaching English language and culture in addition to Native language and culture created the conditions for students to succeed in school. Cummins listed four educational areas that need to be addressed to empower Indian students:

- Incorporation of the cultural and linguistic background of the student into the school and its curriculum
- Participation of the community in school activities
- Use of interactionist teaching methods which emphasize an active role for students

- School testing programs that recognize linguistic and cultural differences and that search out student strengths rather than being used to track minority students into special education programs. (See Cummins 1986, 1989, 1992, 2000)

Cummins (1981) found that exposure to television, school, and English-speaking children could help Indian students to speak English fairly well in about two years, as can the transitional bilingual programs that are usually found in the first three or four grades. However, those speaking skills are "context-embedded," meaning that the situation that is being talked about is familiar to the student. Cummins found many classroom situations after grade four, especially those involved with reading textbooks, to be "context-reduced," meaning that all the information must be gained from lectures or textbooks. The academic competence to understand English in a context-reduced situation takes an average of five or six years to learn.

Cummins argued that under the old submersion, new transitional bilingual, and ESL approaches, Indian students often experience so much failure in school that they tended to give up and drop out, never catching up to their white peers. In maintenance bilingual programs such as Rock Point's, ESL instruction is spread over the entire elementary grades, and students get the time needed to gain context-reduced, academic English-language skills.

Rock Point Community School's bilingual program fit well with the research on bilingual education that emerged in the late 1970s. It also closely resembled the successful California Spanish-English programs described by Krashen and Biber (1988). They found that successful Spanish-English bilingual programs in California shared the following characteristics:

- High quality subject matter teaching in the first language, without translation.
- Development of literacy in the first language.
- Comprehensible input in English. Ideally, comprehensible input in English is provided directly by high quality English as a second language classes, supplemented by comprehensible, or "sheltered" subject matter teaching in English. (25)

DEMOGRAPHICS IN THE ERA OF
SELF-DETERMINATION

In 1974 there were 170 Alaska Native villages, 258 Indian reservations and Indian trust areas concentrated in the western United States, and 27 federally recognized tribes with trust areas in Oklahoma (*Federal and State Indian Reservations* 1974). The BIA estimated in 1987 that 48 percent of the potential Indian labor force living on or next to reservations age sixteen and older were unemployed, and of those 38 percent were seeking work. Twenty-six percent were employed and earning more than $7,000 per year (Bureau of Indian Affairs 1987, 1).

In 1980 a little less than half of American Indians lived in rural areas. About a third of a million American Indians lived on reservations, and another hundred thousand lived in the historic areas of Oklahoma. Of the adults over twenty-five years old, 57 percent had not graduated from high school and 16 percent had completed less than five years of school. Twenty-seven percent of reservation American Indians over the age of sixteen were unemployed, 45 percent lived below the poverty level, 21 percent had homes without piped water, and 16 percent were without electricity (*American Indians* 1985).

The 1980 census reported that about one-third of the Indian population, or 500,000 people, were enrolled in school, 500,000 were employed, and 76,865 were unemployed, a 13 percent unemployment rate. It also reported that the mean household income for whites was $21,173 and for American Indians $15,418. Although Indians had a lower average household income, they had a higher average household size, 3.3 persons compared to 2.7 persons (*General Social and Economic Characteristics* 1984).

In 1988 the BIA operated 103 elementary and secondary schools and 9 peripheral (bordertown) dormitories. In addition, it funded 65 elementary and secondary schools and 5 peripheral dormitories operated by Indian tribes or tribal organizations under contract (Bureau of Indian Affairs 1988, 1).

The *Chronicle of Higher Education* reported 82,672 American Indians enrolled in U.S. colleges and universities for 1984. American Indians represented approximately 0.7 percent of the U.S. population and 0.7 percent of the enrollment in higher education ("Racial and Economic Makeup" 1986).

One hundred thousand Indian children between the ages of five and seventeen lived on reservations, of whom about one-third attended BIA schools. More than 80 percent of the 15,729 BIA employees were Native American, or approximately 2.5 percent of all employed Native Americans (*American Indians* 1984). Almost 14,000 American Indians were teachers, librarians, or counselors, representing about 2.7 percent of the workforce, whereas 3.5 percent of the white workforce were teachers (*General Social and Economic Characteristics* 1984).

THE 1988 *REPORT ON BIA EDUCATION*

In 1988 the Bureau of Indian Affairs issued the *Report on BIA Education*, which examined its past and current state. Partly as a result of the BIA's encouragement of day school attendance over boarding schools, the number of BIA boarding school students declined from 24,051 in 1965 to 11,264 in 1988, and from 1968 to 1986 BIA-funded school enrollment declined from 51,448 students to 38,475, whereas Indian non-BIA school enrollment almost doubled (see table 4). By 1987 contract schools enrolled 27.8 percent of students. Whereas in BIA-operated schools 18.4 percent of the staff were teachers and 26 percent were teachers' aides, in public schools the figures were 53.4 percent and 7.4 percent, respectively. BIA-operated schools had a ratio of 4.4 students to each staff member as compared to 9.6 to 1 for public schools. The 1980 census found that the reservation poverty rate was 41 percent and the off-reservation poverty rate about half that. With unemployment rates ranging from 40 to 90 percent, reservation communities saw "schools as a significant and desirable source of employment for tribal members"; however, "the use of BIA education funds to create additional jobs [came] partly at the expense of the education program" and "[l]ow salaries and other difficulties . . . resulted in an annual BIA turnover rate for all BIA educational professionals of more than 20 percent" (*Report* 1988, 119–20).

While the *Report* found student tests scores in BIA-operated and contract schools well below average (see table 5), they were not substantially different from the scores of students in public schools who had a similar background. It described the curriculum of BIA schools as "content-neutral—where skills (reading, mathematics, etc.) are taught

TABLE 4

Public and Bureau of Indian Affairs (BIA) School Enrollments from 1968–1986

Year	Public and Private Schools[1]	BIA-funded Schools[2]	All Schools	Percent BIA-funded
1968	177,463	51,448	228,911	22.48
1970	197,245	52,098	249,343	20.89
1972	232,765	53,646	286,411	18.73
1974	288,208	49,524	337,732	14.66
1976	288,262	45,609	333,871	13.66
1978	329,430	41,324	370,754	11.15
1980	305,730[3]	41,604	347,334	11.98
1982	N/A	40,773	N/A	N/A
1984	364,313[3]	40,693	405,006	10.05
1986	353,462[4]	38,475	391,937	9.82

SOURCE: Report on BIA Education 1988, 29.

1 Does not include BIA-funded schools.

2 BIA-operated and contract schools. Excludes BIA dormitory counts. Prior to 1980, based on enrollment counts taken that were defined and calculated differently from determining average daily attendance (ADA).

3 Government sampling procedures employed in 1980, 1982, and 1984 were modified from earlier years and were not designed to yield a representative sample of Indian students. As a result, no projections of Indian students could be made in 1982, and the 1980 and 1984 projections contain abnormally large standard errors.

4 Preliminary.

by a few examples devoid of cultural or community context" (217). The *Report* concluded,

> One reason for the lack of emphasis on Indian history and culture is the shortage of textbooks and other teaching materials. The market is too limited for mainstream commercial publishers—especially when each tribe may have its own history and outlook. The BIA could undertake to provide financial support for the development of new teaching materials. For example, a textbook focused on the history of American Indians, beginning the story with their arrival from Asia 10,000 years ago, could be used throughout BIA-operated schools. More specialized materials, such as the history of a particular tribe, might have to be developed locally. Indeed, BIA schools might create school and class projects to develop written materials that could then be passed on and used by succeeding generations of students. (228)

TABLE 5

Combined Battery Test Scores of Reading, Language, and Mathematics and Other Subjects, Including the Scores of Some Special Education Students for 1986

Type of School	Grade											
	1	2	3	4	5	6	7	8	9	10	11	12
BIA-Oper. Schools	N/A	22% (2,256)	22% (2,441)	22% (2,412)	20% (2,068)	22% (2,045)	22% (1,796)	20% (1,693)	16% (1,037)	16% (947)	20% (819)	21% (803)
Contract Schools	N/A	18 (433)	16 (468)	19 (441)	18 (393)	17 (412)	19 (537)	18 (491)	16 (573)	16 (491)	17 (353)	20 (309)
All BIA-Funded Schools	N/A	22 (2,689)	21 (2,909)	21 (2,853)	19 (2,461)	21 (2,457)	21 (2,333)	19 (2,184)	16 (1,610)	16 (1,438)	18 (1,172)	21 (1,112)

Source: Report on BIA Education 1988, 73.

Following a national trend, some BIA schools were introducing the "Whole Language" method, which involved reading to students, students reading to themselves daily, students writing every day, students bringing familiar language to the classroom, language experience activities, extended literature activities, and reading strategy instruction with positive effects on students' test scores (*Report* 1988, 46). A community member described the curriculum developed at Ramah Navajo High School, founded in 1970 after Dillon Platero and others from Rough Rock Demonstration School visited and encouraged community members to run their own school,

> We did a literature based program before a lot of other schools even got into it. We had the whole language base program for years before any other school started to. We had authentic assessments with learning records and profiles way back in the 80s and early 90s. . . . I have to say that the whole language really took advantage of the Navajo language [in] its curriculum. The belief was, and this used to be something we use to always talk about, was that you took the strengths of the kids and not have a deficit model. The strength of the children, when they came, was always that they had a life language. And so if it was the Navajo language base, we did the Navajo language program with them in the mornings. We had a child centered program that included having to look at these folks and kids that came to school, their language, their culture. A program that meets their needs, the environment that they come from. We worked on the discipline, we worked on all kinds of social needs that the child had and it was all child centered. (Manuelito 2001, 187)

The *Report* also noted that BIA schools shifted from paying higher than average teacher salaries in the 1970s to lower than average in the 1980s.

> Non-Indian teachers located at isolated BIA schools have tended to be a blend of idealists, reformers, adventurers and the curious. Unfortunately, non-Indian teachers have also included a few of the misfits and failures elsewhere in American education. Some of these teachers ended up in BIA schools because no other school would have them. In other cases, teachers have been fleeing from personal problems and have been seeking to fashion a new life with a dramatic change in circumstance. BIA education has thus

included some of the best and a few of the worst that the American teaching
profession has had to offer. (202)

In 1978, 41 percent of the BIA's 1,039 teachers were Indian. The *Report*
noted:

> The pressures to hire Indian teachers, combined with the limited number
> available, have resulted in some cases in the hiring of poorly-trained
> teachers. As colleges and universities sought to expand Indian enrollments
> in the 1960s and 1970s, some of these institutions were willing to sacrifice
> full academic rigor. (204)

The result was that some could not pass state certification tests. If schools
provided strong support for weaker teachers, they could improve, but
teachers, once hired, can sometimes be forgotten in their classrooms,
harming generations of students. The *Report* rated the BIA's in-service
training and support for teachers "minimal" (211).

In 1978 P.L. 95-561 reorganized the BIA so that the twelve area offices
were largely removed from direct administration of BIA schools and
required the implementation of an Indian Student Equalization Formula
(ISEP) to fund BIA schools based on their enrollment. Congress went
on to require uniform federal standards for all BIA schools, state certification of teachers, and a nationwide program of testing all students.
Before the passage of P.L. 95-561, teachers were recruited in the same
manner as other federal civil servants, but after it, school boards and
principals were given more power to hire and fire teachers. The *Report*
concluded that BIA schools were functioning "as largely autonomous
units. Below the Agency level, in particular, there is little sense of
participation in a joint educational undertaking" (1988, 255).

Shortly after the *Final Report on BIA Education* was issued, the *Final
Report and Legislative Recommendations* was issued by the U.S. Senate's
Special Committee on Investigations of the Select Committee on Indian
Affairs. This investigation was instigated by reports of BIA fraud and
mismanagement, including a series of 1987 articles in the *Arizona Republic*. The 1989 *Final Report and Recommendations* found, "Paternalistic
federal control over American Indians has created a federal bureaucracy ensnarled in red tape and riddled with fraud, mismanagement
and waste. Worse, the Committee found that federal officials in every

agency knew of the abuses but did little or nothing to stop them" (Special Committee 1988, 5)

Among the worst problems found by the Special Committee was the fact that the BIA "permitted a pattern of child abuse by its teachers to fester throughout BIA schools nationwide." Its *Final Report* stated:

> For almost 15 years, while child abuse reporting standards were being adopted by all 50 states, the Bureau failed to issue any reporting guidelines for its own teachers. Incredibly, the BIA did not require even a minimal background check into potential school employees. As a result, BIA employed teachers who actually admitted past child molestation, including at least one Arizona teacher who explicitly listed a prior criminal offense for child abuse on his employment form. (9)

ALASKA AND THE "MOLLY HOOTCH CASE"

In 1931 the Indian Office took over schools for Alaska Natives from the U.S. Office of Education. According to Prucha (1984, 982), "Alaska schools were community schools in a full sense, for the teachers were social workers, medical aides, economic advisers, and recreational directors." In 1938 Alaska had ninety-eight day schools with 4,417 students, and nearly three-fourths of these schools had only one teacher. Three-fourths of the students in Alaska territorial schools were Native. In 1947 a single consolidated boarding school was established by the BIA at the former naval air station in Sitka, and Mt. Edgecumbe remained from 1947 to 1965 the only government high school in Alaska available to Native children from isolated villages, while white students were generally served by local high schools. In the 1960s more than one thousand Native students were also attending Chemawa Indian School in Oregon and Chilocco in Oklahoma. In addition, the state of Alaska funded families who took in Native students from remote villages so that they could attend high school. Under these conditions the high school dropout rate was high, and in 1972 the state of Alaska was sued for not providing secondary schools in Alaskan villages in what became known as the Molly Hootch Case (*Tobeluk v. Lind*). A 1976 consent decree required high schools to be located in 126 Alaskan villages, unless the village did not want one (Cotton 1984). At the beginning of the twenty-first century just under one-fourth of Alaskan students were American Indians or Alaska Natives.

The civil rights and self-determination movements rekindled interest in culturally responsive instruction that flickered during the Indian New Deal and was largely extinguished during the 1950s. Community-controlled schools allowed students to stay closer to home and involved local people in setting school policy and hiring staff. As more and more Indian students graduated from high school, tribal leaders began to look at the high dropout rates of Indian students in colleges and universities and sought to extend tribal control of education to the college level.

CHAPTER ELEVEN

HIGHER EDUCATION

Many Indians have been upset about the elementary and vocational emphasis of BIA education. However, leaving close-knit Indian communities for large, impersonal non-Indian colleges and universities to obtain advanced education can be too traumatic, expensive, and harsh a sacrifice for many Indians. Various solutions to the problem have been proposed, including Indian-only colleges and universities, Native American Studies programs as a "home" for Indians at large universities (Reyhner 1997), and tribal colleges that target their courses and programs to local needs (Tribal Colleges 1989; Boyer 1997).

As indicated in chapter 1, Harvard, the College of William and Mary, and Dartmouth were established with Indian education missions, but the ambitious rhetoric of their founders was not matched by deeds. In the late nineteenth century several new institutions were set up for Indians. Although the surviving schools now educate a majority of non-Indian students, they still retain a substantial Indian student body. In addition, Harvard, Dartmouth, and other colleges and universities responded to the increased interest in Indian education in the 1970s by establishing Native American studies programs. This chapter looks at the various efforts in the nineteenth and twentieth centuries to provide higher education for American Indian students.

OTTAWA UNIVERSITY

The historian William Unrau (1983) has documented that education was used in the nineteenth century to defraud Indians. In 1860 C. C.

Hutchinson worked with a member of the American Baptist Home Mission Society to charter Roger Williams University in Ottawa, Kansas (renamed Ottawa University in 1865), with the help of prominent Baptists. In 1861 Hutchinson was appointed an Indian agent and used his position to get a treaty through that included setting aside almost one-third of the reservation for establishing a university for Indians. He was dismissed the same year but wrangled another appointment as agent for the Ottawa until he was suspended for not keeping adequate financial records. Fifty thousand dollars were spent building the university, which had only one Indian student. An act was passed to sell the university in 1872 and give the proceeds to the Ottawa Indians, but most of the money from the sale went to lawyers. It was not until 1960 that, through the Indian Claims Commission, the Ottawa, now in Oklahoma, received $406,166 in compensation for the fraud that had been perpetrated against them.

CHEROKEE INDIAN NORMAL SCHOOL OF ROBESON COUNTY

A more successful effort at Indian education occurred in North Carolina. One of the earliest institutions of higher education established exclusively for Indian students was the Croatan Normal School. The Lumbee Indians were recognized in 1885 by the North Carolina General Assembly and authorized to have their own schools because they did not want to be educated in segregated schools with blacks. The Croatan Normal School opened its doors with fifteen students in fall 1887.

The school's early curriculum was described by the historians David Eliades and Linda Oxendine (1986) as nonstandard and nontraditional and below an eighth-grade level. Students originally had to be fifteen years old to enter. In 1911 the school was renamed the Indian Normal School of Robeson County because of the negative connotations given by North Carolinians to the word "Croatan." In 1913 it was again renamed, this time Cherokee Indian Normal School of Robeson County, a name it retained until 1941, when it became Pembroke State College for Indians. In 1949 the name was shortened to Pembroke State College. From 1941 to 1953, when it was opened to non-Indians by court-ordered desegregation in schools, Pembroke was the only four-year state-supported college for Indians in the United States.

In 1926 a regular two-year normal course was added to the curriculum, and elementary courses were phased out so that by 1928 the school offered only high school and teacher training studies. The school was opened to all Indians in 1945. It was accredited regionally as a four-year liberal arts college in 1951. As Pembroke State graduated more Indian students, pressure was put on the state universities to open their graduate and professional schools to Indians.

The school remained small until the 1960s. It experienced tremendous growth after the courts forced desegregation, and white students soon outnumbered Indian students. In 1969 the school was renamed Pembroke State University, and in 1971 it became part of the University of North Carolina System. In reaction to the de-Indianization of the university and the Indian militancy of the early 1970s, a Native American Studies department was added in 1972, and that department was authorized to offer a major in 1984—one of only two such majors offered east of the Mississippi River at the time. In 1981 the school's enrollment was 24 percent Indian. This percentage has remained relatively steady, and in 1992, 24 percent of the 3,041 students were again categorized as American Indians.

BACONE'S INDIAN UNIVERSITY

Three years after the founding of the Croatan Normal School, Almon C. Bacone, an instructor at the Cherokee National Male Seminary, helped to found the Indian University in Tahlequah with support from the American Baptist Home Mission Society. The school started with three students in 1880 in the Cherokee Baptist Mission and was chartered by a close vote a year later by the Muscogee-Creek Nation with the stipulation that the school be open to all Indians. John D. Rockefeller, the oil magnate and a friend of Bacone's wife, became the school's major benefactor.

The first annual catalog in 1881 for the Baptist Normal and Theological School declared that "[i]ts primary object is to prepare native teachers and preachers for a more effective Christian work among the Indian tribes" (quoted in Williams and Meredith 1980, 15). The school awarded its first bachelor's degree in 1883, and construction on Rockefeller Hall (see fig. 22) began in 1884 in Muscogee, Oklahoma, with the

THE INDIAN MISSIONARY.

THE INDIAN UNIVERSITY.

This institution was established for the especial purpose of training native teachers and preachers for a more effective Christian work among the Indian tribes. Its building is new and well furnished, its location near Muskogee is central and one of the most desirable in the Territory. Its teachers are in every way competent and the best that can be obtained.

TERMS:—Charge for tuition, per term of twelve weeks, $6.00. Board, per week, $2.50. All students are expected to work for the University on an average one hour each day, if required, for which 50 cents per week will be allowed, thus reducing the cost of board to $2.00.

CALENDAR FOR 1886-7:—First term begins Sept. 29, ends Dec. 23. Second term begins Dec. 27, ends March 16. Third term begins March 30, ends June 22.

A. C. BACONE, A. M. President.

An 1887 advertisement for Bacone's Indian University in the *Indian Missionary*. Courtesy of the Edward E. Ayer Collection, The Newberry Library, Chicago.

old site in Tahlequah becoming the Cherokee Academy. Between 1883 and 1888 there were five graduates, all Cherokee. The 1889–90 Tenth Annual Catalog listed fifteen students in a normal class and ten in a theological class. It reported that sixty students had been prepared for teaching and thirty-three for the ministry. The catalog stated, "Daily Bible instruction is imparted to all. All are required to be present at the weekly prayer meetings, the Sunday School, and the regular Sabbath services" (35). Rule 7 for students was as follows: "The young men and women will not be allowed to walk or ride in company, or have any place of meeting, only as they are brought together in their regular school duties, and religious and society meetings. Their correspondence will be subject to the approval of the teachers" (36). Students could not go to town without permission, and there were to be no amusements on Sunday. The Board of Trustees included the chiefs of the Creek Nation and the Delaware. Seniors took German, juniors Spanish, sophomores French, and freshmen Latin for a year. Graduates received a master's of science degree. The 1889–90 catalog reported twenty-two students, nine of them white, including all three seniors.

Alcoholism was considered the major illness among students, and they were closely supervised; for example, their correspondence was censored, and coeds were required to have teacher escorts outside of the school. Most of the faculty in the early days spoke one of the Indian languages of Oklahoma. Bacone graduates entered a variety of professions, including medicine, law, journalism, and business. There were only ten students in the college department in the 1904–5 school year, and from 1911 to 1916 there were no college-level students. Vocational training in farming was emphasized to prepare students to work their allotments.

In 1910, after Bacone's death, the college was renamed Bacone College. The student body represented fifteen tribes in 1919, twenty-four tribes in 1922, and forty tribes in 1933. In 1925 only Indians were accepted because of overcrowding. In 1928 there were ten Indians on the faculty, and the curriculum emphasized Native music and art. Bacone became known for its school of traditional Indian art. Commissioner of Indian Affairs John Collier recognized its contributions to Indian education when he laid the cornerstone in 1937 for a new boys' dorm.

From 1943 to 1948 the Reverend Early Louis Riley, a Creek Indian and an alumnus, served as president. During World War II, school enrollment declined, and by the end of 1943, 160 students had joined the armed forces. During the summers of 1943 and 1944, Bacone hosted Summer Linguistic Institutes, with more than one hundred students and fifteen faculty members in attendance.

After World War II, the school focused on providing programs that other Indian schools did not offer, and more non-Indian students were enrolled. In the late 1950s the school received regional accreditation. Dean Chavers, a Lumbee with a Ph.D. from Stanford and experience in establishing the Native American Studies program at the University of California, Berkeley, was president from 1978 to 1981. In 1992, 43 percent of Bacone's 623 students were American Indians. Its fall 2001 enrollment of 436 students was 45 percent Indian, representing twenty-three tribes.

TRIBAL COLLEGES

Despite the long histories of Indian higher education at Pembroke State University and Bacone College, these schools served only a tiny fraction of Indians. Both schools remained small, with only a few hundred students or less until after World War II. As the Bureau of Indian Affairs improved its educational system it began to think about postsecondary education. In 1932 Secretary of the Interior Ray L. Wilbur reported that Indian students could get educational loans from federal and tribal funds, get room and board at nearby Indian schools in return for part-time work, and receive federal funding for tuition and scholarships (Fischbacher 1967). However, Indian students enrolling in mainstream colleges had a 90 percent attrition rate (Stein 1992). Some colleges would not even accept Indian students. K. Tsianina Lomawaima describes how her father worked his way through high school and graduated in 1939 with an Honor Society scholarship. He was admitted to a small midwestern college. On arrival, however, "a dean informed him they had no place for Indians and told him to pack his bags and go" (Lomawaima 1994, 170). The failure of off-reservation colleges and universities to recruit and retain Indian students led to the exploration of alternative routes to higher education for American Indians. Tribal colleges were a direct outgrowth of OEO adult education programs and attempts by Indians to control their own schools.

As knowledge of what worked in cross-cultural education increased and began to be applied in schools, it became apparent that mainstream colleges were not designed to develop the skills provided by community-based schools. Thus, immediately after the founding of Rough Rock, Robert Roessel and others turned their attention to the higher education needs of Native students. Specialized colleges and universities for Indian students were not a new idea. However, the system of tribal colleges that developed starting with the founding of Navajo Community College in 1968 was unprecedented.

Navajo Community College

In 1957 the Navajo tribe established a scholarship fund financed by oil royalties. However, more than 50 percent of the students dropped out in their freshman year. This high failure rate led Navajo leaders to explore the possibility of setting up their own college. In the early 1960s, Navajo educator Dillon Platero, traditional elder and chairman of the tribal council's Education Committee Allen Yazzie, and tribal councilman Guy Gorman worked to establish a Navajo institution of higher education as a solution to the problem of high dropout rates. In 1965 they helped to convince the OEO, a Johnson-era War on Poverty agency, to finance a feasibility study. The study concluded that a tribally controlled community college should be established. Across Indian country OEO programs after 1965 provided leadership, career-ladder opportunities, and funded graduate education for young Indians.

With the example of Rough Rock Demonstration School in mind, formal and informal meetings were held, with the result that a non-Indian with grant writing skills, Robert Roessel, former director for the Center for Indian Education at Arizona State University and director of Rough Rock Demonstration School (see chap. 10), was brought into the planning process. A proposal was submitted to the OEO at the start of 1968 that was strongly supported by OEO officials in Washington, D.C. The OEO funding bypassed the BIA, which tended to be obstructionist. A public meeting was held in May 1968 in Window Rock at which Navajo tribal chairman Raymond Nakai strongly supported the founding of a community college.

On July 17, 1968, the Navajo tribal council passed a resolution founding Navajo Community College (NCC). An interim Board of Regents was appointed. In recognition of the work he did to gain initial funding for the college, Roessel stepped down from directing Rough Rock Demonstration School and was appointed the first president of NCC. Classes began in January 1969 in the BIA high school facility at Many Farms, Arizona. NCC started as an open admission institution, and 309 students (196 full-time equivalent [FTE] students) enrolled at NCC that first spring. Approximately 60 percent passed their courses the first semester, a much better percentage than Indians had attending mainstream institutions. By 1978 the enrollment had reached 1,241 students (1,034 FTE), 110 of whom were non-Indian. Roessel's Navajo wife, Ruth, became director of the Navajo Studies Department.

Yazzie Begay donated family lands at Tsaile, Arizona, and ground was broken in 1971 for a permanent campus, which opened in 1973. Ironically for a community college, this location was some distance from any Navajo population center, making it necessary for most students to live in dorms or to commute thirty miles or more one way to the main campus. Branch campuses were soon established in population centers, including Shiprock, Tuba City, and Chinle.

A staunch advocate of local control, Roessel soon stepped aside as president and became the college's chancellor, and in July 1969 Dr. Ned Hatathli became the first Navajo president. Both Roessel and Hatathli envisioned Navajo Studies as the centerpiece of the college and intended to replace non-Indian staff as qualified Indians became available. However, Roessel "was distressed" when non-Indian faculty members at NCC were denied a voice in school decision making (Szasz 1977, 177). Hatathli, disregarding the source of funding for the college, declared, "This is an Indian owned and an Indian operated institution, and we certainly don't want any people other than Indian to dictate to us what is good for us" (quoted in Szasz 1977, 177–78). While in 1970 the faculty was only 40 percent Indian, Hatathli considered the non-Indian faculty as just "working themselves out of a job" (quoted in Szasz 1977, 178). Faculty served without tenure on one-year contracts. Because of geographic isolation, cultural differences, and sometimes outright anti-white hostility, there was a high turnover of non-Indian faculty. Navajo faculty members tended to have less formal education than the non-Indian faculty but brought an intimate knowledge of Navajo language and culture to their teaching.

Although Szasz (1977) emphasized Roessel's role in starting NCC based on interviews and published sources, former tribal college president and Montana State University professor Wayne J. Stein (1992) put more emphasis on the role of Navajo leaders. However, assigning credit is a fruitless debate, since both local community support and the tribal leadership of Guy Gorman, Allen Yazzie, Dillon Platero, and others were needed as well as the expertise of Roessel and the support of government officials both in the BIA and the OEO. Navajo Community College was the result of collaboration between local desires and outside expertise; however, the tension created by that interplay continues today in the debate about what role tribal colleges should play.

On the one hand, extremists would reject much of mainstream thinking on what should comprise a college curriculum. On the other hand, there is a potential in the words of American Indian Movement leader Ward Churchill (1992, 36) that tribal colleges will do "the training of the colonized to colonize themselves." This conflict over what Indian tribal colleges would be was played out early on the NCC campus. Tribal traditionalists saw the tribal college playing a leading role in preserving tribal culture; modernists saw tribal colleges preparing students to get jobs or to leave the reservation to enter mainstream four-year colleges. On December 15, 1971, the U.S. Congress passed the Navajo Community College Act (P.L. 92-189) to provide federal support for the college.

Hatathli died unexpectedly in 1972 while still president of NCC. According to an account in the biography of one of his relatives:

> He died at a young age in the bedroom of his home of a shotgun blast. He had been drinking, friends say, and was despondent. He had just been passed over for a job as head of the BIA area office, a high-ranking job in the BIA bureaucracy. It is not clear whether his death was suicide or an accident. (Benedek 1995, 242)

After Hatathli's death, the new president, Thomas Atcitty, moved NCC, with the support of the new tribal chairman, Peter MacDonald, toward a more mainstream non-Indian community college against the wishes of the Board of Regents. MacDonald grew up herding sheep, and he first attended the BIA day school at Teec Nos Pos in northeastern Arizona pretty much on his own initiative. However, later he ran away twice from the boarding school at Shiprock, New Mexico, because of the "teasing, taunting, [and] the regimentation" there, and he became a "sixth grade dropout" (MacDonald and Schwarz 1993, 45, 87). After serving as a code talker in the Marine Corps, he was allowed to enroll in Bacone, at that time a Baptist Indian junior college, on the G.I. Bill in spite of his lack of a high school education.

After getting a General Equivalency Diploma at Bacone, MacDonald majored in sociology and studied both Christianity and Indian history. On graduation from Bacone he majored in engineering at the University of Oklahoma. He worked nights at the state mental hospital and was encouraged by the BIA to enter a trade school when his G.I. Bill funding ran out. MacDonald chose instead to work two years to save enough money so that he could return to the University of Oklahoma in 1955. He completed an electrical engineering degree in 1957.

After being wooed by several companies, MacDonald accepted a job at Hughes Aircraft. His autobiography describes a successful career at

Hughes, where he learned about Polaris missiles and other cutting edge technology. He also was impressed by the lifestyle of the corporate leaders at Hughes, who had offices on "Mahogany Row" (1993, 107). Despite opportunities for advancement at Hughes, the new Navajo tribal chairman, Raymond Nakai, convinced MacDonald to take a sabbatical leave to head OEO programs on the Navajo Reservation. He used that position as a springboard to the tribal chairmanship in 1971. As tribal chairman, MacDonald worked to separate the tribal government from BIA control and to get a better deal for the tribe on their oil, gas, and coal contracts. He wrote in his autobiography:

> Looking back, I realize that the BIA program was poorly planned and unrelated to the needs of the Navajo children. The hostile attitude toward my people was emotionally devastating, of course. We were taught that we were superstitious savages, and we were forced to go to church without being given an understanding of the Christian religion. We were made to feel that our parents, our grandparents, and everyone who had come before us was inferior. . . . We were constantly told that we were truly inferior to them and that we would always be inferior. (1993, 49)

MacDonald refused to accept an inferior position, and he learned to appreciate the good things in life. He also wanted the Navajo elite to have the same luxuries as the non-Indian world. He and his wife sponsored the Navajo Academy for the best high school students, and his final political downfall came when during his fourth term he made his office literally into a Mahogany Row and was imprisoned in 1990 for accepting bribes and inciting a riot after efforts were made by the tribal council to dismiss him from office. President Bill Clinton pardoned MacDonald, releasing him from jail, just before he left office in 2001.

MacDonald wanted Navajo Community College to have greater prestige, and admission standards were instituted. Atcitty, while gaining national recognition serving as a leader of the tribal college movement, was absent frequently from Tsaile and lost touch with his home base. He helped to found the American Indian Higher Education Consortium and later became its president. Robert Roessel (1979) bitterly resented that under Atcitty Navajo Studies ceased to be a separate entity and was to be integrated into the various traditional college departments. A coalition of faculty, students, and staff petitioned successfully

for Atcitty's resignation in January 1977. In 1976, 77 percent of the 304
college employees were Indian, and about 65 percent of the faculty
were non-Indian. After two short-term presidents, the Navajo educator
Dean C. Jackson became NCC's sixth president, serving from 1979 to
1989. Jackson, who had chaired a committee developing a Navajo (Diné)
philosophy of education while at Window Rock Public Schools, brought
curricular balance and administrative stability back to the institution
and promoted a Diné philosophy of learning:

> The educational philosophy of Diné College is Sa'ah Naagháí Bik'eh
> Hózhóón, the Diné traditional living system, which places human life in
> harmony with the natural world and the universe. The philosophy pro-
> vides principles both for protection from the imperfections in life and for
> the development of well being. (*Diné College NCA* 2002, 25)

Jackson needed such a philosophy. As president, he was forced to deal
with a federal funding cut, from $6 million to $3 million per year, for
operating expenses.

Sometimes, in reaction to the many years of coercive assimilation in
BIA schools that devalued all that was Indian, tribally controlled schools
went to the other extreme and devalued everything that was "white."
Deborah House, who took Navajo Studies classes and taught at NCC in
the 1990s, wrote:

> [N]on-Navajo students (Anglo, Hispanic, and others) were encouraged to
> disparage their own upbringing and cultural experiences. Furthermore,
> their language, literature, religion, family life, and ethnic identities are
> routinely, and at times painfully, denigrated and devalued by Navajo and
> non-Navajo instructors, administrators, and other students. (2002, 38)

House found that although there was a great deal of talk about the
importance of revitalizing Navajo language and culture at NCC, very
little was actually being done. The ideal Navajo lifestyle that was
promoted in some NCC classes—"sheepherding and growing a small
garden, living in a hogan, and driving a team of horses"—was not
really viable, especially considering the great increase in Navajo population over the last century (House 2002, 87). According to the 2002

North Central Accreditation (NCA) Self Study, "[I]n recent years the DEP [Diné Educational Philosophy] office has provided little or no support for faculty in integrating the philosophy into instruction" (*Diné College NCA* 2002, 27).

In 1997 NCC was renamed Diné College. "Diné" means "the people" in the Navajo language and is their name for themselves. In addition to the main Tsaile campus, there were seven satellite campuses in 2002. Finding the money to keep these campuses in repair was a major problem, as was balancing the financial needs of the main campus with the demands of local constituencies for local services. In part as a result of the conflicting demands and severe financial constraints, the 1990s were characterized by administrative instability, according to the the Diné College 2002 NCA Self Study report. In 1996 a four-year teacher education program was started, with the cooperation of Arizona State University. However, independent accreditation for this program was denied because of the college's lack of resources. FTE enrollment averaged 1,387 students per semester between 1997 and 2002, an enrollment substantially higher than that at any other tribal college.

Other Tribal Colleges

Deganawidah-Quetzalcoatl (D-Q) University near Davis, California, established originally as a joint Hispanic-Indian school in 1971, was among the pioneer tribal colleges. Jack D. Forbes, a Powhatan-Delware, helped to found the California Indian Education Association in 1967, and that group worked to set up an Indian college. After a nonviolent takeover of an abandoned army installation, the founders were able to get the facility turned over to the college. But funding was precarious in the early years. Most of the students were urban Indians, and Lakota was the only Indian language taught at the college. The activist founders hired the AIM leader Dennis Banks as an instructor in 1975 and as assistant to the president in 1976 (employment was a condition set by then California Governor Jerry Brown to keep Banks from being extradited to South Dakota to face charges stemming from the second Wounded Knee incident). In 1978, to obtain funding through the Tribal College Act, the Hispanic board members resigned.

Oglala Lakota College (OLC) on the Pine Ridge Reservation in South Dakota was started in 1969 by volunteers in association with the University of Colorado. In the 1978 mission statement the trustees stressed "the importance of maintaining the Lakota culture and fostering tribal self determination" while also preparing students "to understand the ways of the larger society" (quoted in Stein 1988, 99). To serve better the dispersed communities on the reservation, the college had nine centers rather than one central campus. The vision of the four-year teacher preparation program at OLC is "[t]o graduate highly qualified, professional, motivated, committed teachers who possess and who will teach *Wolakota* in a multicultural, changing world" (2001, 79). (*Wolakota* refers to the whole person in balance and in harmony spiritually, physically, mentally, and socially.)

OLC is currently working on an assessment format that identifies seven ability-based outcomes. The college's goal is for students to be able to demonstrate and use these qualities as a source of empowerment for lifelong learning. They are the ability to (1) develop and maintain an individual wellness program and nurture the mind, body, heart, and spirit; (2) model self-identity, founded on cultural practices, customs, values, and beliefs; (3) demonstrate basic understanding and usage of the Lakota language; (4) demonstrate community involvement or service; (5) reflect and document real-life examples of character (courage, honesty, generosity, etc.); (6) demonstrate and document effective communication skills; and (7) demonstrate and document professional abilities of critical thinking and problem solving. Assessment results are being gathered throughout the collegewide network using a Medicine Wheel view of abilities that emphasize *wolakolkiciyapi* (living in peaceful balance).

Sinte Gleska College on the Rosebud Sioux Reservation in South Dakota was chartered in 1971 and began with six centers. From the beginning, Sinte Gleska had a large non-Indian enrollment, sometimes representing over 50 percent of the student body. One of the founders, Gerald Mohatt, went on to help to form the American Indian Higher Education Consortium in 1972. In 1973 Lionel Bordeaux became its president. The tribal chairman tried to dismiss him several times, but he was still president in 2003. A four-year program in human services and education was started in 1977.

AMERICAN INDIAN
HIGHER EDUCATION CONSORTIUM

The American Indian Higher Education Consortium (AIHEC) was founded in 1972 at a meeting of representatives from all existing Indian postsecondary institutions. Gerald One Feather of Oglala Sioux Community College was chosen as its first president. The organizers' first priority was to start an American Indian accreditation agency, but finding a stable funding source quickly became the overriding priority and external accreditation helped the struggling colleges to establish credibility with Congress. In addition, the North Central and North Western Association of Schools regional accreditation associations proved very supportive of the infant tribal colleges and helped boards of trustees and college administrators to distance themselves from tribal politics and to gain legitimacy in the eyes of the outside world.

In her 1994 Ed.D. dissertation, "The Tribally Controlled Community Colleges Act of 1978: An Expansion of Federal Indian Trust Responsibility," former Little Big Horn College president Janine Pease-Windy Boy (Crow) gave a blow-by-blow analysis of AIHEC's work to find a stable source of funding for tribal colleges. Tribal college presidents Lionel Bordeaux of Sinte Gleska College, James Shanley of Standing Rock College, Thomas Atcitty of Navajo Community College, and Phyllis Howard of Fort Berthold College led the fight for a tribal college act. Between 1973 and 1975 AIHEC's executive director, David M. Gipp, and Bordeaux visited every congressional representative whose district had a tribal college lobbying for support (Stein 1990). Key support came from South Dakota Senator James Abourezk, who had grown up on the Rosebud Reservation.

According to Pease-Windy Boy, the BIA and the U.S. Office of Education consistently opposed the tribal college bill, and there was Indian opposition as well. Patricia Locke, a Hunkpapa Lakota and White Earth Chippewa, of the Western Interstate Commission on Higher Education and president of the National Indian Education Association in 1977, initially fought a tribal college amendment to the 1975 Indian Self Determination and Educational Assistance Act because it "undermined tribal sovereignty and self-determination" (Pease-Windy Boy 1994). Her efforts contributed to a name change from Indian-controlled to tribally controlled community colleges and the requirements that they be chartered by a tribal government, have all-Indian boards of trustees, and majority Indian student enrollment.

AIHEC leaders unselfishly supported new, struggling tribal colleges even though it meant spreading inadequate federal funding even thinner. Between 1968 and 1978 the seventeen colleges listed in table 6 were established that have survived into the twenty-first century. In 1978 stable if not bountiful funding for these colleges was achieved, despite BIA opposition, with the passage of the Tribally Controlled Community College Assistance Act (P.L. 95-471). It was sponsored by Senator Abourezk and signed by President Jimmy Carter. In that Act Navajo Community College received special funding status. In 1994 federal legislation awarded tribal colleges land grant status. In 1999 AIHEC listed twenty-eight tribally chartered colleges, most of them fully accredited, and three federally chartered Indian colleges in twelve states; four offered bachelor's degrees and two offered master's degrees. Accreditation requirements have helped tribal colleges to remain independent of tribal politics.

AMERICAN INDIAN AND NATIVE AMERICAN STUDIES

Responding to calls by university administrators and American Indian representatives, the South Dakota State Legislature authorized the founding of the Institute of American Indian Studies at the University of South Dakota in 1955. The Institute collected oral histories and, among other books, published *An Indian Philosophy on Education* (1974), edited by John Bryde. That book was described as "the first publication of its kind[,] . . . a collection of essays by American Indian professionals describing how American Indian children should be educated" (Bruguier and White 2001, 7).

As Indians moved to cities because of the BIA's relocation program promising jobs, many found that promise hollow. Some of the disappointed immigrants became community activists who along with college students began to protest the treatment of Indians in various ways. One of the most highly publicized protests was the takeover of Alcatraz Island in San Francisco Bay by activists and students from the University of California, Berkeley, the University of California, Los Angeles,

TABLE 6

Original Tribal Colleges Still Open (Some Now with New Names) in 2003

	Date Chartered	1979 Enrollment	
Navajo Community College, Tsaile, Ariz.	1968	1,118	
Oglala Sioux Community College, Kyle, S. Dak.	1970	282	
Sinte Gleska College, Rosebud, S. Dak.	1971	173	
Standing Rock Community College, Ft. Yates, N. Dak.	1972	111	
Turtle Mountain Community College, Belcourt, N. Dak.	1972	107	
Fort Berthold Community College, New Town, N. Dak.	1973	60	
Lummi Community College, Lummi Island, Wash.	1973	85	(1980)
Nebraska Indian Community College, Winnebago, Neb.	1973	115	(1997)
Sisseton Wahpeton Community College, Sisseton, S. Dak.	1973	96	
Little Hoop Community College, Ft. Totten, N. Dak.	1974	51	
Cheyenne River Community College, Eagle Butte, S. Dak.	1975	138	
Dull Knife Memorial College, Lame Deer, Mont.	1975	231	
Blackfeet Community College, Browning, Mont.	1976	304	
Little Big Horn College, Crow Agency, Mont.	1977	102	
Salish Kootenai College, Pablo, Mont.	1977	507	
D-Q University, Davis, Calif. (originally founded 1971)	1977	163	(1978)
Fort Peck Community College, Poplar, Mont.	1978	135	

SOURCE: Adapted from Oppelt 1984, 42–43.

and San Francisco State College. It was these institutions that first established Native American Studies (NAS) programs and associated courses (De La Torre 2001).

During the 1970s, NAS programs were established in colleges and universities across the United States and Canada. Within these programs, courses were developed in Native American literature, American Indian legal-political studies, Native American arts, Native American religion and philosophy, Native American education, American Indian languages, American Indian tribal and community development, and related areas (Forbes and Johnson n.d. [1971?]). Jack D. Forbes, who was involved in establishing the NAS programs at the University of California, Davis, wrote in 1969 that the "thrust of Indian Studies is not primarily to study the Indian community but to develop practical programs for and by the Indian community" (Forbes and Johnson n.d. [1971?], 29).

HIGHER EDUCATION GOALS

The central question for tribal colleges in particular and Indian education in general is whether the education supplied will be for the purpose of assimilation into the non-Indian world or for a purpose that is
more in line with Indian cultures. W. Larry Belgarde, founding president
of Turtle Mountain Community College, examined the struggle between
tribal members operating the colleges and the demands of the federal
funding agencies that provided the resources necessary for the colleges'
existence. Using Turtle Mountain Community College and Little Big
Horn College as case studies, Belgarde documented that "[t]he colleges
have installed formal administrative structures that resemble those of
the external society but have moved towards using Indian social norms
for day to day interaction" (vi). The colleges need to conform to outside
norms both to continue receiving funding and to confer on their students an education that is recognized by outside employers. However,
the higher education structure allows considerable autonomy, and
strong tribal studies departments have grown up in many colleges, and
Diné College has a tribal press that focuses on the publication of oral
history and other materials on Navajo culture.

Tribal colleges serve students who would not otherwise have a chance
to go to college and retrieve students who have gone off to mainstream
colleges and failed. They were in the vanguard of improving the quality
of life on their reservations. A two-year study of tribal colleges by the
Carnegie Foundation concluded, "The idea of Indian-controlled colleges
offers great hope to the Native American community and the nation as a
whole" (*Tribal Colleges* 1989, 87). Longtime president of Sinte Gleska
College, Lionel Bordeaux (1991, 12), declared that "these founders [of the
tribal colleges] foresaw the need to preserve the Indian culture so cultural
preservation is really the foundation of the tribal colleges."

In the 1990s there was a move by some tribal colleges to become
four-year institutions. Sinte Gleska College became Sinte Gleska University in 1992. Sinte Gleska and Oglala Lakota College in South Dakota
developed four-year teacher preparation programs, and Sinte Gleska
also developed a master's degree program in education (Bordeaux
1991). Both Diné College in Arizona and Haskell Indian Nations University in Kansas began developing teacher education programs in the
mid-1990s.

TABLE 7

Degrees earned per year by American Indians and Alaska Natives: 1981–1998

	1981	1985	1990	1995	1997	1998
Associate's degrees	2,584	2,953	3,530	5,492	5,927	6,220
Bachelor's degrees	3,593	4,246	4,392	6,606	7,409	7,894
Master's degrees	1,034	1,256	1,101	1,621	1,924	2,049
Ph.D.'s	130	119	99	130	173	187

SOURCE: US. Census Bureau, *Statistical Abstract of the United States* 2001, 175.

Unlike many white college graduates, many American Indian college graduates have had unsuccessful K–12 school careers. A Montana case study showed that their high school teachers did not encourage them to go to college, most had low grade point averages, and they heard little or nothing positive about Natives in their classrooms. Yet with family support, they went on to receive associate of arts, bachelor's, and master's degrees. Tribal colleges and organizations such as the American Indian Science and Engineering Society visited high schools and demonstrated to students that American Indians could be successful in technological society and at the same time retain their tribal cultures (Davis 1992). Table 7 shows the rapid increase in the number of degrees earned by American Indians and Alaska Natives between 1981 and 1998.

CHAPTER TWELVE

New Directions in Indian Education, 1989–2003

The policy of self-determination for Indians has survived, despite changes in administration, budget cuts, and doubts about the place of minorities in the United States. U.S. Indian reservations shared the neglect of its inner cities, but tribes persisted in the uphill struggle to take control of their education. Despite seriously inadequate funding, by 1991 there were twenty-two tribally controlled community colleges and seventy-four schools operated by Indian tribes and tribal organizations and funded by the Bureau of Indian Affairs (Office of Indian Education Programs 1991). These colleges and schools did not completely turn around Native education, but they certainly moved it in the direction of Indianizing Indian education.

There is also no question that the problems of Native education in the United States described in the 1969 Senate subcommittee report, *Indian Education: A National Tragedy, a National Challenge* (Special Subcommittee on Indian Education 1969), which helped to lead to self-determination, were not resolved by that change in policy. The 1991 Audit Report of the U.S. Department of the Interior's Office of Inspector General showed that students in BIA schools on average achieved far below non-Native students and generally did not receive high-quality education (Office of Inspector General, 11). Bureauwide, average percentiles ranged from a low of the twenty-fourth percentile for third and ninth grades to a high of the thirty-second percentile in the twelfth grade. Students in only 2 out of 153 schools had average scores at or above the fiftieth percentile (Office of Inspector General 1991, 11).

However, there were promising signs for the future. Demographically, after four centuries of precipitous population decline, the U.S. Native population increase that started at the turn of the twentieth century accelerated. Between 1970 and 1990 the U.S. Census reported a doubling of the American Indian and Alaska Native populations. Three specific events of the early 1990s indicate that the policy of self-determination was moving forward: The Native American Languages Act, the U.S. Secretary of Education's Indian Nations at Risk Task Force, and the first-ever White House Conference on Indian Education.

NATIVE AMERICAN LANGUAGES ACT OF 1990

On October 30, 1990, President George H. W. Bush signed the Native American Languages Act, Title I of Public Law 101-477. Congress found in this act that "the status of the cultures and languages of Native Americans is unique and the United States has the responsibility to act together with Native Americans to ensure the survival of these unique cultures and languages." Congress made it the policy of the United States to "preserve, protect, and promote the rights and freedom of Native Americans to use, practice, and develop Native American languages. . . . The right of Indian tribes and other Native American governing bodies to use the Native American languages as a medium of instruction in all schools funded by the Secretary of the Interior" is recognized. Furthermore, the act declared, "[T]he right of Native Americans to express themselves through the use of Native American languages shall not be restricted in any public proceeding, including publicly supported education programs."

The Native American Languages Act had three important implications. First, it was a continuation of the policy of Indian self-determination. Second, it was a reversal of the historical policy of the U.S. government to suppress Native languages in BIA and other schools. Third, it was a reaction to the attempt to make English the official language of the United States. The Act represented the grassroots support of Native people for their heritage and was a real departure from the old BIA attitude that "tradition is the enemy of progress," which led to the punishment of students for speaking their Native languages. The Act was a tribute to Native people's determined resistance to the forces of cultural assimilation and their answer to renewed calls for assimilation from the conservative English-only movement that wants a constitutional amendment to make English the official language of the United States (see, e.g., Crawford 1990, 2000).

The Native American Languages Act was an outgrowth of the Native desires that are expressed eloquently in tribal education policies, which have supported bilingual education and Native-language revival. In the preface to the Navajo Tribal Education Policies enacted by the Navajo Tribal Council in 1984, tribal chairman Peterson Zah declared, "We believe that an excellent education can produce achievement in the basic academic skills and skills required by modern technology and still educate young Navajo citizens in their language, history, government and culture" (Navajo Division of Education 1985, vii). The policies supported local control, parental involvement, Indian preference in hiring, and instruction in the Navajo language (Navajo Division of Education 1985, 4–9). The code states:

> The Navajo language is an essential element of the life, culture and identity of the Navajo people. The Navajo Nation recognizes the importance of preserving and perpetuating that language to the survival of the Nation. Instruction in the Navajo language shall be made available for all grade levels in all schools serving the Navajo Nation. Navajo language instruction shall include to the greatest extent practicable: thinking, speaking, comprehension, reading and writing skills and study of the formal grammar of the language. (9)

The Tribal Education Policies also required schools serving Navajo students to have courses in Navajo history and culture.

The Northern Ute Tribal Business Committee (1985) passed resolution 84-96 in 1984 declaring,

> The Ute language is the official language of the Northern Ute Nation and may be used in the business of government—legislative, executive and judicial—although in deference to, and out of respect to speakers of English, English may be utilized in official matters of government.
>
> We declare that the Ute language is a living and vital language that has the ability to match any other in the world for expressiveness and beauty.

Our language is capable of lexical expansion into modern conceptual fields such as the field of politics, economics, mathematics and science.

Be it known that the Ute language shall be recognized as our first language, and the English language will be recognized as our second language. We assert that our students are fully capable of developing fluency in our mother tongue and the foreign English language and we further assert that a higher level of Ute mastery results in higher levels of English skills. (16)

The Northern Ute Tribe required Ute-language instruction in preschool through twelfth grade, encouraged "pre-service training in Ute language theory and methodology for teachers," and required three credits of in-service training in Ute language for teachers within one year of employment.

Internationally, researchers have found that bilingualism is an asset rather than the handicap it was previously thought (Baker 1988; Cummins 1989). It is not necessary to forget a home language to learn a second "school" language and be academically successful in that second language. It takes time, approximately six years on average, to become fully—that is, academically—competent in a second language, but through proper instruction—such as has been carried out at Rock Point Community School on the Navajo Nation (see chap. 10)—students can learn English and academic subjects and still learn to read and write their tribal language (Collier 1989; Cummins 1989; Reyhner 1990).

INDIAN NATIONS AT RISK TASK FORCE

The Indian Nations at Risk (INAR) Task Force chartered by Secretary of Education Lauro Cavazos in 1990 issued its final report in 1991. The Task Force gathered testimony at seven regional public hearings and at the annual conference of the National Indian Education Association, made thirty school site visits, and commissioned twenty-one papers from national experts on American Indian and Alaska Native education on subjects such as current conditions, funding, dropout prevention, and curriculum.

In the Final Report's transmittal letter, the Task Force's co-chairs, former Secretary of Education Terrel H. Bell and former Alaska

Commissioner of Education William G. Demmert Jr., a Tlingit-Sioux, wrote:

> The Task Force believes that a well-educated American Indian and Alaska Native citizenry and a renewal of the language and culture base of the American Native community will strengthen self-determination and economic well-being and will allow the Native community to contribute to building a stronger nation—an America that can compete with other nations and contribute to the world's economies and cultures. (INAR 1991, iv)

The Task Force was composed of one school superintendent, two representatives from state education agencies, three representatives of Native organizations, including a former president of the National Indian Education Association, two representatives from Indian colleges, and four tribal leaders, including three present or former tribal chairpersons. Only two Task Force members were non-Indians, one of them the co-chair, Bell.

Based on their work and President Bush's six National Education Goals, the Task Force established ten goals for Native education (see table 8). Among the added goals are maintaining Native languages and cultures (goal 2), high-quality Native and non-Native school personnel (goal 6), restructuring schools (goal 9), and parental, community, and tribal partnerships (goal 10).

The Task Force co-chairs identified four reasons that Indian Nations are at risk:

1. Schools have failed to educate large numbers of Indian students and adults [as indicated by] high dropout rates and negative attitudes toward school;
2. Schools have discouraged the used of Native languages [with the result that] the language and culture base of the American Native are rapidly eroding;
3. The diminished lands and natural resources of the American Native are constantly under siege; and
4. Indian self-determination and governance rights are challenged by the changing policies of the administration, Congress, and the justice system. (INAR 1991, iv)

TABLE 8
Indian Nations at Risk Task Force National Education Goals for American Indian and Alaska Natives, October 1991

1. Readiness for School: By the year 2000 all Native children will have access to early childhood education programs that provide the language, social, physical, spiritual, and cultural foundations they need to succeed in school and to reach their full potential as adults.
2. Maintain Native Languages and Cultures: By the year 2000 all schools will offer Native students the opportunity to maintain and develop their tribal languages and will create a multicultural environment that enhances the many cultures represented in the school.
3. Literacy: By the year 2000 all Native children in school will be literate in the language skills appropriate for their individual levels of development. They will be competent in their English oral, reading, listening, and writing skills.
4. Student Academic Achievement: By the year 2000 every Native student will demonstrate mastery of English, mathematics, science, history, geography, and other challenging academic skills necessary for an educated citizenry.
5. High School Graduation: By the year 2000 all Native students capable of completing high school will graduate. They will demonstrate civic, social, creative, and critical thinking skills necessary for ethical, moral, and responsible citizenship and important in modern tribal, national, and world societies.
6. High-Quality Native and non-Native School Personnel: By the year 2000 the numbers of Native educators will double, and the colleges and universities that train the nation's teachers will develop a curriculum that prepares teachers to work effectively with a variety of cultures, including the Native cultures, that are served by schools.
7. Safe and Alcohol-Free and Drug-Free Schools: By the year 2000 every school responsible for educating Native students will be free of alcohol and drugs and will provide safe facilities and an environment conducive to learning.
8. Adult Education and Lifelong Learning: By the year 2000 every Native adult will have the opportunity to be literate and to obtain the necessary academic, vocational, and technical skills and knowledge needed to gain meaningful employment and to exercise the rights and responsibilities of tribal and national citizenship.
9. Restructuring Schools: By the year 2000 schools serving Native children will be restructured to effectively meet the academic, cultural, spiritual, and social needs of students for developing strong, healthy, self-sufficient communities.
10. Parental, Community, and Tribal Partnerships: By the year 2000 every school responsible for educating Native students will provide opportunities for Native parents and tribal leaders to help plan and evaluate the governance, operation, and performance of their educational programs.

The Task Force reported that during the 1989–90 school year, 39,791 Native students (10 percent of the total) were attending 166 BIA funded schools, 9,743 (3 percent) were attending private schools, and 333,494 (87 percent) were attending public schools. Testimony gathered at the Task Force hearings indicated that many of these Native students attended schools with "an unfriendly school climate that fails to promote appropriate academic, social, cultural, and spiritual development among many Native students." Schools also had a Eurocentric curriculum, low teacher expectations, "a lack of Native educators as role models," and "overt and subtle racism." These factors contributed to Native students having the highest high school dropout rate (36 percent) of any minority group in the United States (INAR 1991, 7–8).

On the positive side:

> The Task Force learned that there is a direct relationship between students' understanding of their culture and role in society and their ability to function comfortably in society and to achieve academic success. When students' relationships with the larger society are strained, their chances for academic success appear to diminish. . . .
>
> Often schools have failed to make clear to students the connection between what they learn in school and what they must know to live comfortably and contribute to society. (INAR 1991, 20)

The Task Force recommended "establishing the promotion of students' tribal language and culture as a responsibility of the school" and "training of Native teachers to increase the number of Indian educators and other professionals" (22). Furthermore, they recommended that school officials and educators "integrate the contemporary, historical, and cultural perspectives of American Indians" and "give education a multicultural focus to eliminate racism and promote understanding among all races" (24).

State governments were encouraged to "allocate specific funding for schools serving Native children to develop and use linguistically, culturally, and developmentally appropriate curricula" (26), and the federal government was asked to "seek legislation to authorize the establishment of a national research and school improvement center for Native education" (29). In addition, colleges and universities needed to "encourage scholarly work on curricula and textbook development that incorporates Native perspectives" (31). To solve the problems that Native people face, the Task Force particularly recommended

> support for new early childhood education and parent training programs, support for teacher education and other professional training for larger numbers of American Indian students and adults, support for Indian community colleges, and the development of new and exemplary education projects designed to carry out school improvement recommendations to meet the unique cultural and academic needs of Native students. (INAR 1991, v)

All in all, the Final Report strongly supported the need for linguistically and culturally appropriate education for American Indian and Alaska Native students and echoed the Native American Languages Act. It reflected a trend toward viewing schools as subcultures and the results of ethnographic classroom research. In Native education this research highlighted the cultural conflict occurring in classrooms in which teachers come from a different culture than the students. Untrained teachers—untrained in the sense of not being sensitive to cultural differences—often misinterpret and misunderstand the actions of their students. This ranges from misinterpreting the practice of some Native students not to look directly into one's eyes to misunderstanding that subtle differences in students' spoken and written English that reflect elements of a tribal language they may no longer speak.

For too long Native education was viewed as a one-way street, with Natives learning from the white society. At the worst this was forced assimilation; at best it was white people's arrogant assumption that Indians needed their help. In fact, there is a long history, largely ignored, of European and other immigrants learning from American Indians and Alaska Natives. Books such as Jack Weatherford's *Indian Givers* (1988) and *Native Roots* (1991) outline many of these contributions to the U.S. economic and political systems. These gifts have sometimes been exaggerated, but ignoring them is far worse.

The studies commissioned by the INAR examined the high Native student dropout rate (Reyhner 1992a). The common assumptions that Native students drop out mainly because they are failing academically or abusing drugs or alcohol were not borne out by the research. Studies of Navajo students by Paul Platero (1986) and Donna Deyhle (1989) found that students most frequently cited boredom as their reason for leaving school. They got tired of being told to read their textbooks, which were often written for students with more advanced reading capabilities, and being told to answer the questions at the end of the chapter. They felt their teachers were more interested in the subject manner than in them.

Overall, in the Task Force hearings held across the country in 1990 and 1991, parents, tribal leaders, and educators stressed the need for a cultural revival in Native communities to fight problems of drug and alcohol abuse, unemployment, and dysfunctional families. Testimony was repeatedly given on the need for more Native community involvement in Native education. Too often parents were asked to be "cake bakers and cops"—to help with school fund-raising and to get their kids to school on time. Until Native communities felt a sense of ownership in their schools, Native education would continue to be a failed, colonial enterprise. In addition, the INAR hearings brought out again and again the fact that racism was still alive and well in the United States and was hurting Native children. Another recurrent theme was the need for increased funding of Native education programs.

WHITE HOUSE CONFERENCE ON INDIAN EDUCATION

The White House Conference on Indian Education took place in Washington, D.C., in January 1992. It was authorized by P.L. 100-297 to "explore the feasibility of establishing an independent Board of Indian Education that would assume responsibility for all existing federal programs relating to the education of Indians" and "to develop recommendations for the improvement of educational programs relevant to the needs of Indians." The president, the Speaker of the House, and the president pro tempore of the Senate each selected one-third of the 234 conference delegates to discuss ways to improve Native education. One-fourth of the delegates were to be currently active educators on Indian reservations; one-fourth were required to be educators from urban areas with large concentrations of Indians; one-fourth were required to be federal and tribal government officials; and at least one-fourth were required to be Indians. In fact, the vast majority of the conference delegates were Indians.

In the months before the conference state preconferences were held across the nation in states with large Native populations to discuss issues such as whether there should be a national board of Indian education and a national Indian university and what should be the national goals of Indian education. Much of these discussions echoed the concerns expressed at the INAR hearings. The New Mexico preconference delegates reported, "[W]hen the idea of the White House Conference was first presented to us, there was much negativity and frustration expressed because it was thought of as another federal project that would collect the information, publish a report and place it on a shelf in Washington" (*Report for the White House Conference* 1991, ii). They continued:

> In reference to the quality and training of teachers, conference participants felt that some teachers are currently employed in the public schools primarily on the basis of their certification, with little consideration given to other important factors that directly affect the education of Indian children. Improved training and selection of teachers for public schools serving predominantly Indian populations was identified as a continuing need. In addition, the curriculum content found in most public schools was characterized as having been developed for mainstream America, without regard for cultural differences. Participants stressed the importance of enhancing the basic curriculum through the inclusion of local culture, history and language and that Native American parents and tribal leaders assist in the development of these curricula. (7)

The Washington State preconference concluded that a national board of Indian education would have little power and add more bureaucracy to inhibit tribal self-government. They concluded that Indian education should have a "holistic approach focusing on all segments of Native communities and all aspects of being human (emotional, physical, spiritual, and intellectual)" (*Special Report* 1991, 10).

Montana conferees called for flexibility to meet the diverse needs of tribal people and for the training of more Indian teachers, counselors, and administrators. They also felt a national board of Indian education would hurt local control and expand the bureaucracy and "white tape" (*Meeting the Challenge* 1991). However, Kansas's preconference report called for "a national certification procedure" for Indian teachers (*Kansas White House Conference* 1991, n.p.). Montana called for an emphasis on schools "to promote holistic education with the total community as their constituents" (*Meeting the Challenge* 1991, 10). The Montana group declared that education "is highly suspect among many Indian people. They sense the dichotomy between being educated, and being taught that to be Indian is not all right" (*Meeting the Challenge* 1991, 4). The need for better funding of Native education was a common theme across the nation.

Building on the work of the state preconferences, the White House Conference delegates adopted 113 resolutions covering a variety of topics, ranging from the governance of Indian education to safe, alcohol- and drug-free schools, building on the work of both the Effective Schools movement and the Indian Nations at Risk Task Force.

Following the White House Conference, the federal government showed little further initiative until in 1998 President Clinton issued Executive Order 13096 on American Indian and Alaska Native Education, which set six goals: (1) improving reading and mathematics; (2) increasing high school completion and postsecondary attendance rates; (3) reducing the influence of long-standing factors that impede educational performance, such as poverty and substance abuse; (4) creating strong, safe, and drug-free school environments; (5) improving science education; and (6) expanding the use of educational technology. To help achieve those goals, the American Indian and Alaska Native Research Agenda was formulated. Among the priority research topics set in the Agenda was a call for research on the "effects on educational outcomes for students and schools of incorporating American Indian and Alaska Native language and culture into the school curriculum" (*Research Agenda* n.d., 19).

The need for more research to improve American Indian and Alaska Native student achievement was highlighted by a 2001 General Accounting Office study that found "their performance on standardized tests and other measures is far below the performance of students in public schools," even though in 1999 the 171 BIA-funded schools serving 47,080 students generally spent more per pupil than did public schools. The study found that 17 percent of BIA students still resided in school

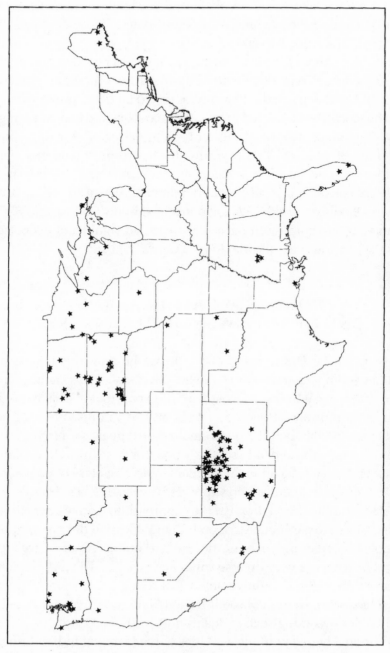

Location of BIA schools in the 1999–2000 school year. Courtesy of the U.S. General Accounting Office 2001, 4.

dormitories. While most BIA schools were in the states of Arizona, New Mexico, North Dakota, South Dakota, and Washington, there were also schools in Maine, Florida, and many other states. Figure 23 shows the location of BIA schools in 2000.

The BIA's Office of Indian Education Programs reported that in the 2000–2001 school year there were sixty-five schools operated directly by the BIA and one hundred twenty operated by tribes under P.L. 93-638. The schools were located in twenty-three states and had an average daily attendance rate of 90 percent. State or regional associations accredited 96 percent of them. In math 44 percent of students were considered proficient and 6 percent advanced. In language arts 45 percent were considered proficient and 5 percent advanced. These BIA-funded schools reported 3,496 incidents of substance abuse and 8,471 instances of violence, both figures represented significant decreases from the previous year (School Report Cards 2003).

INDIAN EDUCATION AT THE
END OF THE TWENTIETH CENTURY

The work of the INAR Task Force showed how local Native communities could take the work of the Effective Schools researchers and others and make it fit their needs. The Task Force took the six national goals for education released by President Bush in his *America 2000* (1991) plan and shaped them into ten national goals for Native education. These goals helped to set the format for the White House Conference on Indian Education. At that conference Secretary of Education Lamar Alexander accepted and supported the INAR goals. These goals reflected a multicultural, English Plus approach to Native education.

The White House Conference on Indian Education did not support a national board of Indian education, in part out of fear of centralized control of what are very diverse tribes and schools. The jury remains out on a national Indian university; tribal colleges fear losing already scarce resources, though Haskell Indian Nations University has the potential for becoming such an institution.

Additional hope lay in the activities of the National Indian Education Association, which now holds alcohol-free conferences and celebrated its thirtieth anniversary in 1999. More interest in Indian education created new scholarly interest in the field, revitalizing journals and organizations started in the 1960s and 1970s and starting new ones. Anyone reading the *Journal of American Indian Education* and the *Canadian Journal of Native Education* as well as the many allied publications of related organizations such as the National Association for Bilingual Education and the TESOL organization at the national and local levels can see the revitalization of interest in Native and minority education. All teachers of Native students, whether tribal college graduates or not, keep informed about new research and practices in Native education through school-based in-service training, reading professional literature, and attending professional conferences.

Although in many ways unique, Canada's experience with Indian reserves, residential schools, and assimilationist policies parallel the U.S. experience. Public hearings held in 1992 by the Canadian Royal Commission on Aboriginal Peoples brought forth concerns similar to those of U.S. Natives. There was a universal call for more aboriginal control of education, more aboriginal teachers, more cross-cultural training and education programs, and more Native language, culture, and history in schools. Other testimony called for students to learn about the land so that they could become more self-sufficient.

On January 8, 2002, President George W. Bush signed the reauthorization of the Elementary and Secondary Education Act, known as the No Child Left Behind Act of 2001. Title VII of this Act states:

> It is the policy of the United States to fulfill the Federal Government's unique and continuing trust relationship with and responsibility to the Indian people for the education of Indian children. The Federal Government will continue to work with local educational agencies, Indian tribes and organizations, postsecondary institutions, and other entities toward the goal of ensuring that programs that serve Indian children are of the highest quality and provide for not only the basic elementary and secondary educational needs, but also the unique educational and culturally related academic needs of these children. (P.L. 107-110, Sec. 7101)

The Act contains extensive provisions for ensuring educational accountability for Indian and other students, which led critics to label it the "No Child Left Untested Act." Critics expressed grave concerns that making "at risk" students meet high educational standards under the threat of not graduating would lead them to drop out of school. This is especially a concern since the tests being used to determine student success are mostly one-size-fits-all and reflect the academic content that legislators and other policy makers think is appropriate for mainstream American students.

In 2002 the Bush administration floated a plan to "privatize" the remaining BIA schools using "for profit" companies such as the controversial Edison Schools that promise to increase test scores with no increased expenditures (BIA "Privatization" Plan 2002, 4). Many Indian leaders saw this as a return to the conservative termination agenda of the 1950s, with the government seeking to get out of its trust responsibility for the education of Indian children. Mainstream critics of the No Child Left Behind Act, such as Gerald W. Bracey (2002), document a general conservative political attack on public schools, which means plans to privatize Indian schools are, as so often has been the case with American Indian policy, just a by-product of a larger national movement.

CHAPTER THIRTEEN

ENTERING THE TWENTY-FIRST CENTURY

Before the European invasion, traditional education for American Indians began in their extended families. Children were taught survival skills, allowing them to obtain food and shelter in an often hostile environment and to live in harmony with nature and their relatives (Morey and Gilliam 1974). Apprenticeship provided a means of higher education for those seeking to become healers and religious leaders. These traditional educational practices produced people fit to survive and prosper in the North American environment. With the coming of Europeans, the living conditions of Native Americans changed rapidly through the introduction of guns, horses, Christianity, new diseases, and many other foreign intrusions.

Christian missionaries tried to convince Native peoples to give up their old way of life. Federal Indian policy swung between supporting tribal governments and trying to destroy them. Although from the 1830s to the end of the century the tribes in present-day Oklahoma were allowed to operate their own schools, the U.S. government soon took them over, much as it had taken their land. Only in the last few decades of the twentieth century did Indians gain a measure of local control over both BIA and public schools that primarily enrolled Indian students.

The government's allotment policy in the nineteenth century and its termination policy in the mid-twentieth century constitute one extreme of the pendulum's swing. Indian Commissioner John Collier's Indian New Deal of the 1930s and the self-determination policy at the end of the twentieth century constitute the other extreme. Most recently, self-determination has led to an increased number of Indian-controlled schools.

Over the years the goals, content, methods, and delivery of Indian education have changed. The historical goal of coercive assimilation of Indian students into the dominant society has often led to students being forbidden to speak their tribal languages and having their tribal traditions labeled sinful. Had the goal of assimilation been realized, there would be no culturally recognizable Indian people today. However, many Indian children did not find success in schools that refused to recognize their indigenous languages and cultures, and many Indian elders worked strenuously to preserve their heritage. As Indian education enters the twenty-first century, accreditation associations require universities to have multicultural components in their teacher preparation programs to encourage students to learn to respect and appreciate the diverse world cultures.

In colonial times Christianity was synonymous with civilization, and both Indian and white students learned to read in order to read the Bible. If Indian languages were used, it was to speed conversion to Christianity. In the school textbooks that became popular in the nineteenth century, Indians were usually portrayed as savages. In the twentieth century, although Indian schools taught some courses in Indian culture, history, and languages, the curricula and textbooks, even in many Indian-controlled schools, still overwhelmingly reflected the dominant, non-Indian culture.

In the Spanish, French, and English colonies, Christian missions provided formal Indian schooling. In the nineteenth century increasing government funding of church-affiliated Indian schools greatly increased their number, but the Supreme Court stopped the practice at the end of the century, and most of the mission schools were replaced by BIA schools. Since then, the growing separation of church and state has led to the secularization of the curricula in both public and Indian schools. State-oriented public schools increasingly replaced federally run schools in the twentieth century. Since 1966 there has also been a revival of tribally controlled schools operated under contracts and grants from the BIA. In 1994, for the first time, the number of tribally controlled Bureau funded schools outnumbered the number of schools still directly operated by the BIA (Tippeconnic 1995). In 1998 the BIA's directory listed seventy-four BIA-operated elementary and secondary schools and ninety-seven BIA-funded schools operated by Indian tribes and tribal organizations. Another fourteen peripheral dorms with students attending public schools were also in operation.

Over the years teachers' training and teachers have become more professional. By the end of the nineteenth century BIA teachers were required to pass a Civil Service examination, though they were not required to have college degrees. In the last two decades of the twentieth century, some states required a fifth year after the bachelor's degree for full teacher certification. Raising professional standards for teachers, including licensing examinations, has been a mixed blessing for Indians. Teachers today are not tested on Indian culture or on the specific skills necessary for teaching Indians, and the use of culturally inappropriate tests makes it more difficult for Indians to enter the teaching profession.

Whatever their training, teachers who have been responsive to their students have been more successful than those who have slavishly taught from textbooks and curricula that may or may not reflect the culture of their students. The results of a study of a successful mission school for Alaskan Native students indicated that a key factor in the school's success was that teachers and other school staff took an interest in the lives of their students. Friendly, informal discussions increased the students' knowledge. Students from this school did well in college, even though they did not score high on standardized tests (Kleinfeld 1979).

Many reservation schools now have large numbers of Indian teachers; yet efforts to modify fundamentally the curriculum have not taken place except in a few schools such as Rock Point Community School. In the past three decades of "self-determination" Indian people have obtained a voice in determining their own destiny through elected parent committees, school boards, and tribal councils. However, as the federal government cut funding at the end of the twentieth century to many programs to balance the budget and control the deficit, the question these groups needed to address was whether schools can turn out self-assured, employable Indian graduates who can provide leadership in making reservations self-sufficient.

Often the purpose of local Indian control was to provide employment on reservations rather than to provide a high-quality education (McCarty 1987, 1989; Szasz 1977). Some reservations have unemployment rates as high as 80 percent. The pressing need for employment in order to survive has often overridden what is not a clear-cut educational mandate in the first place.

All the above changes in purpose, curriculum, pedagogy, and governance have still not made it possible for the average Indian student to do as well as the average non-Indian student in school. This relative academic failure of Indian students has led to study after study, including the 1928 Meriam, 1969 Kennedy, and 1992 Indian Nations at Risk Task Force Reports, that investigated why Indian students have not, on average, been academically successful. Reformers used these reports over the years to promote a variety of special programs funded by the federal government. Some, such as the 1934 Johnson-O'Malley and 1972 Indian Education Acts, are for Indian students only. Others, including Title I, Bilingual Education, and Special Education, apply to all students who meet the achievement, language, or handicap criteria.

The challenges faced by the United States and Canada to improve the education of their American Indian and Alaska Native citizens and give them the freedom to determine their own political and cultural destiny is not unique. Worldwide, the survival of indigenous peoples and their cultures is a compelling political issue. The breakup of the Soviet Union and Yugoslavia shows the strong claims minorities make for self-determination. Elsewhere, Kurds, Basques, and other indigenous peoples demand independence. The continued poverty and social problems of these minority groups are linked, rightly or wrongly, to their political and educational disempowerment.

The common practice in the United States, Canada, and elsewhere to use teachers and schools to destroy minority cultures and to indoctrinate children into mainstream cultures that continue to maintain ethnocentric and racist attitudes, despite their "melting pot" philosophies, is a travesty of what education should be. Regardless of the views of the children's families, Indian children were embued with the idea that the dominant "white" culture epitomized perfection, but their elders remind them of the reality that they are not and can never be white. It is long past time to remember what Luther Standing Bear ([1933] 1978, 252) declared about young Indians needing to be "doubly educated" so that they may learn "to appreciate both their traditional life and modern life." Three decades later, Polingaysi Qöyawayma noted,

[Indians] should be regarded as valuable assets to the nation and to the world, for that is what they can be, once their talents and special abilities are recognized and encouraged.

But don't ask them to peel off their brown skins and become white men. Peel though they might, there'd always be another layer of brown underneath. No. Rather, ask them to be themselves, help them to realize the value of their own heritage. Too much time has been spent in trying to teach them to cast aside the Indian in them, which is equivalent to asking them to cease being. An Indian can no more be a white man than a white man can be an Indian. And why try? There is infinite good in the Indian culture pattern. Let's look at this thing objectively, understanding each other with charity; not disparaging the differences between us, but being gratefully aware of the good qualities we may adopt, one from the other. (1964, 174)

This multicultural theme in Indian education can be found early in the history of the United States. For example, in 1905 John D. Benedict, superintendent of schools in Indian Territory, stated:

The greatest need of Indian education today is a corps of teachers trained to understand Indian life and environment, its habits of thought, its possibilities, its prejudices, its peculiarities, and its tendencies; trained in the kind of knowledge the Indian needs to know; trained to do the things which the Indian should learn to do; and trained in methods of importing needed knowledge in such a manner as will appeal to the mind of the Indian child. (*Addresses* 1905, 950)

He noted that successful public school teachers with "high examination grades and excellent recommendations, have failed as Indian teachers, while others with less knowledge of grammar, but knowing something of the work which they are expected to do, and something of the difficulties which they have to encounter, have succeeded" (*Addresses*, 950). Furthermore, he stressed that teachers need to also work with adults and that "[i]nstead of educating him [the Indian] away from his home life, the school should train him to a better appreciation of his home advantages, and should inculcate in him a desire to improve, to beautify, to elevate, and to enjoy his home" (*Addresses*, 951). And in his 1937 novel, *The Enemy Gods*, the anthropologist Oliver LaFarge wrote:

I think you make a mistake, too. If you learn all the white man's way and forget the Navajo, if that happens to our young men, then we die, we are destroyed, as surely as if by warfare. The man who will serve his people in the years to come, the man who will strengthen them, is the man who can learn all of the one without losing the other. (46)

The United Nations recognized both the predicament and the aspirations of indigenous minorities by declaring 1993 the International Year for the World's Indigenous People. The current policy of Indian self-determination in the United States, while not perfect, approaches the ideal of freedom and cultural democracy envisioned in the United Nations' Universal Declaration of Human Rights.

Guy B. Senese (1991) expressed the cynical view of self-determination when he concluded that the amount of self-determination was directly proportional to the amount of federal funding available and that it was an attempt to strengthen tribes and their economies so that the federal government would be able to terminate its trust responsibilities. The economic development foisted on reservations involved nonunion, relatively unskilled work. The reservation BIA schools participated by emphasizing basic skills and vocational education. In other words, as Senese (1991, 113) wrote, "Self-determination through community control and development assumes the quintessential purpose of ideology—the active involvement of a people in their own exploitation."

We would argue that Senese is looking at the glass as half empty rather than half full. Tribal schools and colleges are helping to change the negative environment on many reservations to an environment of hope. The renewal of traditional Native cultures in and out of school is reestablishing a sense of community and is fighting the materialistic, hedonistic, and individualistic forces of the popular culture. American Indians' concerns about land, culture, and community are concerns that all Americans need to share if we are to assure a future for our children. The Assembly of Alaska Native Educators has been particularly active in promoting culturally relevant education for Native peoples. In 1998 they adopted *Alaska Standards for Culturally Responsive Schools*, in 1999 *Guidelines for Preparing Culturally Responsive Teachers for Alaska's Schools*, in 2001 *Guidelines for Nurturing Culturally-Healthy Youth* and *Guidelines for Strengthening Indigenous Languages*, and in 2002 *Guidelines for Culturally-Responsive School Boards*.

Efforts to contextualize Indian education by including Native language and culture in the classroom is hampered both by the distrust of many Indians of white-dominated schools and by national efforts in the United States to improve test scores and to adopt specific "standards" regarding what should be taught in the classroom. The Navajo Nation in 2000 adopted its own "Diné Cultural Content Standards for Students," but these standards, like the state standards, are only beginning to be linked to curriculum materials for teachers and students.

Efforts to indigenize Indian education have taken the form of federally funded teacher training programs across the United States. These programs enrolled more than four hundred American Indian and Alaska Native students in 2002. However, the question remains whether these new teachers will receive specific preparation for teaching Native students and whether once in the classroom they will be able to resist the testing and standards mandates that point to a one-size-fits-all approach to American education.

There are no overnight solutions to the problems of Indian education that prompted initiatives such as the passage of the Native American Languages Act, the appointment of the Indian Nations at Risk Task Force, and the calling of the White House Conference on Indian Education. The rhetoric is in place both in Canada and in the United States, but there is still a long way to go to turn words into actions for all Native children.

Recent events in Indian education are indicative of the efforts by Indian people to reverse centuries of repression of their languages and cultures. The anthropologist William Leap (1982) could find no tribe that had allowed Native language restoration to outrank teaching English in importance. Another anthropologist, Malcolm McFee (1968), pointed out that assimilation is not a one-way street to progress and that Native Americans can learn to participate successfully in white society and at the same time retain their languages and traditional Indian values to become what he has described as the "150%" person. This must be the goal of Indian education.

Historically, Indian education has been mostly subtractive in nature. But when additive elements have existed, Native and non-Native, as in the work of Thomas Mayhew Jr., Samson Occom, Alfred L. Riggs, Luther Standing Bear, John Collier, Polingaysi Qöyawayma, Wayne Holm, and many others, Indian education has been more successful.

In the relatively short history of self-determination, Native people, on the whole, have favored schools that teach their children non-Indian ways without forcing them to forget their Indian ways. The Indian influence in Indian education is increasing, and the battle now is to make sure Indian education never returns to being a one-way, subtractive process of cultural assimilation.

The "vanishing" American is no longer vanishing through population decline or assimilation. The 2000 U.S. Census counted 2,476,000 American Indians and Alaska Natives, or 0.9 percent of the country's total population. Since 1970 the U.S. Native population has increased about one half million per decade, and this population is becoming increasingly educated.

The legacy of linguistic and cultural repression remains today among the expanding American Indian and Alaska Native population. Having internalized the old boarding school attitude that any time spent on ancestral languages is time wasted, some parents object to modern bilingual education for their children. Christian converts can think that teaching Native studies means promoting Native religions to their children, and, based on past experience, many Native people are suspicious of any government-sponsored programs. Those attitudes and suspicions must be allayed and not allowed to cripple badly needed reforms in the education of Native children.

Today, at the dawning of the twenty-first century, when the United Nations, the United States, Canada, and other countries are supporting human rights, including the right of indigenous minorities to their languages, religions, and cultures in eastern Europe and elsewhere in the world, the time has come for equal recognition of the basic human right of America's Native peoples to control the education of their children.

REFERENCES

Abbott, F. H. 1915. *The Administration of Indian Affairs in Canada.* Washington, D.C.: U.S. Government Printing Office.

Adams, David Wallace. 1988. "Fundamental Considerations: The Deep Meaning of Native American Schooling 1880–1900." *Harvard Educational Review* 58(1):1–28.

———. 1995. *Education for Extinction: American Indians and the Boarding School Experience.* Lawrence: University Press of Kansas.

Adams, Evelyn C. 1946. *American Indian Education: Government Schools and Economic Progress.* Morningside Heights, N.Y.: King's Crown.

Addresses and Proceedings of the National Educational Association. 1900–1909. Chicago: University of Chicago Press.

Ahenakew, Freda. 1986. "Text Based Grammars in Cree Language Education." In *Proceedings: Selected Papers and Biographics,* edited by Suzanne Weryackwe, 1–4. Choctaw, Okla.: Sixth Annual International Native American Language Issues Institute.

Ahern, Wilbert H. 1983. "'The Returned Indians': Hampton Institute and Its Indian Alumni, 1879–1893." *Journal of Ethnic Studies* 10(4):101–24.

Allen, Ray. 1970. "Whither Indian Education: A Conversation with Philleo Nash." *School Review* 79:99–108.

America 2000: An Education Strategy. 1991. Washington, D.C.: U.S. Department of Education.

American Indian Higher Education Consortium, Institute for Higher Education Policy. 1999. *Tribal Colleges: An Introduction.* Alexandria, Va.: AIEHC.

American Indians, Eskimos and Aleuts on Identified Reservations and in the Historic Areas of Oklahoma (Excluding Urbanized Areas): 1980 Census of Population. 1985, November. Washington, D.C.: U.S. Department of Commerce, Bureau of the Census. (Subject Report PC80–2–1D, Part 1.)

Annual Report of the Board of Indian Commissioners (ARBIC). 1869–1933. Washington, D.C.: U.S. Government Printing Office.

Annual Report of the Commissioner of Indian Affairs (ARCIA). 1824–1949. Washington, D.C.: U.S. Government Printing Office.

Arizona Department of Education. 1976. *A Study of Public Schools On and Off Indian Reservations in Arizona*. Phoenix: Arizona Department of Education.

Armstrong, O. K. 1945, August. "Set the American Indians Free!" *Reader's Digest* 47: 47–52.

Asher, James. 1977. *Learning Another Language through Actions: The Complete Teacher's Guide*. Los Gatos, Calif.: Sky Oaks Publications.

Baerreis, David A. 1963. Foreword. In *Francis La Flesche, The Middle Five: Indian Schoolboys of the Omaha Tribe*. Madison: University of Wisconsin Press.

Baker, C. 1988. *Key Issues in Bilingualism and Bilingual Education*. Clevedon, U.K.: Multilingual Matters.

Banks, Dennis. 1994. Foreword. In J. Hubbard, *Shooting Back from the Reservation: A Photographic View of Life by Native American Youth*, viii–ix. New York: New Press.

Barreiro, Jose, ed. 1992. *Indian Roots of American Democracy*. Ithaca, N.Y.: Akwe:kon Press, Cornell University.

Bartlett, S. C. 1887, October 6. "The Ruling of the Indian Bureau." *The Independent* 39(2027):1254–55.

Bass, Althea. [1936] 1996. *Cherokee Messenger*. Norman: University of Oklahoma Press.

———. 1937. *A Cherokee daughter of Mount Holyoke*. Muscatine, Iowa:: Prairie Press.

———. 1966. *The Arapaho Way: A Memoir of an Indian Boyhood*. New York: Clarkson N. Potter.

Beatty, Willard. 1942. "Training Indians for the Best Use of Their Own Resources. In *The Changing Indian*, edited by Oliver Lafarge, 128–38. Norman: University of Oklahoma Press.

———. 1947, April 14. "Who Segregates Indians?" *Indian Education* 150:1–5.

———. 1950, April 1. "Choosing School Books." *Indian Education* 194:1–4.

———. 1951. *Education for Cultural Change*. Washington, D.C.: U.S. Department of the Interior, Bureau of Indian Affairs. [Collected articles from the Bureau publication Indian Education.]

———. 1961. "History of Navajo Education." *America Indigena* 21:7–31.

Belgarde, W. Larry. 1993. "Indian Control and the Management of Dependencies: The Case of Tribal Community Colleges." Ph.D. dissertation, Stanford University.

Benedek, Emily. 1996. *Beyond the Four Corners of the World: A Navajo Woman's Journey*. New York: Alfred A. Knopf.

Bergman, Robert, Joseph Muskrat, Sol Tax, Oswald Werner, and Gary Witherspoon. 1969. *Problems of Cross-Cultural Educational Research and Evaluation: The Rough Rock Demonstration School*, edited by Arthur Harkins and Richard Woods. Minneapolis: University of Minnesota Training Center for Community Programs.

Bernstein, Bruce, and W. Jackson Rushing. 1995. *Modern by Tradition: American Indian Painting in the Studio Style*. Santa Fe: Museum of New Mexico Press.

BIA "Privatization" Plan. 2002, March 27. *Navajo Hopi Observer*, 4.

Blodgett, Harold. 1935. *Samson Occom*. Hanover, N.H.: Dartmouth College.

Bloom, John. 1996. "'Show What an Indian Can Do': Sports, Memory, and Ethnic Identity at Federal Indian Boarding Schools." *Journal of American Indian Education* 35(3):33–48.

————. 2000. *To Show What an Indian Can Do: Sports at Native American Boarding Schools*. Minneapolis: University of Minnesota Press.

Boas, Franz. 1911. *The Mind of Primitive Man*. New York: Macmillan.

Bordeaux, L. 1991. "Higher Education from the Tribal College Perspective." In *Opening the Montana Pipeline: American Indian Higher Education in the Nineties*, edited by Deborah LaCounte and Patrick Weasel Head, 11–18. Sacramento, Calif.: Tribal College Press.

Bowden, Henry Warner. 1981. *American Indians and Christian Missions*. Chicago: University of Chicago Press.

Boyce, George A. 1974. *When Navajos Had Too Many Sheep: The 1940's*. San Francisco: Indian Historian Press.

Boyer, Paul. 1997. *Native American Colleges: Progress and Prospects*. San Francisco: Jossey-Bass.

Bracey, Gerald W. 2002. *The War against America's Public Schools: Privatizing Schools, Commercializing Education*. Boston: Allyn and Bacon.

Brandt, Elizabeth A. 1992. "The Navajo Area Student Dropout Study: Findings and Implications." *Journal of American Indian Education* 31(2):48–63.

Brandt, Rose K. 1935. "We Make Our Own Books." *Indians at Work* 2(2):25–27.

Branom, Mendel E. 1919. *The Project Method in Education*. Boston: Richard G. Badger, Gorham Press.

Brody, J. J. 1971. *Indian Painters and White Patrons*: Albuquerque: University of New Mexico Press.

Brown, Dee Alexander. 1970. *Bury My Heart at Wounded Knee: An Indian History of the American West*. New York: Holt, Rinehart & Winston.

Brown, Estelle Aubrey. 1952. *Stubborn Fool: A Narrative*. Caldwell, Idaho: Caxton.

Bruguier, Leonard R., and Scott E. White. 2001. "The Institute of American Indian Studies: A Tradition of Scholarly Pursuit." *Indigenous Nations Studies Journal* 2(2):3–10.

Bureau of Indian Affairs, U.S. Department of the Interior. 1986. *Education Directory*. Washington, D.C.

————. 1987, January. *Indian Service Population and Labor Force Estimates*. Washington, D.C.

————. 1988. *Education Directory: Bureau of Indian Affairs Schools, Tribally Controlled Community Colleges, Contract Schools, Agencies, Area Offices, and Central Office*. Washington, D.C.

Burnette, Robert, and John Koster. 1974. *The Road to Wounded Knee*. New York: Bantam.

Butler, N. M., ed. 1910. "Education and the Indian." In *Education in the United States*, 937–72. New York: American Book Co.

Cantoni-Harvey, Gina. 1977. "Some Observations about Red English and Standard English in the Classroom." In *Studies in Southwestern Indian English*, edited by William L. Leap, 223–33. San Antonio, Tex.: Trinity University.

————. 1983. "ESP in Every Classroom: An Option for a Navajo School." In *Swallow Ten: Tenth Southwest Areal Languages and Linguistics Workshop Proceedings*, edited by G. Cantoni–Harvey and M. F. Heiser, 177–83. San Antonio, Tex.: Trinity University.

Chavis, Ben. 1999. "Off-Reservation Boarding High School Teachers: How Are They Perceived by Former American Indian Students?" *Social Science Journal* 36(1):33–45.

Cherokee Nation v. Georgia. 1831. 5 Peters, 15–20.

Churchill, Ward. 1992. *Fantasies of the Master Race: Literature, Cinema and the Colonization of American Indians.* Monroe, Me.: Common Courage Press.

Clinton, William. 1989, August 6. *American Indian Alaska Native Education* (Executive Order 13096). Washington, D.C.: The White House.

Cohen, Felix. 1945, October 1. "Indian 'Restrictions' are 'Privileges.'" *Indian Education* 122:1–4.

———. 1945, October 15. "White Culture Enriched by Indians." *Indian Education* 123:1–5.

Coleman, Michael C. 1987. "The Responses of American Indian Children to Presbyterian Schooling in the Nineteenth Century: An Analysis through Missionary Sources." *History of Education Quarterly* 27(4):273–497.

Collier, John. 1923a. "America's Treatment of Her Indians." *Current History* (August): 771–78.

———. 1923b. "Our Indian Policy." *Sunset Magazine* (March):13–15, 89–93.

———. 1934a. "A Reply to Mrs. Eastman." *Christian Century* 57:1018–1020.

———. 1934b. Editorials [from *Indians at Work*]. Photocopy in Special Collections, Northern Arizona University, Cline Library.

———. 1947. *The Indians of the Americas: The Long Hope.* New York: W. W. Norton.

———. 1963. *From Every Zenith: A Memoir.* Denver: Sage Books.

Collier, John, Jr. 1973. *Alaskan Eskimo Education: A Film Analysis of Cultural Confrontation in the Schools.* New York: Holt, Rinehart & Winston.

———. 1988. "Survival at Rough Rock: A Historical Overview of Rough Rock Demonstration School." *Anthropology & Education Quarterly* 19:253–69.

Collier, Virginia. 1989. "How Long? A Synthesis of Research on Academic Achievement in a Second Language." *TESOL Quarterly* 23:509–31.

Colton, L. 2000. *Counting Coup: A True Story of Basketball and Honor on the Little Big Horn.* New York: Warner Books.

Comprehensive BIA School Report. 1985, Fall. Washington, D.C.: Bureau of Indian Affairs, U.S. Department of the Interior.

Cotton, Stephen E. 1984. "Alaska's 'Molly Hootch Case': High Schools and the Village Voice." *Educational Research Quarterly* 8(4):30–43. Retrieved March 26, 2003. http://www.alaskool.org/native_ed/law/mhootch_erq.html

Crane, Leo. 1929. *Indians of the Enchanted Desert.* Boston: Little, Brown.

Crawford, James. 1990. "Language Freedom and Restriction: A Historical Approach to the Official Language Controversy." In *Effective Language Education Practices and Native Language Survival,* edited by Jon Reyhner, 9–22. Choctaw, Okla.: Native American Language Issues.

———. 1995. "Endangered Native American Languages: What Is to Be Done, and Why?" *Bilingual Research Journal* 19(1):17–38.

———. 2000. *At War with Diversity: U.S. Language Policy in an Age of Anxiety.* Clevedon, U.K.: Multilingual Matters.

Cremin, Lawrence. 1961. *Transformation of the School: Progressivism in American Education, 1876–1957*. New York: Alfred A. Knopf.

Cummins, Jim. 1981. "The Role of Primary Language Development in Promoting Educational Success for Minority Students." In *California State Department of Education, Schooling and Language Minority Students*. Los Angeles: California State University at Los Angeles.

———. 1986. "Empowering Minority Students: A Framework for Intervention." *Harvard Educational Review* 56:18–36.

———. 1989. *Empowering Minority Students*. Sacramento, Calif.: California Association for Bilingual Education.

———. 1992. "The Empowerment of Indian Students." In *Teaching American Indian Students*, edited by Jon Reyhner, 3–12. Norman: University of Oklahoma Press.

———. 2000. *Language, Power, and Pedagogy: Bilingual Children in the Crossfire*. Clevedon, U.K.: Multilingual Matters.

Dahlberg, Henry. 1968. "Community and School Service." *Journal of American Indian Education* 7(3):15–19.

Dauenhauer, Richard L. 2000. *Conflicting Visions in Alaskan Education*, 3d ed. Juneau, Alaska: Tlingit Readers.

Davis, J. 1992. "Factors Contributing to the Post–secondary Achievement of American Indians." Master's thesis, Eastern Montana College [now Montana State University, Billings].

Dawes, Henry L. 1883. "Solving the Indian Problem." In *Fifteenth Annual Report of the Board Of Indian Commissioners*, 69–70. Washington, D.C.: U.S. Government Printing Office. [Reprinted in Francis Paul Prucha, ed., *Americanizing the American Indians: Writings by the "Friends of the Indian," 1880–1900* (Cambridge, Mass.: Harvard University Press), 27–30.]

Debo, Angie. 1970. *A History of the Indians of the United States*. Norman: University of Oklahoma Press.

DeJong, David H. 1993. *Promises of the Past: A History of Indian Education in the United States*. Golden, Colo.: North American Press.

DeKorne, John C., ed. 1947. *Navaho and Zuni for Christ: Fifty Years of Indian Missions*. Grand Rapids, Mich.: Christian Reformed Board of Missions.

De La Torre, Joely. 2001. "From Activism to Academics: The Evolution of American Indian Studies at San Francisco State, 1968–2001." *Indian Nations Studies Journal* 2(2):11–20.

Deloria, Vine, Jr., and Clifford Lytle. 1984. *The Nations Within: The Past and Future of American Indian Sovereignty*. New York: Pantheon.

Deloria, Vine, Jr., and Daniel R. Wildcat. 2001. *Power and Place: Indian Education in America*. Golden, Colo.: Fulcrum Resources.

Delpit, Lisa D. 1995. *Other People's Children: Cultural Conflict in the Classroom*. New York: New Press, distributed by W. W. Norton.

Dewey, John. 1900. *The School and Society*. Rev. ed. Chicago: University of Chicago Press.

———. 1933. *How We Think*. Rev. and expanded ed. Boston: Houghton Mifflin.

Deyhle, Donna. 1989. "Pushouts and Pullouts: Navajo and Ute School Leavers." *Journal of Navajo Education* 6(2):36–51.

———. 1992. "Constructing Failure and Maintaining Cultural Identity: Navajo and Ute School Leavers." *Journal of American Indian Education* 31(2):24–47.

Diné College NCA (North Central Association) Self Study. 2002. Tsaile, Ariz.: Diné College.

Dodge, Richard Irving. 1882. *Our Wild Indians: Thirty-three Years' Personal Experience among the Red Men of the Great West.* Hartford, Conn.: A. D. Worthington. [Reprint Archer House, New York, 1959].

Driver, Harold E. 1969. *Indians of North America.* 2d ed. Chicago: University of Chicago Press.

Duffy, Sister Consuela Marie. 1966. *Katherine Drexel: A Biography.* Philadelphia: Peter Rilly.

Duncan, Kunigunde. [1938] 1990. *Blue Star: The Story of Corabelle Fellows, Teacher at Dakota Missions, 1884–1888.* St. Paul, Minn.: Historical Society Press. [Originally published by Caxton Printers, Caldwell, Idaho.].

Dunn, Dorothy. 1968. *American Indian Painting of the Southwest and Plains Areas.* Albuquerque: University of New Mexico Press.

Dusenberry, Verne. 1962. *The Montana Cree: A Study of Religious Persistence.* Stockholm: Almqvist & Wiksell.

Eastman, Charles A. (Ohiyesa). 1915. *The Indian Today: The Past and Future of the First American.* Garden City, N.Y.: Doubleday.

———. [1916] 1977. *From the Deep Woods to Civilization: Chapters in the Autobiography of an Indian.* Lincoln: University of Nebraska Press.

Eastman, Elaine Goodale. 1934. "Does Uncle Sam Foster Paganism." *Christian Century* 57:1016–18.

———. 1935. *Pratt: The Red Man's Moses.* Norman: University of Oklahoma Press.

Editorial. 1874. *IAPI OAYE* 3(1):4.

Editorial. 1990. *Education* 10:449–53.

Eliades, David K., and Linda Ellen Oxendine. 1986. *Pembroke State University: A Centennial History.* Columbus, Ga.: Brentwood University Press.

Elk v. Wilkins. 1884, November 3. 112 U.S. Reports, 98–99, 102, 109.

Ellis, Clyde. 1996. *To Change Them Forever: Indian Education at the Rainy Mountain Boarding School, 1893–1920.* Norman: University of Oklahoma Press.

Ellis, Richard N. 1979. "Louis Rook Bruce (1969–1973)." In *The Commissioners of Indian Affairs 1824–1977,* edited by Robert M. Kvasnicka and Herman J. Viola, 333–40. Lincoln: University of Nebraska Press.

Emerson, Gloria. 1970. "The Laughing Boy Syndrome." *School Review* 79:96–98.

Enochs, J. B. 1950. *Little Man's Family: Diné Yázhí Ba'álchíní.* Phoenix, Ariz.: Bureau of Indian Affairs.

Enos, Anya Dozier. 2002. "Deep Sovereignty: Education in Pueblo Indian Communities." Paper presented at the annual meeting of the National Indian Education Association, November 4, 2002, Albuquerque, New Mex.

Erickson, Donald. 1969, April. *Community School at Rough Rock: A Report Submitted to the Office of Economic Opportunity.* (Copy in Special Collections, University of Arizona Library.)

"Experiential Reading." 1943, December 1. *Indian Education* 94:5–8.

Federal and State Indian Reservations and Indian Trust Areas. 1974. Washington, D.C.: U.S. Government Printing Office.

Fedullo, Mick. 1992. *Light of the Feather.* New York: Morrow.

Feraca, Stephen E. 1990. *Why Don't They Give Them Guns? The Great American Indian Myth.* Lanham, Md.: University Press of America.

Fire, John, and Richard Erdoes. 1972. *Lame Deer: Seeker of Visions.* New York: Simon and Schuster.

Fischbacher, Theodore. 1967. "A Study of the Role of the Federal Government in the Education of the American Indian." Ph.D. dissertation, Arizona State University, Tempe.

Fletcher, Alice C., and Francis La Flesche. 1911. *The Omaha Tribe.* Washington, D.C.: U.S. Government Printing Office [Reprint Johnson Reprints, 1970.]

Fogel, Daniel. 1988. *Junípero Serra, the Vatican and Enslavement Theology.* San Francisco: Ism Press.

Folsom, Cora M. 1893. "Record of Returned Indian Students." In *Twenty–two Years' Work at the Hampton Normal and Agricultural Institute at Hampton, Virginia,* 317–493. Hampton, Va.: Normal School.

Forbes, Alexander. [1839] 1972. *California: A History of Upper and Lower California From Their First Discovery to the Present Time.* New York: Kraus Reprint Co. [Reprint of 1937 edition published by J. H. Nash, San Francisco; first published Smith, Elder and Co., London, 1839.]

Forbes, Jack D., and Carolyn Johnson, eds. n.d. [1971?]. *Handbook for the Development of Native American Studies.* Davis: Native American Studies, University of California, Davis.

Ford, Paul Leicester. [1897] 1962. *The New England Primer: A History of Is Origin and Development.* New York: Teachers College, Columbia University.

Foreman, Carolyn Thomas. 1931. "The Choctaw Academy." *Chronicles of Oklahoma* 9(December):382–411.

———. 1932. "The Choctaw Academy." *Chronicles of Oklahoma* 10(March):77–114.

Foreman, Grant. 1938. *Sequoyah.* Norman: University of Oklahoma Press.

Fowler, B. 1930. "President's Message." *Progressive Education* 7:59.

Frissell, H. B. 1901. "Learning by Doing." In *Addresses and Proceedings of the National Educational Association,* 893–96. Chicago: University of Chicago Press.

Franciscan Fathers. [1910] 1968. *An Ethnologic Dictionary of the Navajo Language.* St. Michaels, Ariz.: St. Michael's Mission.

Franklin, Benjamin. 1784. *Two Tracts: Information to Those Who Would Remove to America, and Remarks Concerning the Savages of North America.* Dublin: L. White.

Fuchs, Estelle, and Robert J. Havighurst. [1972] 1983. *To Live on This Earth: American Indian Education.* Albuquerque: University of New Mexico Press.

Fuess, Caude M. 1932. *Carl Schurz: Reformer.* New York: Dodd, Mead.

Gage, Lucy. 1951. "The Romance of Pioneering." *Chronicles of Oklahoma* 29:284–313.

Garland, Hamlin. 1923. *The Book of the American Indian.* New York: Harper & Brothers.

General Social and Economic Characteristics, United States Summary, 1980 Census of Population. n.d. Washington, D.C.: U.S. Department of Commerce, Bureau of the Census. (Characteristics of the Population PC80–1–C1, U.S. Summary.)

Getches, David H. 1977. *Law and Alaska Native Education.* Fairbanks: Center for Northern Educational Research.

Giago, Tim. 1984. *Notes from Indian Country.* Vol. 1. Pierre, So. Dak.: State Publishing Co.

Golden, Gertrude. 1954. *Red Moon Called Me: Memoirs of a Schoolteacher in the Government Indian Service.* Edited by Cecil Dryden. San Antonio, Tex.: Naylor.

Goodale, E. 1891. "Self–Teaching in the Indian Schools." *Educational Review* 1:57–59.

Goodman, Kenneth S., Patrick Shannon, Yvonne S. Freeman, and Sharon L. Murphy. 1988. *Report Card on Basal Readers.* Kantonah, N.Y.: Richard C. Owen.

Goodner, James, Richard G. Woods, and Arthur M. Harkins. 1970. *Characteristics and Attitudes of 1968 Haskell Institute Students.* Minneapolis: Training Center for Community Programs, University of Minnesota.

Grey, Loren. 1982. Foreword. In Zane Grey, *The Vanishing American.* New York: Pocket Books.

Grey, Zane. 1915. *The Rainbow Trail.* New York: Harper & Brothers.

———. 1922. "The Vanishing American." *Ladies Home Journal* (December):21–23, 190–94, 197–99.

———. 1925. *The Vanishing American.* New York: Harper & Brothers.

———. 1928. *Wild Horse Mesa.* New York: Harper & Brothers.

Grinde, Donald A., and Bruce E. Johansen. 1991. *Exemplar of Liberty: Native America and the Evolution of Democracy.* Los Angeles: American Indian Studies Center, University of California, Los Angeles.

Gutek, Gerald Lee. 1968. *Pestalozzi and Education.* New York: Random House.

Hagan, William T. 1979. "Daniel M. Browning, 1893–1897." In *The Commissioners of Indian Affairs, 1824–1977,* edited by R. M. Kvasnicka and H. J. Viola, 205–9. Lincoln: University of Nebraska Press.

Haglund, E. A. 1966. *Indian Integration in Nevada Public Schools.* Carson City: State of Nevada Department of Education.

Haile, Father Berard. [1948] 1998. "The Story of the Ethnologic Dictionary." *Provincial Chronicle* 20:195–99. [Reprinted in *Tales of an Endishodi: Father Berard Haile and the Navajos, 1900–1961,* edited by Murray Bodo, 137–43. Albuquerque: University of New Mexico Press.]

Hailmann, William. 1900. "Education of the Indian." In *Education in the United States,* vol. 2, edited by Nicholas Murray Butler. New York: J. B. Lyon.

Hall, G. Stanley. 1903. "The White Man's Burden versus Indigenous Development for the Lower Races." *Addresses and Proceedings of the National Educational Association,* 1053–56. Chicago: University of Chicago Press.

Harrod, Howard L. 1971. *Mission among the Blackfeet.* Norman: University of Oklahoma Press.

Harvey [Cantoni], Gina P. 1970, Fall. "ESL Help for Teachers in the Navajo Area." *English for American Indians: A Newsletter of the Office of Education Programs Bureau of Indian Affairs,* 23–25.

Hawkins, James E. 1971. Foreword. In *Indian Education: Bilingual Education for American Indians* (Curriculum Bulletin No. 3). Washington, D.C.: Office of Education Programs, U.S. Bureau of Indian Affairs.

Heath, Shirley Brice. 1972. *Telling Tongues: Language Policy in Mexico—Colony to Nation.* New York: Teachers College Press.

Hegemann, Elizabeth Compton. 1963. *Navajo Trading Days.* Albuquerque: University of New Mexico Press.

Heger, Nancy Irene. 1932. "Before Books in an Indian School." *Progressive Education* 9:138–43.

Henry, Jeannette. 1970. *Textbooks and the American Indian.* San Francisco: Indian Historian Press.

Hertzberg, Hazel W. 1971. *The Search for an American Indian Identity: Modern Pan Indian Movements.* Syracuse, N.Y.: Syracuse University Press.

Hewes, Dorothy W. 1981. "Those First Good Years of Indian Education: 1894–1898." *American Indian Culture and Research Journal* 5(2):63–82.

Heyer, Sally. 1990. *One House, One Voice, One Heart: Native American Education at the Santa Fe Indian School.* Santa Fe: Museum of New Mexico Press.

Hinman, S. D. 1869. *Journal of the Rev. S. D. Hinman Missionary to the Santee Sioux Indians.* Philadelphia: McCalla & Stavely.

Hirsch, E. D. 1987. *Cultural Literacy: What Every American Needs to Know.* Boston: Houghton Mifflin.

History of Sheldon Jackson College. 2003. Retrieved March 26, 2003. http://www.sheldonjackson.edu/aboutsjc/index.htm

Hodgkinson, Jennifer. 2002. *Intermountain Indian School—P0327.* Retrieved March 28, 2002. http://library.usu.edu/Specol/photoarchive/p0327.html

Hoffman, Edwina. 1992. "Oral Language Development." In *Teaching American Indian Students,* edited by Jon Reyhner, 132–42. Norman: University of Oklahoma Press.

Holm, Wayne. 1964. "Let It Never Be Said." *Journal of American Indian Education* 4(1):6–9.

———. 1975. "The Development of Reading Materials: The Rock Point (Navajo) Experience." In *Proceedings of the First Inter-American Conference on Bilingual Education,* edited by Rudolph C. Troike and Nancy Modiano, 185–92. Arlington, Va.: Center for Applied Linguistics.

———. 1985. "Community School Charts Achievements." *Indian Affairs* 108(February):2–3.

———. 1989. "On the Role of a Navajo Tribal Education Agency in Navajo Education." *Journal of Navajo Education* 6(3):38–54.

Hopkins, Sarah Winnemucca. 1883. *Life Among the Piutes: Their Wrongs and Claims,* edited by Mrs. Horace Mann. Boston: Cupples, Upham & Co.

Horne, Esther Burnett, and Sally McBeth. 1998. *Essie's Story: The Life and Legacy of a Shoshone Teacher.* Lincoln: University of Nebraska Press.

House, Deborah. 2002. *Language Shift among the Navajos: Identity Politics and Cultural Continuity.* Tucson: University of Arizona Press.

Howard, Margaret Kellog. 1958. "Sunrise to Sunset (Theodore Foster Riggs as told to his niece Margaret Kellog Howard)." *South Dakota Department of History Report and Historical Collection* 29:87–306.

Howard, Oliver O. 1907. *My Life and Experiences among Our Hostile Indians.* Hartford, Conn.: A. T. Worthington. [Reprint New York: DeCapo, 1972.]

Hoxie, Frederick E. 1984. *A Final Promise: The Campaign to Assimilate the Indians, 1880–1920.* Lincoln: University of Nebraska Press.

Iliff, Flora Gregg. 1954. *People of the Blue Water.* New York: Harper & Brothers.

The Indian. 1886, February 17. Printed in Hagersville, Ontario. P. 25.

Indian Affairs 1965: A Progress Report from the Commissioner of Indian Affairs (Philleo Nash). 1968. Washington, D.C.: U.S. Government Printing Office.

Indian Affairs 1968: A Progress Report from the Commissioner of Indian Affairs (Robert L. Bennett). 1968. Washington, D.C.: U.S. Government Printing Office.

Indian Education: A National Tragedy, A National Challenge (The Kennedy Report). 1969, November. Washington, D.C.: U.S. Government Printing Office.

Indian Education: America's Unpaid Debt. 1982. Washington, D.C.: U.S. Government Printing Office (Eighth Annual Report to the Congress of the United States by the National Advisory Council on Indian Education).

"Indian Education at Hampton and Carlisle: 1880." [1880] 1972. Reprinted from *Harper's New Monthly Magazine* in *The American Indian Reader: Education,* edited by Jeannette Henry, 38–50. San Francisco: Indian Historian Press.

Indian Nations at Risk Task Force (INAR). 1991, October. *Indian Nations at Risk: An Educational Strategy for Action* (Final Report of the Indian Nations at Risk Task Force). Washington, D.C.: U.S. Department of Education.

Iverson, Peter. 2002a. *Diné: A History of the Navajos.* Albuquerque: University of New Mexico Press.

———. 2002b. *"For Our Navajo People": Diné Letters, Speeches & Petitions, 1900–1960.* Albuquerque: University of New Mexico Press.

Jackson, Helen Hunt. [1881] 1886. *A Century of Dishonor: A Sketch of the United States Government's Dealings with Some of the Indian Tribes.* Boston: Roberts Brothers.

Jackson, Robert H., and Edward Castillo. 1995. *Indians, Franciscans, and Spanish Colonization: The Impact of the Mission System on California Indians.* Albuquerque: University of New Mexico Press.

Jacob, Evelyn, and Cathie Jordan, eds. 1987. Theme Issue: "Explaining the School Performance of Minority Students." *Anthropology and Education Quarterly* 18(4): 259–391.

James, George Wharton. 1908. *What the White Race May Learn from the Indian.* Chicago: Forbes.

James, Harry C. 1974. *Pages from Hopi History.* Tucson: University of Arizona Press.

Jenkins, Minnie Braithwaite. 1951. *Girl from Williamsburg.* Richmond, Va.: Dietz Press.

Jensen, Katherine. 1983. "Teachers and Progressives: The Navajo Day-School Experiment, 1935–1945." *Arizona and the West* 25:49–62.

Johnson, Broderick. 1968. *Navaho Education at Rough Rock.* Rough Rock, Ariz.: Rough Rock Demonstration School.

————, ed. 1977. *Stories of Traditional Navajo Life and Culture by Twenty-two Navajo Men and Women*. Tsaile, Ariz.: Navajo Community College.

Kabotie, Fred, with Bill Belknap. 1977. *Fred Kabotie: Hopi Indian Artist*. Flagstaff: Museum of Northern Arizona.

Kansas White House Conference on Indian Education, Final Report. 1991. Horton, Kans.: United Tribes of Kansas and Southeast Nebraska.

Kari, Jim, ed. 1973. "Report of a Navajo Bilingual–Bicultural Materials Conference, Albuquerque, N.M., October, 1972." In *Indian Education: Bilingual Education for American Indians*, vol. 2 (Curriculum Bulletin 13), 6–16. Washington, D.C.: Office of Education Programs, U.S. Bureau of Indian Affairs.

Kelly, Lawrence C. 1983. *The Assault on Assimilation: John Collier and the Origins of Indian Policy Reform*. Albuquerque: University of New Mexico Press.

Kenney, Florence. 1995. "Men and Women Lived Their Seasons." In *Messengers of the Wind: Native American Women Tell Their Life Stories*, edited by Jane Katz, 33–45. New York: Ballantine.

Kidwell, Clara Sue. 1987. "Choctaws and Missionaries in Mississippi before 1830." *American Indian Culture and Research Journal* 11(2):51–72.

Kilpatrick, William Heard. 1918. "The Project Method." *Teachers College Record* 19(4): 319–35.

King, A. Richard. 1967. *The School at Mopass: A Problem of Identity*. New York: Holt, Rinehart & Winston.

Kleinfeld, Judith S. 1979. *Eskimo School on the Adreafsky: A Study in Effective Bicultural Education*. New York: Praeger.

Kleinfeld, J., and G. W. McDiarmid. 1983. *Effective Schooling in Rural Alaska: Information for the Rural Effective Schools Project*. Fairbanks: Institute of Social, Economic, and Government Research. (ERIC Document Reproduction Service No. 232 813.)

Klineberg, O. 1963. "Life Is Fun in a Smiling, Fair-skinned World." *Saturday Review*, February 16, 75–77, 87.

Kluckhohn, Clyde. 1962. *Culture and Behavior*. New York: Free Press of Glencoe.

Kluckhohn, Clyde, and Dorothy Leighton. [1946] 1962. *The Navaho*. Rev. ed. Garden City, N.Y.: Doubleday.

Knaut, Andrew L. 1995. *The Pueblo Revolt of 1680: Conquest and Resistance in Seventeenth Century New Mexico*. Norman: University of Oklahoma Press.

Kneale, Albert H. 1950. *Indian Agent*. Caldwell, Idaho: Caxton.

Knobloch, Madge. 1988. *Havasupai Years*. Billings: Eastern Montana College.

Kozol, Jonathan. 1991. *Savage Inequalities*. New York: Crown.

Kraman, Sister Carla. 1984. *A Portrait of Saint Labre Indian Mission through One Hundred Years*. Ashland, Mont.: Saint Labre Indian Mission.

Krashen, Stephen. 1996. *Under Attack: The Case against Bilingual Education*. Culver City, Calif.: Language Education Associates.

Krashen, Stephen, and Douglas Biber. 1988. *On Course: Bilingual Education's Success in California*. Sacramento: California Association for Bilingual Education.

La Farge, Oliver. [1929] 1971. *Laughing Boy*. New York: New American Library.

————. 1937. *The Enemy Gods*. Boston: Houghton Miflin.

La Flesche, Francis. [1900] 1963. *The Middle Five: Indian Schoolboys of the Omaha Tribe.* Lincoln: University of Nebraska Press.

"Language Experiments of Indian Children." 1932. *Progressive Education* 9:144–79.

Las Casas, Bartolomé de. [1542] 1992. *The Devastation of the Indies: A Brief Account.* Translated by Herma Briffault. Baltimore, Md.: Johns Hopkins University Press.

Lau v. Nichols. 1974. 414 U.S. 563.

Lawhead, Helen E. 1932. "Teaching Navajo Children to Read." *Progressive Education* 9:131–35.

Layman, Martha Elizabeth. 1942. "A History of Indian Education in the United States." Ph.D. dissertation, University of Minnesota.

Leap, W. L. 1982. "Roles for the Linguist in Indian Bilingual Education." In *Language Renewal among American Indian Tribes: Issues, Problems, and Prospects*, edited by R. St. Clair and W. Leap, 19–30. Rosslyn, Va.: National Clearinghouse for Bilingual Education.

"Learning Foreign Languages Faster." 1944. *Indian Education* 99(March 1):6–7. [Reprinted from *Schools and Society*, April 3, 1943.]

Ledlow, S. 1992. "Is Cultural Discontinuity an Adequate Explanation for Dropping Out." *Journal of American Indian Education* 31(3):21–36.

Leupp, Francis E. 1910. *The Indian and His Problem.* New York: Charles Scribner's Sons.

Linderman, Frank B. [1932] 1972. *Pretty Shield: Medicine Woman of the Crow.* Lincoln: University of Nebraska Press. [First published under the title *Red Mother.*]

Lindsey, Donal F. 1995. *Indians at Hampton Institute, 1877–1923.* Urbana: University of Illinois Press.

Lippincott, J. A. 1882. "The Indian Training and Industrial School at Carlisle, Pa." *Education* 2:482–89.

Littlebear, Richard. 1999. "Some Rare and Radical Ideas for Keeping Indigenous Languages Alive." In *Revitalizing Indigenous Languages*, edited by Jon Reyhner, Gina Cantoni, Robert St. Clair, and Evangeline Parsons Yazzie, 1–5. Flagstaff: Northern Arizona University.

Lockard, Louise. 1995. "New Paper Words: Historical Images of Navajo Language Literacy." *American Indian Quarterly* 19(1):17–30.

Lomawaima, K. Tsianina. 1994. *They Called It Prairie Light: The Story of Chilocco Indian School.* Lincoln: University of Nebraska Press.

———. 1996. "Estelle Reel, Superintendent of Indian Schools, 1898–1910: Politics, Curriculum, and Land." *Journal of American Indian Education* 35(3):5–31.

Lummis, Charles F. [1884] 1989. *Letters from the Southwest*, edited by James W. Byrkit. Tucson: University of Arizona Press.

———. [1903] 1968. *Bullying the Moqui.* Prescott, Ariz.: Prescott College Press. [Reprint of series in *Out West* magazine.]

MacDonald, Peter, and Ted Schwarz. 1993. *The Last Warrior: Peter MacDonald and the Navajo Nation.* New York: Orion Books.

MacGregor, Gordon. 1948. "Federal Schools Meet Sioux Needs." *Indian Education* 167 (September 15):6–8.

————. 1964. *Warriors without Weapons: A Study of the Society and Personality Development of the Pine Ridge Sioux*. Chicago: University of Chicago Press.

Mankiller, Wilma, and Michael Wallis. 1993. *Mankiller: A Chief and Her People*. New York: St. Martin's Press.

Mann, Henrietta. 1997. *Cheyenne-Arapaho Education, 1871–1882*. Niwot: University Press of Colorado.

Manuelito, Kathryn D. 2001. "Self-Determination in an Indian Community Controlled School." Ph.D. dissertation, Arizona State University.

Mardock, Robert Winston. 1971. *The Reformers and the American Indian*. Columbia: University of Missouri Press.

Marquis, Thomas B., interpreter. 1931. *Wooden Leg: A Warrior who Fought Custer*. Lincoln: University of Nebraska Press.

Marriott, Alice, and Carol K. Rachlin. 1969. *American Epic: The Story of the American Indian*. New York: G. P. Putnam's Sons.

Mathes, Valerie Sherer. 1985. "Dr. Susan La Flesche Picotte." In *Indian Lives: Essays on Nineteenth- and Twentieth-Century Native American Leaders*, edited by L. G. Moses and Raymond Wilson, 61–90. Albuquerque: University of New Mexico Press.

McAlister, Lyle N. 1984. *Spain and Portugal in the New World, 1492–1700*. Minneapolis: University of Minnesota.

McBeth, Sally J. 1983. *Ethnic Identity and the Boarding School Experience of West-Central Oklahoma American Indians*. New York: University Press of America.

McCallum, James Dow, ed. 1932. *The Letters of Eleazar Wheelock's Indians*. Hanover, N.H.: Dartmouth College Publications.

McCarthy, James. 1985. *A Papago Traveler: The Memories of James McCarthy*, edited by John G. Westover. Tucson: University of Arizona Press.

McCarty, Teresa L. 1987. "The Rough Rock Demonstration School: A Case History with Implications for Educational Evaluation." *Human Organization* 46(2):103–12.

————. 1989. "School as Community: The Rough Rock Demonstration." *Harvard Education Review* 59:484–503.

————. 2002. *A Place to Be Navajo: Rough Rock and the Struggle for Self-Determination in Indigenous Schooling*. Mahwah, N.J.: Lawrence Erlbaum.

McCarty, T. L., and R. Schaffer. 1992. "Language and Literacy Development." In *Teaching American Indian Students*, edited by Jon Reyhner, 115–31. Norman: University of Oklahoma Press.

McFee, M. 1968. "The 150% Man, a Product of Blackfeet Acculturation." *American Anthropologist* 70:1096–1107.

McLaughlin, Daniel. 1992. *When Literacy Empowers: Navajo Language in Print*. Albuquerque: University of New Mexico Press.

McLoughlin, William. 1984. *Cherokees and Missionaries*. New Haven, Conn.: Yale University Press.

————. 1990. *Champions of the Cherokees: Evan and John B. Jones*. Princeton, N.J.: Princeton University Press.

McNitt, Frank. 1962. *The Indian Traders*. Norman: University of Oklahoma Press.

Meeting the Challenge: The Report of the Montana White House Conference on Indian Education. 1991. Great Falls, Mont., September 9 and 10.

Melville, Herman. [1857] 1971. *The Confidence-Man.* New York: W. W. Norton.

Meriam, Lewis. 1932. "The Social Outlook of Indian Missions." In *Facing the Future in Indian Missions,* 1–141. New York: Council of Women for Home Missions and Missionary Education Movement.

————, ed. 1928. *The Problem of Indian Administration.* Baltimore, Md.: Johns Hopkins University Press.

Mihesuah, Devon A. 1993. *Cultivating the Rosebuds: The Education of Women at the Cherokee Female Seminary, 1851–1909.* Champaign: University of Illinois Press.

Milloy, John S. 1999. *A National Crime: The Canadian Government and the Residential School System, 1879 to 1986.* Winnipeg: University of Manitoba Press.

Mitchell, Frank. 1978. *Navajo Blessingway Singer: The Autobiography of Frank Mitchell, 1881–1967,* edited by Charlotte J. Frisbie and David P. McAllester. Tucson: University of Arizona Press.

Monroe, Mark. 1994. *An Indian in White America.* Edited by Carolyn Reyer. Philadelphia: Temple University Press.

Mooney, Carolyn J. 1989. "Affirmative-Action Goals, Coupled with Tiny Number of Minority Ph.D.'s, Set Off Faculty Recruiting Frenzy." *Chronicle of Higher Education* 35(47):A1, A10–A11.

Morey, Sylvester M., and Olivia L. Gilliam, eds. 1974. *Respect for Life: The Traditional Upbringing of American Indian Children.* Garden City, N.Y.: Waldorf.

Morgan, Thomas J. 1889. *Studies in Pedagogy.* Boston: Silver, Burdett & Co.

Morris, Harold White. 1954. "A History of Indian Education in the United States." Ph.D. dissertation, Oregon State College.

Morse, Jedidiah. 1822. *A Report to the Secretary of War of the United States, on Indian Affairs, comprising a Narrative of a Tour Performed in the Summer of 1820, under a Commission from the President of the United States, for the Purpose of Ascertaining, for the Use of the Government, the Actual State of the Indian Tribes in Our Country . . .* New Haven, Conn.: S. Converse, Printer.

Morton, Louis. 1962. "How the Indians Came to Carlisle." *Pennsylvania History* 29(January):53–73.

NAACP Legal Defense and Education Fund, with the cooperation of the Center for Law and Education, Harvard University. 1971. *An Even Chance: A Report on Federal Funds for Indian Children in Public School Districts.* New York.

Nader, Ralph. 1969. *Statement of Ralph Nader, Author, Lecturer. Indian Education,* pt. 1, 47–55. Hearings before the subcommittee on Indian Education of the Committee on Labor and Public Welfare. U.S. Senate, 91st Cong., 1st sess. Washington, D.C.: U.S. Government Printing Office.

Native American Languages Act of 1990. 104, 25 U.S.C. 2901–2906. Retrieved Marcy 22, 2002. http://www.ncbe.gwu.edu/miscpubs/stabilize/ii-policy/nala1990.htm

Navajo Division of Education. 1985. *Navajo Nation: Educational Policies.* Window Rock, Ariz.

Navajo Nation Pre-White House Conference on Indian Education, September 11–13, 1991, Final Conference Report. 1991. Window Rock, Ariz.: Navajo Nation Steering Committee, White House Conference on Indian Education.

A New Curriculum for Navajo Beginners. 1970, Fall. *English for American Indians: A Newsletter of the Office of Education Programs, Bureau of Indian Affairs,* 71–80.

New American State Papers: Indian Affairs. 1972. 2:173.

Niethammer, Carolyn. 2001. *I'll Go and Do More: Annie Dodge Wauneka, Navajo Leader and Activist.* Lincoln: University of Nebraska Press.

Nieto, Sonia. 1992. *Affirming Diversity: The Sociopolitical Context of Multicultural Education.* New York: Longman.

Nixon, Richard. 1971. "Special Message to the Congress on Indian Affairs." In *Public papers of the presidents of the United States, Richard Nixon, containing the public messages, speeches, and statements of the president, 1970.* Washington, D.C.: U.S. Government Printing Office.

Nock, David A. 1988. *A Victorian Missionary and Canadian Indian Policy: Cultural Synthesis vs. Cultural Replacement.* Waterloo, Ont., Canada: Wilfrid Laurier University Press.

"No Place for Censors." 1948. *Indian Education* 159:6–7.

North, I. 1891. Quoted in *Word Carrier* 20(5):10–11.

Northern Ute Tribe. 1985. "Ute Language Policy." *Cultural Survival Quarterly* 9(2):16–19.

"Number of Blacks Taking SAT Drops 5 Pct. in 5 Years." 1986. *Chronicle of Higher Education,* September 3. 108.

Oakes, J. 1985. *Keeping Track: How Schools Structure Inequality.* New Haven, Conn.: Yale University Press.

Occom, Samson. 1994. "A Short Narrative of My Life." In *Native American Autobiography: An Anthology,* edited by Arnold Krupat, 105–13. Madison: University of Wisconsin Press.

O'Donnell, James. 1980. "Joseph Brant." In *American Indian Leaders,* edited by R. David Edmunds, 21–40. Lincoln: University of Nebraska Press.

Office of Diné Culture, Language and Community Service, Division of Diné Education. 2000. *T'aa Sha Bik'ehgo Diné Bi Na nitin doo Ihoo'aah* (Diné Cultural Content Standards for Students). Window Rock, Ariz.

Office of Indian Education Programs, Bureau of Indian Affairs. 1991. *Education Directory.* Washington, D.C.

Office of Inspector General, U.S. Department of the Interior. 1991. *Audit Report: Implementation of the Education Amendments of 1978, Bureau of Indian Affairs.* Washington, D.C. (Report No. 91–I–941.)

Oglala Lakota College. 2000. *Oglala Lakota College Catalog, 2000–2001.* Kyle, So. Dak.

Ogbu, John U. 1978. *Minority Education and Caste: The American System in Cross-Cultural Perspective.* New York: Academic Press.

———. 1995. "Understanding Cultural Diversity and Learning." In *Handbook of Research on Multicultural Education,* edited by In J. A. Banks and C. A. M. Banks, 582–93. New York: Macmillan.

Oppelt, Norman T. 1984. "Tribal Controlled Colleges in the 1980s: Higher Education's Best Kept Secret." *American Indian Culture and Research Journal* 8:4, 27–45.

O'Sullivan, John L. 1845, December 27. Editorial. (New York) *Morning News.*

Otis, Joseph Edward. 1924. *The Indian Problem* (Resolution of the Committee of One Hundred, Appointed by the Secretary of the Interior, and a Review of the Indian Problem). Washington, D.C.: U.S. Department of the Interior, Committee One Hundred on Indian Affairs.

Ovando, Carlos, and Virginia Collier. 1985. *Bilingual and ESL Classrooms.* New York: McGraw Hill.

Palladino, L. B. 1894. *Indian and White in the Northwest: A History of Catholicity in Montana, 1831–1891.* Baltimore: J. Murphy.

———. 1922. *Indian and White in the Northwest: A History of Catholicity in Montana 1831–1891.* 2d ed. Lancaster, Pa.: Wickersham.

Parker, Dorthey R. 1992. *Singing an Indian Song: A Biography of D'Arcy McNickle.* Lincoln: University of Nebraska Press.

———. 1996. *Phoenix Indian School: The Second Half Century.* Tucson: University of Arizona Press.

Parman, Donald L. 1972. "J. C. Morgan: Navajo Apostle of Assimilation." *Prologue: Journal of the National Archives* 4:2, 83–98.

———. 1976. *The Navajos and the New Deal.* New Haven, Conn.: Yale University Press.

Parsons, Jackie. 1980. *The Educational Movement of the Blackfeet Indians, 1840–1979.* Browning, Mont.: Blackfeet Heritage Program.

Pascua Yaqui Tribal Council. 1984. *Yaqui Language Policy for the Pascua Yaqui Tribe: Policy Declaration.* Tucson, Ariz.: Tucson Unified School District.

Pavlik, Steve. 1994. "Fads, Gimmicks, and Buzzwords: Critical Commentary on the Restructuring of Navajo Education." *Journal of Navajo Education* 11(3):21–24.

Pease–Windy Boy, Janine. 1994. "The Tribally Controlled Community College Act of 1978: An Expansion of Federal Indian Trust Responsibility." Ed.D. dissertation, Montana State University, Bozeman.

Peery, Dan W. 1932–33. "The Indians' Friend John H. Seger." *Chronicles of Oklahoma,* 10:348–68, 570–91; 11:709–32, 845–68, 967–94.

Peshkin, Alan. 1997. *Places of Memory: Whiteman's Schools and Native American Communities.* Hillsdale, N.J.: Lawrence Erlbaum.

Peters, Richard, ed. 1845. *The Public Statutes at Large of the United States of America.* Vol. 2. Boston: Charles C. Little & James Brown.

———. 1848. *The Public Statutes at Large of the United States of America.* Vol. 3. Boston: Charles C. Little & James Brown.

Peterson, Shailer Alvarey. 1948. *How Well Are Indian Children Educated? Summary of Results of a Three Year Program Testing the Achievement of Indian Children in Federal, Public and Mission Schools.* Lawrence, Kans.: Haskell Institute Print Shop, U.S. Indian Service.

Pettitt, George A. 1946. *Primitive Education in North America.* Berkeley: University of California Publications in American Archaeology and Ethnology.

Philp, Kenneth R., ed. 1986. *Indian Self-Rule: First-hand Accounts of Indian-White Relations from Roosevelt to Reagan.* Salt Lake City: Howe Brothers.

Plank, Gary A. 1993. "The School-leaving of Non-Navajo Educators in the Interior of the Navajo Nation." *Journal of Navajo Education* 10(2):26–34.

Platero, Dillon. 1975. "Bilingual Education in the Navajo Nation." In *Proceedings of the First Inter-American Conference on Bilingual Education,* edited by Rudolph C. Troike and Nancy Modiano, 56–61. Arlington, Va.: Center for Applied Linguistics.

Platero Paperwork, Inc. 1986. *Executive Summary: Navajo Area Student Dropout Study.* Window Rock, Ariz.: Navajo Nation, Navajo Division of Education.

Pond, S. W., Jr. 1893. *Two Volunteer Missionaries among the Dakotas or the Story of the Labors of Samuel W. and Gideon H. Pond.* Boston: Congregational Sunday-School and Publishing Society.

Powell, John Wesley. 1877. *Introduction to the Study of Indian Languages.* Washington, D.C.: U.S. Government Printing Office.

———. 1896. "The Need of Studying the Indian in Order to Teach Him." In *Annual Report of the Board of Indian Commissioners,* 109–15. Washington, D.C.: U.S. Government Printing Office.

Prakash, Madhu Suri, and Esteva, Gustavo. 1998. *Escaping Education: Living as Learning within Grassroots Cultures.* New York: Peter Lang.

Pratt, Richard Henry. 1964. *Battlefield and Classroom: Four Decades with the American Indian, 1867–1904.* New Haven, Conn.: Yale University Press. [First publication of Pratt's autobiography.]

Proceedings of the Great Peace Commission, 1867–1868. 1975. Washington, D.C.: Institute for the Development of Indian Law.

Prucha, Francis Paul. 1979a. *The Churches and the Indian Schools: 1888–1912.* Lincoln: University of Nebraska Press.

———. 1979b. "Thomas Jefferson Morgan, 1889–93." In *The Commissioners of Indian Affairs, 1824–1977,* edited by R. M. Kvasnicka and H. J. Viola, 193–203. Lincoln: University of Nebraska Press.

———. 1984. *The Great Father: The United States Government and the American Indians.* Lincoln: University of Nebraska Press.

———. 1985. *The Indians in American Society: From the Revolutionary War to the Present.* Berkeley: University of California Press.

———, ed. 1973. *Americanizing the American Indians: Writings by the "Friends of the Indian," 1880–1900.* Cambridge, Mass.: Harvard University Press.

———. 1975. *Documents of United States Indian Policy.* Lincoln: University of Nebraska Press.

Qöyawayma, Polingaysi (Elizabeth Q. White). 1941. "Letter to Jean Glasser, June 3, 1941." In *When I Met Polingaysi Underneath the Cottonwood Tree,* edited by Jo Linder. Mesa, Ariz.: Discount Printing.

———. 1964. *No Turning Back: A Hopi Indian Woman's Struggle to Live in Two Worlds. As told to Vada F. Carlson.* Albuquerque: University of New Mexico Press.

"Racial and Ethnic Makeup of College and University Enrollment." 1986. *Chronicle of Higher Education,* July 23, 25–34.

Ravitch, Diane. 2000. *A Century of Failed School Reform.* New York: Simon and Schuster.

Reichard, Gladys A. 1939. *Dezba: Woman of the Desert.* New York: J. J. Augustin.

Report for the White House Conference on Indian Education, New Mexico. 1991. Santa Fe: New Mexico Indian Education Association.

"Report of the Doolittle Commission." [1867] 1900. In *Documents of United States Indian Policy*, 2d ed. expanded, edited by Francis Paul Prucha, 102–6. Lincoln: University of Nebraska Press.

Report of Indian Peace Commissioners. 1868, January 7. House of Representatives, 40th Cong., 2d sess., Exec. Doc. No. 97. (Serial Set, 1337, Vol. 11, No. 97.)

Report on BIA Education: Excellence in Indian Education through the Effective School Process (Final Review Draft). 1988. Washington, D.C.: Office of Indian Education Programs, Bureau of Indian Affairs, U.S. Department of the Interior. (ERIC Document Reproduction Service No. ED 297 899.)

Report on Indian Education, Task Force Five: Final Report to the Indian Policy Review Commission. 1976. Washington, D.C.: U.S. Government Printing Office.

Research Agenda Working Group. 2001, November. *American Indian and Alaska Native Education Research Agenda.* Retrieved March 22, 2002. http://www.indianeduresearch.net/reports.htm

Reyhner, Jon. 1990. "A Description of the Rock Point Community School Bilingual Education Program." In *Effective Language Education Practices and Native Language Survival*, edited by Jon Reyhner, 95–106. Choctaw, Okla.: Native American Language Issues.

———. 1991. "The Effective Schools Research and Indian Education." In *Entering the 90s: The North American experience*, edited by T. E. Schirer, 207–17. Saulte Ste. Marie, Mich.: Lake Superior State University Press.

———. 1992a. *Plans for Dropout Prevention and Special School Support Services for American Indian and Alaska Native Students* (Indian Nations at Risk Task Force commissioned paper 9). Charleston, W. Va.: ERIC Clearinghouse on Rural and Small Schools. (ERIC Document Reproduction Service No. ED 343762)

———, ed. 1992b. *Teaching American Indian Students.* Norman: University of Oklahoma Press.

———. 1994. "Restructuring Navajo Schools." *Journal of Navajo Education* 11(2):10–14.

———. 1997. "The Case for Native American Studies." In *American Indian Studies: An Interdisciplinary Approach to Contemporary Issues*, edited by D. Morrison, 93–110. New York: Peter Lang.

———. 2001. "Cultural Survival vs. Forced Assimilation: The Renewed War on Diversity." *Cultural Survival Quarterly* 25(2):22–25.

Reyhner, Jon, D. Gabbard, and H. Lee. 1995. "Inservice Needs of Rural Reservation Teachers." *Rural Educator* 16(2):10–15.

Reyhner, Jon, and Don Jacobs. 2002. "Preparing Teachers of American Indian and Alaska Native Students." *Action in Teacher Education* 24(2):85–93.

Reyhner, Jon, H. Lee, and D. Gabbard. 1993. "A Specialized Knowledge Base for Teaching American Indian Students." *Tribal College* 4(4):26–32.

Richardson, James D., ed. 1910. *A Compilation of the Messages and Papers of the Presidents.* Washington, D.C.: Bureau of National Literature and Art.

Riesman, David, with Nathan Glazer and Reuel Denney. 1950. *The Lonely Crowd: A Study of the Changing American Character.* New Haven, Conn.: Yale University Press.

Riggs, M. B. 1928. *Early Days at Santee: The Beginnings of Santee Normal Training School founded by Dr. and Mrs. A. L. Riggs in 1870*. Santee, Neb.: Santee N.T.S.

Riggs, Stephen R. 1880. *Mary and I: Forty Years with the Sioux*. Chicago: W. G. Holmes. (Reprinted by Ross & Haines, Minneapolis, 1969).

Riggs, Stephen R., and G. H. Pond. 1839. *The Dakota First Reading Book*. Cincinnati: Kendall and Henry Printers.

Riney, Scott. 1999. *The Rapid City Indian School, 1898–1933*. Norman: University of Oklahoma Press.

Rock Point Community School. 1988. *Internal Evaluation Report*. Rock Point, Ariz..

Roessel, Robert A., Jr. 1960. "An Analysis of Select Navaho Needs with Implications for Navaho Education." Ed.D. dissertation, Arizona State University, Tempe.

———. 1962. *Handbook for Indian Education*. Los Angeles, Calif.: Amerindian Publishing Co.

———. 1967. *Indian Communities in Action*. Tempe: Arizona State University Bureau of Publications.

———. 1968a. "The Right to Be Wrong and the Right to Be Right." *Journal of American Indian Education* 7(2):1–6.

———. 1968b. "An Overview of the Rough Rock Demonstration School." *Journal of American Indian Education* 7(3):2–14.

———. 1977. *Navajo Education in Action: The Rough Rock Demonstration School*. Chinle, Ariz.: Navajo Curriculum Center, Rough Rock Demonstration School.

———. 1979. *Navajo Education, 1948–1978: Its Progress and Its Problems*. Rough Rock, Ariz.: Navajo Curriculum Center, Rough Rock Demonstration School.

———. 2002. *"He Leadeth Me": An Account of How God/Jesus/Holy People Have Led Me Throughout My Life*. Round Rock, Ariz.: Author.

Ronda, James P. 1981. "Generations of Faith: The Christian Indians of Martha's Vineyard." *William and Mary Quarterly* 38:369–94.

Roosevelt, Theodore. 1889. *The Winning of the West*. Vol. 1. New York: G. P. Putnam's Sons.

Rosier, Paul, and Wayne Holm. 1980. *Bilingual Education Series: 8; The Rock Point Experience: A Longitudinal Study of a Navajo School Program (Saad Naaki Bee Na'nitin)*. Washington, D.C.: Center for Applied Linguistics.

RRDS (Rough Rock Demonstration School) *Monthly Reports*. 1966–69.

Returned Student Surveys (RRS). 1917. Manuscript in the Ayer Collection, Newberry Library, Chicago.

Rules for the Indian Schools. 1898. Washington, D.C.: U.S. Government Printing Office.

Ryan, Carmelita S. 1962. "The Carlisle Indian Industrial School." Ph.D. dissertation, Georgetown University.

Ryan, W. Carson, Jr., and Rose K. Brandt. 1932. "Indian Education Today." *Progressive Education* 9:81–86.

Salinas, Elaine. 1995. "Still Grieving Over the Loss of the Land." In *Messengers of the Wind: Native American Women Tell Their Life Stories*, edited by Jane Katz, 79–87. New York: Ballantine.

Salisbury, Neal. 1986. "Red Puritans: The 'Praying Indians' of Massachusetts Bay and John Eliot." In *The American Indian: Past and Present*, 3d ed., edited by R. L. Nichols, 73–88. New York: Alfred A. Knopf. [Reprinted from *William & Mary Quarterly* 3(January 1974):27–54.]

Sánchez, George Isidore. 1948. *"The People": A Study of the Navajos*. Washington, D.C.: U.S. Indian Service.

Sando, Joe S. 1998. *Pueblo Profiles: Cultural Identity through Centuries of Change*. Santa Fe, New Mex.: Clear Light.

Satz, Ronald N. 1979. "Carey Allen Harris, 1836–38." In *The Commissioners of Indian Affairs, 1824–1977*, edited by Robert M. Kvasnicka and Herman J. Viola, 17–22. Lincoln: University of Nebraska Press.

Saville, Muriel. 1970, Fall. *Navajo Kindergarten: English for American Indians* (A Newsletter of the Office of Education Programs, Bureau of Indian Affairs), 26.

Schmeckebier, Laurence F. 1927. *The Office of Indian Affairs: Its History, Activities and Organization*. Baltimore, Md.: Johns Hopkins University Press.

Scholes, France V. 1937. "Troublous Times in New Mexico, 1659–1670." *New Mexico Historical Review* 12:134–74.

School News. 1881–82. Carlisle, Pa.: Carlisle Indian School. (Copies in the Ayer Collection, Newberry Library, Chicago.)

School Report Cards. 2003. Retrieved February 3, 2003. http://www.oiep.bia.edu/faqs_reportcards.html

Scoon, Annabelle R. 1971. "Affective Influences on English Language Learning among Indian Students." *TESOL Quarterly* 5(4):285–91.

Seaman, P. David, ed. 1993. *Born a Chief: The Nineteenth Century Hopi Boyhood of Edmund Nequatewa*, as told to Alfred F. Whiting. Tucson: University of Arizona Press.

Secada, W. G. 1991. "Diversity, Equity, and Cognitivist Research." In *Integrating Research on Teaching and Learning Mathematics*, edited by E. Fennema, T. P. Carpenter and S. J. Lamon, 17–53. Albany: State University of New York Press.

Seger, John H. [1924] 1979. *Early Days among the Cheyenne and Arapahoe Indians*. Edited by Stanley Vestal. Norman: University of Oklahoma Press.

Sekaquaptewa, Helen. 1969. *My and Mine: The Life Story of Helen Sekaquaptewa, as Told to Louise Udall*. Tucson: University of Arizona Press.

Semple, C. M. 1882. "How It Is done at Carlisle." *IAPI OAYE* 11(3):23.

Senese, Guy B. 1991. *Self–Determination and the Social Education of Native Americans*. New York: Praeger.

Sergeant, John. 1743. *Letter from the Rev^d Mr. Sergeant of Stockbridge to Dr. Colman*. Boston: Rogers & Fowle. [Reprinted 1929 from the original in the library of Teas Heye.]

Shaw, Anna Moore. 1974. *A Pima Past*. Tucson: University of Arizona Press.

Shepard, Ward. 1934. "Reorientating Indian Education and Extension in the Wake of the Wheeler-Howard Act." *Indians at Work* 2(1)8–11.

Sievers, Harry J. 1952. "The Catholic Indian School Issue and the Presidential Election of 1892." *Catholic Historical Review* 38(2):129–55.

Skinner, Carl H. 1958. *Good Indians*. New York: Comet Press Books.

Smith, John. [1764] 1932. "John Smith's Letter to a Friend." In *The Letters of Eleazar Whee-lock's Indians*, edited by James Dow McCallum, 73–74. Hanover, N.H.: Dartmouth College Publications.

Smith, Michael T. 1979. "Morris Thompson (1973–76)." In *The Commissioners of Indian Affairs, 1824–1977*, edited by Robert M. Kvasnicka and Herman J. Viola, 341–46. Lincoln: University of Nebraska Press.

Snake, Reuben. 1996. *Your Humble Serpent: Indian Visionary and Activist, as Told to Jay C. Fixes*. Santa Fe, New Mex.: Clear Light.

Spach, Ruth. 2002. *America's Second Tongue: American Indian Education and the Ownership of English, 1860–1900*. Lincoln: University of Nebraska Press.

Special Committee on Investigations of the Select Committee on Indian Affairs, U.S. Senate. 1989. *Final Report and Legislative Recommendations* (Senate Report 101–216). Washington, D.C.: U.S. Government Printing Office.

Special Report: State Preconference Overview from Washington State White House Conference on Indian Education. 1991. *National Advisory Council on Indian Education Newsletter* 8(1):9–10.

Special Subcommittee on Indian Education, Senate Committee on Labor and Public Welfare. 1969. *Indian Education: A National Tragedy, a National Challenge*. (Senate Report 91–501 [Kennedy Report].)

Spindler, George D. 1987. "Why Have Minority Groups in North America been Dis-advantaged by Their Schools?" In *Education and Cultural Process: Anthropological Approaches*, edited by George D. Spindler, 160–72. Prospect Heights, Ill.: Waveland.

Spolsky, Bernard. 1973a. "Advances in Navajo Bilingual Education, 1969–72." In *Indian Education: Bilingual Education for American Indians: Navajo*, vol. 2 (Curriculum Bulletin No. 13), 1–5. Washington, D.C.: Office of Education Programs, U.S. Bureau of Indian Affairs.

———. 1973b, June. *The Development of Navajo Bilingual Education*. ERIC Document, ED 094 559.

———. 1976. "Linguistics in Practice: The Navajo Reading Study Program." *BIA Education Research Bulletin* 4(3):1–10.

Spolsky, Bernard, Agnes Holm, and Penny Murphy. 1970. Preface. In *Indian Education: Analytical Bibliography of Navajo Reading Materials* (Curriculum Bulletin No. 10). Washington, D.C.: Office of Education Programs, U.S. Bureau of Indian Affairs.

Standing Bear, Luther. 1928. *My People the Sioux*. Edited by E. A. Brininstool. Boston: Houghton Mifflin.

———. 1933. *Land of the Spotted Eagle*. Boston: Houghton Mifflin.

Standing Bear v. Crook. 1879, May 12. 25 Federal Cases, 695, 697, 700–701.

Stein, Wayne J. 1988. "A History of the Tribally Controlled Community Colleges: 1968–1978." Ed.D. dissertation, Washington State University.

———. 1992. *Tribally Controlled Colleges: Making Good Medicine*. New York: Peter Lang.

———. 1990. "Founding of the American Indian Higher Education Consortium." *Tribal College* 2(1):18–22.

Stewart, Irene. 1980. *A Voice in Her Tribe: A Navajo Woman's Story*. Anthropological Papers No. 17. Socorro, New Mex.: Ballena Press.

Studies in Immersion Education: A Collection for United States Educators. 1984. Sacramento: California State Department of Education.

Suina, Joseph H. 1988. "When I Went to School." In *Linguistic and Cultural Influences on Learning Mathematics,* edited by Rodney Cocking and Jose P. Mestre, 295–99. Hillsdale, N.J.: Lawrence Erlbaum.

Summary Report 1985 Doctorate Recipients from United States Universities. 1986. Washington, D.C.: National Academy.

Swinton, William. 1875. *A Condensed School History of the United States.* New York: Ivison, Blakeman, Taylor.

Swisher, Karen, ed. 1989. Special Edition (on learning styles). *Journal of American Indian Education* (August):1–88.

Szasz, Margaret Connell. 1977. *Education and the American Indian: The Road to Self-Determination since 1928.* 2d ed. Albuquerque: University of New Mexico Press.

———. 1988. *Indian Education in the American Colonies, 1607–1783.* Albuquerque: University of New Mexico Press.

Talayesva, Don C. 1942. *Sun Chief: The Autobiography of a Hopi Indian.* Edited by Leo W. Simmons. New Haven, Conn.: Yale University Press.

Task Force Five: Indian Education. 1976. *Report on Indian Education: Final Report to the American Indian Policy Review Commission.* Washington, D.C.: U.S. Government Printing Office.

Taylor, S. Lyman. 1973. *A History of Indian Policy.* Washington, D.C.: Bureau of Indian Affairs, U.S. Department of the Interior.

Tennant, Edward A. 1971. "The Bilingual Education Act and the American Indian." In *Indian Education, Bilingual Education for American Indians* (Curriculum Bulletin 3), 33–37. Washington, D.C.: Office of Education Programs, U.S. Bureau of Indian Affairs.

Tenth Annual Catalog of the Officers and Students of Indian University, Bacone, Indian Territory, and other Baptist Indian Schools, 1889–90. Muskogee, Indian Territory: Phoenix Printing Company.

Tharp, Roland G., and Lois A. Yamauchi. 1994. *Effective Instructional Conversation in Native American Classrooms* (Educational Practice Report 10). Santa Cruz, Calif.: National Center for Research on Cultural Diversity and Second Language Learning.

Thompson, Hildegard. 1965. "Experience: Prerequisite to Language." *Indian Education* 28(416):1–3.

———. 1975. *The Navajos' Long Walk for Education: A History of Navajo Education.* Tsaile, Ariz.: Navajo Community College Press.

Thonis, E. W. 1981. "Reading Instruction for Language Minority Students." In *California State Department of Education, Schooling and Language Minority Students.* Los Angeles: California State University at Los Angeles.

Thorpe, Francis Neuton. 1909. *The Federal and State Constitutions.* Washington, D.C.: U.S. Government Printing Office.

Thornton, Russell. 1987. *American Indian Holocaust and Survival: A Population History since 1492.* Norman: University of Oklahoma Press.

Thwaites, Reuben Gold. 1896–1901. *The Jesuit Relations and Allied Documents.* Translated by J. C. Covert. Cleveland: Burrows Brothers Co.

Tibbles, Thomas Henry. [1905] 1957. *Buckskin and Blanket Days: Memoirs of a Friend of the Indians.* Lincoln: University of Nebraska Press.

Tinker, George E. 1993. *Missionary Conquest: The Gospel and Native American Cultural Genocide.* Minneapolis, Minn.: Fortress Press.

Tippeconnic, John W. 1995. Editorial (on BIA education). *Journal of American Indian Education* 35(1):1–5.

Tocqueville, Alexis de. 1966. *Democracy in America.* Translated by George Lawrence. New York: Harper & Row. (First published in French in 1835).

Trennert, Robert A., Jr. 1988. *The Phoenix Indian School: Forced Assimilation in Arizona, 1981–1935.* Norman: University of Oklahoma Press.

Tribal Colleges: Shaping the Future of Native America. 1989. Princeton, N.J.: Carnegie Foundation for the Advancement of Teaching.

Triplett, Frank. 1883. *Conquering the Wilderness.* New York: N. D. Thompson.

Underhill, Ruth M. 1944. "Papago Child Training." *Indian Education* 103(May):5–8.

———. 1953. *Here Come the Navaho!* Lawrence, Kans.: U.S. Department of the Interior, Bureau of Indian Affairs, Branch of Education.

Underhill, Ruth M., and Willard W. Beatty. 1944. "Culture Has Nothing to Do with Blood." *Indian Education* 107:1–3.

U.S. Commission on Civil Rights. 1975, September. *The Navajo Nation: An American Colony.* Washington, D.C.

U.S. General Accounting Office. 2001. *BIA and DOD Schools: Student Achievement and Other Characteristics Often Differ from Public Schools'.* Washington, D.C.

Unrau, William E. 1983. "The Ottawa University: C. C. Hutchinson, the Baptists, and Land Fraud in Kansas." *Arizona and the West* 25:229–44.

Utley, Robert M. 1964. Introduction. In Richard Henry Pratt, *Battlefield and Classroom.* New Haven, Conn.: Yale University Press.

———. 1984. *The Indian Frontier of the American West 1846–1890.* Albuquerque: University of New Mexico Press.

Vick-Westgate, Ann. 2002. *Nunavik: Inuit-controlled Education in Arctic Quebec.* Calgary, Alb., Canada: University of Calgary Press.

Viola, Herman J. 1979. "Thomas L. McKenney, 1824–30." In *The Commissioners of Indian Affairs, 1824–1977*, edited by Robert M. Kvasnicka and Herman J. Viola, 1–7. Lincoln: University of Nebraska Press.

Vogel, V. J. 1972. *This Country Was Ours: A Documentary History of the American Indian.* New York: Harper & Row.

Voget, Fred W. 1995. *They Call Me Agnes: A Crow Narrative based on the Life of Agnes Yellowtail Deernose.* Norman: University of Oklahoma Press.

Vorih, Lillian, and Paul Rosier. 1978. "Rock Point Community School: An Example of a Navajo-English Bilingual Elementary School Program. *TESOL Quarterly* 12(3): 263–69.

Washburn, Wilcomb E. 1971. *Red Man's Land/White Man's Law: A Study of the Past and Present of the American Indian.* New York: Charles Scribner's Sons.

———, ed. 1973–79. *The American Indian and the United States: A Documentary History.* 4 vols. Westport, Conn.: Greenwood.

Washington, Booker T. [1901] 1972. *Up From Slavery.* In *The Booker T. Washington Papers, Vol. 1,* edited by Louis R. Haslan. Urbana: University of Illinois Press.

Watembach, Karen. 1983. "The History of the Catechists of the Catholic Church on the Crow Reservation." Master's thesis, Montana State University.

Wax, Murray L. 1970. "Gophers or Gadflies: Indian School Boards." *School Review* 79:62–71.

———. 1971. *Indian Americans: Unity and Diversity.* Englewood Cliffs, N.J.: Prentice-Hall.

Wax, Rosalie, and Murray Wax. 1968. "Indian Education for What?" In *The American Indian Today,* edited by Stuart Levine and Nancy O. Lurie, 257–67. Baltimore, Md.: Penguin Books.

Weatherford, J. 1988. *Indian Givers: How the Indians of the Americas Transformed the World.* New York: Crown.

———. 1991. *Native Roots: How the Indians Enriched America.* New York: Crown.

Werner, Ruth E. 1972. *Novice in Navajoland.* Scottsdale, Ariz.: Southwest Book Service.

Whiteley, Peter M. 1988. *Deliberate Acts: Changing Hopi Culture through the Oraibi Split.* Tucson: University of Arizona Press.

Whitewolf, Jim. 1969. *Jim Whitewolf: The Life of a Kiowa Indian.* Edited by Charles S. Brant. New York: Dover.

Wigginton, E. 1992. "Culture Begins at Home." *Educational Leadership* 49(4):60–64.

Wilken, Robert L. 1955. *Anselm Weber, O.F.M.: Missionary to the Navaho 1898–1921.* Milwaukee, Wisc.: Bruce Publishing Co.

Williams, John, and Howard L. Meredith. 1980. *Bacone Indian University: A History.* Oklahoma City: Western Heritage Books.

Wilson, Raymond. 1983. *Ohiyesa—Charles Eastman, Santee Sioux.* Urbana: University of Illinois Press.

Wise, Jennings C. 1931. *The Red Man in the New World Drama: A Politico-Legal Study with a Pageantry of American Indian History.* Washington, D.C.: W. F. Roberts.

Wolcott, Harry F. 1967. *A Kwakiutl Village and School.* Arlington Heights, Ill.: Waveland.

Woodruff, Janette. 1939. *Indian Oasis.* Caldwell, Idaho: Caxton.

Woodward, G. S. 1963. *The Cherokees.* Norman: University of Oklahoma Press.

Worcester v. Georgia. 1832. 6 Peters, 534–36, 558–63.

Wright, Irvin Lee (Bobby). 1985. "Piety, Politics and Profit: American Indian Missions in the Colonial Colleges." Ph.D. dissertation, Montana State University, Bozeman.

"Writing for Pleasure." 1944. *Indian Education* 95:5–8.

Yava, Albert. [1978] 1981. *Big Falling Snow: A Tewa-Hopi Indian's Life and Times and the History and Traditions of his People.* Albuquerque: University of New Mexico Press.

Yellow Robe, Chauncey. 1926. *The American Indian* 1(3):5, 12.

Young, Robert W. 1944. "To Read and Write Native Languages." *Indian Education* 98:2–8.

———, comp. 1961. *The Navajo Yearbook:* Window Rock, Ariz.: Navajo Agency.

———, ed. 1957. *The Navajo Yearbook VI.* Window Rock, Ariz.: Navajo Agency.

Young, Robert W., and William Morgan. 1943. *The Navaho Language: The Elements of Navaho Grammar with a Dictionary in Two Parts Containing Basic Vocabularies of Navaho and English.* Phoenix, Ariz.: Education Division, U.S. Indian Service.

———. 1968. *English as a Second Language for Navajos: An Overview of Certain Cultural and Linguistic Factors*. Albuquerque, New Mex.: Albuquerque Area Office, Bureau of Indian Affairs.

Young, Robert W., and William Morgan. 1943. *The Navaho Language: The Elements of Navaho Grammar with a Dictionary in Two Parts Containing Basic Vocabularies of Navaho and English*. Phoenix, Ariz.: Education Division, U.S. Indian Service.

Zah, Peterson. 1983, October 12. *A Blueprint for Navajo Education*. Keynote address presented by Peterson Zah, Chairman, Navajo Tribal Council to the Navajo Education Leadership Conference of the Navajo Division of Education.

Zitkala–Sa (Gertrude Bonnin). [1921] 1985. *American Indian Stories*. Lincoln: University of Nebraska Press.

INDEX